EUROPEAN SOCIAL SECURITY LAW

SOCIAL EUROPE SERIES, Volume 25

EUROPEAN
SOCIAL SECURITY LAW

Frans Pennings

Fifth edition

Antwerp – Oxford – Portland

Distribution for the UK:
Hart Publishing Ltd.
16C Worcester Place
Oxford OX1 2JW
UK
Tel.: +44 1865 51 75 30
Email: mail@hartpub.co.uk

Distribution for the USA and Canada:
International Specialized Book Services
920 NE 58th Ave Suite 300
Portland, OR 97213
USA
Tel.: +1 800 944 6190 (toll free)
Tel.: +1 503 287 3093
Email: info@isbs.com

Distribution for Austria:
Neuer Wissenschaftlicher Verlag
Argentinierstraße 42/6
1040 Vienna
Austria
Tel.: +43 1 535 61 03 24
Email: office@nwv.at

Distribution for other countries:
Intersentia Publishers
Groenstraat 31
2640 Mortsel
Belgium
Tel.: +32 3 680 15 50
Email: mail@intersentia.be

European Social Security Law. Fifth edition
Frans Pennings

© 2010 Intersentia
Antwerp – Oxford – Portland
www.intersentia.com

ISBN 978-90-5095-729-8
D/2010/7849/129
NUR 825

PREFACE

In 2010 a new coordination Regulation came into force. This is a very good reason for making a new, fully revised edition of this handbook.

Part I of this book is dedicated to this coordination Regulation. Regulation 883/2004 and the judgments of the Court of Justice will be described. Furthermore I will analyse the contributions which the Regulation and the judgments have made to the development of coordination law and to the realisation of the objective of free movement for workers. The differences with Regulation 1408/71 will be outlined and proposals for further amendments will be made.

Part II is dedicated to social policy and harmonisation initiatives. Harmonisation instruments are described in general, in order to give a good insight into the possibilities and impossibilities of a 'Social Europe'. Secondly, the judgments of the Court on Article 141 EC, now Article 157 TFEU, and the directives on the equal treatment of men and women in social security are analysed.

Given the need for an update of this handbook on the coordination Regulation, most of the revisions have this time been made to Part I.

The book is the fifth edition of the Introduction to European Social Security Law, from now on: European Social Security Law.

The text of this edition has been revised completely. I am grateful for the comments on the earlier editions.

At the end of this book an index on the case law of the Court and a subject index can be found.

Frans Pennings   Utrecht, September 2010
f.pennings@uu.nl

CONTENTS

Chapter 6.
The Rules for Determining the Legislation Applicable. 71

ABBREVIATIONS

AAW	Algemene Arbeidsongeschiktheidswet [General Invalidity Benefits Act]
ABP	Algemene Burgerlijke Pensioenwet [Public Servants' Superannuation Act]
AG	Advocate-General
AKW	Algemene Kinderbijslagwet [General Child Benefits Act]
Anw	Algemene nabestaandenwet [General Survivors' Benefits Law]
AOW	Algemene Ouderdomswet [General Old Age Pension Act]
AWW	Algemene Weduwen- en Wezenwet [Widows and Orphan's Benefits Act]
BTSZ	Belgisch Tijdschrift voor Sociale Zekerheid [Belgian magazine]
CMLR	Common Market Law Reports
CMLRev	Common Market Law Review
COM	proposal of the European Commission
CRvB	Centrale Raad van Beroep [Central Appeals Court]
CSG	Cotisation sociale généralisée [Generalized Social Levy]
CSV	Coördinatiewet sociale verzekeringen [Social Security (Co-ordination) Act]
DLA	Disability living allowance
EC	European Community
ECR	European Court Reports
ECU	European currency unit
EEA	European Economic Area
EEC	European Economic Community
EFTA	European Free Trade Association
EJSS	European Journal of Social Security
ELR	European Law Review
EP	European Parliament
ESC	European Social Charter
EU	European Union
ILJ	Industrial Law Journal
ILO	International Labour Organisation
ILR	International Labour Review
IOAW	Wet Inkomensvoorziening Oudere en gedeeltelijk Arbeidsongeschikte werkloze Werknemers [Law on income for older and partially incapacitate unemployed persons]

KB	Koninklijk Besluit [Royal Decree]
LIEI	Legal Issues of European Integration
MR	Migrantenrecht
NCIP	non-contributory invalidity pension
NJCM	Magazine of Netherlands Committee for Human Rights
NJB	Nederlands Juristenblad [Dutch magazine]
NLG	Dutch guilders
NTER	Nederlands Tijdschrift voor Europees Recht [Dutch magazine]
NYIL	Netherlands Yearbook of International Law
OJ C	Official Journal of the European Communities, Information and Notices
OJ L	Official Journal of the European Communities, Legislation
OMC	Open Method of Coordination
PS	Periodiek voor sociale verzekering, sociale voorzieningen en arbeidsrecht [Dutch magazine]
RMC	Revue du Marché Commun
RSV	Rechtspraak Sociale Verzekering [Dutch magazine with law reports]
RTDE	Revue Trimistrielle de Droit Européen
RV	Rechtspraak Vreemdelingenrecht [Dutch magazine]
RvB	Social Security Appeals Tribunal [former Netherlands social security court]
SDA	Severe Disablement Allowance
SEW	Tijdschrift voor Europees en economisch recht [Dutch magazine]
SGB	Sozialgesetzbuch [Social security code]
SMA	Sociaal Maandblad Arbeid [Dutch magazine]
SR	Nederlands tijdschrift voor sociaal recht [Dutch magazine]
STb	Staatsblad [Netherlands Official Journal]
SVB	Sociale Verzekeringsbank [Netherlands administration of national insurances]
TFEU	Treaty on the Functioning of the EU
Trb.	Tractatenblad [Netherlands official journal of treaties]
Wajong	Wet Artbeidsongeschiktheidsvoorziening Jonggehandicapten [Invalidity Provision (Young Disabled Persons) Act]
WAO	Wet op de Arbeidsongeschiktheidsverzekering [Netherlands law relating to insurance against incapacity for work]
WW	Werkloosheidswet [Unemployment Insurance Act]
WWV	Wet Werkloosheidsvoorziening [Unemployment Benefits Act]
YEL	Yearbook of European Law

PART I
COORDINATION

CHAPTER 1

INTRODUCTION TO THE CONCEPT
OF COORDINATION

1.1.   GENERAL

Promotion of the freedom of movement of workers has been one of the European Economic Community's (EEC), now EU's, pillars from its very creation in 1957: freedom of movement of persons is seen as favourable for the economic development of the Member States as they can benefit from the effects of the optimal allocation of labour.

Ensuring the freedom of movement of workers across national borders requires active measures. An important part of these measures will have to be in the field of social security, since workers cannot be expected to go abroad if doing so has negative effects on their social security position. Without interference by international legislation, such negative effects are unavoidable since national social security legislation often makes distinctions on grounds of nationality. For instance, only persons who have nationality of the State in question are eligible for the benefit. Another rule often found in national systems is that benefits are paid only to persons residing in the country concerned. Persons who have returned to their country of origin, e.g. after retirement, are not paid benefit. A third category of provisions causing problems to migrants are those which make the acquisition or calculation of benefit conditional upon the completion of periods of insurance, employment or residence, where only periods completed under the legislation of that country are taken into account. In such a system a migrant worker may not be entitled to benefit or may receive a lower benefit than s/he would receive if s/he had stayed in his or her native country.

The effect of cross border movement on social security had already become a subject of concern by the beginning of the 20th Century, when employees' insurance schemes were first established. Problems arose, for instance, for employees who worked in a State other than the State of residence and who claimed an occupational accidents benefit. It appeared to be possible that an employee was insured for occupational accidents benefits in both States, or in no State at all. Such problems had to be solved and therefore coordination provisions were inserted into bilateral trade treaties. Inserting coordination provisions into trade treaties reflected the fact that such rules were seen, in particular, as necessary in order to avoid unfair competition. The treaty provisions had to prevent situations in which one State had to compensate for the effects of cross border working whereas other States escaped such costs. In the treaties it was agreed that nationals of a State which had signed the treaty had to be given the same advantages as those applying to the nationals of the State where the advantage is required. Such a provision is sometimes called 'reciprocity condition'.

In order to deal with national rules which are disadvantageous for cross border movement, international social security rules are essential. These rules are based on the assumption that a worker will not be prepared to go abroad if this would have negative effects on his or her right to benefit. To a certain extent, this assumption is of an abstract character as it is irrelevant whether workers are aware of negative effects of cross border movement at the moment they crossed the border. Many effects, such as on old age pensions, will often occur much later. However, bad experiences will be told to future migrants and thus they will certainly affect the movement of persons. Some effects of movement across the border will occur almost immediately, in particular on the liability of social security contributions. Therefore it is obvious that rules have to be made in order to deal with the effects of migration on social security.

1.2.   THE TERRITORIALITY PRINCIPLE

It is a general phenomenon that a State restricts its responsibility in the area of social security to its own territory and/or its own nationals. The linking of the social security system to the territory of a State is called the *territoriality principle*. This principle is not a legal principle, but it describes the phenomenon that a national social security system applies only to events which occur within the national borders of the State in question. An example is the condition that a person is entitled only to benefit if the risk materialised in the territory of that State. Another example is the condition that a person must have worked or lived for specified periods in the territory of a State in order to be entitled to benefit. A third example is the condition that benefits are paid only in the territory of the State where the right to the benefit was acquired. In other words, a link is made between, on the one hand, the territory of the State and, on the other hand, the group of persons, contributions, benefits and/or risks that are governed by the legislation of that State.

The territoriality principle is an impediment to the realisation of free movement of workers, since when each country uses territorial criteria to define the field of application of its social security system, this leads to problems in relation to cross border movement of workers. The criteria which States use to define the field of application of their social security systems are called the national *rules of conflict*. One example of such a rule of conflict is that only persons residing in the territory of the State are insured. Another example is the rule that all persons employed in the territory of the State are insured. Rules of conflict define the persons or facts to which a national legal system is confined. In social security law, examples of rules of conflict are the following: the place where the worker *works*, where s/he *resides*, or where the *employer* has his or her registered office or place of business, or, for seamen, the flag under which s/he sails.

Rules of conflict of public law, to which social security law belongs, are of a one-sided character. This is because public law is not concerned with relationships between individuals, but with relationships between States. The logical consequence is that a national government cannot decide that its legislation is also applicable outside its territory. Belgium, for instance, cannot decide that a person is entitled to a German passport or to German unemployment benefit.

The importance of the unilateral effect of conflict of public law is shown, for instance, in situations where the rules of conflict of two State have contrary effects. This may happen because national legal systems do not always use the same (territorial) criteria in their rules of conflict: *e.g.* one State may cover all and only workers in its social security system and another State may cover all persons residing in their territory.

As rules of conflict of public law have a unilateral character, a State can decide only whether it includes or excludes persons from its system, but it cannot decide on the rules of conflict of other States. As a result, it is possible, for example, that a person working in a State other than the one in which s/he lives, will fall under two legal systems at the same time, or under none at all. For instance, State x provides that people who work in its territory are insured for old-age pensions and State y provides that residence is the decisive criterion. In the case of a person who works in State x and resides in State y, s/he is covered in two countries; if s/he resides in State x and works in State y s/he is insured in neither State. In other words, when States apply different criteria, *conflicts of law* are likely to occur. When a migrant worker falls under the social security provisions of more than one State at the same time, this is called a *positive conflict of laws*; when a migrant falls under no system at all, this is called a *negative conflict of laws*. Conflicts of law can, precisely because of the unilateral character of the national rules of conflict, only be solved by a supranational coordination regulation.

The effects of the territoriality principle can also be seen in *rules of substance*. Rules of substance concern the conditions and provisions of a national scheme which determine which facts lying outside the territory of a State are relevant to its own benefit rules. For instance, a national scheme may provide that periods of residence abroad are taken into account for the acquisition of a right to benefit in the host country. A provision that persons of a State which signed a reciprocity agreement are treated in the same way as the State's own nationals is an example of a rule of substance. Rules of substance can, unlike rules of conflict, have a multilateral character, as they can refer to facts occurring in other countries.

Differences in national rules of substance can also lead to conflict. This may be the case when a person receives benefit from country x and country y. Country x may be inclined to deduct the benefit of country y from its own benefit. But country y may also do so. These discrepancies also make clear the need for a common regulation, for coordination.

1.3.   A DEFINITION OF COORDINATION

In the previous section the term coordination was used. Here we will give a definition of this term:

> Coordination rules are rules intended to adjust social security schemes in relation to each other (as well as to those of international regulations) in order to regulate transnational questions, with the objective of protecting the social security position of migrants.

This definition mentions not only national social security rules, but also international regulations. This is because coordination pertains also to the relation with other international treaties, since, for instance, in addition to the EU coordination regulations, the European Interim Agreements, ILO Conventions and bilateral treaties (*see* Chapter 19) may contain coordination rules which may affect the same persons.

The definition of the term coordination is important, in particular, where the question arises whether a particular measure is coordination or harmonisation. Harmonisation is the sum of international provisions directed at States which have the objective or obligation that these States adjust their national law to the requirements of the harmonisation provisions.

The difference between harmonisation and coordination is that when national schemes are coordinated, they are left intact, which implies that the differences between the national schemes remain to exist. Coordination rules have to find a solution, however, if national rules are disadvantageous for migrants. This may mean that national rules are supplemented, or that they have to take foreign facts or law into account.

Harmonisation may involve changes to national legislation. These apply for all persons covered by these, not only migrants.

An example to illustrate the difference between coordination and harmonisation is the following: if, in order to be entitled to benefit, claimants must have been insured for ten years, coordination rules may provide that foreign periods are to be taken into account in order to meet this condition. The fact that one country requires ten years, another one year, and a third three years, is not taken away by coordination rules. Here is a difference with harmonisation; a harmonisation rule could involve that there is a uniform condition for benefit. Since differences between schemes are not taken away by coordination, it is possible that a person cannot meet the conditions of a scheme despite the aggregation rules. If he would have satisfied the rules in his or her country of origin, this person is worse off as a result of making use of the right to free movement. Coordination does not take this effect away. Harmonisation could solve this problem.

As regards EU law, neither the coordination Regulation (*see* Chapter 2) nor the Treaty provide a definition of coordination. Nor has the Court of Justice given such a definition in any of its rulings. In several decisions the Court held that the Regulation leaves the Member States the powers to determine the type, and the content, of the provisions of their benefit schemes.[1] When discussing the scope of coordination, the Court even uses this concept in a negative sense: 'coordination does not preclude the powers of the Member States to determine the benefit conditions and the type of benefits, nor does it forbid differences between Member States'.[2]

As will be discussed in Chapter 2 and the following chapters, the Court interprets Article 42 EC (now Article 48 TFEU) in the sense that coordination is aimed at promoting the free movement of workers. This interpretation gives a special meaning to the concept of coordination. We must keep in mind, however, that the Court is not concerned with discussions on coordination in general, but with coordination as it is made possible by Article 42 EC and the coordination Regulation. Thus, in some decisions, the Court speaks of 'the mere coordination at present practised'.[3] Therefore, it is an open question what the approach of the Court would be if the Community legislator introduced a Treaty provision or regulation with a broader coordination objective.

1.4.   TASKS OF A COORDINATION INSTRUMENT

Protection of social security rights of migrant workers implies that at least the following essential problems have to be solved:
1.   conflicts of law have to prevented;
2.   discrimination on grounds of nationality must be forbidden;
3.   if periods of insurance, work, etc. are fulfilled in more than one Member State and this is disadvantageous to the fulfilment of the conditions for benefit and/or the calculation of the amount of benefit, this has to be repaired;
4.   territorial requirements for payment of benefit rights have to be removed.

---

[1]   For example in Case 41/84, *Pinna*, [1986] *ECR* 1.
[2]   Case 22/77, *First Mura judgment*, [1977] *ECR* 169.
[3]   *See Mura* judgment, previous note.

1.4.1. SOLVING CONFLICTS OF LAW

If an employee goes to work in another State, it must be clear which social security system is applicable to him or her. There are, in theory, several different ways for the international legislature to determine the criteria for determining the law applicable. The first way is to offer employers and employees a choice as to which scheme is applicable. In such a system, employers and employees are free to designate a national legal system as applicable to their situation. Under this option, it is also conceivable that parties designate the law of a third country. Such options exist, for instance, in civil law. In such an option rules have to be made for the case where parties have not designated a particular legal system. This option does not prevent provisions requiring that at least rules of public order of the State of work (*e.g.* rules on minimum wages) apply, even if parties have designated the law of another State (which has no minimum wage provisions).

For coordination of social security a coordination system giving the possibility of opting for a particular national system seems less obvious. This is because a third party, not the employer or the employee, but the State would be responsible for the expenses of the competent social security scheme. Therefore freedom of choice would cause problems, especially when a national system is not cost-effective and receives State subsidies.

A second option for the rules for determining the law applicable is that persons are entitled to the most *favourable* solution. Suppose that a person worked for ten years in country x, ten years in country y, and twenty years in country z. In this system, the law of the State where forty years of work result in the largest old age pension would be the competent one. However, if there are large differences between national schemes, this method results in disproportionate benefit charges for the country with the most favourable scheme. Also improper use would be possible in such a system: it becomes attractive to spend a short period in the most favourable country in order to be entitled to benefit from this country. A third problem is that it may be difficult to determine which scheme is the most favourable. What if country x has the most generous disability benefit and country y has the most advantageous old age benefit system?

The earliest bilateral coordination conventions allowed choosing between either separate application of national legislation or the application of the system of coordinated assimilation of pensions. Later, multilateral treaties abandoned this option. Currently the rules of conflict given in international conventions do not give freedom of choice between legislations; they give binding rules on which legislation is applicable. This is the most obvious coordination method in relation to social security and also followed in the EU coordination Regulation.

1.4.2. PROHIBITION OF DISCRIMINATION ON THE BASIS OF NATIONALITY

Equal treatment of migrant workers and nationals is fundamental for each coordination scheme. An important distinction is that between direct discrimination and indirect discrimination.

Direct discrimination means a situation where a distinction is made between persons on the basis of a forbidden criterion, *e.g.* nationality. *Indirect discrimination* concerns a practice of rule which, although not containing a forbidden criterion, leads to disadvantageous effects for specific categories of persons who can be defined by the forbidden criterion (such as migrant workers). It is much more difficult to prove indirect discrimination than direct discrimination, because the forbidden criterion is not explicitly mentioned. A claim that there is indirect discrimination starts with the suspicion that a rule is indirectly discriminatory. This is the case if the rule predominantly affects a particular category, whereas it is irrelevant whether the author of the rule had the intention to discriminate against this group.

An example of rules which raise the suspicion of being indirectly discriminating is a residence requirement: a scheme can require, for instance, that only periods fulfilled in State x count towards satisfying the conditions for benefit payable under that scheme. Although this condition applies to both national and foreign workers, the latter group is disproportionately affected by this condition, as foreign workers are more likely to have fulfilled periods of insurance in another State as well.

Sometimes the suspicion of indirect discrimination has to be supported by statistical data, but this is not always the case. In the judgment of the Court of Justice of the EU, *Commission v. Belgium*,[4] the Court considered that a provision of national law must be considered indirectly discriminating if it affects *by its nature* migrant workers more than national employees and threatens to affect the former group negatively. It did not require statistical proof in this case, but it was sufficient that it can be determined that the contested provision can have the effect of indirect discrimination.

If there is an alleged case of indirect discrimination, the person or organisation who made the rule or who applies it, has the opportunity to show grounds of justification, which must not relate to discrimination. If the person or organisation succeeds in proving such grounds, there is no indirect discrimination. This approach means that the person accused of indirect discrimination has to prove that s/he is innocent; this is a reversal of the burden of proof.

In general, it is difficult to say whether a particular provision can serve as an objective ground of justification. *See*, for the case law on this, Section 8.2 and Chapter 22.

---

[4]   Case 278/94, [1996] *ECR* I-4307.

1.4.3. TERRITORIAL REQUIREMENTS FOR ACQUIRING BENEFIT RIGHTS

Some national schemes provide that a person is entitled to benefit only if s/he or his or her family members live in that State. This is a clear elaboration of the territorial principle. Another example is where a scheme makes the receipt of an industrial accident benefit conditional on the fact that the accident happened on the territory of that State. The right to certain types of benefits is often subject to the condition that the person in question completed periods of residence, periods of contributions or periods of work. When periods completed in other Member States do not count for the fulfilment of such conditions, cross border movement leads to serious problems. Without further rules, a worker may not satisfy the conditions for benefit entitlement and will not receive benefit.

It may also happen that, although an employee succeeds in satisfying the benefit conditions, periods completed in a foreign country do not count in the calculation of the amount of benefit. This worker receives a lower benefit than s/he would if these periods were aggregated. Therefore, an important objective of coordination is to ensure that migrant workers who have been insured in more than one State do not suffer the disadvantages caused by breaks in their career as a result of cross border movement. It is important that the periods completed in a foreign country and those completed under the regulation of the State where benefit is claimed are aggregated.

This requirement does not mean that all periods of insurance of migrants must be assimilated. It requires, however, the possibility of aggregating these periods. Aggregation needs coordination rules, since national schemes vary to a large extent. There are, for instance, systems in which the right to benefit is conditional on the periods in which contributions were paid; other systems require periods of residence. Other systems do not have requirements on periods of residence or work, but only demand that a person resides on the territory of the State in question at the moment the risk occurs for the first time. Aggregation of periods completed under such different types is not a *sine cure* and neither is it clear at first sight how such aggregation is to be effected: how can periods completed abroad be 'translated' into those periods required by the schemes of another State? Coordination regulations have to solve these problems.

1.4.4. TERRITORIAL REQUIREMENTS FOR PAYMENT OF BENEFIT

Some national regulations require that a person who applies for benefit or the person on behalf of whom the claim is made resides in that country. This is a problem for the free movement of workers, as a worker who has acquired a right to benefit will be disinclined to go abroad and often workers are only prepared to go abroad if they remain entitled to their pension when they return to the State of origin. Therefore, a coordination regulation must make it possible for migrant workers to receive the benefits they are entitled to, regardless of the fact that they no longer reside in the territory of the country which is due to pay these benefits.

CHAPTER 2

THE INSTITUTIONAL CONTEXT
OF REGULATION 883/2004

2.1.   THE REQUIREMENTS FOR DECIDING ON A
COORDINATION REGULATION

Since the national governments were unwilling to give up their sovereignty when the EC was founded, the then Treaty Articles which gave decision-making power to the Council provided that a decision of the Council had to be unanimous. In other words, each Member State had a veto right. As a result, the move towards a common market became a tedious process. In order to make the process easier, the Single European Act[1] amended the Treaty of 1957. From now on, for a specific number of decisions only a qualified majority of votes was required, as specified in the Treaty. However, for regulations concerning social security still unanimity in the Council was necessary. Social security is one of the most sensitive topics in EU discussions and decision making, since Member States fear, among other reasons, the costs which will result for their country.

The Treaty of Amsterdam, which came into force on 1 July 1999, did not bring substantial changes in the area of coordination of social security. For social policy as a whole, it was important that provisions of the so-called Social Protocol were inserted in the Treaty; these articles will be discussed in Chapter 20. In addition, the numbering of the articles was changed. Before the Treaty of Amsterdam, the coordination Regulation was based on Article 51 EC Treaty; this became Article 42 EC.[2] The main difference between the text of Article 42 EC and Article 51 EC Treaty was that under Article 42 the European Parliament had to be consulted in accordance with the co-decision procedure. This meant that without the consent of Parliament, coordination regulations cannot be amended or adopted. However, whereas the other Articles of the Treaty which required co-decision provided that majority or qualified voting in the Council was sufficient

---

[1]   Signed at Luxembourg on 17 February 1986.
[2]   'EC Treaty' refers to the text before the Treaty of Amsterdam, 'EC' refers to the Treaty of Amsterdam.

for adopting the proposal, in the area of social security the unanimity rule in Council was maintained.

The coming into force of the Lisbon Treaty[3] on 1 January 2010 involved, again, a new number for the legal basis of the coordination Regulations, i.e. Article 48 TFEU (Treaty on the Functioning of the EU). The major change in the text of this Article was that the Article does not require unanimity of decision making anymore. This is an important deviation from the unanimity rule in force so far. However, the second sentence of this Article contains a 'brake provision': where a member of the Council declares that a draft legislative act on coordination would affect important aspects of the social security system, including its scope, cost or financial structure, or would affect the financial balance of that system, it may request that the matter be referred to the European Council (constituted of Heads of State or prime ministers). In that case the legislative procedure is suspended. After discussion the European Council has, within four months of this suspension, to refer the draft back to the Council (constituted of Ministers of Social Affairs), which has to terminate the suspension of the ordinary legislative procedure, take no action, or request the Commission to submit a new proposal.

Thus, the new provision does not entail a veto right anymore, but rather gives a dissenting Member State the right to a negotiation period and 'appeal' to the European Council. The Council can overrule this Member State by maintaining the instrument adopted; how the provision will be used in practice still remains to be seen.

Another reason why it can still not be said that decision making is (fully) possible by qualified majority is that the personal scope of the coordination Regulation is broader then that addressed in Article 48. Article 48 is limited to employees and self-employed persons. For the non-active workers another provision of the Treaty has to be invoked as a legal basis, i.e. Article 352 TFEU. This Article still requires unanimity. Also here it is still unclear how this double legal basis will influence the decision making process.

2.2. THE COURT OF JUSTICE

The judgments of the Court of Justice have played an important role in the development of coordination law. The Court has the task of ensuring a uniform interpretation of EU law in all Member States.[4] If a national court considers, in a procedure pending before that court, that the meaning of an EU rule is unclear,

---

[3]   OJ C 115/1 of 9 May 2008.
[4]   The decisions of the Court are published in the *European Court Reports* (hereafter abbreviated as ECR). This collection provides the authentic texts. It is published in all languages of the Union. Judgments of the Court (from June 1997) can also be found on the web site of the Court: curia.europa.eu; all judgments, including older ones, can be found on europa.eu/documentation/legislation/index_en.htm.

this court *can* refer this question to the Court of Justice and ask for a so-called preliminary ruling under Article 267 TFEU. When any such question is raised in a case pending before a court of a Member State, against whose decisions there is no further judicial remedy under national law,[5] that court *has* to bring the matter to the Court of Justice. It is only after the ruling of the Court, that the procedure before the national court can be continued. Hence, the Court has an indirect function; individual subjects cannot appeal to this court, unless a certain decision is specifically directed at them.

2.3. THE LEGAL BASIS FOR THE COORDINATION REGULATION

As follows from Section 2.1, the legal basis for making coordination rules in the area of social security is primarily Article 48 TFEU. This Article is part of Title IV of the Treaty, entitled The Free Movement of Persons, Services and Capital, and, more specifically, of Chapter 1 of this Title, called 'Workers'. Situating Article 48 is relevant, since its position in the Treaty may be important to is interpretation. Indeed, the Court often refers to the place of (the predecessors of) Article 48 when giving arguments for its interpretation of the Regulation: because of its wording and its place, Article 48 is to be interpreted in view of securing freedom of movement, especially of employees, and not merely as a technical coordination provision.[6]

> Article 48 TFEU provides that:
> 'The European Parliament and the Council shall, acting in accordance with the ordinary legislative procedure, adopt such measures in the field of social security as are necessary to provide freedom of movement for workers; to this end, they shall make arrangements to secure for employed and selfemployed migrant workers and their dependants:
> (a) aggregation, for the purpose of acquiring and retaining the right to benefit and of calculating the amount of benefit, of all periods taken into account under the laws of the several countries;
> (b) payment of benefits to persons resident in the territories of Member States.
> Where a member of the Council declares that a draft legislative act referred to in the first subparagraph would affect important aspects of its social security system, including its scope, cost or financial structure, or would affect the financial balance of that system, it may request that the matter be referred to the European Council. In that case, the ordinary legislative procedure shall be suspended. After

---

[5]   This need not be the highest court in a hierarchy, but the highest court which can decide on an issue in a particular field of law.

[6]   *See*, for instance, Case 92/63, *Nonnenmacher*, [1964] ECR 1261.

discussion, the European Council shall, within four months of this suspension, either: (a) refer the draft back to the Council, which shall terminate the suspension of the ordinary legislative procedure; or (b) take no action or request the Commission to submit a new proposal; in that case, the act originally proposed shall be deemed not to have been adopted.

From the place of Article 48 the Court derived, as we will see in Chapter 4, that it can be a legal basis only for coordination rules on persons having nationality of a Member State.[7] Rules on third country nationals cannot be based on this legal basis.

Also Article 45 TFEU is relevant to coordination. This Article prohibits any discrimination on grounds of nationality between workers of the Member States in relation to employment, remuneration and other conditions of employment. It does not apply to employment in the public service. Article 45 is often referred at in order to give an interpretation of a provision of the Regulation or to deal with coordination issues beyond the scope of Article 48. We will pay special attention to Article 45 in Chapter 10.

Coordination could be limited to the protection of the social security rights of migrant workers. In this approach, the coordination rules do not require an active policy to promote the free movement of workers. The Court, however, derives from Article 48 that the mobility of workers has to be *promoted*. Hence, the rules of the Regulation are interpreted by the Court in the light of the objective of promoting free movement.[8] In the next chapters we will see several examples of this in the judgments of the Court.

Article 48 gives the powers to take measures which are 'necessary in the area of social security to provide the freedom of movement of workers' and mentions a series of arrangements which have to be taken in any case. The powers of the Council are not limited to these types of arrangements, as was confirmed by the Court in the *Patteri* judgment.[9] However, measures based on Article 48 must relate to the free movement of workers. It is not possible to base other types of measures, *e.g.* to realise a 'social Europe', on Article 48.

Article 48 has to prevent national social security rules from impeding free movement. Whether a measure is necessary has to be decided, in the first instance, by the European Commission, being the body which prepares proposals for amending the Regulation. Subsequently, it is up to Parliament and the Council to decide on the necessity of a measure,[10] and also a Member State can raise objections.

---

[7]   Case 95/99, *Khalil,* [2001] ECR I-7413.
[8]   See, for instance, Case 67/79, Fellinger, [1980] ECR 1980, 535.
[9]   Case 242/83, [1984] ECR 3171.
[10] The Administrative Commission, see Section 2.6, can make proposals to the European Commission to amend the Regulation.

If the Court of Justice finds, in a preliminary reference or in an infringement procedure, that a measure is not necessary in this sense, this could mean that the Council did not have the power to make that particular rule. So far, the Court has not yet come to such a conclusion. Nor is this situation likely to occur because if a measure is not deemed necessary, it is very unlikely that it would survive the voting procedure in the Council. Measures which are 'not necessary' are not likely to be adopted given the general reluctance of Member States to agree on social measures.

The phrase 'which are necessary for the free movement' has appeared to be important in the case law of the Court of Justice. If there is an interpretation question concerning the Regulation, the Court tends to refer to the objective of Article 48 and answers the question in the light of this article to ensure free movement. It then usually interprets the disputed term of the Regulation in a way which most favours this mobility. Examples are the interpretations of the terms employed person and self-employed person in the *Unger* case[11] and the *Van Roosmalen* case[12] respectively (discussed in Chapter 4 of this book). In respect of the material scope of the Regulation, the interpretation of the term *social security* is an example of this attitude of the Court (*see* the *Frilli* case[13] in Chapter 5 of this book).

Article 48 requires measures. For this purpose the legislator chose the instrument of a *regulation*. As is provided in Article 288 TFEU, a regulation has general application, it is binding in its entirety and is directly applicable in all Member States. A regulation differs from that of the *directive*, which is binding as to the result to be achieved, upon each Member State to which it is addressed, but the national authorities retain the freedom of the choice of forms and methods to achieve this result. Directives do not have a horizontal effect. It is the State which has to guarantee that individuals can realise the rights awarded to them in the directive. Regulations can have horizontal effect. Regulation 883/2004, for instance, can be invoked when defending benefit claims against benefit administrations and, in some cases even against employers (Section 5.2).

2.4.   ARTICLE 48 TFEU DIRECTLY APPLIED IN COORDINATION CASES

Article 48 TFEU provides that the Council must adopt measures in the field of social security. The coordination Regulation gives, however, a limitative list of benefits to which it applies.

---

[11]   Case 75/63, [1964] ECR 369.
[12]   Case 300/84, [1986] ECR 3097.
[13]   Case 1/72, [1972] ECR 457.

In the *Vougioukas* judgment,[14] the Court based a coordination rule directly on the predecessor of this Article (Article 42 EC) in order to deal with a type of benefit not included in the Regulation. The case concerned special schemes for civil servants, which were excluded from Regulation 1408/71 at the time (i.e. until 25 October 1998). The dispute in this case concerned the rule that periods of employment fulfilled under a special scheme in countries other than Greece were not relevant to the Greek pension for civil servants. Mr Vougioukas had undertaken periods of work under German special schemes and now claimed a Greek pension. The Court considered that in order to safeguard the effective exercise of the right to freedom of movement, the Council was required to set up a system to enable workers to overcome obstacles with which they might be confronted in national social security rules. The Community legislature, however, had, at the time of the judgment, not yet adopted such measures for civil servants. As a result, the Regulation left a considerable lacuna in the Community coordination of social security schemes. The Court considered that technical difficulties, which may have justified the exclusion of civil servants' schemes at the time when the Regulation was adopted, could not justify indefinitely the lack of any coordination of special schemes for civil servants. Therefore the Council had not fully discharged its obligation under Article 42 EC. Although the exclusion of civil servant schemes remained valid, this did not entail that a request for aggregation be refused when it may be satisfied, in direct application of Articles 39 to 42 EC (now 45 to 48 TFEU), without recourse to the coordination rules adopted by the Council. The Court based this consideration, as it often does, on the objective of Article 42 EC: this objective would not be attained if, as a result of exercising their right to freedom of movement, workers were to lose social security advantages granted to them by the legislation of a Member State. This might dissuade Community workers from exercising their right to freedom of movement. The Court ruled that periods abroad have to be aggregated for the purpose of acquiring benefit rights in the case of civil servants, even though Regulation 1408/71 did not provide for a coordination system for civil servants' schemes.

So far this has been an exceptional case. In principle, however, it could be applied also in other situations where the Regulation does not give rules where these are required by Article 42 and where the coordination rule necessary could be easily applied, i.e. where no technical implementing rules are necessary.

---

[14]   Case 443/93, [1995] *ECR* I-4033.

2.5. A VERY SHORT HISTORY OF THE COORDINATION REGULATIONS

The measures required by Article 48 are elaborated in Regulation 883/2004, whose full title is: Regulation (EC) No 883/2004 of the European Parliament and of the Council of 29 April 2004 on the coordination of social security systems. This is sometimes called the Basis Regulation. In addition, the so-called Implementing Regulation is relevant, *i.e.* Regulation 987/2009, Regulation of the European Parliament and of the Council laying down the procedure for implementing Regulation (EC) No 883/2004 on the coordination of social security systems.[15] Regulation 988/2009, published in the same *Official Journal* as the implementing Regulation, introduced some amendments to Regulation 883/2004 and included the Annexes.

Regulation 883/2004 replaced Regulation 1408/71,[16] which on its turn replaced Regulation 3,[17] which was drawn up in 1958. Regulation 3 was one of the earliest EEC regulations, as coordination of social security was already at that time seen as essential for the free movement of workers. The speed by which Regulation 3 was ready can also be explained by the fact that by 1958 the text for a European Convention on social security for migrant workers was just completed (Convention of 9 December 1957). This Convention was related to Article 69(4) of the Treaty of the European Coal and Steel Community. After the EEC was established, this text was used for drafting the Regulation required by Article 51 EC Treaty, which was the legal basis for the coordination rules at the time (later Article 42 EC, now Article 48 TFEU). So a regulation was used instead of a Treaty; given the institutional framework a regulation is easier to adopt and to implement than a Treaty.

In 1971 Regulation 3 was replaced by Regulation 1408/71. This Regulation has frequently been amended and many judgments of the Court of Justice concerned this regulation. As a result the regulation has become very complicated and this was considered problematic for migrant workers and also for legal aid advisors and judges the regulation was difficult to apply. This complexity is the more problematic as it may impede the main objective of the Regulation, *i.e.* the promotion of free movement of workers. Some of the main causes of the complexity are:

– the text of the Regulation cannot and must not be interpreted without taking the judgments of the Court of Justice into account. The case law has grown considerably in length and complexity in the course of time;
– the Regulation provides for many exceptions to its main rules;

---

[15] Regulation 883/2004 was published in OJ L 166/1 of 2004. The implementing regulation, Regulation 987/2009, was published in OJ L 284/1 of 2009.
[16] Regulation 1408/71 was published for the first time in OJ 149 of 5 July 1971.
[17] OJ 30 of 16 December 1958.

- the lack of an explanatory memorandum to the Regulation. This means that all provisions had to be interpreted as they stand, unless the Court has interpreted them.

Moreover the Regulation had important limitations. It did not apply to non-active persons (apart from members of the family and persons who stopped working). Also the material scope of the Regulation was limited.

On 21 December 1998, the European Commission published a proposal for a new coordination Regulation.[18] Prior to the proposal the Commission had in all Member States conferences organised on the current problems with Regulation 1408/71.[19]

The proposal for a new regulation did not only contain a simplified text, but also several politically very sensitive proposals. These led to difficult discussions in several meetings of the Council. When no agreement could be reached so-called parameters were developed, which were accepted during the Laeken Summit in December 2001, which make clear on which elements there was consensus.[20] The establishment of the parameters appeared successful, since in subsequent meetings of the Council agreement could be reached on chapters of the draft Regulation and finally on the full text. Finally this led to Regulation 883/2004, published in the Official Journal of 30 April 2004. The Regulation was thus adopted very shortly before the European Union was extended by 10 new Member States on 1 May 2004. As the new Member States were not member of the Union at the time of the adoption of the Regulation, they did not have the right to vote on it.

After Regulation 883/2004 was adopted, work started on the implementing regulation. A proposal was published in January 2006. Also the negotiations on this proposal took a considerable time. Finally the text was adopted in June 2009, Regulation 987/2009. Now both regulations have been adopted, Regulation 883/2004 could come into force, and this took place on 1 May 2010.

The text of the new Regulation differs importantly from that of the 1998 proposal, but the differences with Regulation 1408/71 are much smaller. It has important improvements in the text of the Regulation, which is now less complex. Also the extension of the personal scope and the drafting of the personal scope (extension to all nationals) are improvements. Disappointingly little progress has

---

[18] COM (1998) 779. See, on the proposal, E. Eichenhofer, 'How to Simplify the Coordination of Social Security', *EJSS* 2000, p. 229; M. Sakslin, 'Can the Principles of the Nordic Conventions on Social protection Contribute to the Modernisation and Simplification of Regulation (EEC) No. 1408/71', in Swedish National Social Insurance Board and European Commission, *25 Years of Regulation (eec) No. 1408/71 on Social Security for Migrant Workers – A Conference Report, Stockholm 1997*, p. 197; F. Pennings, 'The European Commission Proposal to Simplify Regulation 1408/71', EJSS 2001, p. 45 ff.

[19] The final report on the results of the conferences was published in D. Pieters (ed.), *The Coordination of Social Security at Work*, ACCO, Leuven 1999. For the preparatory materials, *see* P. Schoukens (ed.), *Prospects of Social Security Coordination*, ACCO, Leuven 1997.

[20] Council document 15045/01.

been made vis-à-vis the extension of the material scope, which is almost the same as that of the old Regulation. It appeared that consensus was hard to reach on modernisations.[21] We will discuss these changes in more detail in the following chapters.

2.6.   THE STRUCTURE OF REGULATION 883/2004

As is usual with international instruments, Regulation 883/2004 starts with a Preamble, mentioning the considerations of the Council which led to this Regulation. These considerations are sometimes relevant to the interpretation of provisions of the Regulation.

Title 1 of the Regulation contains Articles 1 to 16. In Article 1, the meaning of some of the terms used in the Regulation is given. Article 2 defines which categories of persons are covered by the Regulation (the personal scope); this subject will be discussed in Chapter 4. Article 3 refers to the type of branches and schemes within the field of application of the Regulation (the material scope), to be discussed in Chapter 5. Article 4 forbids discrimination on grounds of nationality (*see* Chapter 8); whereas Article 5 requires equal treatment of benefits, income, facts or events. Article 6 concerns the aggregation of periods. Article 7 provides that, unless otherwise provided for by the Regulation, residence rules for cash benefits are waived. This is one of the measures required by Article 48 TFEU; this article ensures that benefits are paid to persons not resident in the territory of the Member State under whose regulation these benefits were acquired when this person resides within the territory of another EU or EEA Member State. Unlike Article 10 of Regulation 1408/71 Article 7 of the new Regulation does not give a limitative enumeration of the types of benefits for which it applies (invalidity, old-age and survivors' cash benefits, pensions for accidents at work or occupational diseases and death grants), but it makes a reservation for categories of benefits. In fact this amounts to the same result: for types of benefits other than long-term benefits the Regulation provides for a limitation of export or non-export. Examples are Article 64 for unemployment benefits and Article 17 for sickness and maternity benefits.

Article 9 of the Regulation requires or allows Member States to notify, for the purpose of the application of some specific articles of the Regulation, the national schemes referred to in these articles. For instance, Article 3 mentions the types of benefits covered by the Regulation and Member States must declare which of their national schemes correspond to these benefits. The national minimum benefits, to which Article 58 applies, must also be mentioned in declarations.[22]

---

[21]   See, for an assessment of the modernisation aspect of the new regulation, also F. Pennings, 'Conclusion: Simplification, Modernisation and Regulation 883/2004', EJSS 2009, p. 235 ff.

[22]   These declarations are published in Annexes to the Regulation.

The meaning of these declarations was at stake in the *Beerens* case.[23] In this case it was unclear whether the benefit scheme at issue, was within the material scope of the Regulation. The Court considered that Article 5 of the Regulation (now Article 9) provides that the Member States must mention in declarations the regulations referred to in Article 4 of Regulation 1408/71 (now Article 3 of Regulation 883/2004). The Court held that if a certain benefit is *not* mentioned in a declaration according to Article 5, this is not sufficient to decide that such benefit is not covered by the Regulation. If such benefit satisfies the material characteristics for benefits falling within the scope of the Regulation (as developed by the Court – *see* Chapter 5) it falls within the material scope, even if it is not mentioned. If an Act is *positively* mentioned in the declaration, it is certain, the Court ruled, that it is covered by the Regulation.

Article 8 concerns the relationship of the Regulation to international treaties. As several international treaties may be applicable for EU Member States, it is relevant to define their relationship and the Regulation. According to Article 8, Regulation 883/2004 generally has priority over such international social security treaties. In Chapter 18 we will discuss this issue in more detail and the exceptions to this rule. This article also allows Member States to make, as the need arises, conventions with each other based on the principles of the Regulation and in keeping with the spirit thereof. This may be important to solve issues not dealt with in the Regulation and to deal with administrative issues.

Title II of the Regulation gives the rules for determining the applicable legislation (Article 13 to Article 16). This subject is dealt with in Chapters 6 and 7 of this book.

Title III contains more specific rules for the various types of benefits. In this Title, the requirements of Article 48 TFEU are elaborated in separate chapters for each type of benefit. These chapters contain, among other things, rules on the aggregation of periods of insurance for qualifying for benefit entitlement and rules for the calculation of benefits.

Finally, Articles 71 and 72 have to be mentioned, concerning the Administrative Commission. The Administrative Commission consists of government repre-sentatives and its task is, *inter alia*, to deal with all administrative questions and questions of interpretation arising from the provisions of the Regulation (Article 72). This commission also has the task to submit to the European Commission any relevant proposals concerning the coordination of social security schemes. The decisions of this Commission have significant value in the management of administrative practices. However, following from the Court's decisions, the le-gal force of Administrative Commission's decisions is of a relative nature only. In one of its judgments,[24] the Court held that a decision of this commission can be a useful instrument for social security institutions, but it cannot oblige these

---

[23]   Case 35/77, [1977] ECR 2249.
[24]   Case 98/80, *Romano*, [1981] *ECR* 1241.

institutions to follow a particular method or interpretation of Community legislation. In the following chapters, the decisions of the Administrative Commission will sometimes be referred to.

In view of the new Regulation the Administrative Commission has redrafted its previous decisions and has also taken some new decisions which were deemed necessary for the application of the new Regulations. These were jointly published in the *Official Journal* 2010, C 106.

The Regulation ends with transitional provisions. These are relevant to know when and to which extent periods completed before the date of coming into force of the Regulation are to be taken into account. We will refer to these provisions, if necessary, in the relevant chapters.

CHAPTER 3

THE CONDITIONS FOR APPLICABILITY
OF REGULATION 883/2004

3.1. INTRODUCTION

Before Regulation 883/2004 can be applied on a particular situation, it is important to check whether all conditions for application of this regulation are fulfilled. These are:

- not all the facts of the case are restricted to one single Member State;
- the person concerned is within the personal scope of the Regulation;
- the benefit concerned is within the material scope of the Regulation;
- the situation is within the territorial scope of the Regulation.

Since the discussion of the personal and material scope requires considerable space, it is dealt with in separate chapters (Chapters 4 and 5). The first and fourth issues are discussed in this chapter.

3.2. THE FACTS OF THE CASE MUST NOT BE RESTRICTED TO ONE MEMBER STATE

The Regulation is applicable if a person moves to another Member State. However, it does not require that the person concerned himself or herself *moves* to another Member State. Also if s/he was born having the nationality of another Member State, or if his or her children or spouse move to another Member State, the Regulation applies. In case of mobility, the *reason* for the movement of a worker is irrelevant. Consequently, movement need not be for economic reasons: visiting one's family in another Member State is, for example, sufficient to have the Regulation applied.[1] The Regulation is also applicable if an employed person had never moved across the border before s/he retired and who then goes to another

---

[1]   *See*, for instance, the *Unger* judgment, Section 4.2.

Member State.[2] Thus pensioners who never worked in another Member State also benefit from the Regulation.

The Regulation is only applicable if the facts of the case are not limited to one Member State. If there is no cross-border situation, the person concerned cannot invoke the Regulation, even if s/he is confronted with national rules with discriminatory effects. This was confirmed in the *Petit* judgment.[3] In this case an employee was confronted with conditions on the use of language to be used in legal procedures in Belgium. Mr Petit had filed a petition with the Labour Court in French. The Belgian law on languages to be used in legal proceedings prescribed the Dutch language in a case like this. The use of another language would make the case of the person concerned inadmissible. Mr Petit had Belgian nationality and had never been employed in a state other than Belgium. The Court of Justice considered that it has consistently held that the rules of the Treaty ensuring the free movement of workers and the coordination Regulation were not applicable to activities all elements of which are restricted to the territory of a single Member State only.

This criterion was also at stake in the *Government of the French Community and Walloon Government v Flemish Government Judgment*.[4] The case concerned the Flemish care insurance, which introduced insurance for certain costs occasioned by a state of dependence for health reasons. Examples are expenses involved in home help services or in the purchase of equipment or products needed by the insured person. Initially, the insurance was limited to persons residing in the Dutch-speaking region. The European Commission started infringement proceedings against this residence condition. Consequently, the scheme was adapted and extended to include persons working in the territory of the Dutch speaking part and residing in a Member State other than Belgium. The applicant Governments pleaded infringement of Regulation 1408/71, claiming that to exclude from that scheme persons who, although working in the Dutch-speaking region, reside in the French speaking part of Belgium, amounts to a restrictive measure hindering the free movement of persons.

First the Court had to answer the question whether the dispute concerned only a purely internal situation. It confirmed that it is settled case-law that the Treaty rules governing freedom of movement for persons and the measures adopted to implement them cannot be applied to activities which have no factor linking them with any of the situations governed by Community law and which are confined in all relevant respects within a single Member State. The Court

---

[2]   *See*, for instance, the *Spruyt* judgment, Case 284/84, [1986] *ECR* 685; the *De Rijke-Van Gent* judgment, Case 43/86, [1987] *ECR* 3611.
[3]   Case 153/91, [1992] *ECR* I-4973.
[4]   Case C-212/06, [2008] *ECR* I-1683. *See*, on this judgment also H. Verschueren, 'De regionalisering van de sociale zekerheid in België in het licht van het arrest van het Europese Hof van Justitie inzake de Vlaamse zorgverzekering', *Belgisch Tijdschrift Sociale Zekerheid*, 2008, No. 2 p.177-232; I. van der Steen, 'Zuivere interne situaties: geen omwenteling, wel inperking', *NTER*, nr. 11, 2008, p. 301 ff.

then argued that two kinds of situations must be distinguished. The first is that of Belgian nationals working in the territory of the Dutch-speaking region, but who live in the French or German speaking region and have never exercised their freedom to move within the European Community. Community law clearly cannot be applied to such purely internal situations nor can the principle of citizenship of the Union be applied here.

The second situation is nationals of Member States other than Belgium working in the Dutch-speaking region but living in another part of the national territory, and Belgian nationals in the same situation who have made use of their right to freedom of movement, can be excluded from the care insurance. The second category falls within the scope of Community law.

The Court further argued that legislation such as that of the Flemish care insurance may produce restrictive effects on the freedom of movement. Migrant workers contemplating to take up work in the Dutch speaking part might be dissuaded from making use of their freedom of movement and from leaving their Member State of origin to stay in Belgium, by reason of the fact that moving to certain parts of Belgium would cause them to lose the opportunity of eligibility for the benefits which they might otherwise have claimed. This is further discussed in Chapter 10.

Thus, in principle, the Court kept to its former approach, that the facts of the case must not be limited to a purely internal situation. However, it analysed the situation thoroughly in order to see whether there are categories whose situation is not purely an internal national one. As a result, social security schemes restricted to certain regions have to take categories into account falling within the ambit of Community law, that is to say, both nationals of another Member State who work in the region concerned and nationals in the same situation who have made use of their right to freedom of movement.

3.3. THE TERRITORIAL SCOPE OF REGULATION 883/2004

Regulation 883/2004 is not only applicable in the territory of the European Union, but also in that of the European Economic Area (EEA). The EEA comprises the Member States of the European Union and those Member States of the European Free Trade Association (EFTA) which have not yet become a member of the EU, *i.e.* Norway, Liechtenstein and Iceland.

The EEA Treaty provides that important parts of EU law in force on 1 August 1991 became applicable to these countries. It contains a number of provisions which are to a large extent identical to provisions of the Treaty and it has a number of annexes where EC regulations and directives which are also applicable in the EEA are mentioned. In Annex VI, the relevant EU law, *i.e.* the coordination

Regulation, is mentioned. In this Annex, provisions are also given in order to take account, where necessary, of the systems of the EFTA States.

The provisions of the Agreement must be interpreted in conformity with the corresponding rulings of the Court of Justice of the EC (Article 6 EEA Treaty).

Article 28 of the Agreement provides that freedom of movement for workers shall be secured among EU Member States and EFTA States. Such freedom of movement entails the abolition of any discrimination based on nationality of EU Member States and EFTA States as regards employment, remuneration and other conditions of work and employment. This Article corresponds with Article 45 TFEU.

The coordination Regulation applies, on the basis of an Agreement between the EU and Switzerland, also to Switzerland.

Regulation 883/2004 is thus relevant to the territory of the EU, the EEA and Switzerland. First we will discuss the effects of this fact for the material scope.

A question arose as to whether schemes concerning a (former) colonial territory of a Member State were also covered by this definition. This issue concerns the territorial scope of the Regulation. The question was answered in the *Bozzone* judgment.[5] Walter Bozzone was an Italian national who worked in the former Belgian Congo until 1960. He then applied in Belgium for an invalidity allowance and settled in Italy. His claim was based on the Colonial Decree 1952 governing invalidity insurance of colonial employees. Initially he was granted this allowance, but it was terminated in January 1961 on the grounds that he did not actually and habitually reside in Belgium. Could Article 10 of the Regulation (which precludes requirements on territoriality) be invoked by a person who was exclusively employed in the colony of a Member State?

The Court considered that the coordination Regulation applied to workers who are or who had been subject to the legislation of one or more Member States. The Court considered that the person concerned first enjoyed the benefit of the Colonial Decree, which was affirmed by a Belgian Law of 1960 ensuring the continuity of this scheme. As a whole, the Court concluded, those provisions therefore constitute 'national legislation' within the meaning of the Regulation and, as a result, Bozzone could invoke the Regulation in order to receive the disputed benefit in Italy.

The Court was also requested to answer the question of whether a scheme applying to a person who worked outside the territory of a Member State, including the (former) colonies, falls within the scope of the Regulation. This case concerned a person who was working as a priest in Africa, while being insured under the Dutch social security system (this opportunity exists of workers in developing projects). This lead to the *Van Roosmalen* judgment,[6] in which the

---

5   Case 87/76, [1977] *ECR* 687.
6   Case 300/84, [1986] *ECR* 3097.

Court remarked that the main criterion of the term 'legislation' is not the place of the occupational activities, but the relationship between the person – regardless of the place of activities – and the social security scheme of the Member State under which he completed his periods of insurance. Thus, it is not relevant that the insured person performed his activities within or outside the territory of the Community; a national scheme which extends its field of application to persons working outside the Community must be considered as legislation within the meaning of Article 2 of the Regulation. This case law was confirmed in the *Buhari Haji* judgment.[7] Thus Van Roosmalen, who fell incapacitated outside the Nteherlands, could still claim incapacity benefit under a Dutch scheme, even though the risk materialised outside the Netherlands.

---

[7]   Case 105/89, [1990] *ECR* 4211.

CHAPTER 4

THE PERSONAL SCOPE OF REGULATION 883/2004

4.1. INTRODUCTION

Article 48 TFEU provides that the Council has to adopt such measures in the field of social security as are necessary to provide freedom of movement of employed and self-employed workers. This legal basis thus includes self-employed persons and is in this respect an extension compared to its predecessor.

The personal scope of the Regulation has been extended through the time. Regulation 3 was limited to giving coordination rules for wage-earners and assimilated workers and for a long time the personal scope of Regulation 1408/71 was also limited to this category. In 1981, however, its personal scope was extended to cover self-employed persons. This extension was based on Article 235 EC Treaty (now Article 352 TFEU).[1]

The personal scope of Regulation 883/2004 is not limited to the economically active population. Article 2 reads that this Regulation shall apply to nationals of a Member State, stateless persons and refugees residing in a Member State who are or have been subject to the legislation of one or more Member States, as well as to the members of their families and to their survivors. It shall also apply to the survivors of persons who have been subject to the legislation of one or more Member States, irrespective of the nationality of such persons, where their survivors are nationals of a Member State or stateless persons or refugees residing in one of the Member States.

In the next section I will give a historical overview of the personal scope under Regulation 3 and Regulation 1408/71. Section 4.3 will deal with the personal scope of Regulation 883/2004.

---

[1]   Regulation 1390/81 of 12 May 1981. The Court has accepted this extension, *see* the *Van Roos-malen* judgment, Case 300/84, [1986] *ECR* 3097.

4.2. AN HISTORICAL OVERVIEW OF THE PERSONAL SCOPE OF REGULATIONS 3 AND 1408/71

The personal scope of Regulation 3 was limited to 'wage-earners and assimilated workers' (Article 19(1)). The Regulation gave, however, no definition of this term. Therefore, the Court had to give an interpretation of wage-earners and assimilated workers in the *Unger* judgment.[2] Although this is already a very early judgment and the applicable rules were changed radically later, it still is very relevant as it shows the approach by the Court very clearly.

In the *Unger* judgment the Court held that the term worker has a Community meaning. The case concerned a person who resigned from her job and who was subsequently admitted to the Dutch continued voluntary insurance sickness scheme. During a family visit to her parents in Germany, she fell ill. Her state of health required immediate medical treatment. After her return to the Netherlands, she claimed payments of sickness benefit and the costs of expenses of treatment in this period. Benefit was refused, however, for the period she stayed in Germany and therefore she wished to rely on Regulation 3 in order to have her expenses paid.[3] Since she could rely on Regulation 3 only if she belonged to its personal scope, the Court had to give an interpretation of the term wage earner. The Court considered that the Regulation was made in order to meet the requirements of Article 51 EC Treaty (now Article 48 TFEU). The establishment of complete freedom of movement for workers constitutes the principal objective of this Article and thereby conditions the interpretation of the Regulations adopted in the implementation of that Article, the Court argued. If the definition of the term wage earner were a matter falling within the competence of national law, it would be possible for each Member State to modify the meaning of this concept and to eliminate at will the protection afforded by the Treaty to certain categories of persons. If the meaning of such a term was to be unilaterally fixed and modified by national law, Articles 48 (now Article 45 TFEU) and Article 51 EC would be deprived of all effect and the objectives of the Treaty would be frustrated. These considerations are quoted here, as they clearly show how the Court's interpretation of provisions of the Regulation is linked to the objectives of the Treaty.

Although the term wage earner had a Community meaning, this meaning could not be found in the Regulation. Instead, we had to look at national law to see whether a person was a wage earner. However, it was not national *labour* law which had to be applied, so whether a person has a contract of employment was irrelevant.

---

[2]   Case 75/63, [1964] *ECR* 177.
[3]   Regulation 3 did not contain a definition of employed person – in the terms of this Regulation: *wage earner*. Mrs Unger would fall within the personal scope of Regulation 1408/71, which gave a definition: Article 1(a)(i) includes persons who are 'insured on an optional continued basis'.

Instead, in order to be a wage earner a person must be or have been subject to a social security scheme for employed persons. An example is an unemployment benefit scheme for employees. If a person is covered by such a scheme, s/he was an employee for the Regulation, even if s/he did not have a contract of employment. Thus it was decisive how a national social security scheme defined its personal scope. However, if the national scheme included particular categories of persons, these were also covered by the Regulation. As a result, persons assimilated with employed persons under a national social security scheme were also covered. For instance, several national systems treat home workers, even when they do not have a contract of employment, under some conditions as employees. Musicians, sportsmen and insurance agents working without a contract of employment are also sometimes covered by compulsory employees' insurance. In order to be considered an employed person, it is irrelevant whether the person concerned perform(ed) occupational activities, but it was important that s/he was or had been covered by a social security scheme for employed persons.[4]

It is, however, also possible that, due to his or her low income or small number of working hours, a person is excluded from a national scheme, even if s/he has a contract of employment. Consequently, now s/he is not covered by any national social security scheme for workers, s/he is not an employee for the regulation. Consequently, it was up to the national legislature to decide which categories are covered by a social security scheme for employees.

An interesting question was whether it is required that a person is engaged for a minimum number of hours a week in order to be considered an employee. This was one of the questions asked in the *Kits van Heijningen* judgment.[5] The question was whether a person in this position, *i.e.* who works only four hours a week, could invoke the Regulation. The Court pointed out that the Regulation did not contain provisions which exclude certain categories of workers who only work part-time from its scope. Therefore, it ruled that coordination Regulation applied to all persons satisfying the conditions of Articles 1 and 2, irrespective of the number of hours they work.

The Court also gave a broad interpretation to the term self-employed persons, this was in the *Van Roosmalen* judgment.[6] Mr Van Roosmalen was a Dutch priest who was sent to Belgian Congo where he applied for voluntary insurance under the Dutch General Invalidity Benefits Act (AAW). After his return to Europe,

---

[4] Under German law, for instance, a person who brings up a child under the age of three is compulsorily insured under the Old Age and Invalidity Pension Act, a form of employees' insurance. If a person falls under this insurance on the grounds of raising a child, he is an employed person for the purpose of the Regulation, even if he does not work and has never even worked (see also the *Sürül* judgment, Case 262/96, [1999] *ECR* I-2685, to be discussed in Section 17.2. This judgment concerned Decision 3/80 of the Association Council EEC Turkey, but the interpretation of the terms of this Decision and Regulation 1408/71 is the same, and therefore the judgment is a useful example.

[5] Case 2/89, [1990] *ECR* 1755.

[6] Case 300/84, [1986] *ECR* 3097.

he came to live in Belgium where he was found to be disabled because of back troubles which he had incurred in Zaire. He was refused Dutch disability benefit on the grounds that a person is only eligible for AAW if he has been disabled for at least fifty-two weeks in the Netherlands. If the Regulation were applicable, this territoriality condition would not be allowed. It was, therefore, important to him that he could be qualified as a self-employed person. Van Roosmalen did not receive an income from his order, but was supported by his parishioners. The Court considered that the term 'self-employed person' was characterised, following the definitions of the Annex relating to the Netherlands, by the type of activities a person performs or has performed, provided these are occupational activities.[7] The term 'occupational activities' must be interpreted in a broad sense: it is not necessary that the person concerned receives direct consideration for his or her activities. Contributions from parishioners count for this purpose if they enable the priest to support himself partially or completely. As this was the case for Mr Van Roosmalen, he was considered a self-employed person for the purpose of the Regulation.

Until 25 October 1998, civil servants fell only within the personal scope of the Regulation in so far as they were or have been subject to the statutory social security schemes which were within the material scope of the Regulation. Article 4(4) provided that the special schemes for civil servants were excluded from the material scope of the Regulation. Regulation 1606/98 repealed the latter provision.[8] Also civil servants who are exclusively covered by special schemes for civil servants, are now covered by the Regulation.

As from 1 May 1999, students also fell under the personal scope of the Regulation.[9] In Article 1(ca), the term *student* was defined: a person who studies or receives vocational training leading to a qualification officially recognised by the authorities of a Member State, and who is insured under a general social security scheme or a special social security scheme applicable to students. Those who fall under the Regulation as an employed or self-employed person or member of the family are excluded. The advantages of falling under the scope of the Regulation are limited for students: the rules for determining the legislation applicable do, for instance, not apply to them. They benefit from the Regulation, however, as the rules in the area of sickness benefits applicable to employees do also apply to students provided they are insured in a general scheme or special scheme for students.

---

[7]   Mr Van Roosmalen was voluntarily insured and therefore under the scope of the Regulation.
[8]   *OJ* L 209 of 25 July 1998, p. 1.
[9]   This is the result of Regulation 307/99 of 8 February 1999, *OJ* L 38, p. 1.

4.3. THE PERSONAL SCOPE OF REGULATION 883/2004

4.3.1. INTRODUCTION

Article 2 reads that:

(1) This Regulation shall apply to nationals of a Member State, stateless persons and refugees residing in a Member State who are or have been subject to the legislation of one or more Member States, as well as to the members of their families and to their survivors.

(2) It shall also apply to the survivors of persons who have been subjectf to the legislation of one or more Member States, irrespective of the nationality of such persons, where their survivors are nationals of a Member State or stateless persons or refugees residing in one of the Member States.

It follows that for stateless persons and refugees it is required that they reside in a Member State; other categories fall under the personal scope even if they reside outside the territory of the EU.

Thus Article 2 is not restricted to employees or self-employed persons, but covers all nationals of a Member State. We will discuss the condition that the person concerned is or has been subject to the legislation of one or more Member States and the nationality discussion below.

4.3.2. THE REQUIREMENT OF BEING SUBJECT TO THE LEGISLATION OF A MEMBER STATE

The criterion that a person must be or have been subject to the legislation of a Member State means that a person who is not and who has not been covered by the legislation of a Member State is not under the personal scope. For instance, a national of an EU Member State who is covered by a non-EU scheme only or by the scheme of the European Commission, is not covered by the Regulation. Also for the determination of the rights of family members it is relevant that the person from who they derive their rights is subject to the legislation of a Member State.

The legislation meant here is the legislation referred to in Article 3 of the Regulation. For instance, if a person is covered by social assistance only, s/he is not within the personal scope of the Regulation.

The Court ruled in the *Kuusijärvi* and *Martínez Sala* judgment – translated into the terms of the new Regulation – that any person insured under one of the social security schemes mentioned in Article 3 is under the personal scope. This is satisfied if the person is covered, even if only in respect of a single risk, by a general or special social security scheme, irrespective of the existence of an employment relationship. Although the Court uses the term 'insured', it obviously means to say that the person was covered ('subject to'). The Court explains that the condition is certainly satisfied, in the case of a person who is unemployed in a Member State and is in receipt there of unemployment benefits under the legislation of that Member State. So if a person is insured by meeting the conditions for insurance (or coverage) of a particular scheme, e.g. on the basis of a contract of employment, working as a self-employed, residence, etc., s/he is subject to the scheme. If s/he receives or claims benefit under a particular scheme to which s/he has been covered in the past, s/he is also under the personal scope.

This interpretation is relevant to the part of Article 2 that a person is subject to legislation. Article 2 also allows that a person who has been subject to the legislation of one or more Member States is covered.[10] This part is relevant in case a person wishes to invoke the coordination rules in respect to claim benefits which s/he acquired when s/he was covered by the legislation of a Member State. For instance, a person was subject to a particular legislation, in the past, acquired benefit rights, is subsequently no longer subject to legislation and later claims these pension rights (e.g. an old age pension). Then s/he is also under the personal scope.

4.3.3. THE NATIONALITY CONDITION

According to Article 2, one of the requirements for falling within the personal scope of the Regulation is that a person must be a national of one of the Member States. Nationals of one of the European Economic Area countries and Switzerland are assimilated with nationals of EU Member States. By 'nationality' is meant the formal legal position of an individual as appears from the official Registry Office or passport. Long term residency or 'citizenship' are therefore the same as being national of a Member State.

The question was raised at *which moment* a person has to satisfy the nationality condition. This was answered in the *Belhouab* judgment.[11] Mr Belhouab was born as French national in Algeria. He worked during 155 months in France and, since

---

[10] One might argue that the English use of the tense is not fully correct as present continuous suggests that a person must be subject in the past and is still covered. Other language versions use a different tense: French : 'Le présent règlement s'applique aux ressortissants de l'un des États membres, aux apatrides et aux réfugiés résidant dans un État membre qui sont ou ont été soumis à la législation d'un ou de plusieurs États membres, ainsi qu'aux membres de leur famille et à leurs survivants.'
German: 'Diese Verordnung gilt für Staatsangehörige eines Mitgliedstaats, Staatenlose und Flüchtlinge mit Wohnort in einem Mitgliedstaat, für die die Rechtsvorschriften eines oder mehrerer Mitgliedstaaten gelten oder galten, sowie für ihre Familienangehörigen und Hinterbliebenen.'
Spanish : 'El presente Reglamento se aplicará a las personas nacionales de uno de los Estados miembros y a los apatridas y refugiados residentes en uno de los Estados miembros, que estén o hayan estado sujetas a la legislación de uno o de varios Estados miembros, así como a los miembros de sus familias y a sus supérstites.'
[11] Case 10/78, [1978] *ECR* 1915.

1961, he worked in Germany. When Algeria became independent in 1962 he lost his French nationality. In 1974 he applied for a German mineworker's pension. The Court decided that the periods in which a person worked, paid contributions or acquired benefit rights are relevant to answering the question of whether he satisfies the conditions for benefit. Thus, the moment of the claim is not of decisive importance.

Another question concerns the situation where a person *becomes* a national of a Member State: can s/he have the periods fulfilled before s/he became national of the Member State counted for the purpose of fulfilling the benefit conditions or calculating the level of benefit? *Example:* A person with Iraqi nationality works from 1980 to 1990 in Belgium and changes to Belgian nationality in 1989. If s/he subsequently moves to Germany to work in that country as an employed person, but becomes disabled within one month, can s/he rely on the Regulation in order to fulfil the waiting conditions of the German disability benefit? In the *Belhouab* judgment, discussed before, the Court refers to the rules on transitional law of the Regulation (Article 94), which says that periods of insurance fulfilled before the Regulation came into force are also relevant, provided, according to the Court, the employed person was a national of one of the (later) Member States at the time of insurance. If the Iraqi person were Swedish instead, he could have the periods fulfilled from when Sweden became a Member State counted. In the example as it is, the Iraqi cannot have the periods fulfilled in the past counted towards the calculation of his benefit rights.

A rare situation is that of a person who worked as a national of a State, but lost this status before this State entered the EU, *see* the *Buhari Haji* judgment.[12] Mr Buhari was born in 1914 in Nigeria and had British nationality until 1964. At that time, he acquired Nigerian nationality. From 1937 until 1986, he worked in the Belgian Congo. Until this State became independent, he paid contributions to the Belgian social security authorities. When he applied for a Belgian retirement pension it was refused. The Court considered that the nationality criterion of the Regulation could not be considered to be fulfilled when the employee concerned had, during the period in which he performed his occupational activities and paid contributions, the nationality of a Member State which was not yet a Member of the EC and who lost the status of national of that State before the State entered the EC. The Court argued that this approach was legitimate because, in this situation, freedom of movement as guaranteed in EC Treaty was not involved.

---

[12]   Case 105/89, [1990] *ECR* 4211.

4.3.4. STATELESS PERSONS AND REFUGEES

Also stateless persons and refugees are mentioned in Article 2. In the *Khalil* judgment,[13] the question was raised whether (what is now) Article 48 TFEU was a sufficient legal basis to include this group in the Regulation. The case concerned a number of stateless persons and political refugees who applied for child benefit in Germany. As from 1994 this benefit was refused to foreigners who did not have a residence entitlement or residence permit. The case concerned, among others, Kurdish and Palestinian refugees from Lebanon, who had lived already during ten years in Germany when they were confronted with this Law. Could these applicants invoke Regulation 1408/71, which would mean that the condition on the residence permit was not permitted?

The answer of the Court to the question whether stateless persons and refugees could be included in the Regulation was clearly in the affirmative. The Court considered that the treatment of refugees was subject of the Geneva Convention, which the original six Member States of the European Economic Community had ratified. This Convention of 1951 provides that the contracting Stares have to ensure that refugees lawfully staying in their territory are treated in the same way as nationals in respect to social security. The same principle was laid down in the New York Convention of 1954 concerning stateless persons. Subsequently this principle was laid down in some coordination agreements which preceded Regulation 1408/71. The Regulation included this principle. Coordination excluding stateless persons and refugees would have meant that the Member States, in order to ensure compliance with their international obligations, had to establish a second coordination regime designed solely for the very restricted category of stateless persons and refugees. The technique chosen to insert these provisions in Regulation 1408/71 is much more efficient and consistent with the EC Treaty. Consequently, Article 2 could be upheld.

The second question in the *Khalil* judgment was whether refugees or stateless persons may rely on the Regulation where they have traveled to that Member State directly from a non-member country and have not moved within the Community. The Court referred to its case law, the *Petit* judgment[14] in particular, in which it concluded that Article 51 EC Treaty (now Article 48 TFEU) and Regulation 1408/71 do not apply to situations which are confined within a single Member State. Such is in particular the case where the situation of a worker has factors linking it solely with a non-member country and one single Member State. Consequently, the refugees and stateless persons in this case could not rely on the rights conferred by the Regulation now they were in a situation which is confined in all respects within one Member State. This means that stateless persons and

---

[13]   Case 95/99, [2001] ecr I-7413.
[14]   Case 153/91, [1992] ECR I-4973.

refugees can benefit from this decision only when their situation involves two Member States.

4.4. THIRD COUNTRY NATIONALS ARE COVERED BY A SEPARATE REGULATION

In Section 4.3 we saw that the nationality condition is essential to being covered by the coordination Regulation. This also applies to Regulation 883/2004. The nationality condition has been severely criticised for excluding the so-called third country nationals. Third country nationals are nationals of countries which are not a Member State of the EU (or EEA or Switzerland). As we saw before, this condition means, for instance, that for a Moroccan who first works in France and subsequently in Belgium, his periods completed in France cannot be used in order to satisfy the conditions for Belgian unemployment benefit.

The European Commission issued several proposals to extend the personal scope of Regulation 1408/71 to third country nationals, but these were not accepted. One proposal was made in 1995, another in 1997,[15] and a third was the Proposal for Simplification of the Regulation.[16] A major point of discussion was whether Article 42 EC (now Article 48 TFEU) could be a suitable legal basis for this extension.[17] This issue was solved in the *Khalil* judgment,[18] discussed in the previous section. From this judgment it follows that Article 48 TFEU cannot be a legal basis for the extension of the personal scope to third country nationals, as the Court decided that the scope of this Article is limited to EU nationals, since only these enjoy the freedom of movement of the Treaty.

Thereupon, the Commission made a new proposal, this time based on Article 63(4) EC (now Article 79 TFEU). This Article concerns the conditions for admission and residence of third country nationals to the Community. This legal basis for making a Regulation was accepted by the Council and in 2003 Regulation 859/2003 was adopted.[19]

---

[15] OJ C 242 of 19 September 1995; OJ C of 10 January 1998, Com 1997, 561. *See*, on this topic, Y. Jorens, *De rechtspositie van niet-EU-onderdanen in het Europese Socialezekerheidsrecht*, Brugge, 1997; Y. Jorens and B. Schulte (eds.), *European Social Security Law and Third Country Nationals*, Brugge, 1998.
[16] Com 1998, 779.
[17] *See*, on this issue also D. Pieters, 'Enquiry into the Legal Foundations of a Possible Extension of Community Provisions on Social Security to Third-Country Nationals Residing and/ or Working in the European Union', in: P. Schoukens (ed.), *Prospects of Social Security Co-ordination*, Leuven 1997, p. 15; and S. Roberts, '"Our view has not changed": the uk's Response to the Proposal to Extend the Co-ordination of Social Security to Third Country Nationals" *European Journal of Social Security*, 2000, p. 189, who explains the reason of the UK government not to be in favour of extension the scope of the Regulation to third country nationals.
[18] Case 95/99, [2001] ECR I-7413.
[19] *OJ L* 124. See the preparatory work in Com 2002, 59.

The question arises, of course, why some Member States were so heavily opposed against taking (what is now) Article 48 TFEU as a legal basis, but were willing to accept Article 63(4). The reason is that the Treaty provides that Title IV EC, of which Article 63 is part, does not bind the United Kingdom, Ireland and Denmark, unless these countries explicitly accept regulations based on a provision of this Title.[20] Therefore they had the right to opt out.

After the Regulation was adopted the United Kingdom and Ireland joined the countries which are bound by the new Regulation. Denmark did not bind itself. The Regulation does not apply to the EEA Member States and Switzerland either.

Regulation 859/2003 has, apart from a transitional provision, only one provision, which extends the provisions of Regulation 1408/71 and Regulation 574/72 to nationals of third countries who are not already covered by those provisions solely on the ground of their nationality, as well as to members of their families and to their survivors provided they are legally resident in the territory of a Member State and are in a situation which is not confined in all respects within a single Member State.

Thus third country nationals have to be legally resident in the territory of a Member State and they must be in a situation which is not confined in all respects within a single Member State. This means that only if a situation concerns facts in at least two Member States (*e.g.* a worker from France who goes to work in the UK) the Regulation is applicable. If, however, a person came from a non-EU State and remained in one and the same EU Member State, the Regulation is not applicable. This limitation can also be found the *Khalil* judgment, and earlier in the *Petit* judgment. Still, this limitation could be criticised, as, different from these two cases, the new Regulation is not based on Article 48 TFEU, but on Article 63(4) EC. This separate legal basis is not related to the right to free movement, which is an EU right, so why require that at least the facts of two Member States have to be involved?

The effect of this requirement is different for third country nationals than for EU nationals, such as Mr Petit in the *Petit* judgment,[21] as the former persons are from a third country and therefore much more likely to be discriminated against on grounds of nationality. Examples are situations such as in the *Sürül* judgment,[22] in which national law excludes foreigners from their national security system. The third country nationals cannot invoke the Regulation in, for instance, a case of discrimination on grounds of nationality which occurs within a Member State if s/he does not work, reside or stay in another Member State. If the worker himself moves to another Member State, or if his or her spouse or children are in another Member State, the situation is not confined to one single Member State.

---

[20] This is laid down in Protocols to the Treaty of Amsterdam.
[21] Case 153/91, [1992] ECR I-4973.
[22] Case 262/96, [1999] *ECR* I-2685.

An interesting question is what the position of Denmark is in this respect. It is clear, of course, that a third country national cannot invoke the Regulation if s/he first works in Belgium and then moves to Denmark, in order to have periods of insurance aggregated. However, what about the reverse situation? If s/he moves to Belgium, can s/he have his or her Danish periods added to the Belgian ones? Or, even more basically, suppose that s/he wishes to invoke the Regulation since benefit is refused because of nationality, and s/he was first in Denmark, can this person invoke Regulation 859/2003? Or does the period in Denmark not count for the condition that the facts must not be limited to one Member State?

Cornelissen argued that it is doubtful that Denmark has to be taken into account for the requirement of having two countries. The extension of Regulation 1408/71 to cover third-country nationals only applies to Member States that have adopted Regulation 859/2003 and this extension therefore only applies to cases affecting third-country nationals where the cross border element is between these particular Member States.[23] He bases his position on recital 15 of Regulation 859/2003, which reads: 'To achieve these objectives it is necessary and appropriate to extend the scope of the rules coordinating the national social security schemes by adopting a Community legal instrument which is binding and directly applicable in every Member State that takes part in the adoption of this Regulation'. [24]

I have a different view on this. Although the recital makes clear that Denmark does not have to accept the application of the Regulation in its territory, that does not explain why – in my example – Belgium does not have to take the period completed in Denmark into account. After all, the Recital does not say that 'the scope is extended *to* all countries taking part in the adoption of the scheme'. Furthermore, from the rationale of the requirement of cross border elements, it is not necessary to ignore the period fulfilled in Denmark. The other countries have adopted the coordination rules for these migrants, so what is then a good reason not to take the period in Denmark into account? This is only different if Denmark would be confronted with extra costs as result of this interpretation.

Also Recital 12 does not lead to exclusion of the periods in Denmark. It reads that the provisions of Regulation 1408/71 and Regulation 574/72 are not applicable in a situation which is confined in all respects within a single Member State. This concerns, *inter alia*, the situation of a third country national who has links only with a third country and a single Member State.

This recital does not make an explicit connection with Denmark, where, if the interpretation that Denmark does not count for this Regulation, is correct, it

---

[23]   R. Cornelissen, 'Third-Country Nationals and the European Coordination of Social Security', *EJSS* 2008, p. 360.
[24]   Also the Dutch benefit administration, Sociale verzekeringsbank, follows the approach that Denmark does not count. See its *Beleidsregels* (policy rules) on svb.nl.

would have been logical to mention it here. So far the Court has not been asked to give a ruling on this issue.

A second question is what is meant by 'legally resident'. The interpretation that it is sufficient to meet the criteria for legally staying or residing in a Member State according to its national law or following from international law seems to fit best with the purpose of the Regulation.[25] This suggests that stricter conditions, such as a permanent permit, may be inconsistent with this condition.

So far there have not been any cases before the Court of Justice on the interpretation of legally resident for this Regulation. In Chapter 10 we will see some cases in which the Court did not pose strong requirements for legally resident in the application of Regulation 1612/68 and Article 18 EC. It is not clear whether this case law also applies to Regulation 859/2003.

Regulation 883/2004 is limited to nationals of EU Member States in the same way as Regulation 1408/71. Therefore, a regulation like Regulation 859/2003 is necessary in order to have coordination rules applied to third country nationals. In 2007 a proposal was made.[26] So far it has not been adopted and it seems to be the subject of difficult discussions in the Council. As long as no new regulation is adopted, Regulation 859/2003 remains in force and it remains to refer to Regulation 1408/71 (Article 90(1)(a) of Regulation 883/2004). The complicated co-existence of two coordination Regulations can therefore continue to last for a considerable time. If some of the countries who opted in Regulation 859/2003 do not accept a new one, it becomes even more difficult.

4.5. MEMBERS OF THE FAMILY AND SURVIVORS

Article 2 of Regulation 883/2004 does not only cover nationals, but also members of their families and survivors. Although by the extension of the personal scope of the Regulation many members of the family, including those who were not employees or self-employed persons themselves, are now covered on their own right, the reference to members of the family is still relevant. This is in particular the case for persons not having nationality of one of the Member States.

Article 2(1) covers nationals of a Member State and members of their families and their survivors. Thus, the members of the family and survivors need not have nationality of a Member State themselves. For this purpose the reference to this category is still relevant.

Article 2(2) refers to survivors of persons who have been subject to the legislation of one or more Member States, irrespective of the nationality of such

---

[25] R. Cornelissen, 'Third-Country Nationals and the European Coordination of Social Security', *EJSS* 2008, p. 359.
[26] Com(2007) 439 final.

employed or self-employed persons, where their survivors are nationals of one of the Member States, or stateless persons or refugees residing within the territory of one of the Member States. This is a different category: the survivors themselves are national of a Member State, whereas the person from whom they derive their right is not.

The term *member of the family* is defined in Article 1(i). It provides that member of the family is any person defined or recognised as a member of the family or designated as member of the household by the legislation under which benefits are provided. Thus the social security legislation of the country that pays benefits is decisive. As a result of this rule there may be differences between the Member States.[27]

Suppose there are two neighbouring countries, country A and B. Country A recognises same sex marriages and Country B does not. Suppose also that a couple lives in country A, and one of them works in country B, which does not recognise same sex marriages. The partner is not member of the family for the scheme of B.[28]

Sometimes schemes do not make a distinction between the members of the family and other persons to whom it is applicable. In this case the spouse, minor children and dependent children who have reached the age of majority are considered members of the family. If a scheme considers a member of the family or member of the household only if s/he lives in the same household as the insured person this condition shall be considered satisfied if the person concerned is mainly dependent on the insured person or pensioner. For instance, a severely handicapped person, who has reached the age of majority and lives on his or her own, can thus still be considered as member of the family.

Even if one falls within the scope of the Regulation as a member of the family or survivor, this does not mean that one can rely on the Regulation with respect to all types of benefits. Initially, the Court followed the so-called *Kermaschek* doctrine.[29] In this it considered that members of a family can only rely on provisions concerning benefits payable *qua* members, such as family allowances or survivors' benefits. As a result Ms Kermaschek could not aggregate periods of work in the Netherlands to claim unemployment benefit in Germany. Although Ms Kermaschek worked as an employed person, she did not have the nationality

---

[27]   Article 1(i)(1)(ii) provides that with regarded to sickness, maternity and paternity benefits any person defined or recognised as a member of the family or designated as a member of the household by the legislation of the Member State in which s/he resides is a member of the family. This special rule is relevant since for sickness benefits in many schemes also members of the family are insured. These members may live in a different Member State than the one whose legislation is applicable to the person who is the main insured person. For these members the country where they live is decisive. This is also discussed in Section 11.4.2.

[28]   See previous note: for sickness benefit this outcome is the opposite.

[29]   Case 40/76, [1976] *ECR* 1669.

of a Member State and therefore she had to rely on the Regulation, at the time, as member of the family.[30]

In the *Cabanis* judgment[31] the Court partially departed from the *Kermaschek* doctrine. This decision concerned a woman of French nationality, a widow of a migrant worker. After her husband died in 1978, she was entitled to a reduced Dutch old age pension only. The Dutch benefit agency offered her a voluntary insurance, but the contribution conditions for this insurance were less attractive for persons with a nationality other than Dutch. Was this discrimination allowed? The Court considered that in the light of the *Kermaschek* case law a widow of a migrant worker could not invoke Article 3 of Regulation 1408/71 in order to fight the discriminatory conditions of the voluntary insurance. The Court continued to argue, however, that the fact that the spouse could not rely on the equal treatment rule would adversely affect the freedom of movement of workers. This would run counter to the purpose and spirit of the Community rules on free movement. The distinction drawn between rights in person and derived rights, the Court considered, renders the fundamental rule of equal treatment inapplicable to the surviving spouse of a migrant worker. Another problem is that this distinction undermines the fundamental requirement that Community rules should be applied uniformly. This could be the case if the applicability of provisions to individuals depends on whether national law relating to the benefits in question treats the rights concerned as rights in person or as derived rights. Therefore, the Court concluded, the doctrine of the distinction between rights in person and derived rights has to be partially abandoned.

The *Cabanis* judgment limits the *Kermaschek* doctrine to those cases in which a member of the family invokes provisions of the Regulation which *apply exclusively to employed persons*. Examples of such exclusive provisions are Articles 61 to 75 of the present Regulation concerning unemployment benefits. Thus, we must not look at the type of benefit, but at the provision of the Regulation a person wishes to invoke: how is its wording?

In the *Hoever and Zachow* judgment,[32] the Court decided that the *Cabanis* decision did not apply only if the discrimination clause is invoked. This judgment involves that members of the family can also invoke Article 73 dealing with family benefits, as this is not an exclusive provision (*see* also Section 16.1).

---

[30]   In the *Fracas* judgment (Case 7/75, [1975] *ECR* 679), the Court followed a different approach. The case concerned a completely incapacitated son of an Italian worker, for whom a Belgian benefit for the handicapped was requested. These were payable to Belgians only. The Court decided that the nationality requirements could not be upheld, as otherwise the worker would be induced not to remain in the Member State where he has established himself and where he was employed. This approach was also followed in the *Inzirillo* judgment, which concerned a handicapped child (Case 63/76, [1976] *ECR* 2057). In later decisions, the Court followed the *Kermaschek* doctrine again, *see* the *Deak* judgment (Case 94/84, [1985] *ECR* 1873) and the *Zaoui* judgment (Case 147/87, [1987] *ECR* 5511).

[31]   Case 308/93, [1996] ECR I-2097.

[32]   Cases 245/94 and 312/94, [1996] ECR I-4895.

In the *Ruhr* case,[33] the *Cabanis-Issarte* case law was followed in respect to the coordination rules on unemployment benefits – what is now Article 63 of the Regulation. These rules only apply to employed persons having nationality of a EU Member State. Ms Ruhr was a Polish national who was married to an employed person with German nationality and living in Germany. Ms Ruhr used to work in Luxembourg. Having lost her job, she registered as a person seeking work in Germany.

The Court followed the *Cabanis-Issarte* case law and affirmed that the provisions on unemployment benefits apply solely to employed persons. As to the question whether this conclusion was liable to hamper the right to freedom of movement of Ms Ruhr's husband, the Court held that he, as a German national residing in Germany, had not exercised his right to freedom of movement and that, even if he would have done so, this would not have altered the legal position of Ms Ruhr. Although this judgment it is not surprising, given the recent *Cabanis* judgment, the result in this case is unsatisfactory. Ms Ruhr had paid contributions to the Luxembourg benefit scheme, but she was refused unemployment benefit solely for reasons of her nationality. Regulation 859/2003 solves such cases, but came too late for Ms Ruhr.

The *Cabanis* case law was also relevant in the *Hosse* judgment.[34] The case concerned a care benefit, which was not paid for a daughter of a German frontier worker, working in Austria and residing in Germany. The Court decided that the Austrian benefit was exportable (see Section 5.6). The Court then considered that it is apparent from the documents before the Court that the entitlement to the care allowance under the SPGG is an entitlement of Silvia Hosse's own, not one derived from her father. The Court referred to the *Cabanis-Issarte* judgment, in which it decided that a member of the worker's family cannot rely on provisions of the Regulation which apply solely to workers and not to members of their families. That is not the case with (what is now) Article 17 of the Regulation (see Chapter 11 below), the purpose of which is precisely to guarantee the worker and the members of the family residing in a Member State other than the competent State the grant of the sickness benefits provided for by the applicable legislation, in so far as the members of the family are not entitled to those benefits under the legislation of the State in whose territory they reside.

To summarise: the *Kermaschek* doctrine can be characterised as *no, unless*: members of the family and survivors cannot invoke the Regulation, unless in case of benefits meant especially for them. The *Cabanis* doctrine can be denoted as *yes, unless*: members of the family and survivors can rely on the Regulation, unless the provisions are meant especially (taking into account the wording) for employees or self-employed persons.

---

[33]   Case 189/00 [2001] *ECR* I-8225.
[34]   Case C-286/03 Hosse [2006] ECR I-1771.

CHAPTER 5

THE MATERIAL SCOPE OF REGULATION 883/2004

5.1. INTRODUCTION

The coordination Regulation can be applied only in respect of benefits which are within its material scope. The material scope of Regulation 883/2004 is defined in Article 3; it reads that the Regulation applies to all legislation concerning the following branches of social security:

a) sickness benefits;
b) maternity and equivalent paternity benefits;
c) invalidity benefits;
d) old-age benefits;
e) survivor's benefits;
f) benefits in respect of accidents at work and occupational diseases;
g) death grants;
h) unemployment benefits;
i pre-retirement benefits;
j) family benefits.

This is a limitative list of the benefits, and by this the material scope is defined. Benefits not mentioned here, such as study grants and housing benefits, are not covered. Furthermore, the material scope is limited to *legislation* on these benefits. We will discuss this term in Section 5.2. If a benefit is part of legislation and fits with one of the types mentioned *supra*, the Regulation applies to this benefit, regardless of whether the benefit belongs to a general or special social security scheme, and whether it is contributory or non-contributory. Thus, benefits paid from taxes also fall within the Regulation's scope.

Sometimes it is difficult to determine how a particular benefit is to be qualified; this issue will be discussed in more detail in Section 5.3.

5.2. THE TERM LEGISLATION AND THE EXCLUSION OF CONTRACTUAL SCHEMES

The material scope of the Regulation is limited to benefits governed by legislation. The meaning of the term legislation can be found in Article 1(l) of the Regulation. This Article provides that legislation means: laws, regulations and other statutory provisions, and all other implementing measures relating to the social security branches covered by Article 3(1).

Thus, the term legislation has a broad meaning and, by referring to implementing measures, also refers to ministerial and royal decrees, regulations made by the benefit administration etc.

The term legislation excludes, according to the same Article, contractual provisions other than those which serve to implement an insurance obligation arising from the laws and regulations mentioned supra or which have been the subject of a decision by the public authorities which makes them obligatory or extends their scope, provided that the Member State concerned makes a declaration to that effect, notified to the President of the European Parliament and the President of the Council of the European Union. Such declaration has to be published in the *Official Journal* of the European Union. Consequently, a collective agreement which serves to implement a law is also covered, provided that the Member State makes a declaration to this effect and notifies the President of the European Parliament and the President of the Council. Under the same condition of notification also contractual provisions which have been made subject of a decision by the public authorities which makes them obligatory or extends their scope are covered. Thus, if a collective agreement including social security provisions is made obligatory or extended *and* notified to the said Presidents, it is within the material scope of the Regulation.

If collective agreements and supplementary pension schemes do not satisfy the mentioned conditions they are not within the scope of the Regulation. In some countries, collective agreements govern a substantial part of social security, but, as a result of these provisions, these do not fall under the Regulation, even if the collective agreement concerned has been declared generally binding.

So far, not much use has been made of the possibility of bringing collective agreements within the scope of the Regulation. An exception is France, which, by means of a declaration, brought its collective agreements on unemployment benefit and the supplementary pension schemes ARRCO and AGIRC within the scope of the Regulation.

Apart from these exceptions, collective agreements do not fall within the scope of the Regulation; as a result, export of benefits established by a collective agreement is not required by the Regulation. Nor can periods fulfilled abroad be used to satisfy waiting periods in supplementary pension schemes. For posted workers, for instance, the problem arises that contributions levied on the basis of collective agreements for supplementary benefits in the State of employment may overlap with the benefits for which they remained insured in the State of residence. The coordination Regulation cannot help in this.

The above mentioned 1998 Proposal of the Commission on the modernisation of the Regulation provided that agreements declared generally binding fall within the material scope of the coordination regime; a declaration by the Member State concerned was no longer have been required. This rule was meant to terminate the exclusion of important parts of social security from the co-ordination rules. The effects of extending the co-ordination rules to collective agreements and other contractual schemes are, however, hard to oversee, since all kinds of provisions can be found in collective agreements. Holiday pay, study and training grants, sabbatical leaves, loyalty stamps and bad weather stamps are examples of supplementary social security. Sometimes collective agreements provide for supplements to statutory social security (increases to the benefit rates) or replace statutory protection which was withdrawn (e.g. to compensate the results of privatisation). Therefore it was too simple to bring these advantages within the scope of all the coordination rules.

However, some co-ordination rules could very well be applied to advantages governed by collective agreements, such as the non-discrimination clause and the provision on export of benefits.[1] Other co-ordination rules can lead to problems if they are applied to these advantages. One example is a sabbatical leave provision which requires a waiting period of seven years of work for the same employer. An employer cannot be expected to allow an employee to aggregate the periods of work for other employers for the purpose of satisfying this condition, since this employer has to pay the full costs of the sabbatical. The same problem arises in the case of loyalty benefits. Problems arise also in the case of employees working in two countries. If the rules for determining the legislation applicable apply to these agreements as well, the employee concerned falls under one collective agreement only, insofar as its social security provisions are considered. The effects are hard to oversee and some of the effects are undesirable. Member States could prevent these problems by no longer extending collective agreements, but that would be an unattractive effect.[2]

In Regulation 883/2004, the approach of Regulation 1408/71 towards non-statutory social security is fully maintained. The progress made in extending the co-ordination rules to these types of benefit is disappointing. So far very little use has been made of the declarations, even in cases when there are no obvious problems. Recital 6 of the Preamble of Regulation 883/2004 reads that the close link between social security legislation and those contractual provisions which complement or replace such legislation and which have been the subject of a

---

[1]   In fact, non-discrimination rules, such as Article 7(2) Regulation 1612/68, often have already this effect as they apply also to collective agreements.

[2]   See also Frans Pennings, 'Inclusion and Exclusion of Persons and Benefits in the New Co-ordination Regulation', in M. Dougan and E. Spaventa (eds.), *Social Welfare and EU Law*, Oxford 2006, p. 241-261.

decision by the public authorities rendering them compulsory or extending their scope may call for similar protection with regard to the application of those provisions as that afforded by the new Regulation; as a first step, the experience of Member States who have notified such schemes might be evaluated. This recital was inserted into the text after adoption of an amendment proposed by the European Parliament. However, the Council added a cautious last phrase, which reads that, first, appropriate national experiences have to be studied. The question is whether such an evaluation is really necessary. There are very few declarations, and the schemes concerned – which have national scope – seem to fit very well into the co-ordination system.[3]

It is preferable that Member are encouraged to issue declarations on a more generous scale in order to bring contractual schemes within the scope of Regulation 883/2004. A way to do so is that Member States are given the burden of proof to explain why a declaration cannot be given to bring a generally binding scheme within the scope of the Regulation. At present there is no such obligation yet. If they are not able to give a satisfactory reason, the scheme should be brought within the scope of the Regulation.

5.3. THE CLASSIFICATION OF BENEFITS

5.3.1. INTRODUCTION: A LIMITED MATERIAL SCOPE

In the Proposal for modernisation and simplification of the coordination Regulation of 1998[4] it was proposed to restrict the material scope of the Regulation no longer to the risks mentioned in what is now Article 3. The Proposal provided that 'this Regulation is applicable on all social security legislation concerning the following contingencies, in particular...'. However, this Proposal did not survive the discussions in the Council; Regulation 883/2004 follows the approach mentioned supra, which is the same as that of Regulation 1408/71. The description of the material scope in the 1998 Proposal had interesting implications: it would include also recently developed categories of benefits, including parental benefits, health insurance benefits and benefits for leave. Since Article 48 TFEU requires measures 'in the field of social security', there are good arguments for an open definition of the material scope. However, an unrestrictive definition of the material scope encounters also important problems. Since the term social security is not defined in the Regulation, it would be very difficult to decide whether a

---

[3]   Still, the recital leaves more room than the text of the parameters (the parameters were discussed in Section 2), as now it is no longer argued that co-ordination of supplementary social security has to take place outside the Regulation.
[4]   COM (1998) 779.

particular advantage would be part of it. For instance, would housing grants fall within its scope? And tax rebates? And study grants?

In addition, like Regulations 1408/71 and 883/2004, the 1998 Proposal also covers the statutory obligations of employers in relation to social security, e.g. the statutory obligation of employers to pay wages. Since the 1998 Proposal did not limit the types of benefits which were covered, all employers' obligations would fall within the scope of the Regulation. Holiday pay and fidelity payments are examples of advantages which could fall under the Regulation.

As was said, Regulation 883/2004 does not follow this approach. For this Regulation, the extension of the material scope is limited to pre-retirement benefits and paternity benefits. However, since the scope of the Regulation remains limited to statutory schemes, contractual pre-retirement schemes (most pre-retirement schemes are of this type) fall outside the scope of the Regulation. Consideration 33 of the Preamble of Regulation 883/2004 reads that, given the fact that statutory preretirement schemes exist in a very small number of Member States only, aggregation rules are not necessary. Apart from the fact that this is not a fully logical consideration, it shows that the extension of the material scope is very limited.

5.3.2. THE CRITERIA FOR CLASSIFYING BENEFITS

Let us now have a closer look at the benefits mentioned in Article 3(1). Although at first sight the list seems to be unproblematic, it is not always easy to determine to which category a specific benefit belongs. In the *Hoever and Zachow* judgment[5] the Court of Justice argued that the distinction between benefits included in and excluded from the scope of the Regulation is based essentially on the constituent elements of the benefit in question, in particular its purposes and the conditions on which it is granted, and not on how it is classified in the national legislation.

Also for determining the category to which a benefit belongs, the constituent elements, in particular its purposes and the conditions, are decisive. In the *Hoever and Zachow* case the German child-raising allowance (*Erziehungsgeld*) was to be classified. The German Government maintained that the child-raising allowance did not have the same purpose as a family benefit within the meaning of the Regulation, since the child-raising allowance is intended, by conferring a personal right, to remunerate the particular parent who both takes on the task of raising a child and personally fulfils the conditions for grant of the allowance. The Court did not accept this argument, since the benefit's aim was to meet family expenses. Child-raising allowance is paid only where the family of the person concerned comprises one or more children.

---

[5]   C-245/94 and C-312/94, [*1996*] *ECR*, p. I-4895.

This approach was also followed in the *Kuusijärvi* case.[6] This time the Swedish *föräldrapenning* (parental benefit) was concerned, which was paid by reason of the birth of a child. Under the provisions of the Law, a parent was entitled to parental benefit for a maximum of 450 days and this applied until the child reached the age of eight. The Swedish Government declared this as a maternity benefit for the purpose of the Regulation. The Court decided, however, that the benefit concerned was a family allowance. Although it is true, the Court considered, that the mother is eligible for parental benefit with effect from the 60th day before the day on which the child is due to be born, it is nevertheless the case, therefore, that during by far the greater part of the period for which parental benefit is payable, the right to that benefit belongs to the parent who primarily has care of the child; that right may therefore also accrue to the father. Moreover, the amount of benefit is, subject to certain conditions and reservations, directly determined by the amount of the earned income of the parent concerned. Provided that the parent concerned was affiliated to a social insurance office for at least 240 consecutive days before the birth or the due date of the birth, that parent is entitled, for 360 of the 450 days during which parental benefit is payable, to an allowance in a sum which is greater than the minimum guaranteed amount of SKR 60 per day and is generally equivalent to 75 per cent of the income which s/he previously earned. Those detailed rules show that parental benefit is intended, on the one hand, to enable the parents to devote themselves, in alternation, to the care of the young child until that child has started to attend school and, on the other, to offset to some extent the loss of income entailed for the parent devoting himself or herself to the care of the child in temporarily giving up his or her occupational activity.

Another type of benefit whose qualification was discussed and severely disputed is the German Care insurance Law (*Pflegeversicherungsgesetz*). This happened in the *Molenaar* judgment.[7] The Care Insurance Law was designed to cover the costs entailed if insured persons become reliant on care, that is to say if a permanent need were to arise for those insured to resort, in large measure, to assistance from other persons in the performance of their daily routine. Care insurance gives entitlement, first, to benefits designed to cover costs incurred for care provided in the home by a third person. Was this a sickness benefit, an old age pension or an invalidity benefit? The Court considered this benefit as a sickness benefit. We will discuss this benefit also in Chapter 11.

The classification of benefits is first of all important in order to know whether a particular benefit falls within the material scope of the Regulation. For instance, if *Erziehungsgeld is* not a family benefit or another type of benefit mentioned in Article 3, it is not within the material scope of the Regulation. Secondly the classification as a particular type is relevant in order to know which coordination

---

[6]   Case 275/96, [1998] *ECR* I-3443.
[7]   Case 160/96, [1998] *ECR* I-880.

rules apply; the coordination rules for, for instance, maternity benefits are different from those for family benefits. This difference can be decisive for the question whether a benefit is exportable or not and also for other issues.

5.3.3. THE COVERAGE OF BENEFITS WHICH FORM PART OF SCHEMES OUTSIDE THE MATERIAL SCOPE AND THE COVERAGE OF SCHEMES CONTAINING RULES NOT RELATED TO SOCIAL SECURITY BENEFITS

If a provision is part of an Act which is *beyond* the material scope of the Regulation, this does not necessarily mean, the Court ruled, that that provision itself is outwith its material scope. An example can be seen in the *Paletta* judgment,[8] discussed in a following section (Section 5.3.6). Although the provision, at stake in this judgment, which obliged employers to continue to pay wages was part of a labour Act, it was considered as a social security benefit, even though the Labour Act as a whole was not. This was since the obligations of the employer in relation to the benefits mentioned in Article 3(1) of the Regulation also fall within its scope.

A second question was whether all provisions of an Act which falls within the scope of the Regulation are covered by the Regulation. This question was raised in the *Rheinhold and Mahla* case[9] concerning the liability of an employer to pay social security contributions if his subcontractor fails to do so. The dispute arose in the case of a firm, established in the Netherlands, which worked in Belgium as a subcontractor for Rheinhold, a Belgian company. When the subcontractor went bankrupt, the benefit administration required Rheinhold to pay the non-paid contributions on the basis of a Dutch law which rules that the contractor is liable for paying contributions due by the subcontractor if the latter fails to do so. The question now was to whether the Regulation could be invoked to realize this claim in a cross border situation.

The Court answered that national schemes of social security are completely subject to Community law. Consequently, the scope of the Regulation is not confined to the rules on benefit mentioned in Article 4 (now Article 3(1)). Thus, the disputed Dutch law was within the material scope of the Regulation. However, the next question is whether the *liability* provisions of this Act fall within the material scope of the Regulation. The Court considered that if an Act is *within* the scope of the Regulation, this does not mean that all provisions of that Act fall under the Regulation. Decisive for answering the question whether the provision falls under the Regulation is whether it has a direct and sufficiently relevant connection to the provisions which fall under Article 4(1) of the Regulation. The disputed

---

[8]   Case 45/90, [1992] *ECR* I-3423.
[9]   Case 327/92, [1995] *ECR* I-1223.

provision did not concern an obligation of an employer established in another Member State to pay the social security contributions required by Dutch social security legislation. Instead, the provision concerned the obligation of a third party established in another Member State to pay to the benefit administration a certain amount which corresponds with the contributions not paid by an employer established in the Netherlands. The Court considered that there is a certain connection between social security obligations of the employer and the responsibility of the main contractor, but this is an indirect one. The liability concerned is not based on an employer-employee relationship but on the fact that the main contractor has made use of the services of the subcontractor, who has not paid the social security contributions. Strictly speaking this contractor is not obliged to pay the social security contributions but has to compensate the loss in income suffered by the benefit administration. There is therefore no direct and sufficiently relevant connection with the material scope of the Regulation. This could be different, the Court added, if fraud on the part of the main contractor could be shown, fir instance, if the main contractor was, in reality, the real employer of the workers. This was not the case here. Thus the Regulation could not be invoked.

5.3.4. TAXATION AND THE COORDINATION REGULATION

Another question brought before the Court was whether specific types of taxes fall within the scope of the co-ordination regulation. This was dealt with in the *Commission versus France* case,[10] which concerned the French Social Debt Repayment Contribution (CRDS). The primary purpose of the contribution was to finance the deficits accumulated by the French general social security scheme. This contribution went to a special public fund which was placed under the joint supervision of the Minister for the Economy and Finance and the Minister for Social Security. The European Commission brought this case before the Court as the contribution was also levied on persons living in France and working in another Member State. As a result these persons could be subject to charges for financing social security in more than one Member State and this was contrary to a basic principle of the Regulation.

The Court considered that by levying the contribution on persons living in France and working in another Member State, the French Republic disregarded the rule set out in Article 13 of the Regulation (the rule for determining the legislation applicable). Article 13 provides that the legislation of a single State is to apply insofar as that same income has already borne all the social charges imposed in the Member State of employment. The Court did not accept the

---

[10]   Case 34/98, [2000] *ECR* I-995.

French argument that the contribution should be categorised as a tax, thereby falling outwith the scope of the Regulation. The fact that a levy is categorised as a tax does not mean that, as regards the Regulation, that same levy cannot be regarded as falling within the scope of that Regulation and caught by the prohibition against overlapping legislation. The Court argued that it follows from the *Rheinhold and Mahla* judgment, discussed *supra*, that the national social security schemes are subject in their entirety to the application of the rules of Community law. Consequently, the decisive factor for the purpose of applying the Regulation is that there is such a direct and sufficiently relevant link between the provision in question and the legislation governing the branches of social security listed in Article 4 of the Regulation. The CRDS meets this criterion, as it is not a levy designed to meet general public expenses. Instead, its purpose is specifically and directly to discharge the deficit of the general French social security scheme. It forms part of a comprehensive reform of social protection in France aimed at ensuring the future financial equilibrium of that system. The Court considered that this link was not broken by the allocation of the sums in question for the purposes of financing the French social security scheme. Otherwise the prohibition against overlapping legislation would be deprived of all effectiveness. Neither the fact that the proceeds of the levy are paid to the fund rather than to the social security institutions directly, nor the fact that the levy is collected in the same way as income tax, affected the Court's conclusion. The CRDS therefore falls within the scope of the Regulation. Consequently, the Commission was right in arguing that the application of the French levy to residents working in another Member State was contrary to Community law.[11]

This case law is also relevant to Regulation 883/2004, as it is based on the effectiveness of the rules for determining the legislation applicable (*see* also the next chapter).

5.3.5. LIABILITY OF EMPLOYERS AND THE SCOPE OF THE REGULATION

Article 3(2) provides that schemes relating to the obligations of an employer or ship owner also fall within the material scope. This provision was also part of Regulation 1408/71, although in the latter Regulation it read: 'to schemes concerning the liability of an employer or ship owner in respect of the benefits referred to in Article 4(1)'. We may assume that these two phrases have the same meaning.

---

[11] The same approach was followed in a second infringement procedure, *Commission versus France*, Case 169/98, [2000] *ECR* I-1049.

The relation between the Regulation and employers' liability in case of sickness was subject of the *Paletta* v. *Brennet* case.[12] This case concerned the obligations of the employer (under German law) to continue to pay wages during sickness. Mr Paletta, his wife and two children, all of Italian nationality, were employed by Brennet, a German firm. In 1989 all four Paletta family members reported to be ill at the end of their holiday in Italy. The local Italian benefit office had them examined by medical doctors and the Paletta's were provided with declarations stating that they were ill. The employer, however, was suspicious; Mr Paletta appeared to have been ill during his holidays in three consecutive years. The employer therefore refused to pay wages on the grounds that he did not feel obliged to rely on the medical information on Paletta given by the Italian institution.

This case will be dealt with in more detail in Chapter 11 which concerns sickness benefits. Here, it is relevant whether the obligation on the employer to continue to pay wages in the case of sickness, on the basis of the national law, is subject to the provisions of the Regulation. The Court answered this question in the affirmative. It considered that for this interpretation question it is irrelevant that a particular benefit can be qualified as 'wages'. Payments by the employer can, at the same time, be considered sickness benefits within the meaning of Regulation 1408/71 and also wages. The answer to the question whether a payment falls under the field of application of the coordination Regulation is essentially determined by the constitutive elements of that payment, and, particularly, by the objectives and conditions for acquiring a right to benefit, rather than by the payment's name. We have seen this formula also in other cases, see Section 5.3.1.

In the light of these criteria, the Court continued, the payments concerned fall within the scope of the Regulation, as they are only granted in the event of illness; they suspend the payment of sickness benefits for a period of six weeks as provided for by the German Social Security code.

5.4. BENEFITS FOR VICTIMS OF WAR OR ITS CONSEQUENCES

The Regulation does not apply to benefits in relation to which a Member State assumes the liability for damages to persons and provides for compensation, such as those for victims of war and military action or their consequences; victims of crime, assassination or terrorist acts; victims of damage occasioned by agents of the Member State in the course of their duties; or victims who have suffered a disadvantage for political or religious reasons or for reasons of descent (Article 3(5)).[13]

---

12   Case 45/90, [1992] *ECR* I-3423.
13   This provision was inserted by Regulation 988/2004.

Under Regulation 1408/71, of this category, only benefit schemes for victims of war or its consequences were excluded. This exclusion was dispute in the *Fossi* judgment.[14] Mr Fossi was an Italian national residing in Italy, who worked in the German mines during the Second World War. He was refused a mineworkers' pension which was introduced in order to facilitate the economic and social integration of refugees and persons deported under the Nazi regime. Therefore, these benefits are outside the material scope of the Regulation.[15] We will discuss these benefits also in Chapters 9 and 10.

5.5. SOCIAL AND MEDICAL ASSISTANCE

Social and medical assistance is excluded from the material scope of the Regulation by Article 3(5). The term social and medical assistance is less clear than it seems at first sight. The Regulation does not give a definition of this term. According to the case law of the Court, the name of a scheme is not decisive in determining the question whether the benefit is excluded from the Regulation or not, as we have already noted in Section 5.3.1. Also *income support* and *minimum income* can therefore be social assistance for the Regulation.

One of the first cases in which the Court had to give an interpretation of the term social assistance was the *Frilli* judgment.[16] Mrs Frilli, an Italian national, was employed in Belgium and had, after retirement, continued to reside there. She received a low retirement pension in respect of that employment and applied for the Belgian guaranteed income for old people. This benefit was meant to guarantee a minimum income to the elderly with insufficient means. The costs of the benefit were entirely borne by the State and only granted on request, after a means test has been carried out. Mrs Frill's claim for this benefit was refused as the law required Belgian nationality for entitlement to this benefit.

In order to invoke the non-discrimination provision of the Regulation, it was relevant whether the disputed benefit was within the material scope of the Regulation. The Court considered that by virtue of certain of its features, the national legislation on the disputed benefit had certain affinities with social assistance – in particular where it prescribed need as an essential criterion for its application and did not stipulate any requirement as to periods of employment, membership or contribution. Nevertheless it approximated to social security because it did not prescribe consideration of each individual case, which is a characteristic of assistance, and because it conferred on recipients a legally defined position. Such legislation in fact fulfils a double function of guaranteeing a subsistence level to persons wholly outside the social security system and providing an income

---

[14] Case 79/76, [1977] *ECR* 667.
[15] *See* also the *Even* judgment, Case 207/78, [1979] *ECR* 2019.
[16] Case 1/72, [1972] *ECR* 471.

supplement for persons in receipt of inadequate social security benefits. Thus these benefits are hybrid benefits: they have both the characteristics of public assistance and social security benefits. This makes it difficult to distinguish them from social assistance and social security respectively. When a worker, having completed periods of employment in a Member State resides in that State and is entitled to a pension there, the legislative provisions for the guaranteed income falls, as regards these workers, within the Regulations adopted in the application of Article 42 EC (now Article 48 TFEU) the Court continued, even where such legislation might fall outside this classification with respect to other categories of recipients. Therefore the nationality condition was not allowed for these persons.

It follows from this judgment, that an important criterion for deciding whether a particular benefit is within the scope of the Regulation, is that claimants have a legally defined position which gives them a right to benefit. Therefore, where the benefit administration has no discretion in granting benefit, this benefit cannot be treated as social assistance within the meaning of the Regulation.

There is another important additional criterion for deciding whether a particular benefit is covered by the Regulation: the benefit scheme concerned is related to one of the contingencies of Article 3(1) – listed in Section 5.1 *supra*. This criterion appeared from the *Hoeckx* judgment.[17] Mrs Hoeckx, of Dutch nationality, applied in Belgium for a minimum subsistence income. The conditions for the Belgian subsistence benefit required that one had resided in Belgium for at least five years before the date of the application; this condition applied to non-Belgians only. The Court held that in order to fall within the scope of the Regulation, the national legislation had to be connected with one of the branches of social security enumerated in Article 3(1). A branch not listed in this Article could not be qualified as such, even if the claimant had a legally defined right to benefit. The Belgian subsistence income was paid to persons without sufficient means, and, therefore, of a general character. Therefore, it could not be brought within one of the risks covered by the Regulation.[18]

Consequently, the Regulation does not apply to a benefit which is not meant to compensate for specifically one of the contingencies listed in Article 3(1) of Regulation 883/2004.

A case in which the Court applied the criteria, with the result that the disputed benefit fell within the material scope, was the *Acciardi* judgment.[19] In this case, the Court had to decide whether a Dutch benefit, the Law on Income for Older and Partially Incapacitated Unemployed Persons (IOAW), fell within the material scope of the Regulation. The Netherlands government considered this benefit as social assistance.

---

[17] Case 249/83, [1985] *ECR* 982.
[18] On this case, *see* also the application of Regulation 1612/68, Section 9.3.
[19] Case 66/92, [1993] *ECR* I-4567.

The Court considered that if the conditions on the income received by the claimant and his spouse are satisfied one has a legal right to benefit. So a means test does not exclude that there is a legal right to benefit, provided that the criteria of the test are objectively defined. The second criterion, i.e. that the benefit relates to those listed in the Regulation, was also satisfied. The Law in question restricted the right to this benefit to unemployed persons and the right to benefit ended as soon as the beneficiary reached the statutory retirement age. One became entitled to this benefit immediately after the expiration of the right to unemployment benefit and the Law imposed several conditions on the beneficiary which ensured that he was available for work, such as making him to register at the employment office, that he was to actually seek work as an employed person and that he would accept an offer of suitable work. All these circumstances were relevant to the decision that this benefit was an unemployment benefit.

As we saw in the *Frilli* case, benefits, such as the guaranteed income for the elderly, are only within the scope of the Regulation in respect of 'employed persons and assimilated persons who have completed periods of employment under the legislation of a Member State and are resident in that State and receiving a pension'. In the *Newton* judgment this rule was confirmed.[20] The Court gave the following reason for this approach: if in the case of persons who had never been subject to the legislation of that State, such legislative provisions were to be regarded as falling within the field of social security, within the meaning of Article 42 EC (now 48) and the Regulation, the stability of the system instituted by national legislation, whereby Member States manifest their concern for the handicapped persons residing in their territory, could be seriously affected. The Regulation does not establish a common system of social security, but lays down rules coordinating the different national social security schemes with the purpose of ensuring freedom of movement for workers. Consequently, the Court argued, although the provisions of that Regulation must be construed in such a manner as to secure the attainment of that objective, they cannot be interpreted in such a way as to upset the system instituted by national legislation such as for the *mobility allowances*. This decision meant that Mr Newton, who had not worked in the United Kingdom, could not export the British *mobility allowance*.

The relevance of this case law has decreased after the introduction of the special non-contributory benefits, *see* the next section. Many, if not most, of the hybrid benefits are now dealt with by the provisions on the special non-contributory benefits. However, not all benefits are listed as special non-contributory benefits, an example is the benefit disputed in the *Acciardi* case, mentioned *supra*. For these benefits the *Frilli* case law may still be relevant. However, whether the condition mentioned in *Newton* still applies is disputable, since Regulation 883/2004 is no longer confined to employed and self-employed persons. Moreover, one could argue that if a Member State wishes to exclude a hybrid benefit from export, it

---

[20]   Case 356/89, [1991] *ECR* 3017.

could do so by having it qualified as a special non-contributory benefit. If it does not do so, it must accept that the general provisions of the Regulation apply for all persons covered by the Regulation.

5.6. SPECIAL NON-CONTRIBUTORY BENEFITS

5.6.1. THE PROVISIONS RELEVANT TO THE SPECIAL NON-CONTRIBUTORY BENEFITS

Member States appeared to have problems with the case law on the hybrid benefits discussed in the preceding section; they were, in particular, against the export of these benefits. In the *Frilli* case, for instance, Article 10 of Regulation 1408/71 could be invoked, which meant that this benefit was exportable. In order to regulate this effect, in 1992 Regulation 1408/71 was revised and a new Article 4(2a) was inserted to regulate the special non-contributory benefits.[21] In Regulation 883/2004 the relevant articles are Article 3(3) and Article 70. We will discuss this issue on the basis of the latter Articles.[22]

Article 3(3) of Regulation 883/2004 provides that the Regulation applies also to the special non-contributory benefits covered by Article 70. Article 70 is the sole Article of Chapter 9, the Chapter dedicated to the special non-contributory benefits. As a result of this Article, hybrid benefits satisfying the criteria for special non-contributory benefits are within the scope of the Regulation, but they can be treated differently than the other social security benefits falling under the Regulation.

Article 70 reads that it applies to special non-contributory cash benefits which are provided under legislation which, because of its personal scope, objectives and/or conditions for entitlement, has characteristics both of the social security legislation referred to in Article 3(1) and of social assistance. For the purposes of this Chapter, Article 70 continues, special non-contributory cash benefits means those which:

(a) are intended to provide either: (i) supplementary, substitute or ancillary cover against the risks covered by the branches of social security referred to in Article 3(1), and which guarantee the persons concerned a minimum subsistence income having regard to the economic and social situation in the Member State concerned; or (ii) solely specific protection for the disabled, closely linked to the said person's social environment in the Member State concerned, and

(b) where the financing exclusively derives from compulsory taxation intended to cover general public expenditure and the conditions for providing and for calculating the benefits are not dependent on any contribution in respect

---

[21]   By Regulation 1247/92, *OJ L* 136 of 30 April 1992, pages 1-6.
[22]   Article 4(2a) was amended, but for our purpose it is not relevant to discuss this issue here.

of the beneficiary. However, benefits provided to supplement a contributory benefit shall not be considered to be contributory benefits for this reason alone.

(c) a third condition is that these benefits are listed in Annex X.

For these benefits the export provision (Article 7) does not apply; neither do the other Chapters of Title III apply, i.e. the specific coordination rules for the benefits dealt with in this title. Article 70(4) provides that these benefits shall be provided exclusively in the Member State in which the persons concerned reside, in accordance with its legislation and they have to be provided by and at the expense of the institution of the place of residence. Consequently, the special non-contributory benefits are not exportable and the legislation of the State of residence determines whether a person receives these benefits or not.

This rule has negative effects for persons leaving a Member State having such type of benefit: they are no longer entitled to these as long as they stay outside the country. The rule has also advantages for persons coming from outside such State, these persons become entitled to these benefits, even if the risk (e.g. disability) materialised already when they were outside the territory of this country.

Article 70 of Regulation 883/2004 is, compared to the provisions of Article 10(a) of Regulation 1408/71, very short. This is not surprising, because of the general principles which are now part of the Regulation. Paragraphs 2, 3 and 4 of Article 10a concerned the aggregation of periods, including periods of residence completed in another Member State, and the principle of equal treatment of benefits and facts. These rules are now found in Articles 5 and 6 of Regulation 883/2004.

Section (b) of Article 5 reads that where, under the legislation of the competent Member State, legal effects are attributed to the occurrence of certain facts or events, that Member State shall take account of like facts or events occurring in any Member State as though they had taken place in its own territory. Thus if a scheme requires that a person is only entitled to, for instance, a benefit for people disabled already for the age of eighteen on condition that they were residing in that country at that time, this condition is also satisfied if a person resided at that age in another Member State. Another effect of the principle of equal treatment of benefits and facts applies to pensions received in another Member State which the persons concerned would wish to supplement by a special non-contributory cash benefit.

5.6.2. THE INTERPRETATION OF THE WORD 'RESIDE'

The special non-contributory benefits are paid in the State of residence. In the *Swaddling* judgment[23] the meaning of the term reside was part of the dispute. In January 1995, after an unsuccessful attempt to find work in France, Mr

---

[23]   Case 90/97, [1999] *ECR* I-1075.

Swaddling returned to the United Kingdom, where he lives with his brother. He has declared that he no longer wishes to take a job which entails spending long periods of time abroad and, on 9 January 1995, he applied to the Adjudication Officer for income support. This was refused as he did not satisfy the condition of being habitually resident in the UK. For the purposes of the national legislation, 'habitual residence' presupposed an appreciable period of residence in the United Kingdom in addition to the settled intention of residing there. Mr Swaddling had become habitually resident in the United Kingdom eight weeks after his return there. Therefore the case concerned these first eight weeks.

The Court considered that Article 10a of Regulation 1408/71, now Article 70 of Regulation 883/2004, provides that benefit is paid according to the legislation of the country where the person resides. Article 1(j) of Regulation 883/2004 defines 'residence' as 'habitual residence.' This term refers to the State in which the person concerned habitually resides and where the habitual centre of their interests is to be found. In that context, the Court ruled, account should be taken, in particular, of the employed person's family situation; the reasons which have led him to move; the length and continuity of his residence; the fact (where this is the case) that he is in stable employment; and his intention as it appears from all the circumstances.[24] For the purposes of that assessment, however, the length of residence in the Member State in which payment of the benefit at issue is sought cannot be regarded as an intrinsic element of the concept of residence. In the present case the employed person has made clear that he intends to remain in his State of origin. In these circumstances he cannot be deemed to not satisfy the residence condition merely because the period of residence completed in his State of origin is too short. Consequently, this Article precludes the Member State of origin in this case from requiring the waiting-period for income support. Thus the British interpretation of 'residence' was overruled by the (interpretation of the) relevant provision of the coordination regulation.

5.6.3. THE QUALIFICATION AS SPECIAL NON-CONTRIBUTORY BENEFIT

Whether a benefit is a special non-contributory benefit is sometimes object of very serious discussions, if the Member State in question claims that a particular benefit is special non-contributory, since it does not want to export the benefit. Other parties then tend to restrict this category of benefit, since it infringes the important principle of export of benefits. In order to be a special non-contributory benefit, a benefit has to be listed in Annex X. Therefore, the Community legislature has to decide on this.

---

[24]   For case law on this article *see* also the *Paolo* judgment, discussed in Chapter 15.

Initially, under Regulation 1408/71, the Community legislature was quite lenient in allowing benefits to be listed in the annex. Also the Court was not critical on this issue yet. In the *Swaddling*,[25] *Snares*,[26] and *Partridge*[27] judgments, the Court accepted the benefits listed in the Annex and thus the non-exportability of these benefits. A reason for this can be that the questions of the referring courts did not concern this issue whether they were correctly listed in the Annex.

In the *Leclere* judgment,[28] however, the Court had to consider whether a benefit was validly listed in the Annex. The benefit concerned was a maternity benefit. The Court argued that this benefit was paid to every pregnant woman and to every woman who had given birth, on the sole condition that she was officially resident in Luxembourg when entitlement to it arose. Consequently, it was not a benefit intended to provide supplementary, substitute or ancillary cover against the risks covered by the branches of social security referred to in (what is now) Article 3 of the Regulation. It was, therefore not a special non-contributory benefit, the Court concluded, and therefore export of this benefit was required.

Also in the *Jauch* judgment[29] the Court decided that a benefit was not validly listed in the Annex of special non-contributory benefits. The benefit concerned was the Austrian care allowance. The Court considered that inclusion in the Annex is not sufficient to answer the question whether it is a non-contributory benefit. For the interpretation of the rules provisions which derogate from the principle of exportability of benefits must be interpreted strictly. Therefore the non-export provision can apply only to benefits which satisfy the conditions for the special non-contributory benefits. If a benefit falls under the categories listed in Article 4 of Regulation 1408/71 (now Article 3 of Regulation 883/2004), it cannot be a special benefit.

A benefit may be regarded as a social security benefit in so far as it is granted, without any individual and discretionary assessment of personal needs, to recipients on the basis of a legally defined position and relates to one of the risks expressly listed in Article 4(1) of Regulation 1408/71. The Court then argued that the care insurance benefit was essentially intended to supplement sickness insurance benefits, to which they are, moreover, linked at the organisational level, in order to improve the state of health and quality of persons reliant on care. For this reason they are to be considered as sickness benefits within the meaning of the Regulation and cannot be seen as special benefits. Moreover, the statutory pension and accident insurance institutions pay the cash benefits; this is compensated by a reduction of the sickness insurance contribution payable by the pension insurance contributions. This link, albeit indirect, with sickness insurance contributions makes that care allowance is a contributory benefit.

---

[25]   Case 90/97, 1999] *ECR* I-1075.
[26]   Case 20/96, [1997] *ECR* I-895.
[27]   Case 297/98, [1998] *ECR* I-3467.
[28]   Case 43/99, [2001] *ECR* I- 4265.
[29]   Case 215/99, [2001] *ECR* I-1901.

Consequently, these benefits are not special non-contributory benefits. They must, therefore, be provided irrespective of the Member State in which a person reliant on care is resident.

In the *Hosse* judgment[30] this approach was confirmed, even though it concerned a provincial scheme for, in particular, members of the family. The case concerned the severally disabled daughter of a German frontier worker, who (i.e. the frontier worker) worked in Austria and resided in Germany. The daughter was not paid this benefit, since it was listed in the Annex.[31] Like in the *Jauch* case, the Court considered that social security benefits and special non-contributory benefits are mutually exclusive, so first it has to be decided whether the benefit concerned is a social security benefit. A care allowance such as the Austrian one is intended to compensate, in the form of a flat-rate contribution, for the additional expenditure resulting from the recipients' condition of reliance on care, in particular the cost of the assistance it is necessary to provide them with. The amount of the care allowance depends on the degree of reliance on care. It corresponds to the time spent on care, expressed in terms of hours per month. Assessment of reliance on care is regulated in detail in a measure laying down a classification according to degrees of reliance. The other income of the person reliant on care has no effect on the amount of the care allowance. The allowance is paid to persons who do not receive any pension under the Federal provisions. Those persons are essentially members of the families of socially insured persons, recipients of social assistance, disabled workers, and persons receiving pensions from the provinces and municipalities. Consequently, while this care allowance may have a different system from that applicable in the *Jauch* judgment, it none the less remains of the same kind as those benefits and must be regarded as sickness benefits. Therefore it cannot be classified as a special benefit.

There were also cases where the Court decided that the benefit concerned was a special non-contributory benefit. In the *Skalka* judgment[32] the Court argued that a special benefit is defined by its purpose. It must either replace or supplement a social security benefit and be by its nature social assistance justified on economic and social grounds and fixed by legislation setting objective criteria. The Austrian Compensatory supplement involved was paid if the standard benefit was too low. It ensures the provision of an income supplement to those persons receiving insufficient social security benefit by guaranteeing a minimum means of subsistence to those persons whose total income falls below a statutory threshold. As it is intended to guarantee a minimum subsistence income for pensioners, the

---

[30]   Case C-286/03 Hosse, [2006] *ECR* I-1771.
[31]   More precisely, Article 4(2) of Regulation 1408/71 provided that this Regulation did not apply to the provisions concerning special non-contributory benefits, referred to in Annex II, Section III, the validity of which is confined to part of its territory. However, even though this was a type of benefit limited to regional areas and listed in a special Annex, for the Court the main issue was whether it was a special benefit, and for this purpose its approach was not different from that in the *Jauch* case.
[32]   Case C-160/02, [2004] *ECR* I-5613.

benefit is by nature social assistance. Such a benefit is always closely linked to the socio-economic situation of the country concerned and its amount, fixed by law, takes account of the standard of living in that country. As a result its purpose would be lost if it were to be granted outside the State of residence.

For the question whether it is a non-contributory benefit, the relevant determining criterion is how the benefit is actually financed. Therefore it has to be considered whether that financing comes directly or indirectly from social contributions or from public resources. In this case the costs are borne by a social institution which then receives reimbursement in full from the relevant Land, which in turn receives from the Federal budget the sums necessary to finance the benefit. At no time do the contributions of insured persons form part of this financing arrangement. Therefore it is not a contributory benefit. For this reason the benefit did not have to be exported. A comparable approach was followed in the *Perez Naranjo* judgment.[33]

5.6.4. REVISION OF THE ANNEX AS A RESULT OF THE LECLERE JUDGMENT

As a result of the *Leclere* Judgment the European Commission initiated a study to see whether all benefits listed in the Annex were validly included. It also had to consider whether all the proposals by the Accession States to list benefits in the Annex could be accepted. This led to a new text of Article 4(2a) and a revision of Annex IIa to Regulation 1408/71 by Regulation 647/2005 of 13 April 2005.[34]

Applying criteria drawn from the case-law of the Court, the Commission did not include in that new list: invalidity benefits, including those intended for the maintenance or improvement of earning capacity; benefits granted to disabled children, the primary objective of which is to meet the extra family expenses caused by the presence of a disabled child in the home; care benefits, characterised by the Court in the *Jauch* judgment as sickness benefits in cash for the purpose of improving the state of health and quality of life of persons reliant on care, even if those benefits may cover independent aspects of the sickness itself.

At the request of Finland, Sweden and the United Kingdom, the Council nevertheless agreed to reinsert in the list the Finish child care allowance; the Swedish disability allowance and care allowance for disabled children; and the British disability living allowance (DLA), attendance allowance (AA), and carer's allowance (CA) and these were included in Regulation 647/2005. Subsequently, the Commission sought the annulment of that Regulation in so far as it refers to

---

[33]   Case C-265/05, [2007] *ECR* I-347.
[34]   *OJ* L 117/1, 2005.

the benefits at issue. This led to the judgment *Commission versus Parliament and Council.*[35]

As regards the Finish child care allowance benefit the Court considered that under the Regulation, a benefit can be deemed to be special only if its purpose is solely that of specific protection for the disabled, closely linked to the social environment of those persons in the Member State concerned. The benefits concerned do not have that sole function. In fact, although they unquestionably promote the independence of the persons who receive them and protect the disabled in their national social context, they are also intended to ensure the necessary care and the supervision of those persons, where it is essential, in their family or a specialised institution. They cannot, therefore, be classified as special benefits. The purpose of the Finnish and Swedish care allowances for children is to enable the parents of disabled children to provide for the care, supervision of and possibly re-habilitation of those children. The fact that entitlement to those allowances would not be subject to having worked or made contributions for a certain length of time, that they would be awarded on a case-by-case basis depending on the needs of the child and in accordance with criteria fixed by the legislation, and that, in addition, they would form part of a package of benefits and services for disabled persons and would, on that account, be closely linked to the economic and social context in the Member States concerned, is not such as to influence their main purpose, which is of a medical nature. Accordingly, those allowances must be classified as sickness benefits. The Swedish disability allowance is granted to disabled people for whom a reduction in their mobility occurred between the ages of 19 and 65. It is intended to finance the care of a third person or to allow the disabled person to bear the costs caused by his or her disability and to improve that person's state of health and quality of life, as a person reliant on care. Benefits granted objectively on the basis of a statutorily defined position and which are intended to improve the state of health and quality of life of persons reliant on care have as their essential purpose supplementing sickness insurance benefits and must be regarded as 'sickness benefits'. The Swedish disability allowance must consequently be classified as a sickness benefit. As regards the British DLA, AA and CA, those benefits are all by nature, although only partially so in the case of the DLA, care allowances. Their purpose is to help promote the independence and social integration of the disabled and also, as far as possible, to help them lead a life similar to non-disabled persons. The criterion which determines entitlement to those benefits is the need for care. Entitlement to the DLA or AA does not depend on being unable to work and the three benefits at issue are granted regardless of the level of income of their recipients, simply at different rates. Only the DLA can be considered to include a social assistance

---

[35] Case C-299/05, [2007] *ECR* I-8695. See also H. Verschueren, 'Special Non-contributory Benefits in Regulation 1408/71, Regulation 883/2004 and the Case Law of the ECJ', *EJSS* 2009, p. 229.

component. The other two benefits at issue have a single purpose which is akin to that of the Swedish disability allowance, namely to help the disabled person to overcome, as far as possible, his or her disability in everyday activities. Accordingly, those three allowances as well as the preceding allowances must be regarded as sickness benefits, even though the DLA includes a distinct part relating to mobility. The 'mobility' component of the DLA, which might be regarded as a special non-contributory benefit, is severable, so that that component alone could be included on the list in the Annex as amended if the United Kingdom decided to create an allowance which concerned that component alone. The fact that the DLA, AA and CA, unlike the benefit at issue in the *Jauch* and *Hosse*, do not have as there the essential purpose supplementing sickness insurance benefits does not affect the categorisation of those allowances.[36] Accordingly, the Commission is justified in claiming that the benefits as issue are not allowed to be listed in the Annex.[37]

Thus the Court of Justice only considers as special those benefits which are solely meant to guarantee the beneficiaries a minimal income taking into account the social and economic environment of the society in which they live. This is not the case with benefits intending to cover additional expenses for care encountered by the disabled. Only benefits guaranteeing a minimum income and benefits aiming to facilitate the integration of the beneficiary into the society of the Member State where he resides are special benefits.

5.6.5. NON-EXPORTABILITY OF THE SPECIAL NON-CONTRIBUTORY BENEFITS AND FREE MOVEMENT

A remarkable decision on the special non-contributory benefits was the *Hendrix* judgment,[38] in which the Court ruled that the application of the non-export provision must be consistent with provisions on freedom of movement for workers. The case concerned the Dutch Wajong benefit, which is paid to persons who were already disabled before the age of eighteen.

In the judgment *Kersbergen-Lap and Dams-Schipper*[39] the Court had already decided that the Wajong benefit was validly listed in the Annex. The Wajong benefit was considered a replacement allowance intended for those who do not satisfy the conditions of insurance for obtaining invalidity benefit. By guaranteeing a minimum income to a socially disadvantaged group (disabled young people),

---

[36]   The Court added that the fact that the Court ruled in the *Snares* and *Partridge* judgments that the DLA and AA were, in the legal context at the time, allowances coming under Article 4(2a) (b) of Regulation 1408/71 does not affect the analysis which the Court may make of those allowances in the post-*Jauch* legal context.

[37]   Case C-299/05, *Commission v. European Parliament and Council* [2007] ECR I-8695.

[38]   Case C-287/05, [2007] *ECR* I-6909.

[39]   Case C-154/05, [2006] ECR I-6249.

the Wajong benefit is by its nature social assistance justified on economic and social grounds. Moreover, it is granted according to objective criteria defined by law. Further, that benefit is closely linked to the socio-economic situation in the Netherlands since it is based on the minimum wage and the standard of living in that Member State. It followed that a benefit under the Wajong must be classified as a special benefit. Further, the Court considered that the resources necessary for financing the Wajong benefit are provided by the Treasury and therefore from public funds. Consequently, the Court established that the benefit under the Wajong must be regarded as being non-contributory in nature.

The special element in the *Hendrix* case was that as a result of the loss of his Wajong benefit Mr Hendrix lost his job; the reason was that the grant of Wajong meant that the employer was relieved from the obligation of the minimum wage. The benefit supplemented the low wage. After termination of the right to Wajong benefit, the obligation to pay the minimum wage relived. As a result the employer dismissed him. Thus crossing the borders meant that he lost his job.

Because of this impact on his right to free movement, the Dutch court asked the Court of Justice to consider the relation of the non-export clause with the provisions on free movement. The Court decided that payment of the Wajong benefit may validly be reserved to persons who reside in the territory of the Member State which provides the benefit.

Subsequently, the Court considered the relation between the rules on the non-contributory benefits and Article 39 EC, now Article 45 TFEU, and Regulation 1612/68. We will discuss these provisions in Chapter 10 in more detail, but here it is relevant to mention that the Court ruled that the fact that Mr Hendrix, after taking up residence in Belgium, continued to work in the Netherlands and then changed employer in that Member State gives him the status of a migrant worker (note that he did not take up a job across the border, but merely changed his residence). This brings him within the scope of Community law and, in particular, within the scope of its provisions relating to freedom of movement for workers. It is true, the Court considered, that the benefit under the Wajong is one of the special non-contributory benefits. However, as the Court has consistently held in its case law, the provisions of the Regulation enacted to give effect to Article 42 EC, now Article 48 TFEU, must be interpreted in the light of the objective of that Article. This objective is to contribute to the establishment of the greatest possible freedom of movement for migrant workers. It follows that the condition of residence attached to receipt of the benefit under the Wajong can be put forward against a person in the situation of Mr Hendrix only if it is objectively justified and proportionate to the objective pursued. The Wajong benefit is closely linked to the socio-economic situation of the Member State concerned, as was already decided in *Kersbergen-Lap*, and it follows that the condition of residence as such, laid down in the national legislation, is objectively justified. It is also necessary, the Court continued, that the application of such a condition does not entail an infringement of the rights which a person in the situation of Mr

Hendrix derives from freedom of movement for workers which goes beyond what is required to achieve the legitimate objective pursued by the national legislation. The national regulation expressly provides that the condition of residence may be waived when the condition leads to an 'unacceptable degree of unfairness'. The Court took this provision into account and decided that it is the responsibility of national courts to interpret, so far as possible, national law in conformity with the requirements of Community law[40]. The referring court must therefore be satisfied, in the circumstances of this particular case, that the requirement of a condition of residence on national territory does not lead to such unfairness, taking into account the fact that Mr Hendrix has exercised his right of freedom of movement as a worker and that he has maintained economic and social links to the Netherlands.

In the subsequent procedure, the Dutch court decided, taking into account this judgment, that the Wajong benefit had in this case to be exported.[41] This was since terminating benefit in this case can result in the loss of a job, and this is a serious impediment of the right of free movement.

It is unlikely that a case comparable with that of Mr Hendrix will occur often. Still it is possible, in particular in the case of persons receiving this type of benefit and being frontier worker, and, members of their family. Moreover, we have to learn from this case, that the rules and outcomes of the application of the rules of the Regulation have always to stand the test with Article 45 TFEU (see also Chapter 10 *infra*).

---

[40] As it had already decided in other cases, e.g. Case C-106/89 *Marleasing* [1990] ECR I-4135.

[41] CRvB 7 February 2008, *AB* 2008, 204.

CHAPTER 6

THE RULES FOR DETERMINING
THE LEGISLATION APPLICABLE

6.1.   INTRODUCTION

The rules for determining the applicable legislation are, among other things, relevant to the question to which State a person has to pay contributions and which country is the competent one for granting benefit. More specifically, these rules determine which social security legislation is applicable. The general provisions of Regulation 883/2004 on the legislation applicable can be found in Articles 11 to 16 in Title II.

Section 6.2 will discuss the main characteristics of the rules for determining the legislation applicable if a person works in one State only. In Section 6.3 workers who are not working anymore (post-active workers) are dealt with. In Section 6.4 the persons who are not active (other than the post-active workers) are discussed. In Section 6.5 persons who work simultaneously in two or more Member States are the topic. Finally we will mention some special types of rules: for the non-contributory benefits and on the relation between compulsory and voluntary insurance. Chapter 7 will be dedicated to a special category of the rules for determining the legislation applicable: the posting rules.

6.2.   THE MAIN CHARACTERISTICS OF THE RULES FOR DETERMINING THE LEGISLATION APPLICABLE

6.2.1.   THE STATE OF EMPLOYMENT PRINCIPLE

Most rules for determining the legislation applicable provide that the legislation of the Member State in which a person is working is applicable. The reason for choosing the system of the State of employment is obvious.[1] First of all, the choice for the *lex loci laboris* (State of Employment Principle) implies that all persons employed by an employer are subject to the same contribution and benefit system. Consequently, employers are not able to employ foreign workers on cheaper conditions than national employees. Another approach, which would allow paying them lower contributions for foreign workers and/or allowing them to pay these contributions to the institution in the sending State, would mean that these foreign workers are cheaper and will thus be recruited on a large scale. This will put pressure on the national system to lower its contributions and thus also its benefits. All in all it will lead to a general deterioration of the benefit system of the receiving country. This would be inconsistent with the Treaty, which requires promoting social progress.[2]

Since the personal scope of the Regulation has been extended to all nationals subject to a social security system, and is thus no longer restricted to economically active persons, the *lex loci laboris* principle has become less obvious than before. The Regulation now gives special rules for categories of non-active persons which are based on the State-of-residence principle (Section 6.4). However, the main rule is still the State-of-employment principle and is necessary for the reason of avoiding social dumping.

During the preparatory discussions on the draft of Regulation 883/2004, some authors proposed to introduce the State-of-residence principle, in particular for residence schemes and schemes for the protection of the self-employed.[3] These proposals were not followed.

The general principle, that workers from other Member States must not be discriminated against on basis of nationality, is laid down in Article 45 TFEU and is also applicable on labour conditions (elaborated in Regulation 1612/68, discussed in Chapter 9). Given that the State-of-employment principle is laid down in Article 45 TFEU, it would be extremely difficult to adopt a different approach for the coordination Regulation.

---

[1]   *See*, for an overview of proposals for an alternative, Frans Pennings, 'Co-ordination of Social Security on the Basis of the State-of-employment Principle: Time for an Alternative?', *Common Market Law Review*, 42(1), 2005, p. 67-89.

[2]   For the objectives of the Treaty, see Article 3 of the Lisbon Treaty.

[3]   Anna Christensen and Mattias Malmstedt, '*Lex Loci Laboris* versus *Lex Loci Domicilii* – an inquiry into the normative Foundations of European Social Security Law', *European Journal of Social Security* 2000, p. 69; D. Pieters (ed.), *The Co-ordination of Social Security at Work*, Leuven, 1999; D. Pieters, "An overview of Alternative Solutions for Overcoming the Problematic Issues of Co-ordination", in: Ministry of Labour and Social Security and European Commission (ed), *The Free Movement of the Self-Employed within the European Union and the Co-ordination of National Social Security Systems*, Athens 2001, p. 127.

6.2.2. THE EXCLUSIVE EFFECT OF THE RULES FOR DETERMINING THE LEGISLATION APPLICABLE

Introduction

The rules for determining the legislation applicable have *exclusive effect*. This means that at any given time the legislation of *only one* Member State is applicable; in other words, no other legislations can be applicable.

This exclusive effect is laid down in Article 11(1) of the Regulation. This Article provides that persons to whom this Regulation applies shall be subject to the legislation of a single Member State only.

The State whose legislation is determined as being applicable is called the *competent State*. The Regulation defines the competent Member State indirectly: it is the Member State in which the competent institution is situated. The competent institution is the institution with which the person concerned is insured at the time of the application for benefit (Article 1(q)). For knowing where a person is insured, the rules for determining the legislation applicable are decisive.

During the period that the legislation of a State is applicable to a person, that person is subject to that legislation. This means that, if the applicable legislation provides so, the person has to pay contributions to the benefit administration of that State, and s/he acquires benefit rights in that State, such as to an old age pension.

The meaning of the exclusive effect can be seen in the following example. Suppose that the rules for determining the applicable legislation provide that a person is insured under the system of country *x*. However, s/he also has a link with country *y*, because s/he resides in that country and the law of this country provides that all residents are covered for its national insurance schemes and thus have to pay contributions. The exclusive effect of the rules for determining the applicable legislation means that the national rules of conflict of country *y* are overruled. Thus the person concerned is subject only to the law of country *x*. S/he cannot claim benefits under the scheme of State y, even if it has a residence scheme and the person is residing here. Thus, the rules can also have negative effects for the migrant workers. Suppose s/he is not entitled to disability benefit because of a short working past in the State of work, and would be entitled to such a benefit in the State of residence. As a result of the Regulation the rules of the latter state are not applicable. On the whole, however, the rules are advantageous to free movement, since if they would not exist migrants would often have to pay contributions in more than one country.

In respect of some categories of benefits the Regulation provides that the claimant is also entitled to *receive* benefits from other Member States, e.g. old-age pensions. These rules are laid down in Part III of the Regulation. This does not contradict the exclusive effect of the rules for determining the legislation applicable: the person concerned is still *covered* by one legislation *at the same time*, but s/he is entitled to benefits *based* on earlier periods. Thus it is possible that a person *receives* benefit from one country (e.g. his former State of employment) and is *subject* to the legislation of another country (e.g. his State of residence), where s/he has to pay contributions, acquires further benefit rights and/or is entitled to benefits which are paid only during the period a person is insured (such as family benefits). Thus receiving benefit and being subject to a legislation are two different issues.

Claimants have to satisfy the conditions of the legislation which is designated as the applicable one if they wish to make a claim under that legislation. The Regulation provides, however, assistance in satisfying of these conditions, for instance by giving rules on the aggregation of periods of insurance for specific benefits (Article 6 of the Regulation).

The rules for determining the legislation applicable are of a compulsory nature and leave no choice for the person concerned between the legislations of country x or country y. It can happen that, even with the help of the rules for the aggregation of insurance periods, a person is not able to satisfy the conditions for benefit under the scheme of the competent State. Even if s/he would satisfy the conditions for benefit in his or her State of residence or his or her State of origin, this cannot help the person concerned. The rules for determining the legislation applicable are inexorable. As a result a person may be insured under a scheme with less attractive conditions than the one of his or her State of origin or State of residence. This impediment to free movement cannot be taken away by the Regulation, as it results directly from differences between national systems. The objective of the Regulation is only coordination, and not harmonisation of national social security schemes. Below, however, we will discuss recent case law on the freedom of Member States to award benefits despite the rules of the Regulation (the *Bosmann* judgment).

First, it has to be remarked that the Regulation gives assistance to satisfying the qualifying conditions of social security systems, which takes to some extent the effects of the differences between national systems and the negative effect of the exclusive effect away. We mentioned already the aggregation rules; below we will also discuss the overruling of residence conditions. Still, there can be other conditions which may have as effect that a person is not admitted to a scheme determined by the rules of the Regulation. An example, already from older times. is the *Coonan* judgment.[4] Mrs Coonan, of Irish nationality, entered employment in the United Kingdom after the age of 65. A condition for being insured for British sickness benefits is that one is insured for British old age benefits. Mrs Coonan was, however, because of her age not admitted to the old age benefit scheme. As a result, she could not participate in the sickness insurance scheme either. The question was whether the rules for determining the legislation applicable could overrule the rules for affiliation with the sickness insurance scheme. The Court

---

[4]   Case 110/79, [1980] *ECR* 1445.

decided that this could not be the case, as the Regulation does not preclude the Member States from having the competence to determine the conditions for affiliation themselves. It did not discuss the question of whether the conditions concerned were indirectly discriminating against migrant workers. However, it is quite likely that nowadays the outcome of this case would have been different, as the assimilation rule of Article 5 requires assimilation of events etc. for the purpose of the Regulation, *see* Section 8.3. Thus, the effects of the differences between the systems on migrant workers are diminished. Still, it can happen that a person, despite the aggregation rules, does not qualify for benefit, whereas s/he would have been entitled to benefit in the State of residence or origin.

Regulation 1408/71 allowed some exceptions to the exclusive effect of the rules for determining the applicable legislation; the new Regulation reinforced the exclusive effect by eliminating these exceptions. This removal fits well with the objective of simplifying the coordination rules. We will discuss these rules below (Sections 6.4 and 6.6.3).

The Right of Member States to Grant Benefit even if the Legislation applies of another Member State

A very early judgment of the Court which dealt with the exclusive effect was the *Nonnenmacher* judgment.[5] This judgment was given under Regulation 3. In this Regulation the rules on determining the legislation applicable were not worded in a way that their exclusive effect was indisputable. In the *Nonnenmacher* judgment, the Court considered that in the absence of specific clauses, plurality of benefits under two national laws was not prevented. Article 12 of Regulation 3 did not prohibit the application of the law of a Member State other than the one on whose territory the person concerned worked, unless it compelled this person to contribute to the financing of a social security institution which did not grant any extra benefits for the same risk and the same period.

This approach is not followed under Regulation 1408/71 and Regulation 883/2004. The wording of Article 13 of Regulation 1408/71 and Article 11 of Regulation 883/2004 make clear that the rules for determining the applicable legislation have exclusive effect. For Regulation 1408/71 this was confirmed by the Court in the *Ten Holder* judgment.[6] From the facts of this judgment it also appears that the consequences of exclusive effect are not always advantageous for the individual. Ms Ten Holder, a woman of Dutch nationality, was employed in Germany for some time. When she became ill, she was granted German sickness benefit, *Krankengeld*. At a certain moment, she returned to the Netherlands. After the maximum duration of *Krankengeld* had expired, she applied for a Dutch invalidity benefit, since she did not satisfy the qualifying conditions for a German

---

[5]   Case 92/63, [1964] *ECR* 583.
[6]   Case 302/84, [1986] *ECR* 1821.

incapacity benefit. Since the Dutch scheme was a residence scheme, she would have been entitled to this benefit on the basis of mere residence in this country, provided that that legislation was applicable. The Court held that the legislation of the State of employment, *i.e.* Germany, was to be applied in this situation. This legislation continued to be applicable until the person concerned entered employment in another Member State.

The consequence of this interpretation was that Ms Ten Holder was not entitled to the Dutch benefit. The fact that she did not satisfy the conditions of the German social security provisions was irrelevant. The only benefit she could claim was Dutch public assistance, since that benefit did not fall under the Regulation, and therefore the rules for determining the applicable legislation did not prevent her from applying for this benefit. We will come back to this judgment in Section 6.3.

The *Ten Holder* judgment was confirmed, *inter alia*, in the *Perenboom* judgment.[7] This time the exclusive effect was advantageous to the claimant, as the dispute concerned the levying of contributions. In this case, the person was assessed on one income, but was subject to double contribution charges. The Court ruled this as inconsistent with Article 13 of Regulation 1408/71. Therefore, only the competent State is authorised to impose contributions.

The recent *Bosmann* judgment[8] led, however, again to discussion on the exclusive effect of the rules for determining the legislation applicable. The case concerned a Belgian woman, working in the Netherlands, and residing in Germany. Her two children were over the age of eighteen. Under the Dutch rules they were not eligible for family benefits, as to persons over this age who are students study grants are paid. However, Dutch study grants were not paid to persons not studying in the Netherlands. The question raised to the Court was whether Article 13(2)(a) lends itself to an interpretation which permits an employed person in Ms Bosmann's situation to receive child benefit in the State where she resides (Germany), if it is established that she cannot, because of the ages of her children, be granted such a benefit in the competent Member State.

The Court answered to this question that Community law does not require the competent German authorities to grant Ms Bosmann the family benefits in question. However, it added, neither can the possibility of such a grant be excluded, because under the German legislation Ms Bosmann may be entitled to child benefit solely because of her residence in Germany, which is for the national court to determine. The Court referred to the legal basis of the Regulation – Article 42 EC (now Article 48 TFEU) – which aims to facilitate freedom of movement for workers and entails, in particular, that migrant workers must not lose their right to social security benefits or have the amount of those benefits reduced because they have exercised the right to freedom of movement conferred on them by the

---

[7]   Case 102/76, [1978] *ECR* 815.
[8]   Case C-352/06, [2008] *ECR* I-3827.

Treaty. In the light of those factors, the Court answered that the Member State of residence cannot be deprived of the right to grant child benefit to those residents within its territory.

This approach seems different from that in the *Ten Holder* judgment (discussed *supra*). The Court considered that the *Ten Holder* judgment could not put in question the interpretation of the Regulation in the *Bosmann* case. The *Ten Holder* case concerned a case where the competent Member State's authorities refused to grant a benefit. Consequently, this judgment cannot serve as a basis for precluding a Member State, which is not the competent State, from being able to grant such a benefit to one of its residents. The benefit in the *Bosmann* case is not subject to conditions of employment or insurance and the possibility of such a grant arises, in actual fact, from its legislation.

However, it is not so easy to reconcile the Court's remarks on the *Ten Holder* case with a close reading of the considerations of that judgment. In consideration 21 and 22 of the *Ten Holder* judgment, the Court remarked that the provisions of Title II constitute a complete system of conflict rules, the effect of which is to divest the legislature of each Member State of the power to determine the ambit and the conditions for the application of its national legislation so far as the persons who are subject thereto and the territory within which the provisions of national law take effect are concerned. The Member States are not entitled, the Court continues, to determine the extent to which their own legislation or that of another Member State is applicable since they are under an obligation to comply with the provisions of Community law in force. That rule is not at variance with the Court's decisions, the Court added, in particular the *Petroni* judgment[9] (discussed in Chapter 12 of this book) which meant that the application of Regulation 1408/71 cannot entail the loss of rights acquired exclusively under national legislation. That *Petroni* principle does not apply to the rules for determining the legislation applicable, but it applies to the rules of Community law on the overlapping of benefits provided for by different national legislative systems. It cannot therefore have the effect, contrary to Article 13(1) of Regulation 1408/71, of causing a person to be insured over the same period under the legislation of more than one Member State, regardless of the obligations to contribute or of any other costs which may result therefrom for that person.

Thus the Court made clear in the *Ten Holder* judgment that a Member State is no longer free to pay benefits if its legislation is not applicable according to the rules for determining the legislation applicable. The facts in *Ten Holder* and *Bosmann* case are not so different from each other that they can explain the difference in outcome. In both cases the benefit authorities refused to pay benefit (otherwise there had not been a dispute). Admittedly, the German court seemed in the *Bosmann* case in favour of awarding the claim, but the benefit authorities themselves were opposed to this. Also the Dutch court in the *Ten Holder* case

---

[9]   Case 24/75, *Petroni*, [1975] *ECR* 1149.

considered that, from the standpoint of Netherlands law alone, the plaintiff could be regarded as insured on 1 October 1976 under the general law; it was only the Regulation which deprived Ms ten Holder from benefit. According to the Advocate General there would not have been entitlement under German law.

In any case, we can conclude that in the *Bosmann* judgment the Court did not adequately account for its deviation from previous case law. The only relevant difference between the two cases is that the Dutch invalidity benefit was based on (a residence) insurance, whereas the German benefit was not based on insurance. This difference cannot really account for the differences between the outcomes, since the rules on the legislation applicable apply on all types of schemes within the scope of the Regulation.[10]

The meaning of the *Bosmann* judgment seems to be limited. It leaves the exclusive effect of the rules for determining the legislation applicable intact; it solely does not prohibit a Member State to pay benefits even if its legislation is not applicable. The national court of that State has to decide whether its national legislation requires payment of the benefit concerned. The question then arises whether the national court, in its interpretation, may take the rules of the Regulation into account. In other words, can it say: given the applicability of the Regulation and the exclusive effect of the rules for determining the legislation applicable, that for this reason the national rules as not applicable? Or is only the national text relevant? It seems likely that only the national text is relevant, as otherwise the Regulation would require entitlement in two Member States, which would be contrary to the exclusive effect of the Regulation and which was not required by the Court in the *Bosmann* judgment. Member States can therefore easily make their legislations 'Bosmann proof', if they wish to do so. However, in some Member States there are deliberately made schemes which allow payment of benefits in addition to those of the competent State in order to take away the negative effects which exist – in their view – for migrant workers. These are allowed under this case law.

6.2.3. THE BINDING EFFECT OF THE RULES FOR DETERMINING THE LEGISLATION APPLICABLE

The Case Law under Regulation 1408/71

If a particular national legislation is determined by the Regulation, it is of essential importance that this national legislation does not exclude persons from its scope

---

[10]   It is interesting to note that the problem for Ms Bosmann arose from the fact that the Dutch study grants are not within the scope of the Regulation. Extending the material scope of the Regulation is a more appropriate way to solve the problems which occurred in Ms Bosmann's case, but, as we have seen in Chapter 5, there is little political support for doing so.

by opposing residence conditions. For instance, a self-employed person of Belgian nationality works in the Netherlands, but resides in Belgium. The legislation applicable is the Dutch social security law. In order to be insured for the old age benefit, it is required to be resident in the Netherlands. The self-employed person in this example does not fulfil this condition. The Dutch rules mean that this person would not be subject to the Dutch legislation.

Article 13(2) of Regulation 1408/71 provided that '... a person employed in the territory of one Member State shall be subject to the legislation of that State *even* if s/he resides in the territory of another Member State' (italics added). Article 13(2)(b) gives a corresponding rule for self-employed persons. The word *even* ensured that in this example the Belgian self-employed person is subject to the Dutch social security legislation, even though s/he does not satisfy the residence conditions of this system. The phenomenon of overruling residence conditions is called the *binding effect* of the rules for determining the legislation applicable. Thus the rules for determining the legislation applicable overrule the national conflict rules requiring residentship insofar as the latter rules have an effect which is contrary to the former rules. As an effect the person concerned is insured, even if this would not be the case under national legislation. The binding effect of the rules of Regulation 1408/71 for determining the legislation applicable was confirmed in the *Kuijpers* decision.[11] Another example of binding effect is found in the *Kits van Heijningen* judgment.[12] The question was whether Mr Kits van Heijningen, although a part-time worker, could be refused Dutch family benefit. Mr Kits was not a resident of the Netherlands, and the only condition of the Dutch Law for receiving child benefit was that the insured person resided in the Netherlands. The Court answered that Article 13(2) provides in express terms that the legislation of a Member State continues to be applicable to a person who performs activities as an employed person, even if he resides in the territory of another Member State. This provision would lose all *practical effect* if national legislation could impose conditions on residence.

The binding effect of the rules for determining the legislation applicable overrules conditions related to the *territoriality principle*. Examples of territoriality conditions are: residence conditions, the condition that one has to register with an organisation in a particular Member State, conditions concerning the place of establishment of the employer, and conditions concerning the place where the work is performed.

The binding Effect and Regulation 883/2004

Unlike Article 13 of Regulation 1408/71, Article 11 of Regulation 883/2004 does not contain the terms '*even* if s/he resides in the territory of another Member State'.

---

11   Case 276/81, [1982] *ECR* 3027.
12   Case 2/89, [1990] *ECR* 1755.

Instead, the latter Regulation realises the binding effect by its general rule on the assimilation of benefits, income, facts or events. Article 5(b) of this Regulation provides that where, under the legislation of the competent State, legal effects are attributed to the occurrence of certain facts or events, that Member State shall take account of like facts or events occurring in any Member State as though they had taken place in its own territory. Thus Article 5 overrules residence conditions in a national scheme: if a scheme requires that a person is resident of that country, residence in another country has to be considered as residence for the application of that scheme.

6.2.4. THE PRACTICAL EFFECT DOCTRINE

In the *Kits van Heijningen* judgment, discussed in the previous section, the Court considered that the rules for determining the legislation applicable would lose practical effect if an interpretation other than given by the Court was followed. Another example of the doctrine of practical effect can be found in the *De Paep* judgment.[13] In this case, a rule for determining the applicable legislation applied which has so far not been discussed: this rule assigned applicable to mariners the legislation of the State whose flag the vessel flies. This rule cannot be found in Regulation 883/2004 anymore. Mrs De Paep, of Belgian nationality, was the owner of the ship on which her husband and her son were employed. Due to sustained damage, this ship was declared unseaworthy. Nevertheless it was taken to a new owner in the United Kingdom by the husband and the son, who remained employed by the Belgian firm. The ship was lost and the husband and son were killed. According to the Belgian law on employment contracts for seamen, the contract of employment ended as soon as the ship was officially declared to be unseaworthy. On these grounds, the husband was no longer employed by the Belgian firm when the accident happened. To be entitled to a Belgian benefit for industrial accidents, it was necessary that the person concerned sailed under the Belgian flag. As this condition was not fulfilled, Mrs De Paep was refused benefit. The Court considered that the provision which assigned the legislation of the State of the flag would loose practical effect if the conditions for affiliation with the national legislation of the State in whose territory an undertaking operates were held against persons to which this Article applied. The objective of rules of conflict was not only to prevent two or more legislations from being applicable at the same time but also to avoid the situation where no legislation was applicable at all (negative conflict of laws).

The doctrine of the practical effect may also be relevant under Regulation 883/2004 if the conditions of a national scheme prevent the scheme determined by the Regulation from being effective in a particular case. The doctrine of the

---

[13]   Case 196/90, [1991] *ECR* I-4815.

practical effect seems to depend, however, to a large extent on a case to case approach; it is hard to say in general which interpretation follows from this doctrine.

In Chapter 5 we discussed the *Commission v. France* judgment,[14] which concerned the question of whether a particular type of French benefit fell within the scope of the Regulation. The question was whether frontier workers, who had to pay social security contributions in the State of employment and taxes in France which had to finance the French social security system, could invoke Article 13. The Court considered that by levying the contribution on the employment income of employed and self-employed persons resident in France, but working in another Member State, the French Republic disregarded the rule set out in Article 13 of Regulation 1408/71 that the legislation of a single State is to apply. The Court considered that the decisive factor for the purpose of applying the Regulation is that there is a direct and sufficiently relevant link between the provision in question and the legislation governing the branches of social security listed in Article 4 of the Regulation. This link is not broken by the choice of the specific detailed allocation of the sums in question for the purposes of financing the French social security scheme. Otherwise the prohibition against overlapping legislation was deprived of all effectiveness. So also in this case the doctrine of practical effect was referred to.

6.2.5. THE INESCAPABILITY OF THE RULES FOR DETERMINING THE LEGISLATION APPLICABLE

When a particular legislation is determined applicable, it is not possible to escape this legislation by arguing that one has no advantages from being insured under that system. This approach was confirmed by the Court in the *Molenaar* judgment.[15] The case concerned Mr and Mrs Molenaar, who were employed in Germany, but resided in France. They were compulsorily insured against sickness in Germany, but informed that they would not be entitled to care insurance benefits, since this scheme required residence in Germany (if these benefits were classified as sickness benefits in kind, Article 19 of Regulation 1408/71 linked these benefits to the State of residence). Therefore, they claimed, they were not obliged to pay contributions for this insurance.

The Court considered that migrant workers do not have the right to be exempted, in whole or in part, from the payment of contributions for the financing of care insurance. There is no rule of Community law which requires the competent institutions to ascertain whether an employed person is likely to be able to take advantage of all the benefits of a sickness insurance scheme before registering that

---

¹⁴   Case 34/98, [2000] *ECR* I-995.
¹⁵   Case 160/96, [1998] *ECR* I-880.

person and collecting the appropriate contributions. The right to benefit must be assessed on the date when entitlement arises and not in connection with the duty to pay contributions. The place of residence is relevant to entitlement, but it is not yet clear at the time when contributions have to be paid where the person will be resident at the time a claim arises, the Court argued. Moreover, recognition of a right to exemption would amount to accepting, as regards the scope of the risks covered by sickness insurance, a difference in the treatment of insured persons based on whether or not they resided in the territory of the State in which they were insured. No such consequence can arise from the Treaty.

We can conclude from this that persons falling under a legislation of a Member State must satisfy the conditions of that legislation, including the conditions on contributions. Whether they are entitled to benefit when the contingency materialises depends on the conditions of that legislation. In Chapter 11 we will come back to this case, in order to discuss whether the Molenaar couple was entitled to this type of benefit or not.

6.2.6. SPECIAL RULES FOR DETERMINING THE LEGISLATION APPLICABLE FOR SPECIFIC BENEFITS

For some categories of benefits the Regulation has specific rules to determine in which State benefit has to be claimed. These rules are found in Title III. For wholly unemployed frontier workers, for instance, the applicable legislation is that of the State of residence (Article 65). Also for family benefits there are specific rules. We will discuss these in later chapters.

The application of these rules presupposes the prior determination of the applicable legislation in accordance with the provisions of Title II of the Regulation, *see* the *Adanez-Vega* judgment.[16] This is important, since if a special rule provides, for instance, that it applies if a person does not reside in the competent State, we first have to know which State is competent. Therefore we have to apply Title II first and then Title III.

6.3. THE LEGISLATION APPLICABLE FOR PERSONS WORKING IN ONE MEMBER STATE ONLY

Article 11 of the Regulation provides that persons to whom this Regulation applies shall be subject to the legislation of a single Member State only. Article 11(3) provides that subject to Articles 12 to 16:

---

[16]   Case C-372/02, [2004] *ECR* I-10761.

(a) a person pursuing an activity as an employed or self-employed person in a Member State shall be subject to the legislation of that Member State;

(b) a civil servant shall be subject to the legislation of the Member State to which the administration employing him is subject.

For the application of these provisions it is relevant to know what is meant by 'pursuing an activity as an employed or self-employed person'. A definition of these terms can be found in Article 1 of the Regulation. Article 1(a) provides that 'activity as an employed person' means any activity or equivalent situation treated as such for the purposes of the social security legislation of the Member State in which such activity or equivalent situation exists. Thus the national social security legislation is relevant to know whether a person works as an employed person. For example, if a person is covered by an insurance scheme for employees, s/he is an employed person for the Regulation. A person who is, although working under a contract of employment, not covered by an employees' scheme is therefore not an employed person for the Regulation. The same approach applies for activities as a self-employed person. Such activity is any activity or equivalent situation treated as such for the purposes of the social security legislation of the Member State in which such activity or equivalent situation exists.

A civil servant is a person considered to be such or treated as such by the Member State to which the administration employing him is subject. It is the labour law and/or administrative law which is relevant to decide whether a person is civil servant or not. In some countries also persons outside the ministries or local government can be a civil servant, e.g. persons employed by universities. These persons are also civil servant for the Regulation. This status becomes relevant, in particular, if s/he also works in another Member State as employed person (Sections 6.7 and 6.8).

6.4. THE LEGISLATION APPLICABLE FOR PERSONS WHO CEASED WORKING

In order to be understand better the rules of Regulation 883/2004 applicable to persons who ceased working, the historical background of these rules under Regulation 1408/71 is useful to know (Section 6.4.1). The rules of the present Regulation are discussed in Section 6.4.2.

6.4.1. THE CASE LAW UNDER REGULATION 1408/71

The Ten Holder, Daalmeijer and Kuusijärvi Judgments

From the *Ten Holder* judgment,[17] discussed in Section 6.2.2, it followed that an employed or self-employed person continued to be subject to the social security scheme of a Member State, until s/he started to work as an employee or self-employed person in another Member State.[18] This judgment was criticised, *inter alia*, as it involved that persons could not claim benefits which were available for other residents in the State where they live. Indeed, Mrs Ten Holder could not claim Dutch disability benefit, even though she satisfied the conditions for this benefit under national law. The reverse situation applied if a person was insured in the Netherlands and then moved to another Member State. If s/he did not enter employment in this new State, s/he remained insured under the Dutch social security system. In other words, s/he remained entitled to benefits payable on the basis of residence schemes of the State where s/he last worked if s/he did not take up work in the new State, since residence schemes do not require periods of work in order to acquire benefit rights. The rules for determining the legislation applicable overruled the residence requirements of these schemes, which were the only ways of 'protection' against outsiders.

For the States concerned it was sometimes difficult to effectively obtain contributions from persons who lived abroad; some of these schemes were non-contributory and thus they gave a free ride for persons who did not take up work in their new country. Therefore the effect of the *Ten Holder* judgment was seen as problematic.

In reaction to these problems, in the *Daalmeijer* judgment[19] the Court departed from the *Ten Holder* approach for some categories of workers and self-employed. It ruled that Article 13 of Regulation 1408/71 no longer applied to a person who had *permanently terminated* his working activities. The objective of Article 13 was to solve conflicts of law which can occur when for a certain period the place where a person resides and the place where s/he works are not in the same Member State. These conflicts no longer occur for persons who have permanently terminated their working activities. On the basis of this argument the Court developed the *Daalmeijer* criterion.

Prior to the *Daalmeijer* judgment, the European Commission had already taken the initiative of making an amending Regulation in order to solve the problems resulting from the *Ten Holder* ruling. This Regulation was adopted in 1992 and introduced Article 13(2)(f).[20] This new Article read that 'a person

---

[17]   Case 302/84, [1986] *ECR* 1821.
[18]   *See* also Case 215/90, *Twomey*, [1992] *ECR* I-1823.
[19]   Case 245/88, [1991] *ECR* I-555.
[20]   COM (1990) 335 of 24 July 1990, *OJ* 1992 *L* 206.

to whom the legislation of a Member State ceases to be applicable, without the legislation of another Member State becoming applicable to him in accordance with one of the rules laid down in the foregoing subparagraphs or in accordance with one of the exceptions or special provisions laid down in Articles 14 to 17, shall be subject to the legislation of the Member State in whose territory s/he resides in accordance with the provisions of that legislation alone.' In other words, in the case of a person who was not engaged in employment, and who ceased to be subject to the legislation of a Member State without being subject to the legislation of another State, the legislation of the State of residence became applicable.[21] The new article left it to the national States to define when a person is no longer covered by that State if s/he did not work there anymore. When drafting this Article, the Community legislature discussed the possibility of defining more precisely in which cases the legislation of the previous work State remained applicable, e.g. in case of short interruptions of employment, such as sickness. The Member States could, however, not agree on such a definition.

The *Kuusijärvi* judgment[22] was a new stage in the development. Ms Kuusijärvi, a Finnish national, worked in Sweden for eleven months. Thereafter she received unemployment benefit until 1 February 1994, the date on which her child was born. She was then granted Swedish child allowance and parental benefit. On 1 July 1994, she left for Finland, where she established her residence, but she did not take up work. Her application to continue to draw parental benefit after moving to Finland was rejected on the grounds that she had left Sweden to establish her residence in Finland. Swedish law provided that an insured person who left Sweden continued to be regarded as resident in Sweden only if the stay abroad was not intended to exceed one year. The question was whether Article 13(2)(f) solely concerned the situation of a person who had definitely ceased all occupational activity (such as in the *Daalmeijer* case) or also applied in the case of Ms Kuusijärvi who had (probably) not ceased her occupational activities permanently.

The Court ruled that Article 13(2)(f) did not apply only in the case of a person who had permanently ceased his occupational activities. So also Ms Kuusijärvi was no longer subject to the Swedish law, due to the definitions of this law of who was no longer covered.

This decision led to some astonishment: Member States seemed to be given *carte blanche* to exclude all persons not residing in that State from affiliation with the social security system, even in cases of short interruptions of employment.

---

[21]   *See* H. Verschueren, 'De sociale bescherming van economisch niet (meer) actieve personen die zich binnen de Europese Unie verplaatsen', in: A Van Regenmortel et al. (eds), *Sociale zekerheid in het Europa van de markt en de burgers: enkele actuele thema's*, Bruges, 2007, p. 213 ff.

[22]   Case 275/96, [1998] *ECR* I-3419.

Regulation 883/2004 defines more precisely when the legislation of the previous State is no longer applicable and thus tries to avoid the undesirable effects which were possible under the old case law (see Section 6.4.2).

The Van Pommerden-Bourgondiën judgment

The *Van Pommerden-Bourgondiën* judgment shed some more light on the question when it can be said that a person is no longer subject to the legislation of the State where s/he worked before.[23] The case concerned a Dutch woman, residing in Belgium, who worked in the Netherlands, until she became incapacitated for work in 1997 and received a Dutch full incapacity benefit. Until the year 2000 persons receiving such benefit were insured under the Dutch residence schemes, including the Dutch old age insurance. Under the new rules Ms Van Pommerden-Bourgondiën was no longer compulsorily insured for these residence schemes, except for the Dutch Health Care Act and the Long-term Health Insurance Act. The Dutch rules thus terminated the coverage by Dutch social security only partly; she was offered to buy voluntary insurance for the risks for which she was no longer compulsorily insured (such as old age).

The question raised to the Court was whether Member States could cease to apply part of its legislation pursuant to a person who has ceased all occupational activity in its territory and does not reside there anymore, and keep him compulsorily insured in respect of other branches of social security. The Court answered that it followed from Article 13(2)(f) of Regulation 1408/71 that the legislation of the Member State of residence applied only if no other legislation was applicable. Those provisions did not prevent Netherlands legislation from continuing to apply to Ms Van Pommeren-Bourgondiën. In other words, Article 13(2)(f) did not apply in such a case, but instead Article 13(2)(a) was applicable. The latter rule did not prohibit continued optional insurance within the compulsory insurance system. As a result, the principle that a single social security system applies, i.e. that the rules of determining the legislation applicable have exclusive effect, was not called into question. However, the Court ruled, the optional system (voluntary insurance) must be compatible with Article 39 EC (now Article 45 TFEU). This is the case only if the conditions for this insurance are not less favourable then those relating to compulsory insurance. In this case this condition was not fulfilled, since, among other things, the optional insurance was more expensive. Therefore the Netherlands had to offer voluntary insurance at the same conditions as compulsory insurance.[24]

---

23   Case 227/03, [2005] *ECR* I-6101.
24   Subsequently, the Netherlands made a transitional rule for this purpose and then stopped all insurance of those who did not reside or work in its territory anymore.

6.4.2. REGULATION 883/2004 AND POST-ACTIVE PERSONS

The text of Article 11 of Regulation 883/2004 gives a new approach towards post-active persons. The term 'post-active' is used here in order to distinguish this category from the non active persons, i.e. persons who have never worked or who stopped working and do not fall under Article 11(2). The rules on the non-active persons will be discussed in Section 6.5.

Article 11(2) provides that: 'For purposes of this Title, persons receiving cash benefits because of or as a consequence of their activity as an employed or self-employed person shall be considered to be pursuing the said activity. This shall not apply to invalidity, old-age or survivors' pensions or to pensions in respect of accidents at work or occupational diseases or sickness benefits in cash covering treatment for an unlimited period.'

Article 11(3)(a) provides that a person pursuing an activity as an employed or self-employed person in a Member State shall be subject to the legislation of that Member State.

Thus, in combination with Article 11(3)(a), Article 11(2) has the effect that persons receiving benefit, except for the mentioned excluded types, remain covered by the legislation of the country where they last worked, provided that these benefits are received as a consequence of their activity as an employed person or self-employed person.

Article 11(2) gives criteria for determining situations in which a person no longer falls under the legislation of the previous country of employment. Compared to the rules of Regulation 1408/71 this is an improvement. The new text involves that receipt of benefit such as sickness benefit implies that one is still employed, i.e. covered by the legislation of the State of employment, provided this benefit is paid in relation to being an employee or self-employed person.

For some categories of persons the new text may be a deterioration of their legal position: under the previous rules a Member State could provide that persons remain covered by their legislation if they resided in another Member State and received disability benefit. The new text no longer provides for this opportunity.

The new rules will lead to outcomes which differ from those under Regulation 1408/71. In the *Kuusijärvi* case, for instance, the parental leave benefit concerned was related to employment. As a result entitlement to this benefit means that the State of employment remains applicable and Ms Kuusijärvi would have remained under the Swedish legislation.

As we will see in Section 6.11 a special transitional rule applies to those whose legal position would change as a result of the new rules for determining the legislation applicable.

6.5. THE APPLICABLE RULES FOR UNEMPLOYED PERSONS

Article 11(3)(c) of Regulation 883/2004 provides that a person receiving unemployment benefits in accordance with Article 65 under the legislation of the Member State of residence is subject to the legislation of that Member State. As a result the legislation of the State of residence applies to unemployment benefit recipients.

6.6. THE APPLICABLE RULES FOR NON-ACTIVE PERSONS

The personal scope of Regulation 883/2004 is not limited to persons working as an employed or self-employed person, but includes all nationals of the Member States, provided that they are or have been subject to the social security legislation of one or more Member States. Persons who are not subject to Article 11(3)(a)-(d) – i.e. persons who perform activities as an employed or self-employed, or are considered to pursuing such activity on the basis of Article 11(2); civil servants, persons receiving unemployment benefits; persons called for service in the armed forces or civilian service – are subject to the legislation of the State of residence. This does not prevent other provisions of this Regulation guaranteeing them benefits under the legislation of one or more other Member States from being applicable. Thus also for non-active persons the legislation applies of the State of residence.

6.7. PERSONS WORKING SIMULTANEOUSLY IN TWO OR MORE MEMBER STATES

Some situations are more complicated than that of an employee who works in one Member State only. Before these rules will be described, it is important to remind of the effect of these rules in these situations. As we have seen, the rules for determining the legislation applicable have exclusive effect. Therefore the designation of the legislation of State x instead of that of State y means that the person concerned is covered by the legislation of State x only. As a result the social security system of State x applies, according to the rules of that system, to the activities and the income derived from these activities in both countries. In other words, the contribution rules of State x are applied on the total income earned in both countries, which has to be paid to the State x.

6.7.1. WORKING AS AN EMPLOYEE IN TWO OR MORE MEMBER STATES

If a person works in more than one Member State the State-of-employment principle cannot determine the applicable legislation, since the person is working in the two States. Regulation 1408/71 provided that the applicable legislation in that case was that of the State of residence of the employee, provided that s/he performs part of his or her activities in that State. There were, under that Regulation, no minimum requirements on the amount of work performed in that State in order to designate the legislation of that State. Employees could thus also take up work in their State of residence with the sole purpose of being (remaining) insured in that State. That would be the case if, for instance, they did not want to be covered by another system, for instance because it was more expensive, less attractive or simply because they did not want a change of system. One could doubt whether the Regulation should allow such an easy evasion of the State of employment principle, but thus were the rules.

There were also situations in which a person fell under a system other than that of the State of employment without being aware of this. This could happen if the person adopted a (very) small job in his State of residence. An example was that of a teacher who corrected assignments of his students or a person doing telework at home one day a week. If this is found out many years later one can imagine that this is an unpleasant surprise for an employer; for all these years contributions were paid to the wrong State. This could lead to complicated situations. The new Regulation has a different approach.

Regulation 883/2004 distinguishes the following situations:

– *An Employee has one Employer, who employs Him or Her in Two or More Member States.*
In this situation the legislation is applicable of the State where s/he resides, if s/he pursues a substantial part of his or her activity in that Member State (Article 13(1)(a)). Thus, different from Regulation 1408/71, the new Regulation requires substantial activities. The small difference in wording between the old and the new Regulation has important effects: the part of the activities performed in the State of residence has to be substantial to make the legislation of the residence State applicable.

The implementing Regulation gives some guidance on how to interpret the term substantial. Article 14(8) provides that for the purposes of the application of Article 13(1) and (2) a substantial part of employed or self-employed activity shall be pursued in a Member State if a quantitatively substantial part of all the activities of the employed or self-employed worker is pursued there, without this necessarily being the major part of these activities.

Article 14 continues with an important criterion: the proportion of activity pursued in a Member State is in no event substantial if it is less than 25 per cent of all the activities pursued by the worker in terms of turnover, working time or remuneration or income from work.

This provision does not give very sharp rules and it only indicates when work is not substantial and it leaves alternative ways to define what is substantial. In other words, since the Council could not reach consensus on precise criteria, it leaves it to the Member States to define, on the basis of the mentioned criteria, when an activity is considered as substantial or not.

The effect of this rule may be, depending on the situation and the applicable criteria, that for full-time workers working one day a week in their State of residence is often insufficient to have the legislation of that State apply to him.

Subject to this provision, residence is used as a criterion to determine the applicable legislation. The residence criterion is remarkable as it is a different criterion than used for the other rules for determining the legislation applicable. An alternative way of deciding the applicable legislation in case of simultaneously working in two Member States, could also have been in terms of work, e.g. where does the worker earn most or work most hours? Instead, the place of residence is the decisive criterion.

If a person works in more than one Member State for a single employer, and does not pursue a substantial part of his activities in the State of residence, the legislation applies of the Member State in which the registered office or place of business of the undertaking/employer is situated. This is provided by Article 13(1) (b).

Thus, this rule does not assign the legislation of the State where the person works, but that of the registered office or place of business of the employer. This could be in the State of employment, but also in the State of residence of the employee or even in a third State.

The Implementing Regulation also gives rules on how to decide that the criteria of application of the legislation of the State of residence or another State are fulfilled. This applies also in other situations governed by Article 13 of the basic Regulation where there may be uncertainty. Article 16 of the Implementing Regulation provides that a person who pursues activities in two or more Member States has to inform the competent authority of the Member State of residence. This institution has to determine the legislation applicable to the person concerned. That initial determination is provisional only. The institution then informs the designated institutions of each Member State in which an activity is pursued of its provisional determination. The provisional determination becomes definitive within two months of the institutions designated by the competent authorities of the Member States concerned being informed of it, unless the legislation has already been definitively determined, or at least one of the institutions concerned informs the institution designated by the competent authority of the Member State of residence by the end of this two-month period that it cannot yet accept the determination or that it takes a different view on this. Where uncertainty about the determination of the applicable legislation requires contacts between the institutions or authorities of two or more Member States, at the request of one or more of the institutions designated by the competent authorities of the Member States concerned or of the competent authorities themselves, the legislation applicable to the person concerned shall be determined by common agreement.

– *The Employee works for more than one Employer in more than one Member State*

If the employee has various employers, who have their registered office or place of business in different States, the State of residence of the employee is the competent one, regardless of the size of activities in that State (Article 13(1)(a)).

In this case the legislation of the State of residence applies if the employee works in this State as well. This means that the problems existing under Regulation 1408/71 are not fully solved: employees can still take up work in their State of residence with the single purpose of escaping the system of the State of employment, or they can influence their benefit position by taking up work without being aware of it. The new rules therefore solve only the problems which occur if a person works for one employer in two or more Member States.

Since the terms 'undertaking' and 'employer' are not defined, in many situations confusions can occur, such as in the case where two separate legal persons employ a person, and these legal persons in fact belong to the same enterprise. It will be clear that sometime such confusion is made use of, or even created, for those who wish to make use of the cheapest social security system.

Article 14(11) of the Implementing Regulation deals with the situation that a person pursues his activity as an employed person in two or more Member States on behalf of an employer established *outside the territory of the Union*, and this person resides in a Member State without pursuing substantial activity there. This person is subject to the legislation of the Member State of residence.

6.7.2. WORKING AS A SELF-EMPLOYED PERSON IN TWO OR MORE MEMBER STATES

If a self-employed person works in more than one State, the same approach applies as for employed persons. Article 13(2)(a) of Regulation 883/2004 provides that a person who normally pursues an activity as a self-employed person in two or more Member States is subject to the legislation of the Member State of residence if s/he pursues a substantial part of his or her activity in that Member State. Here again the criterion of substantial activity is used. Section b of this Article, concerning the situation that the person resides in neither of the Member States, necessarily uses a criterion other than the rule applicable on employees: if the person does not reside in one of the Member States in which s/he pursues a substantial part of his activity, the legislation of the Member State applies in which the centre of interest of his or her activities is situated. Article 14(9) of the implementing Regulation defines what is meant by the centre of interest: this is determined by taking account of all the aspects of that person's occupational activities, notably the place where the person's fixed and permanent place of business is located, the habitual nature or the duration of the activities pursued, the Member State in which the person concerned is subject to taxation on all his income, irrespective of the source, and the intention of the person concerned as revealed by all the circumstances.

This rule leaves open which criteria are to be applied and it is up to the States concerned to decide. This is a weak part of the Regulation, but apparently it was not possible to reach a more specific agreement on this. In the preceding section the procedure was described which has to be followed in case of disputes.

6.7.3. WORKING IN ONE STATE AS EMPLOYED PERSON AND IN THE OTHER AS SELF-EMPLOYED

Persons working in one State as an employed person and in the other as self-employed are subject to the system of the country where they work as employed person. This is again a different criterion for giving priority to rules for determining the legislation applicable: assigned is this time the legislation of the country where the person works as an employed person. The rationale behind this criterion is that most States have a better protection for employed persons than for self-employed persons.

Under Regulation 1408/71 some countries with an extensive social security system for the self-employed asked for, and obtained, an exception to this rule; this was laid down in Article 14(c)(a) of that Regulation, that provided that in the cases mentioned in Annex VII, a person was subject to the legislation of the Member State where s/he worked as employed person and to the legislation of the Member State where s/he worked as self-employed. This rule was therefore an exception to the principle of exclusive effect. As a result of this rule the State where the person worked as self-employed applied its legislation on the self-employed activities performed in its territory; the other State applied its legislation on the activities as employed person.[25] The rationale for this serious infringement of the exclusive

---

[25] For the application of this rule, it was important to know how to qualify an activity as an activity of an employed person or a self-employed person. In the *De Jaeck* case (Case 340/94, [1997] *ECR* I-461) Mr De Jaeck, of Belgian nationality, resided and worked as a self-employed person in Belgium. He was also director and sole shareholder of a limited company in the Netherlands, where he generally worked two days a week. The question was whether he was considered employed or self-employed in the Netherlands. If he was self-employed in the Netherlands, Article 14a(2) of the Regulation would be applicable, and contribution in his State of residence, Belgium, could be required only. If he was employee in the Netherlands, contribution was required in both Belgium and the Netherlands (Article 14c(b)). The terms

effect of the rules for determining the legislation applicable was that otherwise persons might evade the contributions payable for self-employed activities by adopting a job as an employed person in a neighbouring country which did not have a system for the self-employed. As a result, the social security system of the latter country would levy contributions on the income for activities as employed person only; the income for activities as self-employed would be unaffected. This effect was to be prevented by this rule.

In the *Hervein and Lorthiois* case[26] the Court decided that Article 14c(b) of Regulation 1408/71 was valid in view of Articles 39 and 42 EC, now Articles 45 and 48 TFEU.

Regulation 883/2004 no longer allows deviations from the exclusive effect of the rules for determining the legislation applicable. Article 13(3) provides that a person who normally pursues an activity as an employed person and an activity as a self-employed person in different Member States is subject to the legislation of the Member State in which s/he pursues an activity as an employed person or, if s/he pursues such an activity in two or more Member States, to the legislation determined in accordance with paragraph 1. Thus, the Regulation uses the main rule for this situation, which existed already under Regulation 1408/71, but without exceptions. The present rule is therefore an improvement from the point of view of the principle of unity of rules for determining the legislation applicable. However, it would be better if the Regulation also here provided that the activities as an employed person have to be substantial in order to shift the applicable legislation to the State where the person is employed. This would help to prevent abuse being made of the rule. In order to prevent such an abuse, the criteria for substantial activities may even be higher than applicable for the other situations governed by the Regulation, such as simultaneous working as employed person in two countries.

The latter part of the provision reads 'or, if s/he pursues such an activity in two or more Member States, [he is subject] to the legislation determined in accordance with paragraph 1'. The effect of this rule can be seen in the following example. A person works twenty hours a week as employed person in State A, eight hours a as employed person and also as a self-employed person in State B. If the activities as employed person in State B are not considered substantial (and we may assume that this is the case), the legislation of State A applies.

'employed person' and 'self-employed person' of the Regulation refer, the Court argued, to the definitions of these terms in the social security legislation of the Member States, and not to the definitions of these terms in labour law.

[26]   Cases C-393/99 and C-394/99, [2002] *ECR* I-2829.

6.8. THE LEGISLATION APPLICABLE TO CIVIL SERVANTS

Article 14*e* of Regulation 1408/71 concerned the case where a person was simultaneously employed as a civil servant in one State and employed or self-employed in one or more other States. This person was insured in the State in which s/he was insured *in a special scheme for civil servants*. Article 14*f* of this Regulation concerned the person who is simultaneously employed in two or more Member States as a civil servant and insured in at least one of those States in a special scheme for civil servants. This person was subject to the legislation of each of these Member States. This rule infringed on the principle of unity of the system of determining the applicable legislation and on the exclusive effect of these rules.

The rules on the applicable legislation of Regulation 883/2004 on civil servants are different from those of Regulation 1408/71. Article 13(4) of Regulation 883/2004 provides that the civil servant is subject to the legislation of the Member State *to which the administration employing him is subject*. Thus Regulation 883/2004 does not make the application of the rule dependent on whether there is a special scheme for civil servants. This makes a difference for countries which do not have such schemes. The Regulation is applicable also to civil servants in general schemes.

Example. A person is employed by Utrecht University in the Netherlands, where the staff has the status of civil servant. He performs his activities in Italy during a period of four years in order to study the remains of a Roman temple. This person is subject to the law of the State where this university is established, i.e. the Netherlands. If this person also works as an employed person in Italy, that does not change the situation. Even if his job at Utrecht University is one day a week and a job in Italy four days a week, he is subject to Dutch law.

Regulation 883/2004 does not give a specific rule for the situation in which a person works in two States as a civil servant. Still, it is not impossible, in particular not for persons working for other than State ministries, for instance, for universities. Most probably in this case the rule applies which the Regulation has on employed persons working in two or more Member States. That means that this person is subject to the system of one country only, i.e. in principle the State where s/he resides if s/he performs a substantial part of his activities in that State.

6.9. THE RULES APPLICABLE TO SPECIAL NON-CONTRIBUTORY BENEFITS

The special contributory benefits were discussed in Section 5.7. For these benefits, there is a special rule for determining the legislation applicable, Article 70(4).

With respect to the special non-contributory benefits this rule provides that the legislation of the State of residence applies.

6.10. THE COORDINATION SYSTEM FOR COMPULSORY AND VOLUNTARY INSURANCE

For the situation in which a person is covered by both a compulsory and voluntary scheme the Regulation has a special rule, Article 14 of the basic Regulation. This provides that Articles 11 to 13 do not apply to voluntary insurance or to optional continued insurance unless, in respect of one of the branches referred to in Article 3(1), only a voluntary scheme of insurance exists in a Member State. Where, by virtue of the legislation of a Member State, the person concerned is subject to compulsory insurance in that Member State, s/he may not be subject to a voluntary insurance scheme or an optional continued insurance scheme in another Member State. However, in respect of invalidity, old age and survivors' benefits, the person concerned may join the voluntary or optional continued insurance scheme of a Member State, even if s/he is compulsorily subject to the legislation of another Member State, provided that s/he has been subject, at some stage in his career, to the legislation of the first Member State because or as a consequence of an activity as an employed or self-employed person and if such overlapping is explicitly or implicitly allowed under the legislation of the first Member State.

If the legislation of any Member State makes admission to voluntary insurance or optional continued insurance conditional upon residence in that Member State, the equal treatment of residence in another Member State as provided under Article 5(b) shall apply only to persons who have been subject, at some earlier stage, to the legislation of the first Member State on the basis of an activity as an employed or self-employed person.

6.11. PERSONS WORKING OUTSIDE THE TERRITORY OF THE EU

Sometimes also persons working outside the territory of the Union, but subject to a social security scheme of a Member State may fall under the rules for determining the legislation applicable. An example of such a situation is the *Aldewereld* judgment.[27] Mr Aldewereld, of Dutch nationality, was recruited by an enterprise established in Germany. Immediately after his recruitment he was sent to Thailand. After some time Mr Aldewereld received a request to pay contributions to the Dutch national insurance scheme. If he had been working

---

[27]   Case 60/93, [1994] *ECR* I-2991.

in Germany, this payment could not have been required because of the effect of the rules for determining the legislation applicable. How was this problem to be solved now he was not working in the territory of the European Union?

The Court answered that the sole fact that an employee is employed outside the territory of the Community does not prevent the applicability of Community rules on the free movement of workers as long as the employment relationship remains sufficiently narrowly linked with that territory. In the case of Mr Aldewereld there was such a link, because this employee from the Community was engaged by a company from another Member State. In the case of Mr Aldewereld, the legislation of the State of residence of the employed person could not be applied, because this legislation did not have any points of connection with the employment relationship. Thus, in this case, the legislation of the State where the employer is established, was applicable, and not the Dutch one.

6.12. TRANSITIONAL RULES

As we have seen in the previous sections, the application of the rules for determining the legislation applicable may have outcomes different from those under Regulation 1408/71. As this may negatively affect persons to whom the Regulation already applies at the moment of coming into force of Regulation 883/2004, a special transitional rule applies (Article 87). Regulation 1408/71 remains applicable to these persons for a maximum period of ten years after 1 May 2010 if the application of Regulation 883/2004 would lead to the application of a different social security legislation whereas the facts of the case have not changed. The person concerned can ask, however, for the application of Regulation 883/2004.

CHAPTER 7

POSTING

7.1. POSTING OF EMPLOYEES

7.1.1. CONDITIONS FOR POSTING

If the legislation of the State of employment were also applicable to employees who are sent by their employer to work for a short period in another Member State, this would seriously affect the attractiveness of making use of the right to free movement. For instance, a Dutch professor of social security law goes to Brussels to give a lecture at the University of Brussels. Suppose he had to pay social security contributions (on his wage from his Dutch employer) for this day of work in Belgium. This would lead to many administrative formalities and in practice not to any benefit rights. In order to prevent such problems, an exception is made to the main rule that the legislation of the State of employment is applicable: this is the posting rule.

Note that for the posting rule to apply it is not required that there is posting in the meaning of labour law. Instead, the conditions have to be fulfilled which are laid down in Article 12(1) of Regulation 883/2004. The Regulation does not define the term posting; from Article 12 we can learn that posting refers to a situation in which an employer sends his employee to another Member State in order to do temporary activities for this employer for his account.

The full text of Article 12 reads: a person who pursues an activity as an employed person in a Member State on behalf of an employer which normally carries out its activities there and who is posted by that employer to another Member State to perform work on that employer's behalf shall continue to be subject to the legislation of the first Member State, provided that the anticipated duration of such work does not exceed twenty-four months and that s/he is not sent to replace another person. These elements of the posting provision are discussed below.

– The employee is sent to work on that employer's behalf;
– The employer normally carries on activities in sending State;
– The employee pursues activities as employed person and is subject to the legislation of the sending State;
– The employee is not sent to replace another person;
– The employee is sent for a maximum period of twenty-four months.

When the rules of Article 12 are fulfilled there is a right to make use of the posting rules. These rules apply *ex lege* when the conditions are fulfilled. In other words, it is compulsory law, not solely a facility for those who wish to make use of it.

The Employee is sent to work on that Employer's Behalf

By this condition is meant that the employer in the sending State sends the employee to work in the host State for his (the sending employer's) own account. It does not prevent a local client, for whom the work is done, from giving instructions to this employee.

The work is regarded as being performed for the employer of the sending State if it this work is being performed for that employer and there continues to exist a direct relationship between the worker and the employer that posted him or her. In Decision A2 the Administrative Commission writes that in order to establish whether such a direct relationship continues to exist, assuming therefore that the worker continues to be under the authority of the employer which posted him, a number of elements have to be taken into account. These include responsibility for recruitment, employment contract, remuneration (without prejudice to possible agreements between the employer in the sending State and the undertaking in the State of employment on the payment to the workers), dismissal, and the authority to determine the nature of the work.[1]

The Administrative Commission derives from this condition that the provisions of Article 12(1) do not apply in particular:
(a) if the undertaking to which the worker has been posted places him or her at the disposal of another undertaking in the Member State in which it is situated;
(b) if the worker posted to a Member State is placed at the disposal of an undertaking situated in another Member State;
(c) if the worker is recruited in a Member State in order to be sent by an undertaking situated in a second Member State to an undertaking in a third Member State.[2]

Thus interpretation apparently follows from the fact that there must be a direct relationship between worker and sending employer. Thus the user company cannot invoke the posting rules. Still, the sending company could itself send the worker to a third Member State, whereas the social security law remains to apply as long as the conditions of Article 12 allow.

Under Regulation 1408/71 a person had 'to be normally attached' to an undertaking; in the case law of the Court of Justice this condition was interpreted

---

[1] Decision A2, Article 1, para 3, OJ C 2010, 106/6.
[2] Decision A2, Article 4, OJ C 2010, 106/7.

by means of the criteria mentioned above which follow from the direct relationship between sending employer and employee.[3]

In the *Herbosch Kiere* judgment[4] the Court considered that, when the institutions of the sending State find that there is an organic link between the employer in the sending State and the employee, this is binding on the institutions of the State to which the worker is posted. The opposite result would undermine the principle that workers are to be covered by only one social security system, would make it difficult to know which system is applicable and would consequently impair legal certainty.

The Employer normally carries out his Activities in the sending State

A company can make use of the posting rules only if it performs substantial activities in the territory of this State. For instance, a business based in the UK, which wants to recruit Polish workers in order to benefit from the lower Polish social security contributions and which opens a letter box company in Poland, with the sole objective of posting Polish workers to the UK, cannot make use of the posting rules. This rule is particularly relevant to agencies for temporary work (see also Section 7.1.2).

The criterion of substantial activities was developed in the *Fitzwilliam* judgment[5], where the Court clarified the criterion that companies have to perform substantial activities in the sending State in order to be able to make use of the posting rules. Fitzwilliam was an Irish agency for temporary work, which placed temporary workers both in Ireland (in all sectors of the economy) and in the Netherlands (in agriculture only). During the years from 1993 Fitzwilliam's turnover was higher in the Netherlands than in Ireland. Given the volume of Fitzwilliam's business in the Netherlands, the Dutch benefit administration considered that the workers sent by Fitzwilliam to the Netherlands were wrongly affiliated to the Irish social security system. The Dutch benefit administration required a service-providing undertaking to have a certain volume of activity in the Member State in which it is established in relation to the activity in the host State in order to satisfy the condition that it has substantial activities in the State of establishment. For this purpose activities in the same branches of the economy have to be compared, in this case the turnover in agriculture.

The Court considered that only an undertaking which habitually carries on significant activities in the Member State where it is established may be allowed to make use of the posting rules. The competent institution of that State must examine all criteria characterising the activities of that enterprise. Those criteria include the place where the undertaking has its seat administration, the number

---

3   Case 35/70, Manpower, [1970] *ECR* 1251; Case 202/97, Fitzwilliam, [2000] *ECR* I-883.
4   Case C-2/05 [2006] *ECR* I-1081.
5   Case 202/97, [2000] *ECR* I-883.

of administrative staff working in the Member State of establishment and in the other Member State, the place where the majority of contracts with clients are concluded, the law applicable to the employment contracts with the workers, on the one hand, and the contracts with the clients, on the other, and the turnover during an appropriately typical period in each Member State concerned. This list is not exhaustive; the choice of criteria must be adapted to each specific case. However, the nature of the work entrusted to the workers is not one of those criteria. Consequently, in order to determine that the enterprise carries on significant activities it was not relevant that the workers in the Netherlands predominantly worked in agriculture and the workers in Ireland mainly in other areas. Nor was it required that the majority of the turnover has to be acquired in the State of establishment; the criterion is solely that the activities must be of a significant nature. In this case this criterion appeared to be satisfied.

This approach was confirmed in the *Plum* judgment.[6] In 1989, Mr Plum founded a company called Senator in the Netherlands. His purpose in founding that company was to meet the increasing competition within Germany from Netherlands construction companies, whose labour and social costs were lower than those of German undertakings. Senator carried out building projects exclusively in Germany. The Court ruled that the posting rule does not apply to workers of a construction company established in one Member State who are posted to carry out construction work in the territory of another Member State in which, apart from purely internal management activities, that undertaking performs all its activities. Those workers are subject to the social security legislation of the Member State in whose territory they actually work.

Article 14 of the Implementing regulation confirms this case law. It clarifies that the words 'which normally carries out its activities there' refer to an employer who ordinarily performs substantial activities, other than purely internal management activities, in the territory of the Member State in which it is established, taking account of all criteria characterising the activities carried out by the undertaking in question. The relevant criteria must be suited to the specific characteristics of each employer and the real nature of the activities carried out.

The Employee is subject to the Legislation of the sending State

A third condition is that a person has to be subject to the legislation of the sending State; Article 12 provides that the posted person 'shall continue to be subject to the legislation of the first Member State'. This means that immediately before the start of the posting period the person must be subject to the legislation of the sending State.[7] The Court decided that this rule also applies in cases where an

---

6   Case C-404/98, [2000] *ECR* I-9379.
7   The Administrative Commission provided that for the application of Article 14(1), as an indication, having been subject to the legislation of the Member State in which the employer is

agency recruits a person to post him immediately to another Member State;[8] this will be discussed in more detail in Section 7.1.2.

Article 14 of the Implementing Regulation provides that the posting rule of the basic Regulation applies also to a person who is recruited with a view to being posted to another Member State, provided that, immediately before the start of his employment, the person concerned is already subject to the legislation of the Member State in which his employer is established. So the person does not have to be insured in the sending State on the basis of working for the recruiting company itself, but s/he had to be subject to that legislation immediately before the beginning of the posting. Thus, for example, a Polish person cannot be brought to Romania and then immediately be posted under Romanian law to Italy. This is a criterion which did not necessarily follow from Regulation 1408/71 and its case law.

Sometimes the condition 'shall be continue to be subject' is interpreted as that a worker must be socially insured before a posting takes place.[9] There is, however, a difference between 'subject to the legislation' and 'being socially insured'. Suppose, for instance, that a person is over 65 and under the national legislation of the sending State no longer insured for social insurance. S/he is subject to the legislation of that State, even if that legislation provides that s/he is not insured. In such a case the legislation of the sending State continues to apply, so that the person concerned is not subject to the legislation of the host State. Another interpretation would be contrary to the right of free movement, since if these persons were to be subject to the legislation of the host State they would not wish to go there.

In case of posting, the employer and employee have to apply for a posting certificate (called: portable document A1) from the competent institution of the sending Member State. As we will see in Section 7.1.3 the certificate is no requirement for the posting rules to be applicable.

The Employee is not sent to replace another Person

A fourth condition is that a person must not be sent to replace another person. Regulation 1408/71 read that a person must not be sent to replace another person who has completed his term of posting; Regulation 883/2004 does not contain the words 'who has completed his term of posting'. This means that it has become more difficult to replace a person by another person. An explanation for this

---

established for at least one month can be considered as meeting the requirement referred to by the words 'immediately before the start of his employment'. Shorter periods would require a case-by-case evaluation taking account of all the other factors involved (Decision A2). It is not clear what the precise meaning of this relevance is, since the criteria for assessing the situation in case of a shorter period are not given.

8   Case 35/70, Manpower, [1970] *ECR* 1251; Case 202/97, Fitzwilliam, [2000] *ECR* I-883.
9   P. Schoukens and D. Pieters, 'The Rules within Regulation 883/2004 for Determining the Applicable Member State Legislation', EJSS 2009, issue 11.1.

difference may be that the maximum posting period is longer under the new Regulation.

The Employee is not sent for more than 24 Months

The fifth condition sets a maximum to the posting period. Under Regulation 1408/71 the maximum period of posting was twelve months, which could be extended by another period of twelve months in case of unforeseen circumstances. Under Regulation 883/2004 the maximum period is twenty-four months. Under the new rules, replacement of a person shortly before his term would be completed would lead to long posting periods in respect of the same job.[10]

From this condition it follows that the anticipated duration of the work must not exceed twenty-four months. Thus, if it is clear from the beginning that the work cannot be done within 24 months, the posting rules are not applicable at all and the person concerned falls immediately under the social security legislation of the State of employment. If the work was not expected to last more than 24 months, but there is an unexpected delay and the person continues to work, s/he falls under the law of the system of the State of employment after the expiration of the posting period of 24 months, unless an agreement is made on basis of Article 16 of the Regulation (see Section 7.5).

The Regulation no longer has the possibility for extending the posting period. Under Regulation 1408/71 for this extension permission by the host State was necessary. Under Regulation 883/2004 there is a single maximum period, no longer extensions and permissions are relevant.

A question which is often raised is whether there must be a certain minimum period between two periods of posting, during which the worker must be working for the enterprise by which s/he is later posted. Given the provisions on the limitation of the duration of posting and its prolongation requiring, such a minimum period would be logical. The Regulation does not answer this question. At the national level, Member States have often inserted provisions in their national law which require minimum periods; these may vary considerably. Decision A2 of the Administrative Commission provides that once a worker has ended a period of posting, no fresh period of posting for the same worker, the same undertakings and the same Member State can be authorised until at least two months have elapsed from the date of expiry of the previous posting period.[11] Derogation from this principle is, however, permissible in specific circumstances. This is the requirement which applies if the same worker is sent to the same enterprise in the same State. Posting to different Member States which

---

[10]   Suppose that it were possible to replace a person before the period was completed, one could do so when a person had been posted for 23 months.

[11]   Decision A2, Article 3c (OJ C 106 of 2010).

immediately follow each other give rise to a new posting; brief interruptions of the activities (holidays, sickness) do not constitute a new period.

7.1.2. POSTING BY AN AGENCY FOR TEMPORARY WORK

As was already mentioned in the previous section, it is possible to post workers who have been especially hired for this job. This is done, in particular, by agencies for temporary work. Differences between social security contribution rates of Member States may be an important reason for the use of the posting rules. In the *Manpower* case the Court was asked whether a temporary work agency can make use of the posting rules, in particular in the situation where a person has never worked in the sending State. The Court ruled that the provisions on posting apply also in the case of an employed person who has not worked in the State where the enterprise is established, but who is recruited exclusively to be sent abroad. Also in that situation an organic link is required between the undertaking and the employed person and it is required that the enterprise normally performs its activities in the territory of the first Member State.[12] If these criteria are satisfied, temporary employment agencies can make use of the posting rules. Under the new Regulation a person must have been insured in the sending state.

Under Regulation 1408/71 a special rule applies for agencies for temporary work with regard to the calculation of the posting period. The posting provisions apply, in principle, for twelve months. If the employee returns for a short period to the sending State in order to work in that State and subsequently returns, it is straightforward to extend the maximum period of posting (twelve calendar months) with the period of interruption. This rule does not make part of Regulation 883/2004.

7.1.3. POSTING AND SOCIAL DUMPING

Posting is a politically sensitive subject. This is logical, since it is a deviation from the main rule, *the lex loci laboris*. As a result it is possible to make use of differences in contribution levels between the host State and the sending State. Although the posting rule is not meant for this purpose, it makes it possible to make use of contribution differences and this can lead to 'social dumping'. This is a problem, the more since some of the posting conditions are hard to check: is a person working on a construction site really not sent in order to replace a person who was posted before him?

In the light of the objective of the posting rules it is not possible to change the Regulation in such a way that the host State must approve a request for posting.

---

[12]   Case 35/70, [1970] *ECR* 1251.

Such a rule would be contrary to the free movement of persons, as Member States might wish to restrict the number of foreign workers in order to protect their own market. Instead, problems with posting can be tackled only by convincing Member States which issue posting certificates too easily to check the conditions better and by checking work sites to see whether the conditions are fulfilled.[13]

7.2. POSTING OF SELF-EMPLOYED PERSONS

Also self-employed persons can be posted. At first sight this is remarkable, since these persons do not have an employer, so they are 'posting' themselves. However, as we saw in the previous section, the posting rule does not refer to the labour law concept of posting, but merely requires that the conditions of Article 12 are fulfilled. The rationale of the posting rule is clear: also self-employed persons must not fall immediately under the legislation of the host State, since that would impede the attractiveness of free movement.

The posting rule for the self-employed can be found in Article 12(2) of Regulation 883/2004. This Article reads that a person who normally pursues an activity as self-employed in a Member State and who goes to perform a similar activity in another Member State shall continue to be subject to the legislation of the first Member State, provided that the anticipated duration of the work does not exceed twenty-four months. Compared with the conditions for posting of employees, there are fewer conditions for posting of the self-employed.

The Case Law under Regulation 1408/71

Before discussing these conditions in more detail, the case law under Regulation 1408/71 in respect of posting of the self-employed requires some attention. A milestone in this case law is the *Banks* judgment.[14] Mr Banks was a British opera singer, who resided in the United Kingdom, where he normally worked and where he was subject to the British social security system as a self-employed person. Between 1992 and 1995 he was engaged by the Belgian Royal Theatre to perform in Belgium; the engagement lasted for less than three months in total. The Theatre withheld from his fees contributions due by reason of him being subject to the general system of social security for employed persons. Mr Banks, however, produced a posting certificate issued by the United Kingdom certifying that he was posted as a self-employed person. He therefore challenged his being made subject to the Belgian social security scheme for employed persons.

---

[13]   *See*, for a study of posting in practice, P. Donders, *Current Practice in Posting According to Regulation 1408/71*, Utrecht, 2002.

[14]   Case 178/97, [2000] *ECR* I-2005.

Thus, according to the Court, self-employed persons can be posted to do work which is considered work as an employed person; it is the sending State which has to determine to which category the person concerned belongs before s/he is posted. The person maintains this quality during the posting period. This approach of the Court can mean that a person who does work as an employed person is neither insured in the scheme for the self-employed in the sending State (since s/he does not work as a self-employed person) nor in the system of the host State, since s/he is posted.[15]

Of course, the professional activities in the *Banks* case were rather exceptional and therefore not really problematic from the point of view of social policy and social dumping. However, posting constructions can concern also other types of work, such as construction work. Workers can be sent with posting certificates for a self-employed person to sites in other countries, where the activities are considered as employed person's work. This may lead to a risk for fair competition. The new Regulation has not solved this problem.

Article 14*a*(1)(a) of Regulation 1408/71 referred to persons who perform *work* in the territory of another Member State. This did not specify whether it was to be work as an employed person or as a self-employed person. The Court followed the argument of Mr Banks, who argued that the word 'work' ordinarily has a general meaning designating without distinction performance of work in either an employed or a self-employed capacity. This meant that a self-employed person can be posted even if this is for activities as an employed person.

Member States had argued that this interpretation would have serious consequences; it would enable any person to become affiliated to the social security scheme for self-employed persons of a Member State in which contributions are modest, with the sole purpose of going to another Member State in order to work there for a year as an employed person without paying the higher contributions in force in that latter State. The Court put this fear into perspective: the person concerned must be normally self-employed in the territory of a Member State and this obligation assumes that the person concerned habitually carries out significant activities in the territory of the Member State where he is established. Similarly, during the period in which he works in the territory of another Member State, that person must continue to maintain, in his State of origin, the necessary means to carry on his activity so as to be in a position to pursue it on his return. Moreover, the activities in the other Member State must constitute a work assignment, that is to say a defined task, the content and duration of which are determined in advance, and the genuineness of which must be capable of proof by production of the relevant contracts.

---

[15]   *See* D. Pieters, 'An overview of Alternative Solutions for Overcoming the Problematic Issues of Co-ordination', in: Ministry of Labour and Social Security and European Commission (ed), *The Free Movement of the Self-Employed within the European Union and the Co-ordination of National Social Security Systems*, Athens 2001, p. 127 ff.

These criteria were laid down in Decision 181 of the Administrative Commission, in 2009 replaced by Decision A2. This decision describes the infrastructure which the self-employed person must maintain in the sending State: the use of an office, payment of social security contributions and taxes, possession of a professional membership card, a VAT number, registration with the chamber of commerce or professional organisation (the relevance of the criteria depends on the legislation of the sending State). As an indication pursuing one's activity for at least two months can be considered as meeting the requirement that the self-employed must already have been working in the sending State for some time before he or she wants to make use of the posting rule. Shorter periods would require a case-by-case evaluation taking account of all the other factors involved.[16]

Conditions for Posting as Self-employed Person under Regulation 883/2004

The approach of Regulation 883/2004 is as follows. Similar as in the case of posting of employees, there is a maximum period for posting: the anticipated period must not exceed twenty-four months. Secondly, Article 12(2) requires that the person goes to pursue a similar activity. This does not mean that the activity has to be of the same legal nature as the one performed in the sending State (which would mean that a self-employed person can be sent to do only self-employed work, which would be a deviation from the *Banks* judgment). The Implementing Regulation explicitly excludes that interpretation: Article 14(4) provides that the criterion for 'similar' shall be that of the actual nature of the activity, rather than of the designation of employed or self-employed activity that may be given to this activity by the other Member State. Thus, a self-employed construction worker cannot be posted as a farmer to another Member State. However, a self-employed farmer can be posted as self-employed famer, even though the work would be considered as employed work in the host State. Similar as under Regulation 1408/71, it is the sending State which qualifies the activities and status of the person concerned.

Thirdly, the person to be posted must normally pursue an activity as a self-employed person. This condition has to be interpreted, as in the *Banks* and *Fitzwiliam* cases, that the person concerned habitually carries out significant activities in the territory of the Member State where he is established. During the period in which he works in the territory of another Member State, that person must continue to maintain, in his State of origin, the necessary means to carry on his activity so as to be in a position to pursue it on his or her return. This also follows from the *Fitzwilliam* case.

---

[16]   Decision A2, Article 2, OJ C 106/6 2010.

7.3. THE RELEVANCE OF A POSTING CERTIFICATE

In order to be able to prove that one is posted to another Member State the fact that one is subject to a social security system in the host State a posting certificate is very useful, which certificate is issued by the competent institution of the host State. Workers and self-employed persons sometimes do not take the trouble to obtain such posting certificate, especially if they work abroad for a short period only. It is probably even the case that in the majority of cases of posting, workers do not have a posting certificate. Still, in some areas where abuse is expected, the legal position of workers may be investigated by the competent services of the host State and the question then rises of the legal meaning of the certificate.

First, the situation is discussed in which a worker does not have a certificate. The posting rules of the Regulation apply, once the criteria of Article 12 are fulfilled. Consequently, having a posting certificate is not a constitutive condition for posting. In line with this conclusion, the Court decided that posting certificates can be awarded with retroactive effect (*see*, for instance, the *Banks* case, discussed in Section 7.2).

Secondly, the question arises of the meaning of a certificate if it is granted, but disputed in the host State. Is it binding on the social security institutions of this Member State and for what period? Is it binding until it is withdrawn by the issuing State, or can the host Member State declare that it is not binding on the grounds that it was issued on the basis of wrong facts?

In the *Fitzwilliam* judgment[17] the Court considered that the certificate is aimed at facilitating freedom of movement for workers and freedom to provide services. The competent institution has to carry out a proper assessment of the facts relevant to the application of the posting rules. Consequently, it has to guarantee the correctness of the information contained in the certificate. It is clear that the obligations to co-operate arising from Article 10 EC (not included in the TFEU, though Article 4(3) basically covers its objective) would not be fulfilled if the institutions of the host State were to consider that they were not bound by the certificate. Consequently, in so far as a certificate establishes a presumption that posted workers are properly affiliated to the social security system of the Member State of establishment, such a certificate is binding on the host State. The opposite rule would undermine the principle that employees are to be covered by only one social security system, would make it difficult to know which system is applicable and would consequently impair legal certainty. Consequently, as long as the certificate is not withdrawn or declared invalid, the competent institution of the host State must take account of the fact that those workers are already subject to the social security system of the State of establishment. However, the Court added, if the competent institution of the host State expresses doubts as to the correctness of the facts on which the certificate was based, the competent

---

[17]   Case 202/97, [2000] *ECR* I-883.

institution of the Member State which issued the certificate must reconsider the grounds for its issue and, if necessary, withdraw the certificate. This is, in particular, the case if the information does not correspond to the requirements of the posting provision. Should the institutions concerned not reach agreement on this issue, it is open to them to refer the matter to the Administrative Commission. If the Administrative Commission does not succeed in reconciling the points of view of the competent institutions on the question of the legislation applicable, the Member State to which the workers concerned are posted may at least bring infringement proceedings under Article 227 EC (now Article 259 TFEU) in order to enable the Court to examine in those proceedings the question of the legislation applicable to those workers and, consequently, the correctness of the information contained in the certificate.

This approach was confirmed in the *Herbosch Kiere* judgment.[18] The Court clarified that also a national court of the hosting State cannot declare a posting certificate invalid. Otherwise there would be a risk that the system based on the duty of cooperation in good faith between the competent institutions of the Member States would be undermined.[19]

This approach is laid down in Article 5 of the Implementing Regulation. This Article reads that documents issued by the institution of a Member State and supporting documents issued by the authorities of another Member State, including the taxation authorities, shall be accepted by the institutions of the other Member States so long as they have not been withdrawn or declared to be invalid by the competent authority or institution of the Member State in which they were issued. Where there is doubt about the validity of a document or the accuracy of the facts on which the particulars contained therein are based, the institution of the Member State that receives the document shall contact the issuing institution to ask it for the necessary clarification and, where appropriate, the withdrawal of the said document. Where no agreement is reached between the institutions concerned in the month following the date on which the institution that received the document submitted its request, the matter may be brought before the Administrative Commission in order to reconcile the points of view within six months of the date on which the matter was brought before it. In Decision A1 of the Administrative Commission the procedure of the dialogue and conciliation concerning validity of documents is laid down.[20]

Note that this procedure does not only apply in case of disputes on posting certificates, but in all cases where documents are issued by a Member State.

---

[18] Case C-2/05 [2006] *ECR* I-1081.
[19] *See* also H. Verschueren, 'Sociale zekerheid en detachering binnen de Europese Unie. De zaak *Herbosch Kiere*: een gemiste kans in de strijd tegen grensoverschrijdende sociale dumping', *BTSZ* 2006, p. 403-449.
[20] OJ C 106/1 of 2010.

7.4.   THE SMALL BORDER LINE BETWEEN POSTING AND WORKING SIMULTANEOUSLY IN TWO COUNTRIES

A person can normally work in one Member State and start activities in another State. When do we have to consider such a situation as posting and when as 'simultaneously working in two Member States'? This question arises, of course, only if the conditions for posting are satisfied.

The Regulation does not clearly define when a situation of posting becomes a situation where a person normally works in two Member States for the same employer. If the period of work in the host State is interspersed with intervals during which s/he works in the State of origin, it can, at a certain moment, be said that s/he normally works in two countries.

Also the approach of the Court in this situation is not clear yet. From the scarce case law[21] we could conclude that it must first be established whether in a given situation the posting criteria are satisfied. Only if these criteria are not satisfied, it has to be considered whether Article 13 (working in two countries) applies. For example, if a person starts to work in another Member State for a period longer than twenty-four months, we cannot call this 'posting' and we can go immediately to Article 13.

As must have become clear, the difference between the Article on posting and the Article on simultaneously working in two States is very important. Regulation 883/2004 provides that applicable legislation of the State of residence is applicable only in case the person works for one employer if substantial activities take place in that State. Therefore, the outcome may be different from that under the posting rule. Furthermore, the administrative procedures to be followed and the applicable legislation may be different depending on the applicable rules. There are also differences in the position of the States. Basically, each State has, in principle, the competence to qualify the activities carried out on its territory in accordance with its own social security legislation, but this is not true for posting. In that case the sending State has competence to qualify the activities. Thus, a self-employed person can be posted as such to another country to carry on activities which the hosting State considers as employed activities. The rules on simultaneous performance of mixed professional activities mean that the country where s/he works as employee is competent. If we consider the situation as one of posting, s/he remains insured as a self-employed person in the sending State.

In the *Banks* case this situation occurred. The Court argued that since, in this case, the posting provision is applicable, the question of whether Banks was simultaneously employed in two Member States did not have to be answered. Consequently, also in the case of concurrence of the provision on mixed activities and the posting provision, the latter has priority. After the expiration of the posting

---

[21]   *E.g.* Case 425/93, Calle Grenzshop, [1995] *ECR* I-269; Case 178/97, Banks, [2000] *ECR* I-2005.

period or when the conditions are no longer satisfied, the rules on simultaneous work can be applied.

7.5. AGREEMENTS ON THE BASIS OF ARTICLE 16

An important exception from the main rules on the legislation applicable is possible on the basis of Article 16. This Article states that 'two or more Member States, the competent authorities of these Member States, or the bodies designated by these authorities may by common agreement provide for exceptions to the provisions of Articles 11 to 15, in the interest of certain categories of persons or of certain persons'. This provision allows agreements on, for instance, employed persons who are sent by their employer to work in another State for a duration exceeding twenty-four months, because of their special knowledge or proficiency, or because of specific objectives of the undertaking or organisation concerned, are posted by a duration exceeding twenty-four months. In many Member States, the competent bodies limit the duration of such agreements to a maximum period of five years.[22]

Article 16 can be applied to any person(s) and, as a result, is not limited to employed and self-employed persons. Consequently, the exceptions to the rules for determining the legislation applicable can be applied to any person(s), regardless of the fact whether they perform occupational activities.

Is it possible to make an Article 16 agreement to repair situations with retroactive effect? This may be necessary if no or the wrong legislation has been applied to a person and if this has to be corrected. It can be the case, for instance, that the posting rule has been applied incorrectly (the posting period exceeds, for instance, 24 months). In that case the contributions have to be reimbursed by the sending State and contributions have to be paid to the State of employment. Since that would be rather complicated, Article 16 gives the possibility to determine the legislation of the sending State with retroactive effect as the applicable one for this whole period.

The question of retroactive effect was raised in the *Brusse* judgment.[23] The Court considered that (what is now) Article 16 allows a deviation from the general rules of Title III and it is up to the Member States to apply it, provided that it is in the interest of the employed person. This includes agreements that have retroactive effect. The decisive criterion is, as we can see in the judgment, whether it is in the interest of the employed person that the agreement is made.

---

[22] See, on some experience in practice, P. Donders, *Current Practice in Posting According to Regulation 1408/71*, Utrecht, 2002.
[23] Case 101/83, [1984] *ECR* 1285.

CHAPTER 8

THE NON-DISCRIMINATON AND ASSIMILATION PROVISIONS OF REGULATION 883/2004

8.1. INTRODUCTION

One of the most important principles underlying the EU Treaty is the prohibition of discrimination on the ground of nationality. This principle is, in the most general form, laid down in Article 18 TFEU. This Article reads: 'within the scope of application of the Treaties, and without prejudice to any special provisions contained therein, any discrimination on grounds of nationality shall be prohibited. The European Parliament and the Council, acting in accordance with the ordinary legislative procedure, may adopt rules designed to prohibit such discrimination.' Another general provision is Article 21, which provides that every citizen of the Union shall have the right to move and reside freely within the territory of the Member States. These Treaty provisions will be discussed in Chapter 10 *infra*.

As regards discrimination of workers more specifically, Article 45 TFEU (previously Article 39 EC) provides that freedom of movement for workers shall be secured within the Union. Such freedom shall entail the abolition of any discrimination based on nationality between workers of the Member States as regards employment, remuneration and other conditions of work and employment. This provision is also applied in social security cases concerning migrant workers. Article 45 is elaborated in Regulation 1612/68 (*see* Chapter 9). In Article 4 of Regulation 883/2004 the principle of equal treatment in social security is enshrined.

The question then arises whether the mentioned provisions can be applied in an arbitrary order, and if not, which order has to be followed. This question is an important one, since the provisions may differ in their outcomes, as we will see in this and the following chapters. The Court addressed this question in the *Masgio* judgment[1] and ruled that the most *specific* non-discrimination provision has to be applied first. This can be seen as a general principle governing the priority order of the application of the non-discrimination provisions.

---

[1] Case 10/90, [1991] ECR I-1119.

Consequently, in case of discrimination on grounds of nationality in social security, first Article 4 of Regulation 883/2004 has to be applied. If the person concerned or the benefit at stake does not fall within the personal or material scope of this Article, it has to be considered whether Article 7(2) of Regulation 1612/68 is applicable (in connection with Articles 45 and 48 TFEU). This will be discussed in Chapter 9. Finally Article 18 TFEU can be applied, in combination with Article 21 TFEU (to be discussed in Chapter 10).

This priority order has the following effect. Suppose that a provision of national social security legislation discriminates on grounds of nationality. Regulation 883/2004 applies in that case, if the person concerned and the benefit concerned fall within the scope of this Regulation. If the coordination Regulation applies, invoking Regulation 1612/68 is not possible anymore, since Article 42 of the latter Regulation gives priority to the instruments based on Article 42 EC (now Article 48 TFEU).

It is also possible to test provisions of Regulation 883/2004 *itself* against Article 45 and/or 48 of the Treaty, since secondary legislation has to be consistent with primary legislation.

If a non-statutory benefit is involved, Regulation 883/2004 is not applicable, since such benefits are not within its material scope. Regulation 1612/68 can then be invoked. The same is true for statutory schemes which are not within the scope of Regulation 883/2004, e.g. study grants.

If a person and/or benefit falls neither within the scope of Regulation 883/2004 nor of that of Regulation 1612/68, Article 18 TFEU (in combination within Article 21 TFEU) may be relevant.

8.2.   ARTICLE 4 OF REGULATION 883/2004

Article 4 of Regulation 883/2004 reads that 'unless provided for by the Regulation, persons to whom this Regulation applies shall enjoy the same benefits and be subject to the same obligations under the legislation of any Member State as the nationals thereof.' This Article corresponds to Article 3 of Regulation 1408/71, with the difference that the latter Article was restricted to persons resident in the territory of one of the Member States. The new Article can also be invoked by persons who reside outside the territory of the EU, provided of course that the Regulation applies to them.

As we have already seen in Chapter 3, in order to rely on the Regulation, the facts of the case may not be limited to one Member State only. This rule was established in the *Petit* judgment.[2] Thus Mr Petit could not invoke the Regulation to combat the rule that documents in a legal procedure had to be in a language which was not his native tongue.

---

[2]   Case 153/91, [1992] *ECR* I-4973.

The question whether a disputed scheme was totally an internal question was also the topic of another case, the *Government of the French Community and Walloon Government v Flemish Government Judgment*.[3] This case concerned the Flemish care insurance, introduced in 1999. The Flemish care insurance is an insurance scheme for the paying of certain costs occasioned by a state of dependence for health reasons. Examples are expenses involved in home help services or in the purchase of equipment or products needed by the insured person. The scheme was limited to persons residing in the Dutch-speaking region and persons working in the territory of the Dutch speaking part and residing in a Member State other than Belgium. The Governments of the Walloon and French Community pleaded infringement of the coordination Regulation. They claimed that to exclude from that scheme persons who, although working in the Dutch-speaking region, reside in the French speaking part of Belgium, amounts to a restrictive measure hindering the free movement of persons.

An important question to answer in this case was whether the dispute concerned only a purely internal situation; we discussed in Chapter 3 that in the judgment the Court answered this question in the affirmative for some categories of workers: those who are nationals of another Member State working in the Dutch-speaking region but who live in another part of the national territory, and Belgian nationals in the same situation who have made use of their right to freedom of movement. Therefore Article 4 of the Regulation was applicable.

Article 4 of the Coordination Regulation prohibits direct discrimination on grounds of nationality. Direct discrimination means that the rule concerned makes a direct reference to nationality. Direct discrimination is always forbidden, unless an admitted (statutory) ground applies. The Regulation does not mention such grounds, but they can be found in the Treaty (Article 45 TFEU), i.e. limitations justified on grounds of public policy, public security or public health. Other limitations, such as administrative problems or costs of the application of the rule, cannot justify discrimination.

In the *Government of the French Community and Walloon Government v Flemish Government* Judgment, discussed supra, the Court considered that the rules of the scheme in question imposed an obstacle for the free movement of workers. This would be contrary of (what is now) Article 45 TFEU. Thus, a scheme within the scope of Article 4 of the coordination Regulation must also satisfy this requirement following from Article 45 TFEU. We will discuss this interpretation more extensively in Chapter 10.

---

[3]   Case C-212/06, [2008] *ECR* I-1683. *See*, on this judgment also H. Verschueren, 'De regionalisering van de sociale zekerheid in België in het licht van het arrest van het Europese Hof van Justitie inzake de Vlaamse zorgverzekering', *Belgisch Tijdschrift Sociale Zekerheid*, 2008, nr. 2, p. 177; I. van der Steen, 'Zuivere interne situaties: geen omwenteling, wel inperking', *NTER*, nr. 11, 2008, p. 301 ff.

Article 4 also forbids indirect discrimination. Indirect discrimination exists where an apparently neutral provision, criterion or practice disadvantages a substantially higher proportion of the members of the group other than the nationals of the country concerned unless that provision, criterion or practice is appropriate and necessary and can be justified by objective factors unrelated to nationality. Suspicion that indirect discrimination is at stake will arise particularly when benefit conditions can be fulfilled much more easily by nationals of the Member State in question than by subjects with another nationality, or when benefit entitlement ends sooner for foreign beneficiaries than for the nationals of that Member State. If such effects occur, there is still only a *suspicion* of discrimination; this can be refuted if objective grounds for justification can be presented.

The most obvious example of indirect discrimination on grounds of nationality is the rule that claimants to a benefit have to be resident of the country concerned: this condition will in general be more easily fulfilled by nationals of that State than by others. For instance, this rule excludes frontier workers (person working in that country, but residing in another one). Although frontier workers do not always have the nationality of another Member State, in most case this will be the case.

It is difficult to say in general when a reason may constitute an objective justification. The general criterion found in the case law of the Court is that the rule or practice concerned has to be necessary, appropriate and proportional for the objective to be reached. For instance, the Court pointed out that the costs of the measure or implementation problems cannot serve as an objective justification, *see,* for instance, the already mentioned *Masgio* judgment.

Another example is the *Toia* judgment.[4] The French Social Security Code provided for an allowance for women with children; this benefit was paid to persons aged at least sixty-five with French nationality who were of insufficient means and who brought up at least five dependent children for at least nine years before their sixteenth birthday. Those children must be of French nationality on the date of entitlement. The French institute argued that the purpose of this benefit was to increase the birth rate in France. The Court considered that this rule could have as result that a mother of foreign nationality might benefit from the allowance in exceptional cases only. Therefore indirect discrimination could be at stake, unless the rule was justified by objective grounds. The reason presented by France could not be such a justification. The benefit in question was an old-age benefit of a non-contributory nature and the coordination Regulation did not make any distinction between the social security schemes on the basis of whether those schemes did or did not pursue objectives of demographic policy. No other arguments showing that the condition concerning the nationality of children

---

[4]   Case 237/78, [1979] *ECR* 2645.

was based on an objective difference had been advanced before the Court and therefore the condition in question constituted indirect discrimination.

Rules that raise the suspicion of indirect discrimination are not always forbidden by the Court, as we can see in the *Coonan* judgment.[5] Mrs Una Coonan was an Irish woman who settled and engaged in paid employment in Great Britain at the age of sixty-three. At that time she had not reached Irish retirement age, whereas she was above the British retirement age. The United Kingdom social security system provided that if a worker continued to be employed as such beyond pensionable age, he was entitled to cash sickness benefits only if he would have been entitled to a particular kind of retirement pension under national legislation in the case that he stopped working. Since entitlement to a retirement pension could derive only from affiliation to a national social security system during the period prior to retirement, it necessarily followed that a person, whether from the United Kingdom or of foreign nationality, who, before reaching pensionable age, had never completed qualifying periods in that Member State or who had completed only an insufficient number of qualifying periods in that State to be entitled to a pension, did not fulfil that condition. If that person continued to work in the United Kingdom, he could therefore not claim, in the event of illness, cash benefits which the legislation awards to workers. That situation could be remedied only if affiliation in another Member State before pension age in the United Kingdom was treated as equivalent to affiliation in the latter Member State. The Court considered that it is for the legislature of each Member State to lay down the conditions creating the right or the obligation to become affiliated to a social security scheme or to a particular branch under such a scheme. The coordination Regulation (i.e. Regulation 1408/71) does not compel Member States to treat as equivalent insurance periods completed in another Member State with those which were completed previously on national territory. The Court did not consider the question whether indirect discrimination was involved in this case, although the Advocate-General had argued that there was reason to do so. Under Regulation 883/2004 it is very likely that under the assimilation rules, the outcome would be different (Section 8.3).

Another example concerns the *Kenny* judgment.[6] Mr Kenny, of Irish nationality, resided in Great Britain. He was imprisoned during a visit to Ireland. While in prison, he became ill and was taken to hospital. After his return to Great Britain, he applied for a United Kingdom sickness benefit for this period. United Kingdom law on this issue excludes imprisoned persons from sickness benefit. Although this law provides that one is ineligible for benefit in case of imprisonment, traditionally this had the meaning of imprisonment *in Great Britain*. The extension of this rule to imprisonment in a foreign country would be a deviation from the original interpretation. The Court argued that although

---

[5]   Case 110/79, [1980] *ECR* 1445.
[6]   Case 1/78, [1978] *ECR* 1489.

a broad interpretation of the term 'imprisonment' seemed most obvious, there might be a considerable difference between rules of penal law and prosecution of Member States. It was therefore possible that a fact in one State could lead to suspension of benefit received from another State, whereas the same fact in the other State would not cause suspension. The Court ruled that the national legislation is allowed to impose conditions, provided that no discrimination is made. The prohibition on discrimination on nationality does not pertain to possible differences in treatment resulting from the differences between the legislations of Member States, provided that these legislations are based on objective criteria and do not take into account the nationality of the person concerned. Here the assimilation rule of Regulation 883/2004 would probably lead to the same outcome.

Finally it is useful to point out that some issues which are covered by the prohibition of indirect discrimination are also addressed by more specific rules of the Regulation. An example is the residence condition, which is also affected by the residence provision of the Regulation (Article 7 – see Section 8.4). As a result, this provision has priority to the non-discrimination clause. The effect of this priority is that no objective justifications are allowed, as Article 7 does not allow objective justifications; if solely Article 4 applies objective justifications put forward by the defendant have to be studied. The absence of the need to discuss objective justifications makes it easier to decide that residence conditions (affected by this provision) are not allowed. However, Article 7 allows also exceptions to the waiving of residence conditions, and these cannot be addressed by Article 4 anymore, now Article 7 and those articles referred to by this Article have priority. Examples are the residence clauses for special non-contributory benefits and unemployment benefits for wholly unemployed frontier workers (discussed in later chapters). Such rules can be challenged only by invoking the Treaty (Article 45 TFEU). In the chapters on these benefits we will see that this test let these provisions of the Regulation intact.

8.3. ASSIMILATION OF RECEIPT OF BENEFIT, EVENTS AND FACTS (ARTICLE 5)

In the previous section we saw that claimants could be confronted by rules such as that entitlement to a retirement pension from a country other than the competent State does not count for qualifying for a particular benefit (*Coonan*). Although it could be argued that the rules in question were indirectly discriminating, the Court did not follow that line of argument, as otherwise the coordination Regulation would have too much of an harmonising effect. After all, a broad interpretation of indirect discrimination might 'endanger' many of the differences between national systems.

Article 5 of Regulation 883/2004 is therefore important as it is a general assimilation rule: it requires equal treatment of benefits, income, facts or events. It reads that unless otherwise provided for by this Regulation and in the light of the special implementing provisions laid down, the following shall apply:

(a) where, under the legislation of the competent Member State, the receipt of social security benefits and other income has certain legal effects, the relevant provisions of that legislation shall also apply to the receipt of equivalent benefits acquired under the legislation of another Member State or to income acquired in another Member State;

(b) where, under the legislation of the competent Member State, legal effects are attributed to the occurrence of certain facts or events, that Member State shall take account of like facts or events occurring in any Member State as though they had taken place in its own territory.

Therefore this article supplements Article 4 to an important extent. The (a) clause seems to be applicable to the *Coonan* situation, where the disputed rule involved that a person was entitled to British cash sickness benefits only if he would have been entitled to British retirement pension in the case that he stopped working.[7] Clause (a) relates also to other situations, including the connection of entitlement to re-integration measures if a person is in receipt of a particular benefit (also if it is from another Member State) or reduction to the costs of public provisions (e.g. public transport) if s/he receives a particular benefit.

The second clause seems to be applicable in cases like that of Kenny in the *Kenny* judgment. Imprisonment abroad has to be treated as if it takes place in the competent State if that is relevant to benefit entitlement.

It is difficult to oversee all the effects of these clauses, as these depend very much on the national schemes involved. We may expect interesting cases and effects resulting from these rules.

8.4. WAIVING OF RESIDENCE CONDITIONS (ARTICLE 7)

Article 7 – which waives residence conditions – was already mentioned in Section 8.2. Residence requirements are problematic in relation to free movement and thus coordination regulations contain rules on this issue. Regulation 1408/71 did not have a general prohibition of residence requirements, but it contained provisions relevant to categories of benefits. An example was Article 10, which waived residence conditions in respect of the long-term benefits involved.

Article 7 of Regulation 883/2004 is a general provision waiving residence conditions. It reads that unless otherwise provided for by this Regulation, cash

---

[7] We may assume that in the light of the purpose of this provision entitlement to benefit is assimilated with receipt of the benefit.

benefits payable under the legislation of one or more Member States or under this Regulation shall not be subject to any reduction, amendment, suspension, withdrawal or confiscation on account of the fact that the beneficiary or the members of his family reside in a Member State other than that in which the institution responsible for providing benefits is situated.

Article 7 allows for some exceptions to the waiving of residence conditions. These can be found in Title III of the Regulation. A major example concerns unemployment benefits, i.e. the rules on wholly unemployed frontier workers and the limited period for which export of this benefit is allowed. Another example concerns the special non-contributory benefits, discussed in Section 5.6. The provisions on these benefits explicitly deviate from Article 7.

8.5. AGGREGATION OF PERIODS (ARTICLE 6)

As we have seen in Chapter 1, Article 48 TFEU requires measures which are necessary for the free movement of workers; one of the measures required concerns aggregation of periods. In Regulation 883/2004, Article 6 gives a general rule on this. It reads that unless otherwise provided for by this Regulation, the competent institution of a Member State whose legislation makes:
–   the acquisition, retention, duration or recovery of the right to benefits;
–   the coverage by legislation; or
–   the access to or the exemption from compulsory, optional continued or voluntary insurance;
conditional upon the completion of periods of insurance, employment, self-employment or residence shall, to the extent necessary, take into account periods of insurance, employment, self-employment or residence completed under the legislation of any other Member State as though they were periods completed under the legislation which it applies.

Some chapters in the Regulation deviate from this provision, e.g. the chapter on unemployment benefits. We will discuss these rules in the relevant chapters.

Article 5 – the assimilation of facts – may seem to overlap with the present provision. However, Article 6 concerns legal qualifications of facts (such as periods of insurance) and Article 5 concerns facts and situations.

8.6. THE GENERAL RULES AGAINST OVERLAPPING

If a person has worked in several countries, it is possible that he has acquired benefit rights with respect to the same contingency. The Regulation has as a main principle that claimants are entitled only to benefit from one country. This approach is called the integration principle. As a result, a person who first worked in France and then in Belgium, is entitled to Belgian sickness benefit only.

This is laid down in a general provision on overlapping of benefits (Article 10). This reads that unless otherwise specified, this Regulation shall neither confer nor maintain the right to several benefits of the same kind for one and the same period of compulsory insurance.

Thus this Article concerns benefits of the same kind for one and the same period of compulsory insurance. This means that a person who is voluntarily insured under a scheme of a country can claim benefit from that country even if he is compulsorily insured in another country.

The provision on overlapping applies unless the Regulation provides otherwise. An important exception concerns long-term benefits (*see* Chapters 12 and 13).

Article 10 is relevant to benefits of the same kind of one and the same person. In other words, this Article does not interfere with national rules against overlapping which refer to the income or benefit of a partner or spouse. This was, under Regulation 1408/71, explained in the *Schmidt* judgment.[8] In this judgement the Court ruled that benefits are of the same kind when their purpose and object as well as the basis on which they are calculated and the conditions for granting them are identical. In this case the concurrence of two benefits was disputed. The first benefit was an old age pension, based on the period of employment which the claimant, Mrs Schmidt, completed in Germany prior to her marriage. The other was an old age pension to which Mrs Schmidt became entitled after her divorce, which was based on the employment of her former husband. The Court considered that it was not disputed that the aim of the Belgian retirement pension granted to a divorcee is to ensure that that person should have adequate means of subsistence now she has no longer an income from her husband. As for the personal retirement pension obtained in Germany, it is intended to ensure that a worker has an adequate income from the date on which he personally retires. Consequently, the benefits at issue in the main proceedings do not have the same purpose and object. Secondly, benefits that are calculated on the basis of the periods of employment of two different persons cannot be treated as benefits of the same kind.

---

[8]   Case 98/94, [1995] *ECR* I-2559.

CHAPTER 9

THE NON-DISCRIMINATION PROVISION OF REGULATION 1612/68

9.1.   INTRODUCTION

Not every person and every benefit is covered by the non-discrimination provision of Regulation 883/2004. Public assistance benefits, for instance, are excluded from the scope of this Regulation. Therefore, the equal treatment provision of the Regulation discussed in this chapter, Regulation 1612/68,[1] may be useful in supplementing the non-discrimination rule of Regulation 883/2004. In order to have a full picture of the application of non-discrimination provisions in social security, the discussion of the coordination Regulation is therefore interrupted by treatment of Regulation 1612/68 and the Treaty provisions in this and the following chapter.

Regulation 1612/68 is based on Article 45 TFEU and elaborates this provision. In the case law of the Court, the Treaty provision is often referred to in order to construe an interpretation of Regulation 1612/68. The objective of Article 45 and the (restricted) exceptions to this Article are thus relevant to the interpretation of Regulation 1612/68.

Regulation 1612/68's only relevant provision to social security is the non-discrimination rule; it does not give provisions on, for instance, aggregation of periods and export of benefits.

This non-discrimination rule (Article 7) reads:

1. A worker who is a national of a Member State may not, in the territory of another Member State, be treated differently from national workers by reason of his nationality in respect of any conditions of employment and work, in particular as regards remuneration, dismissal, and should s/he become unemployed, reinstatement or re-employment
2. He shall enjoy the same social and tax advantages as national workers (..).

---

[1]   *OJ 1968 L 257.*

9.2. THE PERSONAL SCOPE

9.2.1. WORKERS

Regulation 1612/68 is relevant only to workers; the self-employed and non-active persons can therefore not rely on it.[2] The term 'workers' in Regulation 1612/68 is related to Article 45 TFEU, which means that Regulation 1612/68 is restricted to workers in the sense of labour law.

The Court ruled that the term 'worker' has a Community meaning and, since it defines the scope of a fundamental freedom, this term must not be interpreted narrowly. The essential feature of an employment relationship is, according to the *Blum* judgment,[3] that a person performs work for a certain period of time for and under the direction of another person for which s/he receives remuneration. Any person who pursues activities which are effective and genuine, to the exclusion of activities on such a small scale as to be regarded as purely marginal and ancillary, must be regarded as a 'worker'.

From this judgment it follows that also part-timers are workers for the purpose of the Regulation, provided that they perform activities which are effective and genuine. In the *Lair* judgment, the Court ruled that *students* who were former employees can invoke Article 7(2) of Regulation 1612/68, provided that there is a 'demonstrable relationship' between the character of employment previously engaged in and the studies attended.[4]

Thus the relevant criterion is whether activities are effective and genuine, and not marginal only. The Court does not give itself the decision whether activities satisfy this criterion or not. An example is the *Trojani* judgment.[5] This case concerned a French national who went to Belgium in 2000, where he resided, without being registered, first at a campsite and then at a Salvation Army hostel. In the hostel he did, in return for board, lodging and some pocket money, various jobs for about 30 hours a week as part of a personal socio-occupational reintegration programme. He then applied for assistance in Belgium. This claim was rejected as he did not have Belgian nationality. The Court considered that

---

[2] The term 'worker' in Regulation 1612/68 is different from that in Regulation 1408/71, as the latter regulation included persons who were covered by a social security schemes for employees. That meant that persons, although having a contract of employment, could be excluded from the personal scope of the regulation, on the basis that they were not covered by a national scheme, for instance because they earned too much or too little. Also persons assimilated with employees for a national scheme, such as home workers, could thus fall within the personal scope of the Regulation.

[3] Case 66/85, [1986] *ECR* 2121.

[4] Case 39/86, [1988] *ECR* 3161. The student-trainee Brown, however, – not a former worker – could not invoke Article 7(2) as his training (during which he worked as an employee) was regarded as an obligatory part of his technical studies and thus ancillary to his status as a student, Case 197/85, [1988] *ECR* 3205. Persons in the position of Lair and Brown can at present benefit of Article 18 TFEU, see next chapter.

[5] Case 456/02, *Trojani*, [2004] *ECR* I-7573.

any person who pursues activities which are real and genuine, to the exclusion of activities on such a small scale as to be regarded as purely marginal and ancillary, must be regarded as a 'worker'. The *sui generis* nature of the employment relationship under national law is irrelevant. Nor can the level of productivity of the person concerned, the origin of the funds from which the remuneration is paid or the limited amount of the remuneration have any consequence in regard to whether or not the person is a worker for the purposes of Community law. Activities, however, cannot be regarded as a real and genuine economic activity if they constitute merely a means of rehabilitation or reintegration for the persons concerned. It was up to the national court to decide whether the services actually performed by Mr Trojani are capable of being regarded as forming part of the normal labour market. For that purpose, account may be taken of the status and practices of the hostel, the content of the social reintegration programme, and the nature and details of performance of the services. Thus the final decision was left to the national court.

In the *Meeusen* judgment[6] the criteria of worker also led to the assumption that Ms Meeusen was a worker. The case concerned the daughter of a couple of a man, who was the director and sole shareholder of a company established in the Netherlands and his wife, employed by that company for two days a week. As her father was not an employee, the question was whether her mother could qualify as such. This was doubted as the mother was employed by her husband and worked two days a week only. The Court referred to the criteria for worker (effective and genuine, purely marginal and ancillary activities excluded). These were the decisive criteria; the fact that Ms Meeusen was related by marriage to the director of the undertaking does not affect her classification as a worker. We will discuss the effect on the daughter in Section 9.2.2.

A following question was whether frontier workers can invoke Article 7(2). Since Article 7 provides that a worker who is a national of a Member State may not, in the territory of another Member State, be treated differently from national workers by reason of his nationality, it could be argued that a worker, in order to be able to invoke Article 7, must reside in the territory of the State against which the worker wishes rely on this Article. The position of this worker is compared with that of the workers who have nationality of that State. Following this approach, frontier workers could not invoke Article 7 in order to be compared with the workers in the State of employment, as they do not live in the territory of the latter State. The Court, however, interpreted Article 7 in a broader way. It considered that it follows from the fourth recital of the preamble of Regulation 1612/68, that the right of free movement must be enjoyed *inter alia* by seasonal and frontier workers. This recital does not require that recipients be resident within the State's territory. As a result, frontier workers can claim that they are treated equally

---

6   Case 337/97, [1999] *ECR* I-3289.

with the workers in the State of employment, thus enabling them to have benefit exported.[7]

Job Seekers and former Workers

The personal scope of Article 7(2) Regulation 1612/68 does not cover persons seeking work, *i.e.* persons who never worked before. In principle, once the employment relationship has ended, the person concerned as a rule loses his status of worker. This status may produce, however, certain effects after the relationship has ended if they are intrinsically linked with the recipient's objective status as worker. A person who is genuinely seeking work can thus be classified as a worker.[8] As a result a distinction is made between job seekers who have never worked and those who lost work.

An example of unemployed persons who were able to invoke the Regulation is found in the *Commission v. France* judgment.[9] These unemployed workers (frontier workers, living in Belgium) were excluded from the French free pension credits. These unemployed were covered by the Regulation, the Court decided, since there is a direct link between the advantage concerned and their work (see also Section 9.3). Another example of a frontier worker is Mr Meints, who became unemployed; he could invoke Article 7(2) to receive a redundancy payment for agricultural workers from the Netherlands.[10] Under Dutch rules, this benefit was payable in the Netherlands only and consequently it was refused to Mr Meints as he resided in Germany. By invoking Article 7(2) the residence condition in the Dutch scheme was successfully challenged.

Another issue in the case law was whether former workers can invoke Article 7(2) in order to obtain student grants for their children. As we will see in Section 9.2.2, Article 7(2) may relate to members of the family. However, a preliminary question is whether the parent is still a worker. Unlike unemployment benefits, student grants are not related to the employment relationship. Therefore Article 7(2) cannot be invoked. This view was confirmed by the Court in the *Esmoris Cerdeiro-Pinedo Amado* judgment.[11] This judgment concerned a person of Spanish nationality who worked in the Netherlands and then became unfit for work and returned to Spain, where he continued to receive Dutch incapacity benefit. When the family moved to Spain they were refused study grants (which replaced family grants for persons over eighteen). The Court considered that, once the employment relationship has ended, the person concerned as a rule loses his status of worker within the meaning of Article 45 TFEU, although that status

---

[7]   Case 337/97, [1999] *ECR* I-3289.
[8]   Case 85/96, *Martínez Sala*, [1998] *ECR* I-2691. In this case the national court had to investigate whether the conditions for being classified as a worker were fulfilled.
[9]   Case 35/97, [1998] *ECR* I-5325.
[10]   Case 57/96, [1997] *ECR* I-6708.
[11]   Case 33/99, [2001] *ECR* I-4265.

may produce certain effects after the relationship has ended. In the present case, it cannot be claimed that this is the case.

9.2.2. MEMBERS OF THE FAMILY

If Article 7(2) of Regulation 1612/68 were to be interpreted literally, it would be applicable solely to workers and not to the members of his family. The Court, however, followed a broader interpretation of this provision. In the *Cristini* decision[12] it considered that if a Member State could refuse advantages to family members and/or relatives of the worker on the ground of their nationality, the employed person might leave the Member State in which s/he had his or her residence and in which s/he was employed. This would run against the objectives and the spirit of freedom of movement. There is, however, only the obligation to grant a social benefit to members of the family if this can be regarded as a social advantage *pertaining to the employed person*. In determining this, it is important whether the employed person actually supports the family members in question. If a family member is no longer financially dependent on the worker, s/he cannot rely on Article 7(2).[13]

Thus, the daughter of Meeusen, in the *Meeusen* judgment, could claim Dutch study grants, as this advantage to the daughter is also beneficial for the mother, the worker.[14]

Not only the children of the worker are covered by this interpretation, but also relatives in the ascending line, e.g. parents (*see* the *Castelli* judgment[15] and *Frascogna* judgment[16]).

The applicability of Regulation 1612/68 to members of the family is limited in two aspects. One of these can be seen in the *Zaoui* case.[17] Mr Zaoui was of Algerian nationality and was married to a French woman. He was in receipt of a French disablement pension and applied for a supplement. The benefit was refused because he did not have French nationality. Under the then case law, Mr Zaoui could not invoke Regulation 1408/71, since the benefit concerned was not a benefit meant for members of a family. According to the Court, he could not rely on Regulation 1612/68 either, because the Community provisions on freedom of movement cannot be applied to situations which are not those for which Community law

---

12   Case 32/75, [1975] *ECR* 1085.
13   Thus the approach towards members of the family is not the same as under the coordination Regulation (see Chapter 4).
14   Note that she cannot claim this advantage on her own right, by means of Article 18 TFEU, as the latter provision requires equal treatment with persons of the country where this person lives, whereas the daughter lives in another country.
15   Case 261/83, [1984] *ECR* 3199.
16   Case 157/84, [1985] *ECR* 1739.
17   Case 147/87, [1987] *ECR* 5511.

was established. As his wife, being national of one of the Member States, had never made use of the right to freedom of movement within the Community, the Regulation was not applicable. From this decision we can infer that in order to invoke Article 7(2) it is necessary that the employee, from whose position the member of the family will derive rights to Regulation 1612/68, has made use of the free movement of workers.[18]

In the *Taghavi* judgment,[19] we can see another limitation to the applicability of Regulation 1612/68. Ms Taghavi had Iranian nationality, was married to an Italian and lived in Belgium. She wanted to claim the grants for invalid persons on the basis of Belgian law, which stated that, with the exception of some special cases, only Belgians living in Belgium were entitled to these benefits. The question was whether she could rely on Article 7(2) of Regulation 1612/68. The Court considered that the spouse of a *Belgian* employee, not being a national of a Member State of the Community, is not entitled to this benefit. In this case there is no 'social advantage' for national employees which is not paid to foreign workers.[20]

9.3.   THE MATERIAL SCOPE

For some time, it was not clear whether the term 'social advantages' in Article 7(2) was restricted to advantages directly connected with the status of employee or whether the term had a broader meaning.[21] In the *Cristini* judgment the Court clarified this term. Social advantages, in the sense of Article 7(2) of Regulation 1612/68, are all those which, 'whether or not linked to a contract of employment, are generally granted to national workers primarily because of their objective status as workers or by virtue of the mere fact of their residence on the national territory and the extension of which to workers who are nationals of other Member States therefore seems suitable to facilitate their mobility within the Community'. In later judgments the Court has consistently held this interpretation. In the *Cristini*

---

[18]   Note that the approach under the coordination Regulation is different, there it is relevant whether all facts of the case are limited to one Member State.

[19]   Case 243/91, [1992] *ECR* I-4401. *See*, on this judgment, H. Verschueren, 'Het arrest Taghavi en de tegemoetkoming van gehandicapten aan niet-EG-familileden van EG-werknemers', *MR* 1993/4, p. 75.

[20]   It should be pointed out that in the meantime the rules of the *coordination* regulation have changed or are interpreted differently. They include now these situations, so Regulation 1612/68 would not be applicable anymore in these cases. For benefits and persons not within the scope of the coordination Regulation, this case law may still be relevant.

[21]   A restrictive interpretation of this provision can be found in Case 76/72, *Michel S.*, [1973] *ECR* 457. In this decision, the Court ruled that the advantages under the Belgian law concerning social reintegration of disabled persons, which were claimed by a mentally disabled son of an Italian worker, were not subject to Regulation 1612/68. Social advantages were related to employment and therefore they must be to the benefit of the workers themselves rather than the members of their family.

case French reduced railway fares for large families fell within the scope of Article 7(2). This reduction scheme did not have anything to do with the employment of workers, but its objective was to support large families.

In the *Schmid* judgment[22] the Court ruled that Article 7(2) can be applied to social advantages which also fall within the material scope of the coordination Regulation (for the priority rules, *see* Section 9.5).

Public assistance is also covered by Regulation 1612/68. As we saw in Chapter 5, the Belgian guaranteed minimum income benefits were, as social assistance, excluded from the material scope of the coordination Regulation (in the *Hoeckx* judgment); however, Mrs Hoeckx successfully challenged the nationality criteria in the Belgian legislation on the basis of Article 7(2) of Regulation 1612/68.[23]

Also the German child-raising allowance falls within the scope of the Regulation, as it is an advantage which is granted *inter alia* to part-time workers (*Martínez Sala* judgment).[24]

In Section 5.3, we discussed the *Even* judgment,[25] where the disputed benefit for victims of war was not considered to fall within the material scope of the coordination Regulation. The second question was whether such a benefit came within the field of application of Article 7(2) of Regulation 1612/68. The Court answered that Regulation 1612/68 aims to achieve freedom of movement for workers within the Community. The main reason for establishing the disputed benefit was the services which Belgian nationals had rendered in wartime to their own country and its essential objective was to give those nationals an advantage by reason of the hardships they suffered for that country. Such a benefit could not be considered as an advantage granted to a national worker by reason primarily of his status as worker or resident on the national territory. For this reason, this benefit did not fulfil the essential characteristics of the 'social advantages' referred to in Article 7(2) of Regulation 1612/68. Consequently, Mr Even could invoke neither Regulation 1408/71 nor the coordination Regulation.

9.4. THE NON-DISCRIMINATION PROVISION

Regulation 1612/68 precludes both direct and indirect discrimination on ground of nationality. A residence requirement is a form of indirect discrimination which occurs quite often; this requirement was disputed, for instance, in the *Meeusen* judgment.[26] Miss Meeusen, of Belgian nationality and residing at the material

---

[22]   Case 310/91, [1993] *ECR* I-3011.
[23]   Case 248/83, [1985] *ECR* 982. From this case we can implicitly learn that a person who stopped working can invoke the regulation in respect to social assistance, even though otherwise it could be doubted whether social assistance is intrinsically linked with the status of worker (the criterion discussed in Section 9.2.1).
[24]   Case 85/96, [1998] *ECR* I-2691.
[25]   Case 207/78, [1979] *ECR* 2019.
[26]   Case 337/97, [1999] *ECR* I-3289.

time in Belgium, began her studies in August 1993 at the Provincial Higher Technical Institute for Chemistry, Antwerp. Her father and mother were both of Belgian nationality and resident in Belgium. Her father was the director and sole shareholder of a company established in the Netherlands. Her mother was employed by that company for two days a week. The national court took the view that her activity is effective and genuine. On 14 October 1993, Miss Meeusen applied for study finance under the Dutch Study grants Act. The grant was refused on the ground that the child did not live or was not resident in the Netherlands.

The Court considered that study finance awarded by a Member State to children of workers constitutes for a migrant worker a social advantage within the meaning of Article 7(2) of Regulation 1612/68 where the worker continues to support the child. In a situation where national legislation does not impose any residence requirement on the children of national workers for the financing of their studies, such a requirement must be regarded as discriminatory if it is imposed on the children of workers who are nationals of other Member States.

The *Commission v. France* judgment[27] concerned a French scheme in which unemployed persons received free supplementary retirement points, which allowed them to continue to acquire pension rights until they reach normal retirement age. Persons working in France and residing in Belgium were excluded from this insurance. The French Government maintained that Regulation 1612/68 makes no provision for the 'export' of the social advantages to which it refers. The Court considered that this scheme forms an integral part of the advantages granted to workers and falls under Article 7. As the residence condition which applied for the credit point could more easily be fulfilled by French workers – most of whom reside in France – than by workers from other Member States, it is a form of indirect discrimination.

Objective Justifications related to Degree of Integration in the Work State: the Geven Judgment

In a recent judgment, the *Geven* judgment,[28] the Court accepted a restriction to the applicability of Article 7 which was related to the degree to which a person was established in the country of employment. Ms Geven, of Netherlands nationality, was living in the Netherlands with her husband and worked in Germany with a weekly working time varying between 3 and 14 hours and weekly earnings of between 20 and 85 euros. Her application for child-raising allowance was refused. The German Act granted this benefit to any person permanently or ordinarily resident in Germany who had a dependent child in his household, looked after and brings up that child, and has no, or no full-time, employment. In addition, nationals of EU Member States and frontier workers from countries having a

---

27   Case 35/97, [1998] *ECR* I-5325.
28   Case C-213/05, Geven, [2007] *ECR* I-6347.

common frontier with Germany are entitled to child-raising allowance, provided that they are engaged in more than minor employment in Germany; by minor employment was meant work of less than 15 hours a week and with a monthly remuneration not exceeding one seventh of the monthly reference amount (about 300 euro a month).

The Court argued that Ms Geven was within the personal scope of the Regulation; she was in a genuine employment relationship allowing her to claim the status of migrant worker for the purposes of Regulation 1612/68. Therefore, the refusal of benefit constituted a form of indirect discrimination unless it was objectively justified and proportionate to the aim pursued. German child-raising allowance constitutes, the Court considered, an instrument of national family policy intended to encourage the birth-rate in that country. The primary purpose of the allowance is to allow parents to care for their children themselves by giving up or reducing their employment in order to concentrate on bringing up their children in the first years of their life. According to the German Government child-raising allowance is granted in order to benefit persons who, by their choice of residence, have established a real link with German society.

The Court remarked that regardless of whether the aims pursued by the German legislation could justify a national rule based exclusively on the criterion of residence, the German legislature did not confine itself to a strict residence condition, but allowed exceptions for frontier workers. Residence was thus not regarded as the only connecting link with the Member State concerned; a substantial contribution to the national labour market also constituted a valid factor of integration into the society of that Member State.

In those circumstances, the Court considered, the fact that a non-resident worker does not have a sufficiently substantial occupation in the Member State concerned is capable of constituting a legitimate justification for a refusal to grant the social advantage at issue.[29]

The Court did not give a specific reason for this interpretation. Instead it referred to the *Megner and Scheffel* judgment (see also Chapter 22 of this book). In this case the question was whether persons in small jobs could be excluded from coverage for unemployment benefit. Since this rule affected predominantly women – as most part-timers are women – it was a case on Directive 79/9 on equal treatment on grounds of sex in statutory social security. The German Government argued that there was a social demand for these jobs and that therefore these were promoted by excluding them from social security contributions. The Court concluded that, social policy is, in the current state of Community law, a matter for the Member States, who have a wide discretion in exercising their powers in

---

[29] As a person in minor employment she was not insured under a German employees' scheme and thus not an 'employed person' within the meaning of Regulation 1408/71. Therefore she could not invoke that Regulation (if the Regulation had been applicable no criteria on the extent of establishment in the competent State would have applied).

that respect. The Court considered that, in exercising its powers, the German legislature could reasonably consider that the exclusion from the allowance in question of non-resident workers who carry on an occupation in the Member State concerned that does not exceed the threshold of minor employment as defined in national law constitutes a measure that is appropriate and proportionate.

In the *Geven* judgment, however, the Court did not give any argument for the objectification. Different from the *Megner and Scheffel* case, where promotion of employment was the main objective, in the present case no socio-political argument is mentioned.

Therefore this judgment is not really satisfactory, the more while it could 'contaminate' also other cases where persons in minor employment work in another country. Sometimes even such arguments are heard from politicians to exclude persons in minor employment from the coordination Regulation. It is therefore a delicate development.

If we look at the case from some distance, we might, however, acknowledge that it is possible that persons take up work with the sole purpose of obtaining advantages and that even overlapping advantages from two countries are obtained (child care allowance by both spouses; after all, Regulation 1612/68 does not *coordinate* benefit entitlement). However, it would be preferable to avoid such effects by excluding frontier workers in very minor jobs from the personal scope of the Regulation. Although this would be contrary to previous judgments of the Court, but it would have the advantage of not linking this issue with that of objective justifications for indirect discrimination. The link with the objective justification could also affect the coordination Regulation and, additionally, the policy and arguments of a Member State become very relevant, as we can see in the *Geven* case, as this may lead to considerable legal uncertainty.

9.5. THE RELATIONSHIP BETWEEN REGULATION 883/2004 AND REGULATION 1612/68

Article 42(2) of Regulation 1612/68 provides that Regulation 1612/68 shall not affect measures taken in accordance with Article 42 EC (now Article 48 TFEU). It can happen, for instance, that Regulation 883/2004 makes a distinction which can be seen as indirectly discriminatory. An example is the special rules for determining the applicable unemployment benefit legislation for frontier workers, i.e. wholly unemployed frontier workers have to claim unemployment benefit, in principle, in the State of residence. This rule excludes frontier workers from unemployment benefit in the State of employment; as mainly persons having a nationality other than that of the State of employment who are deprived of the right to benefit in this way. Thus it can be called indirect discrimination.

However, since the frontier workers rule is part of Regulation 883/2004 and is accepted by the Court,[30] Regulation 1612/68 cannot be invoked in order to overrule this provision, as article 42(2) of Regulation 1612/68 prevents this.

In the judgment discussed in the previous section, *Commission versus France*, the Court decided that awarding free pension points does not fall under the scope of the coordination Regulation. The advantages concerned were based on an agreement, which was declared generally binding, but which cannot be considered as 'legislation' within the meaning of the Regulation. For this reason it could fall under Regulation 1612/68.

---

[30]   *See* Chapter 15 in which we will discuss the *Miethe* judgment, in which the Court decided that this rule was not contrary to Articles 39 and 42 EC, now Articles 45 and 48 TFEU.

CHAPTER 10

NON-DISCRIMINATION AND FREE MOVEMENT PROVISIONS OF THE TREATY

10.1. GENERAL

The Treaty contains several provisions which are relevant to equal treatment on the ground of nationality. A main provision is Article 45 TFEU, which ensures free movement of workers and non-discrimination in the area of work conditions. This Article is the basis of Regulation 1612/68, discussed in the previous chapter. Decisions of the Court are also directly based on this Article; furthermore it is used to interpret Regulations 883/2004 and 1612/68. This function of Article 45 will be discussed in Section 10.2.

It can happen that a particular national provision or practice does not constitute a form of discrimination as such, but makes crossing borders unattractive, for instance since one loses benefit rights. The Court interpreted Article 45 as not only prohibiting non-discrimination, but also as requiring the removal of obstacles to free movement. We will discuss this issue in Section 10.3.

To self-employed persons Article 49 TFEU is relevant, which will be discussed in Section 10.4.

Finally we will discuss a brand new topic, i.e. European citizenship, laid down in Article 21 TFEU. This provision supplements the free movement and non-discrimination rules for workers; the case law of the Court on this Article will be discussed in Section 10.5.

10.2. ARTICLE 45 TFEU: PROHIBITING DISCRIMINATION ON THE GROUND OF NATIONALITY

Article 45 requires free movement of workers; restrictions on the freedom of movement of workers are allowed only if these can be justified on the basis of public order, public safety or public health. These limited grounds of exception to the non-discrimination rule apply also in the case of the non-discrimination provisions of the Regulations based on Article 45 and 48 (Regulation 883/2004 and Regulation 1612/68).

Article 4 of the coordination Regulation requires non-discrimination, as we have seen in Chapter 8, and Article 7 of Regulation 1612/68 supplements this provision for advantages which are not within the scope of Regulation 883/2004. The meaning of Article 45 lies therefore, in particular, in its status as primary EU law: i.e. provisions of the coordination Regulation must be consistent with this provision.

Two judgments of the Court of Justice are important in demonstrating how the Regulation itself must not infringe the equal treatment provision of the Treaty. These decisions concerned residence requirements in national legislation which appeared to be disadvantageous to migrants. The first is the *Pinna* case.[1] Article 73(2) of Regulation 1408/71 made, at the time, a distinction between France and the other Member States with respect to family benefits. The provision concerned provided that persons employed in France received family benefits at the level of the State of residence, whereas for other Member States the level of the State of employment applies. As a result, persons employed in France received for their children residing, for example, in Greece, child benefit in accordance with the Greek rules, which meant a lower benefit.

The Court declared that this provision (the then Article 73(2) of the coordination Regulation) was invalid insofar as it precluded the award of French family benefits for members of their family residing in the territory of another Member State to employed persons subject to French legislation. The Court considered that the principle of equal treatment prohibits not only overt discrimination based on nationality, but all covert forms of discrimination which, by applying other distinguishing criteria, in fact achieve the same result. That is precisely the case, the Court reasoned, when the criterion set out in Article 73(2) is used to determine the legislation applicable to the family benefits of a migrant worker. Although, as a general rule, the French legislation employs the same criterion to determine the entitlement to family benefits of a French worker employed in French territory, that criterion is by no means equally important for that category of worker, since the problem of members of the family residing outside France arises essentially for migrant workers.[2]

A second judgment is the *Roviello* decision,[3] in which the Court ruled that a particular provision of an Annex to the Regulation was contrary to Article 39 EC, now Article 45 TFEU. On the basis of the rule in the Annex, only periods of employment completed in Germany were taken into account for the calculation of the German occupational disablement pension. Although the disputed rule did not make a distinction on the grounds of nationality, it applied largely to migrant

---

[1]   Case 41/84, [1986] *ECR* 1.
[2]   *See*, for a more detailed discussion of family allowances, Chapter 14.
[3]   Case 237/78, [1988] *ECR* 2805.

workers from other Member States who consecutively worked in those Member States and in Germany. The Court ruled that this condition was incompatible with the principle of equal treatment as guaranteed by the Treaty.

A major issue where the Court did *not* decide that a discriminatory rule of the Regulation was inconsistent with the Treaty concerned unemployment benefit for wholly unemployed frontier workers. The rule distinguishes on basis of residence and thus mainly affects migrant workers. At present it is laid down in Article 65(2) of Regulation 883/2004. Wholly unemployed frontier workers are subject to the legislation on unemployment benefits in the country of residence, even if they seek work in the country of last employment in addition to seeking work in the State of residence. The conditions and the level of benefit are set according to the legislation of the State from which the benefits are due. For frontier workers wishing to be available to the employment services in the State of employment, this rule is unsatisfactory, as it implies that they are deprived of the rights they acquired by virtue of the legislation of the State of employment.

In the *Mouthaan* judgment[4] the Court held that the rule was not inconsistent with the Treaty. It argued that according to the ninth recital of Regulation 1408/71, this Article serves to ensure that a worker placed in one of the situations set out therein may receive unemployment benefits in conditions most favourable to the search for new employment. So here we see that the Court accepts (in fact: invents itself) an objective justification: since the frontier workers have better chances on the labour market in the country of residence it was allowed to determine that their unemployment benefits are also according to the legislation of this country. We will discuss this rule in further detail in Chapter 15.

Provisions of the coordination Regulation may also mean that migrant workers are *better* off than workers who never left their country of origin. This is a problem that mainly occurs as a result of the effects of the calculation rules set out in the Regulation for long-term benefits, discussed in Chapter 12 and 13. The Court argued that such effects are not precluded by Community anti-discrimination provisions; they are merely the result of the fact that the Regulation provides for coordination only, and not for harmonisation.[5]

10.3. ARTICLE 45 TFEU: OBSTACLES TO FREE MOVEMENT ARE NOT ALLOWED

Article 45 TFEU has also been given an interpretation by the Court which goes beyond the mere prohibition of discrimination: Article 45 also prohibits obstacles to free movement. This approach was developed for other freedoms as well, such as the freedom of goods and services. In the area of free movement, the *Terhoeve*

---

[4]   Case 39/76, [1976] *ECR* 1901.
[5]   Case 22/77, *Mura* [1977] *ECR* 1699.

judgment[6] is an example. This judgment concerned the levying of tax on a person who worked during a particular year both in the Netherlands and in the United Kingdom according to Dutch law. Persons who worked the whole year outside the Netherlands would have to pay a considerably lower sum. The Court considered that Article 39 EC (now Article 45 TFEU) implements a fundamental principle contained in the Treaty, *i.e.* the abolition of obstacles to freedom of movement for persons. It precludes measures which might place Community nationals at a disadvantage when they wish to pursue an economic activity in the territory of another Member State. Consequently, obstacles to free movement are prohibited in principle by Article 45 TFEU.

This interpretation was also relevant in the *Government of the French Community and Walloon Government v Flemish Government* Judgment,[7] discussed in Chapter 8. The case concerned the Flemish care insurance, introduced in 1999. The scheme was limited to persons residing in the Dutch-speaking region and persons working in the territory of the Dutch speaking part and residing in a Member State other than Belgium. The Court argued that legislation such as that of the Flemish care insurance may produce restrictive effects on the freedom of movement. Migrant workers contemplating to take up work in the Dutch speaking part might be dissuaded from making use of their freedom of movement and from leaving their Member State of origin to stay in Belgium. In other words, the disputed rules can restrict the choice of the place of residence if the persons concerned do not wish to lose benefit rights.

The Court continued that national measures capable of hindering the exercise of fundamental freedoms guaranteed by the Treaty or of making it less attractive may be allowed only *if* they pursue a legitimate objective in the public interest, are appropriate to ensuring the attainment of that objective, and do not go beyond what is necessary to attain the objective pursued. Thus these three elements have to be satisfied for allowing an obstacle: they must pursue a legitimate objective in the public interest, be appropriate and be necessary for reaching that objective.

The Flemish Government referred exclusively to the fact that there was a division of powers within the Belgian federal structure; the Flemish Community could exercise no competence in relation to care insurance in respect of persons residing in the territory of other linguistic communities of Belgium. This argument was not accepted by the Court.

The Hendrix Judgment

The obligation to take away obstacles was also at stake in the *Hendrix* judgment.[8] In this judgment the non-exportability of a non-contributory benefit was at stake.

---

[6]   Case 18/95, [1999] *ECR* I-345.
[7]   Case C-212/06, [2008] *ECR* I-1683.
[8]   Case C-287/05, *Hendrix*, [2007] *ECR* I-6909.

We discussed this judgment already in Chapter 5. A special aspect of this case was that it concerned a beneficiary of a special non-contributory benefit who was a worker whose right to free movement was affected. Special non-contributory benefits are most often paid to persons not in work, but here the situation was different.

Now the freedom of movement was involved, the non-export rule deserved special attention. The Court ruled that the provisions of the coordination Regulation must be interpreted in the light of the objective of Article 45, which is to contribute to the establishment of the greatest possible freedom of movement for migrant workers. It follows that the condition of residence attached to receipt of the benefit under the scheme for the young disabled (the Wajong benefit, discussed in Chapter 5) can be put forward against a person in the situation of Mr Hendrix only if it is objectively justified and proportionate to the objective pursued. The condition of residence as such, laid down in the national legislation, was objectively justified, as followed already from previous case law (*Kersbergen-Lap*)[9] (Chapter 5). The Court added that it is also necessary that the application of such a condition does not entail an infringement of the rights which a person in the situation of Mr Hendrix derives from freedom of movement for workers which goes beyond what is required to achieve the legitimate objective pursued by the national legislation. Under Dutch law the export was still required if it would otherwise lead to an 'unacceptable degree of unfairness'. The Court concluded that it is the responsibility of national courts to interpret, so far as possible, national law in conformity with the requirements of Community law The referring court must therefore be satisfied, in the circumstances of this particular case, that the requirement of a condition of residence on national territory does not lead to such unfairness, taking into account the fact that Mr Hendrix has exercised his right of freedom of movement as a worker and that he has maintained economic and social links to the Netherlands.[10] Thus we can see that, even if in general a benefit is not exportable, the benefit administration must still keep an eye on situations where the free movement of workers is endangered.

Another issue is that despite the coordination rules persons can still be worse off as a result of crossing the border. We have already mentioned this problem in the preceding chapters. It follows from the legal basis of Article 48 TFEU, which allows coordination only, and not harmonisation, that these effects cannot be taken away. However, the case law on the removal of obstacles to free movement has led to some judgments where in the circumstances at stake the loss of benefits, due to the application of the Regulation, was not accepted. An example is the *Leyman* judgment.[11] This judgment concerned a person who was first insured in

---

[9]   Case C-154/05, [2006] *ECR* I-6249.
[10] In the follow up case, the Central Appeals Court decided that in this case benefit must not be refused (CRvB 7 February 2008, AB 2008, 204, RSV 2008, 86).
[11] Case C-3/08. not yet published in the *ECR*.

Belgium and then in Luxembourg. According to the coordination and national rules, she was awarded a Luxemburg invalidity benefit, which was related to the duration of her insurance, which was low in this case (on this system, *see* Chapters 12 and 13). She was also entitled to a Belgian disability benefit, but this could be paid only after a waiting-period of one year. Persons insured in Belgium receive sickness benefit during this waiting-period, but since she was subject to the Luxembourg system, she had to rely on the small pension only during the waiting period.

The Court considered that, as regards freedom of movement for workers, (what is now) Article 48 TFEU leaves in being differences between the Member States' social security systems. It follows that substantive and procedural differences between the social security systems of individual Member States are unaffected by Article 48. It is not, however, in dispute that the aim of Article 45 TFEU would not be met if, through exercising their right to freedom of movement, migrant workers were to lose social security advantages guaranteed to them by the laws of a Member State. Such a consequence might discourage Community workers from exercising their right to freedom of movement and would therefore constitute an obstacle to that freedom. The law at stake causes a disadvantage for the first year for workers as Ms Leyman compared with workers who are also definitively or permanently incapable of work, but who have not exercised their right to freedom of movement. Workers who are in a situation such as that of Ms Leyman have paid social contributions on which there is no return so far as the first year of incapacity is concerned.

The Court considered that the Treaty offers no guarantee to a worker that extending his activities into more than one Member State or transferring them to another Member State will be neutral as regards social security. Even where its application is less favourable, legislation with such effects is still compatible with Articles 45 if it does not place the worker at a disadvantage as compared with those who pursue all their activities in the Member State where it applies or as compared with those who were already subject to it and if it does not simply result in the payment of social security contributions on which there is no return.[12] So the condition is that the worker is not worse off as compared with the persons who work in one Member State only *and* contributions had been or have to be paid whereas there is no benefit entitlement at all.

The Court concluded that the application of the Belgian law in question is contrary to Community law, given that, firstly, it places that worker at a disadvantage in relation to those who are in the same situation of definitive incapacity to work but who have not exercised their right of freedom of movement and, secondly, it results in payment of social contributions on which there is no return. Where such a difference in legislation exists, the principle of cooperation in good faith laid down in Article 10 EC (now Article 4(3) TFEU as revised)

---

[12]   This was also decided in Cases C-393/99 and C-394/99 *Hervein and Others* [2002], *ECR* I-2829.

requires the competent authorities in the Member States to use all the means at their disposal to achieve the aim of Article 39 EC.

So, if persons are worse off as a result of cross border movement and they receive not benefit, even if they paid contributions for it, this is inconsistent with the Treaty. It is up to the Member States to find a solution.

10.4. ARTICLE 49 TFEU AND EQUAL TREATMENT OF THE SELF-EMPLOYED

The non-discrimination clause of now Article 49 TFEU (previously Article 43 EC) may be of interest for the self-employed. This article was invoked in the *Stöber and Pereira* judgment.[13] In this case, the applicant could not invoke the provision of the coordination Regulation which governs the right to export family benefits (at the time Article 73 of Regulation 1408/71), since he did not satisfy the conditions which then applied for self-employed in Germany. The Court considered that there is nothing to prevent Member States from restricting entitlement to family benefits to persons belonging to a solidarity system constituted by an old-age insurance scheme. However, under the German rules, family benefits are granted to any person habitually or normally resident in Germany, where his dependent children are habitually or normally resident in that this country. Accordingly, that law treats nationals who have not exercised their right to free movement and migrant workers differently, to the detriment of the latter, since it is primarily the latter's children who do not reside in the territory of the Member State granting the benefits in question. Since there was no objective justification given for that difference in treatment, it must be regarded as discriminatory and hence incompatible with Article 43 EC. We can conclude from this judgment that it is allowable to restrict the concept of employees and self-employed persons to particular categories of workers, but a general condition on residence may be indirectly discriminating.[14]

10.5. ARTICLE 21: EUROPEAN CITIZENSHIP

In the previous sections we discussed the Treaty provisions applicable to employees and self-employed persons. As a result of the case law of the Court also persons who do not fall within the scope of these provisions can invoke a non-discrimination provision, this time Article 18 TFEU. Invoking Article 18 TFEU is

---

[13]   Cases 4/95 and 5/95, [1997] *ECR* I-511.
[14]   The Court followed the same approach in the *Merino García* judgment (Case 266/95, [1997] *ECR* I-3279) relating to *employed persons*, for whom there was also a special definition in Annex I.

possible on the basis of the provisions on European citizenship, Articles 20 and 21 TFEU. As the Advocate-General remarked in the *Föster* case, discussed below, the concept of Union citizenship, as developed by the case-law of the Court, marks a process of emancipation of Community rights from their economic paradigm. Community law rights – in particular the right not to be subjected to unjustified discrimination – are no longer bestowed upon citizens solely when they make use of the economic freedoms and assume a corresponding status (worker, provider of services etc.), but directly by virtue of their status as a citizen of the Union.

Before discussing this, it is important to point out the priority order. Article 21 TFEU, which sets out generally the right of every citizen of the Union to move and reside freely within the territory of the Member States, finds specific expression in Article 45 TFEU in relation to freedom of movement for workers. This means that in case Article 45 TFEU is applicable, Article 21 is not applicable. The Court decided so in the *Hendrix* and *Leyman* judgments, discussed in the previous section.[15] This is important as the application of Articles 18 and 45 may have different outcomes.

Article 20 TFEU provides that citizenship of the Union is hereby established. Every person holding the nationality of a Member State shall be a citizen of the Union. Citizenship of the Union shall complement and not replace national citizenship. Article 20(2) further provides that citizens of the Union shall enjoy the rights and be subject to the duties provided for in the Treaties. They shall have the right to move and reside freely within the territory of the Member States.

Article 21 provides that every citizen of the Union shall have the right to move and reside freely within the territory of the Member States, subject to the limitations and conditions laid down in this Treaty and by the measures adopted to give it effect.

Article 18 TFEU provides that within the scope of application of this Treaty, and without prejudice to any special provisions contained therein, any discrimination on grounds of nationality shall be prohibited.

The Martínez Sala judgment

In the *Martínez Sala* judgment,[16] a land mark decision, the combination of these provisions led to an interesting outcome. Mrs Martínez Sala was a Spanish national, who has lived in Germany since May 1968. She had various jobs there at intervals and since October 1989 she has received social assistance. In January 1993, that is to say during the period in which she did not have a residence permit, she applied for child-raising allowance for her child born during that month. Her application was rejected on the ground that she did not have German nationality, a residence entitlement or a residence permit. Since it was uncertain whether

---

[15] Case C-287/05 *Hendrix* [2007] *ECR* I-6909; Case C-3/08, *Leyman*, not yet published.
[16] Case 85/96, [1998] *ECR* I-2691.

she was an employed person for the coordination Regulation or a worker for Regulation 1612/68,[17] the Court relied on (what are now) Articles 18 and 21 TFEU. It argued that Article 21 TFEU attaches to the status of citizen of the Union the rights and duties laid down by the Treaty, including the right, laid down in Article 18 TFEU, not to suffer discrimination on grounds of nationality within the material scope of the Treaty. In order to be able to invoke this Article, the Court added, the facts of the case have to fall within either the material scope or the personal scope of the Treaty. Since the child-raising allowance in question falls within the scope of the coordination Regulation it indisputably falls within the material scope of Community law. In so far as the personal scope is concerned, as a national of a Member State lawfully residing in the territory of another Member State, the appellant in the main proceedings comes within the personal scope of the provisions of the Treaty on European citizenship. Thus, since the child raising benefit, disputed in this case, was in the scope of secondary legislation (Regulations 1408/71 and 1612/68), it was also within the material scope of Article 18. As a result Ms Martínez Sala could invoke Article 18 TFEU in order to combat the refusal of the benefit. Before this decision on Article 18 she would have had no EU instrument for doing so, as the only other instruments were the mentioned Regulations.

The Court then argued that 'a non-national', including a national of another Member State, must be in possession of a certain type of residence permit in order to receive the benefit in question. It considered that for a Member State to require a national of another Member State who wishes to receive a benefit such as the allowance in question to produce a document which is constitutive of the right to the benefit and which is issued by its own authorities, when its own nationals are not required to produce any document of that kind, amounts to unequal treatment. In the sphere of application of the Treaty and in the absence of any justification, such unequal treatment constitutes discrimination prohibited by Article 18 TFEU.

Thus the Court gave an interpretation of the term 'lawful' which does not allow the German conditions on having particular permits; being authorised to stay is sufficient.

Note also that in this case it was not clear whether Ms Martínez Sala was within the personal scope of the Regulations mentioned; when the answer to this question would have been in the affirmative, these Regulations would have had priority. This is relevant to keep in mind, since if the State of residence and the State

---

[17]   The referring court had not furnished sufficient information to enable the Court to determine whether a person in the position of the appellant is a worker within the meaning of Article 45 TFEU and Regulation 1612/68, by reason, for example, of the fact that she is seeking employment. Annex I, point I, C ('Germany'), of Regulation 1408/71, provided in the context of family benefits that only a person compulsorily insured against unemployment or who, as a result of such insurance, obtains cash benefits under sickness insurance or comparable benefits may be classified as an employed person. For this reason there was uncertainty on her status.

of employment are not the same, the application of the Regulations mentioned and Articles 18 and 21 TFEU could have different effects: the Regulations require comparison with the nationals of the State of employment and Articles 18 and 21 TFEU require a comparison with the nationals of the State of residence.

The Grzelczyk and Trojani Judgments

Also in the *Grzelczyk* judgment Articles 18 and 21 TFEU (as is the present numbering) were relevant.[18] The case concerned a French national, who began a course of university studies in Leuven (Belgium). During the first three years of his study, he defrayed his own costs of maintenance on various minor jobs. At the beginning of his fifth final year of study, he applied for payment of Belgium minimum subsistence allowance since because of more demanding study obligations, he did not have the time anymore to earn an income from work.

The national court (and Court of Justice) assumed that Mr Grzelczyk did not satisfy the criterion for worker under Regulation 1612/68. Under national law, a student of Belgian nationality, who found himself in exactly the same circumstances as Mr Grzelczyk, would satisfy the conditions for obtaining the subsistence allowance.

The Court of Justice considered that discrimination solely on the ground of nationality is in principle prohibited by Article 18 TFEU. This Article must be read in conjunction with the provisions of the Treaty concerning citizenship of the Union. A citizen of the Union, lawfully resident in the territory of a host Member State, can rely on Article 18 in all situations which fall within the material scope of EU law. There is nothing in the text of the Treaty which excludes students from being citizens. Consequently, this form of discrimination is not consistent with Community law.

Note that this judgment is relevant only in case students are excluded from social assistance on basis of nationality; if all students are excluded from this benefit there is no problem with discrimination.

Whereas Mr Grzelczyk could not rely on Regulation 1612/68 since he was not a worker, in the case of Mr Trojani (in the *Trojani* judgment)[19] this was uncertain, as he had marginal activities and income. Therefore, it had to be decided whether he could invoke (what is now) Article 18 TFEU on the basis of his European citizenship. Mr Trojani was a French national who went to Belgium in 2000, where he resided, without being registered, first at a campsite and then at a Salvation Army hostel, where in return for board, lodging and some pocket money he did various jobs for about 30 hours a week as part of a personal socio-occupational reintegration programme. He then applied for assistance; this was rejected as he did not have Belgian nationality. First the question had to be answered whether

---

[18]   Case 184/99, [2001] *ECR* I-6193.
[19]   Case 456/02, [2004] *ECR* I-7573.

he could invoke Regulation 1612/68; we discussed this question in Section 9.2.1. The question was subsequently whether a person who cannot rely on Regulation 1612/68, may, in the situation of the claimant, simply by virtue of being a citizen of the European Union, enjoy a right of residence in the host Member State by the direct application of Article 21.

The Court answered that the right to reside in the territory of the Member States is conferred directly on every citizen of the Union by Article 21 TFEU, so Mr Trojani therefore has the right to rely on that provision. That right is not unconditional, however. Among those limitations and conditions, it follows from Article 1 of Directive 90/364 that Member States can require of the nationals of a Member State who wish to enjoy the right to reside within their territory that they themselves and the members of their families be covered by sickness insurance in respect of all risks in the host Member State and have sufficient resources to avoid becoming a burden on the social assistance system of that State during their period of residence. Those limitations and conditions must, however, be applied in compliance with the limits imposed by Community law and in accordance with the general principles of that law, in particular the principle of proportionality.

The Court added that it remains open to the host Member State to take the view that a national of another Member State who has recourse to social assistance no longer fulfils the conditions of his right of residence. In such a case the host Member State may, within the limits imposed by Community law, take a measure to remove him. However, recourse to the social assistance system by a citizen of the Union may not automatically entail such a measure. The criterion for allowing so is whether there will be an unreasonable financial burden for the host Member State.

The Bidar and Föster Judgments

Article 21 TFEU indeed has important effects. Whereas a Member State was previously required to assume full social responsibility and provide welfare for those who had already entered its employment market and who thus made some contribution to its economy, such financial solidarity is now in principle to be extended to all Union citizens lawfully resident on its territory. Yet it should be noted that certain limits remain. As regards assistance covering the maintenance costs of students, the Court accepted in *Bidar* judgment[20] that Member States are permitted to ensure that the grant of social assistance does not become an unreasonable burden upon them and that the grant of such assistance may be limited to students who have demonstrated 'a certain degree of integration'.

This was further elaborated in the *Förster* Judgment.[21] Jacqueline Förster, of German nationality, was confronted with the Dutch rule that study finance may be

---

[20]   Case C-209/03 [2005] *ECR* I-2119.
[21]   Case C-158/07, Jacqueline Föster, [2008] *ECR* I-8507.

granted to students who are national of a Member State if, prior to the application, they have been lawfully resident in the Netherlands for an uninterrupted period of at least five years. Ms Foster settled in the Netherlands in 2005 where she enrolled in 2001 for a course in educational theory. During her studies she had various forms of paid employment. From September 2000 she was granted a grant, since she was regarded as a worker within the meaning of Article 45 TFEU. Between July and December 2003 she was no longer a worker and therefore the decision to grant her maintenance grant was annulled for the period after this date.

The question was therefore whether the policy rule which required five years of residence was prohibited by (what is now) Article 18 TFEU. The Court investigated whether such a requirement can be justified by the objective of the host State's policy of ensuring that students who are nationals of other Member States have to a certain degree be integrated into its society. The Court decided that this condition is appropriate for the purpose of guaranteeing that the applicant is integrated into the society of the host State.

The requirement has also to be proportionate to the legitimate objective pursued by the national law. The Court decided that the condition concerned cannot be held excessive. For this purpose it is relevant that Article 16(1) of Directive 2004/38 provides that Union citizens will have a right to permanent residence in the territory of a host Member State where they have resided legally for a continuous period of five years. The residence requirement for study grants was applied on the basis of clear criteria known in advance. Therefore the residence requirement does not go beyond what is necessary to attain the objective of ensuring that students from other Member States are to a certain degree integrated into the society of the host Member State. Member States are allowed, however, the Court added, to award maintenance to students who do not fulfil the five year residence requirement.

Thus, Article 18 in conjunction with Article 21 does not take away all discrimination on basis of nationality; instead, Member States may require a certain degree of integration of a claimant into its society before this Article can be invoked. Five years is considered a period which is proportional.

One can see this approach of the Court as a threshold against 'social tourism'. It must be kept in mind that this requirement applies only in relation to Article 18 TFEU claims, not in respect of claims on basis of Regulation 883/2004. Although in the *Geven* case (See Chapter 9) also a condition on a certain degree of integration is allowed, the criteria and application are very different from that for Article 18 TFEU.

European Citizenship and Free Movement: the Tas-Hagen Judgment

Article 18 TFEU was also invoked in respect of benefits for victims of war. That was the case in the *Tas-Hagen* judgment.[22] Benefits for victims of war were considered to be beyond the scope of EU law, since they are excluded from the coordination Regulation and, as a result of the *Even* judgment, also from Regulation 1612/68. In the *Tas-Hagen* case, it was not discrimination on the basis of nationality that was challenged, but infringement on the right of free movement. The disputed Dutch law requires that, for persons in the category of the claimants (i.e. who acquired Netherlands nationality in the course of time), they are resident in the Netherlands at the time at which the application is submitted. In December 1986, while still resident in the Netherlands, Mrs Tas-Hagen applied for the grant of a periodic benefit and an allowance to cover various expenses. This application was based on health problems resulting from the events that she had experienced during the Japanese occupation of Indonesia. This claim was rejected as she had not suffered any injury capable of resulting in permanent disability. In 1999 she filed a new application. The benefit administration rejected the application. This time her status as a civilian war victim was recognised, but she was not residing in the Netherlands at the time of the claim. Thus the territorial requirement had not been satisfied. Also Mr Tas' claim was rejected because of the residence condition.

First the Court had to consider whether this situation fell within the scope of Community law, and in particular of Article 21 TFEU. It argued that Article 20(2) attributes to citizens of the Union the rights conferred and duties imposed by the Treaty, including those mentioned in Article 21 TFEU, inter alia the right to move and to reside freely within the territory of the Member States. Some States argued that Article 21 can be relied upon only if the facts of the main proceedings relate to a matter covered by Community law. Since benefits for civilian war victims do not come within the scope of Community law, this was not the case.[23] The Court admitted that compensation for civilian war victims falls within the competence of the Member States; however, Member States must exercise that competence in accordance with Community law, in particular with the Treaty provisions giving every citizen of the Union the right to move and reside freely within the territory of the Member States. The rejection of their applications for benefits was attributable to the fact that, at the time at which they submitted those applications, they had taken up residence in Spain, i.e. that they had made use of the right to move and reside freely within the EU. Therefore the exercise of their right to move and reside freely within the territory of a Member State affected

---

[22]   Case C-192/05, [2006] *ECR* I-10451.

[23]   In the *Government of the French Community and Walloon Government v Flemish Government Judgment* (discussed supra) it was confirmed that these articles, concerning the right of every citizen of the Union to move and reside freely within the territory of the Member States, are not intended to extend the material scope of the Treaty to internal situations which have no link with Community law.

their prospects of receiving that benefit. Such a situation cannot be considered to be a purely internal matter with no link to Community law.

The Court further considered that restriction of the Dutch law on benefits for victims of war can be justified, with regard to Community law, only if it is based on objective considerations of public interest independent of the nationality of the persons concerned and is proportionate to the legitimate objective of the national provisions. The limitation of the Dutch law results from the Netherlands legislature's wish to limit the obligation of solidarity with civilian war victims to those who had links with the population of the Netherlands during and after the war. This aim of solidarity may constitute an objective consideration of public interest. However, it is still necessary for the condition of proportionality to be met: while appropriate for securing the attainment of the objective pursued, it must not go beyond what is necessary in order to attain it. The Court decided that this condition was not met. A condition of residence such as that in issue in the main proceedings cannot be characterised as an appropriate means by which to attain the objective sought, as it is not a satisfactory indicator of the degree of connection of applicants to the Member State granting the benefit when it is liable, as is the case here, to lead to different results for persons resident abroad whose degree of integration into the society of the Member State granting the benefit is in all respects comparable.

10.6. OVERVIEW OF THE RELATION BETWEEN REGULATION 883/2004, REGULATION 1612/68 AND ARTICLE 18 TFEU

In case of alleged discrimination on ground of nationality, first it is to be investigated whether the benefit concerned and the person concerned fall within the scope of Regulation 883/2004. If this is the case, this Regulation has priority.

If Regulation 883/2004 is not applicable, Regulation 1612/68 is applicable. For Regulation 1612/68, it is important to keep in mind that the personal scope is different from that of Regulation 883/2004: a person must be a worker, i.e. performing non-marginal activities. For former workers, the Regulation is applicable only if there is a link between their employment and the advantage concerned.

Both these Regulations require comparison of the worker with the workers in the competent State c.q. State of employment.

Provisions of both Regulations have to be interpreted in the light of Article 45. This means, inter alia, that the must not form obstacles to free movement. If they do, national courts can be required to find a solution in individual cases, even if the provision of the Regulation as such remains intact.

Before the case law on Articles 18 and 21 TFEU some categories of persons could not rely on EU non-discrimination rules, e.g. students performing no work or only marginal activities (stages) and some categories of members of the family. The extension of the coordination Regulation to all nationals makes already the scope of the non-discrimination provision broader, provided that the benefit concerned is within its scope. In respect of third-country nationals it is still required that at least two EU Member States are involved.

The application of Articles 18 and 21 TFEU adds to the extension of the non-discrimination rules. These provisions do not apply to non-EU nationals. The *Förster* case sets limits to this case law, in that it allows conditions on the degree of integration. It is not clear yet in respect of which provisions this case law will apply, or that it will apply in general. Most probable the type and duration of conditions that are allowed will depend on the type of provision. Thus five years are acceptable in the case of study grants, but the number of years for access to primary school, training, municipality provisions for the poor etc. will be shorter. Thus the Article on citizenship can still raise very interesting questions.

CHAPTER 11
SICKNESS BENEFITS

11.1. THE MEANING OF THE TERM SICKNESS BENEFIT

Sickness benefits belong to the first category of benefits mentioned in Article 3 of the Regulation, which defines the material scope of the Regulation. The meaning of the term sickness benefit was questioned for the first time in the *Jordens-Vosters* judgment.[1] Ms Jordens received a disability benefit and a benefit in kind on the basis of the Dutch Incapacity for Work Insurance Act (WAO). The question was whether, although the benefit in kind was not part of the Sickness Benefits Act, it was still covered by the coordination rules on sickness benefit. The Court held that the type of social legislation under which sickness benefits are regulated is irrelevant. Thus, the term sickness benefits applies to medical and surgical provisions even if these are set out in legislation on invalidity benefits. Of course, the term sickness benefits covers only the provisions concerning this benefit and not to the whole legislation containing these provisions.

The question of the meaning of the term sickness benefits was raised again when new types of benefits were created, i.e. the care insurance schemes. We have already touched on these discussions in Chapter 5. The definition question is relevant, since the coordination rules on sickness benefits determine, among other things, whether these benefits can be exported or not. By denying that care benefits are sickness benefits in cash, the Member States from which these benefits were due wished to prevent export of these benefits. The *Molenaar* judgment was the first one on this issue.[2] This judgment concerned the German Care Insurance Law (*Pflegeversicherung*) which was designed to cover the costs entailed if insured persons become reliant on care. The scheme provides for compensation to pay for assistance by a third person in the performance of the daily routine of persons who need permanent care. At the choice of the recipient, this assistance may either be in the form of care dispensed by authorised bodies or in the form of a monthly allowance. Thus these benefits are not traditional sickness benefits, meant to prevent or treat sickness, but to assist a person in his or her daily life. The monthly allowance, known as 'care allowance', enables recipients to choose

---

[1]   Case 69/79, [1980] *ECR* 75.
[2]   Case 160/96, [1998] *ECR* I-880.

the form of aid they consider most appropriate to their condition and the benefits may be paid only to insured persons residing in German territory. Were these old age benefits or sickness benefits? The Court considered that they were designed to develop the independence of the persons reliant on care and aimed at encouraging prevention, rehabilitation and home care. The insurance provides for partial or full payment of certain expenditure provided in the home or in specialised centres or hospitals, equipment, the carrying out of work in the home and the payment of monthly financial aid. In the view of the Court such benefits must be regarded as sickness benefits for the Regulation. In Section 11.2 we will further discuss the question whether such benefits have to be exported or not.

Also the *Jauch* judgment[3] concerned care benefits. These were intended to supplement sickness insurance benefits, to which they are, moreover, linked at the organisational level, in order to improve the state of health and quality of persons reliant on care. For this reason they were to be considered as sickness benefits (and they were not considered as special benefits). The *Hosse* judgment[4] involved a care allowance, intended to compensate, in the form of a flat-rate contribution, for the additional expenditure resulting from the recipients' condition of reliance on care. It was, in particular, meant to compensate for the cost of the assistance it is necessary to provide them with, and the amount of this care allowance depended of the degree of reliance on care. It corresponded to the time spent on care, expressed in terms of hours per month and was paid essentially members of the families of socially insured persons, recipients of social assistance, disabled workers, and persons receiving pensions from the provinces and municipalities. Consequently, also this benefit was considered as a sickness benefit.

Another issue was, asked in another case, whether the term sickness benefits comprises the compulsory payments by employers in the case of sickness, for instance payments on the basis of the German *Lohnfortzahlungsgesetz*? We saw in Chapter 5, that the answer to this question was positive, *see* the *Paletta* judgment,[5] discussed in more detail in Section 11.3.3.

On maternity benefits there have been very few questions so far. Paternity benefits were included in the material scope of the coordination rules by Regulation 883/2004 and, for this very reason alone it follows already that there is no case law yet on these benefits.

---

[3]   Case 215/99, [2001] *ECR* I-1901.
[4]   Case C-286/03, [2006] *ECR* I-1771.
[5]   Case 45/90, [1992] *ECR* I-3423.

11.2. THE DISTINCTION BETWEEN BENEFITS IN CASH AND BENEFITS IN KIND

The coordination rules distinguish sickness benefits in cash and benefits in kind. Benefits *in cash* seek to replace income in the case of sickness, in other words they provide for an income. Regulation 883/2004 gives a definition of 'Benefits in kind' in Article 1(va). These are benefits which are intended to supply, make available, pay directly or reimburse the cost of medical care and products, and services ancillary to that care. This includes long-term care benefits in kind. Examples are drugs, hospital care and wheelchairs.

In order to be a 'benefit in kind', it is not necessary that the benefit is actually 'in kind', it can also be a restitution for medical costs. This was decided in the *Vaassen-Goebels* judgment.[6] A cash payment can, therefore, sometimes be a benefit in kind.[7]

Sometimes payments for provisions can, however, also be benefits in cash, as appeared from the *Molenaar* case.[8] The question was important, since if these benefits were benefits in kind, they were to be provided in Germany only, and the Molenaars were not entitled to them. The Court considered that the care insurance benefits concerned consist, first, in the direct payment or reimbursement of expenses incurred. Such benefits, which are designed to cover care received by the person concerned, both in the home and in specialised centres, purchases of equipment and work carried out are indisputably benefits in kind, the Court considered. Still, however, although the care allowance is also designed to cover certain costs entailed by reliance on care, in particular those relating to aid provided by a third person, rather than to compensate for loss of earnings on the part of the recipient, it nevertheless displays features distinguishing it from sickness insurance benefits in kind. First, payment of the allowance is periodical and is not subject either to certain expenditure, such as care expenditure to the production of receipts for the expenditure incurred. Secondly, the amount of the allowance is fixed and independent of the costs actually incurred by the recipient in meeting his or her or her daily requirements. Thirdly, recipients are to a large extent unfettered in their use of the sums thus allocated to them. In particular, as the German Government itself pointed out, the care allowance may be used by recipients to remunerate a member of their family or entourage who is assisting them on a voluntary basis. The care allowance thus takes the form of financial aid which enables the standard of living of persons requiring care to be improved as a whole, so as to compensate for the additional expense brought about by their condition. The care allowance must therefore be regarded as a sickness insurance

---

[6]   Case 61/65, [1965] *ECR* 257.
[7]   In the *Dekker* judgment (Case 33/65, [1965] *ECR* 1135) it was decided that a scheme which pays sickness benefit contributions for retired persons is not a benefit in kind.
[8]   Case 160/96, [1998] *ECR* I-880.

'cash benefit'. Relevant is, therefore, if it is a payment which is not exchange for a particular medicine or service, but an increase of the income to buy such provisions, it is a benefit in cash. As we will see below, this means that the benefit concerned was exportable.

11.3. BENEFITS IN CASH

11.3.1. AGGREGATION RULES

In Regulation 1408/71 special aggregation rules were given for sickness benefits. These are no longer necessary in the Chapter on sickness benefits of the new Regulation, since the general aggregation rules apply. Under the old Regulation these aggregation rules were interpreted by the Court in the situation where a national scheme provided that benefit can be refused partially or completely if a person is already ill at the commencement of the insurance; in the application of this rule the competent institution must also take account, in accordance with the aggregation rules, of the period completed in other Member States on the basis of periods of affiliation with a statutory scheme, as if these were fulfilled on the basis of the statutory scheme applied by that Member State, the Court ruled in the *Klaus* judgment.[9] The assimilation rule of the new Regulation (Article 5, *see* Section 8.3) will have the same outcome. We can also say that, by giving such a broad interpretation of the aggregation rules, the Court paved the way for the assimilation rules.

11.3.2. BENEFITS IN CASH ARE EXPORTABLE

Article 21 of the Regulation gives coordination rules on cash sickness benefits. It provides that an insured person and members of his or her family residing or staying outside the competent Member State are entitled to cash benefits by the competent institution of that State. Thus the competent State – the State where the person is insured – has to export these benefits. By agreement with the institution of the State of residence or stay these benefits can also be paid by that State; these benefits remain at the expense of the competent State. For instance, if a person who is employed in Spain becomes ill and goes to Germany in order to recover in the house of his or her parents, s/he can claim Spanish sickness benefit in Germany.

---

[9]   Case 482/93, [1995] *ECR* I-3551. *See* also Case 481/93, *Moscato*, [1995] *ECR* I-3525, discussed in Section 13.2.

For *pensioners* receiving (a) pension(s) under the legislation of one or more Member States cash benefits are paid by the competent institution which is responsible for sickness benefits in kind, *see* Section 11.4.2 below.

11.3.3. CLAIMING AND SUPERVISION PROCEDURES

Benefits in cash are granted according to the legislation of the competent State (generally, this is the State of employment). The State of residence is, however, responsible for the medical investigation. Article 27 of the Implementing Regulation provides that if the legislation of the competent Member State requires that the insured person presents a certificate in order to be entitled to cash benefits, the insured person has to ask the doctor of the State of residence who established his or her state of health to certify his or her incapacity for work and its probable duration. The insured person has to send the certificate to the competent institution within the time limit laid down by the legislation of the competent Member State.

Article 27 of the Implementing Regulation also provides that at the request of the competent institution, the institution of the place of residence has to carry out any necessary administrative checks or medical examinations of the person concerned in accordance with the legislation applied by this latter institution. The report of the examining doctor concerning, in particular, the probable duration of the incapacity for work, has to be forwarded without delay by the institution of the place of residence to the competent institution. Article 87 of the Implementing Regulation provides that as an exception to the principle of free-of-charge mutual administrative cooperation in Article 76(2) of the basic Regulation, the effective amount of the expenses of the checks referred to in paragraphs 1 to 5 has to be refunded to the institution which was requested to carry them out by the debtor institution which requested them.

The forwarding of the document by the insured person does not exempt him or her from fulfilling the obligations provided for by the applicable legislation, in particular with regard to his or her employer. In other words, if the person concerned is, for instance, required to notify his or her employer before 9 am that s/he is become ill, s/he has to fulfill this obligation in addition to the obligations imposed by the Regulation.

Article 27 also provides that where appropriate, the employer and/or the competent institution may call upon the employee to participate in activities designed to promote and assist his or her return to employment. Thus this provision concerns reintegration activities, which is an innovation for the coordination rules.

Under Regulation 1408/71 the question was raised whether the competent institution is bound by the report by the State of residence on the state of health of the person concerned. This question was addressed by the *Rindone* judgment.[10] The Court considered that the institution of the State of residence determines the commencement and termination of the incapacity. The competent institution only has the opportunity of checking the findings. A different solution would be problematic for the employed person with regard to the proof that s/he was ill and this would be an impediment to freedom of movement for workers.

This issue is now dealt with by Article 87 of the Implementing Regulation. This Article provides that the institution of the place of stay or residence has to forward a report to the debtor institution that requested the medical examination. The competent institution has the right to have the insured person examined by a doctor of its choice. Thus, this article gives the opportunity of a second opinion. If the competent State does not make use of this possibility, it is bound by the examination of the State of residence.

In the *Rindone* case the question also arose whether the right of the debtor institution to have the beneficiary examined by a doctor of its choice means that the insured person may be required to return to the competent State in order to be examined. The Court ruled that the supervision Article of the Regulation then in force (Regulation 574/72) was not to be interpreted in the sense that the employed person is under an obligation to return to the competent State for examination. Such an obligation would be contrary to the respect owed to the state of health of the person employed. If the competent institution wishes to examine the sick person itself, it will have to send one of its physicians or ask a doctor in the country in question to do so.

The new Implementing Regulation deviates from this case law to the extent that the prohibition to call the patient back is less absolute: the beneficiary may be asked to return to the Member State of the debtor institution only if s/he is able to make the journey without prejudice to his or her health and the cost of travel and accommodation is paid for by the debtor institution. Thus, in each individual case it has to be investigated whether travelling is detrimental to the health of the person concerned. It seems that this approach is more in line with the current approach to sickness benefits, where activation, if possible, has to be undertaken and it may be expected that the Court can live with this. After all, the basic principle of the *Rindone* judgment is maintained.

These rules also apply to a situation in which the *employer* is under the obligation to pay sickness benefit, as follows from the *Paletta* ruling.[11] Mr Paletta, his wife, and his children, of Italian nationality, all four employed by the same employer in Germany, became ill during their holidays in Italy. The employer refused to pay their wages during the required six weeks under the German General Law on Continuation of Payment of Wages on the grounds that he was not bound by the medical report of a foreign country, the reliability of which

---

[10]   Case 22/86, [1987] *ECR* 1339.
[11]   Case 45/90, [1992] *ECR* I-3423.

he seriously doubted. Paletta argued that since the employer did not make use of the right to a second opinion by a physician of his own choice, he was bound by the medical results of the institution of the place of residence, with regard to the establishment of incapacity as well as its duration. The first question was whether the continued payment of wages in the case of illness due on the basis of the German law was a sickness benefit within the meaning of the Regulation. The reply to this was positive, as we have already seen in Chapter 5. The next question was whether the supervision provisions of the Implementing Regulation were relevant to sickness benefits paid by the employer. The Court considered that Regulation 1408/71 stated that the employer is to be regarded as the competent institution as defined in this Regulation with respect to benefits under Article 4(1); under Regulation 883/2004 we can find a comparable definition in Article 1(q)(iv). Consequently, the supervision rule of the Implementing Regulation applied. This result corresponded with the objective of this Article, *i.e.* to remove problems in the furnishing of proof by the employed person and the promotion of the free movement of workers. Consequently, the employer is bound by the certificate of the competent institution of the State of residence if s/he does not avail of the right to a second opinion by a physician of his or her own choice.

The employer, the Netherlands and the German Governments, as well as the European Commission had argued that the employer may not always be able to make effective use of the possibility of a second opinion. In addition, the medical report is not sent directly to the employer, but via the administration of sickness benefits, which causes delay. Another problem mentioned was that the employer often does not know in which place the employed person resides and s/he does not know any physicians in that place. Consequently, the possibility offered by the supervision rule is often an unrealistic one. In answer to these objections, the Court considered that problems of implementation are not to impede the interpretation of an objective of the coordination Regulation.

The *Paletta* judgment was very controversial in the German literature.[12] However, since more and more countries introduce obligations for employers in the administration of and/or responsibility for social security protection, the judgment is still very relevant. Since the underlying rules are basically maintained under the new Regulation and the judgment has thus kept its importance.

After the *Paletta* ruling the German court awarded the claim of the Paletta family. The employer, however, could not live with this and applied for revision of the decision. During that procedure, the national court asked for a new preliminary ruling, which led to the *Second Paletta* judgment.[13] In its questions the national court asked to what extent the national court had to take into account,

---

[12]   *See* B. Schulte, 'Konfliktfelder im Verhältnis zwischen mitgliedstaatlichem und europäischem Recht', in: E. Eichenhofer and M. Zuleeg (ed.), *Die Rechtsprechung des Europäischen Gerichtshof zum Arbeits- und Sozialrecht im Streit*, Schriftenreihe der Europäischen Rechtsakademie Trier, Köln 1995, p. 11.

[13]   Case 206/94, [1996] *ECR* I-2357.

when applying the supervision provision of the coordination Regulation, abuse on the part of the claimant. The Court of Justice did not follow the argument of the national court, which had pointed out that according to German case law the employee had to provide proof that s/he is ill (alongside the medical evidence) where the employer has shown circumstances which raise serious doubt about his or her alleged disability. According to the Court, this national case law is incompatible with the objectives of the supervision Article since, for the employee who has become ill in a State other than the competent State, it would lead to difficulties of proof which Community law wished to avoid.

Instead, the employer can provide evidence on the basis of which a national court can determine whether abuse or deceit is involved. In the case of a positive answer to this, the employee who invokes the supervision Article (Article 22 of the Implementing Regulation), cannot be considered ill. In other words, in the case of deceit or abuse one cannot invoke the supervision Article, but the proof of deceit or abuse has to be provided by the employer. Whether such abuse or deceit is involved, has to be determined with a view to the objectives of the provisions in question.

There is very little or no other case law on abuse or deceit in coordination cases. The *Paletta* judgment may also be the basis for dealing with such cases in areas other than sick pay.

11.4. BENEFITS IN KIND FOR PERSONS NOT RESIDING IN THE COMPETENT STATE

11.4.1. PERSONS NOT RESIDING IN THE COMPETENT STATE

Persons not residing in the competent State are entitled to Benefits in State of Residence

If a person resides in the competent State, s/he receives benefits in kind according to the legislation of that State. This is straightforward, as this will follow already from national legislation.

If a person does *not* reside in the competent State, coordination rules are necessary. This will be discussed in this section. In Section 11.5 we will discuss the situation in which a person needs medical care when s/he stays outside the competent State (or State of residence); Section 11.6 will deal with the situation that a person goes to another Member State in order to obtain care (i.e. care which becomes necessary when staying in the country).

For benefits in kind the coordination rules are different from those applicable to cash benefits. An insured person and members of his or her family who reside in a State other than the competent one receive benefits in kind in the State of residence. Thus, the State of residence is the responsible one; benefits in kind are not exportable. This is different from cash benefits which, as we saw above, are exportable.

Benefits in kind are provided on behalf of the competent institution; they are paid in the State of residence for the account of the competent State. Which benefits have to be awarded depends on the legislation of the State of residence. Persons who do not reside in the competent State include frontier workers, but also non-frontier workers, such as persons who return home with intervals larger than one week and posted workers.

For instance, a person who resides in Spain and is insured in Denmark, receives benefits in Spain according to the Spanish legislation. If, for instance, the Spanish legislation covers drugs for headache, whereas the Danish legislation does not include these, the person can claim them, as it is the Spanish legislation which is applied. If, on the other hand, Danish drugs are provided without cost sharing, and the Spanish legislation requires two euro for each prescription, the person concerned has to pay this sum, even though s/he is insured under the Danish scheme and pays contributions for this insurance. This solution is followed mainly for practical reasons; in another system the institution of the State would have to apply the legislations of all Member States, which would become extremely complicated. This system also implies that the administration of the State of residence decides whether a person is ill or not for the purpose whether s/he is entitled to a benefit in kind.

Persons not residing in the Competent State are also entitled to Benefits in the Competent State

If the insured persons and members of their family stay in the competent State, they are also entitled to benefits in that State, according to the legislation it applies. Thus these persons have the choice: they can either obtain benefits in kind in the competent State or in the State of residence. Of course, they have to satisfy the applicable rules, such as showing a prescription if required.

This choice between the State of residence and the competent State existed under Regulation 1408/71 for frontier workers only; Regulation 883/2004 extends the choice to all persons not residing in the competent State.

11.4.2. MEMBERS OF THE FAMILY OF FRONTIER WORKERS

The Regulation Chapter on sickness benefits has several provisions on members of the family. Remember that the term *member of the family* is defined in Article 1(i), and has a special meaning for sickness benefits. Article 1(i)(1)(ii) provides that with regarded to sickness, maternity and paternity benefits any person defined or recognised as a member of the family or designated as a member of the household by the legislation of the Member State *in which s/he resides* is a member of the family.

Example. Suppose there are two neighbouring countries, country A and B. Country A recognises same sex marriages and Country B does not. Suppose also that a couple lives in country A, and one of them (Elisa) works in country B, which does not recognise same sex marriages, and the other person (Mary) does not perform activities on the basis of which she is covered by the scheme of the State of residence. Consequently, Mary is member of the family of Elisa.

Under Regulation 1408/71, the members of the family of frontier workers did not have the right to choose; they had to solely rely on benefits in kind in the State of residence. This rule was often criticised, since it could have as effect that a parent has a general practitioner in the State of employment and the children and spouse had to choose one in the State of residence. This topic was one of the intensively debated ones during the drafting process of Regulation 883/2004, as some Member States were reluctant to allow members of the family the choice. They were afraid of the extra costs. Finally, a solution was found in that members of the family are entitled to benefits in kind during their stay in the competent State, *unless* this Member State is listed in Annex III. If the competent State is listed in the Annex, entitlement to benefits in the competent State is possible only if they become necessary on medical grounds during their stay (see also Section 11.5).[14] In Regulation 988/2004 this exception for Member States listed in the Annex is limited to 30 April 2014. After all, this solution contributes to the complicated rules of the Regulation and it is preferable that it will be removed.

Remember that Member States can make bilateral agreements to elaborate issues mentioned in the Regulation as long as it is within the spirit of the Regulation. Thus it can happen that countries which opted for the exception to be listed in the Annex make bilateral agreements to give more generous provisions. In this way they allow members of the family of frontier workers residing in specific countries the choice to obtain medical care (e.g. those residing in the

---

[14] Regulation 988/2009 lists Denmark, Ireland, Finland, Sweden and the United Kingdom in the Annex; some other Member States are listed for a temporary period: four years after the coming into force of the Regulation (Article 87(10a) of Regulation 883/2004, as amended. This Article also introduces an evaluation moment for the Member States who are 'permanently' listed in the Annex: Article 87(10b) provides that the list contained in Annex III shall be reviewed no later than 31 October 2014 on the basis of a report by the Administrative Commission. That report shall include an impact assessment of the significance, frequency, scale and costs, both in absolute and in relative terms, of the application of the provisions of Annex III. That report shall also include the possible effects of repealing those provisions for those Member States which continue to be listed in that Annex after the date referred to in paragraph 10a. In the light of that report, the Commission shall decide whether to submit a proposal concerning a review of the list, with the aim in principle of repealing the list unless the report of the Administrative Commission provides compelling reasons not to do so. So the intension of the legislature is to allow the members of the family of frontier workers the right to choose in the future; whether this will be realised will depend on the outcome of this procedure.

neighbouring countries), while not giving the this choice to others. If this is the case, the practical effect of being listed in the Annex is limited.

11.4.3. RETIRED FRONTIER WORKERS

Not only the members of the family of frontier workers were subject of discussion in the drafting process of the new Regulation, but also *retired* frontier workers. Under Regulation 1408/71, the right to choose between medical treatment in the State of residence and in the competent State ended as soon as the frontier worker stopped working. Then s/he had to rely on the State of residence. This could mean that if s/he was, for instance, under treatment by a specialist in the State of employment, s/he had to change doctors after retirement. This was an awkward effect of this rule.

The new Regulation gives a limited solution to this problem (Article 28). It provides that a frontier worker who has retired because of old-age or invalidity is entitled, in the event of sickness, to continue to receive benefits in kind in the Member State where s/he last pursued his or her activity as an employed or self-employed person, in so far as this is a continuation of treatment which began in that Member State. 'Continuation of treatment' means – this Article continues – the continued investigation, diagnosis and treatment of an illness for its entire duration. This also applies mutatis mutandis to the members of the family of the former frontier worker unless the Member State where the frontier worker last pursued his or her activity is listed in Annex III. (Annex III was discussed *supra* in respect of members of the family of frontier workers).[15]

Under some conditions the pensioner has more rights: a pensioner who, in the five years before s/he became entitled to an old age or invalidity pension has been pursuing an activity as an employed or self-employed person for at least two years as a frontier worker, is entitled to benefits in kind in the State in which s/he worked as a frontier worker, provided that this State has opted for this and is listed in Annex V.[16]

Thus in case of members of the family, the Member States listed in Annex III give *fewer* rights than under the main rule. In case of pensioners, the Member States listed in Annex V give *more* rules than under the main rules of the Regulation.

---

[15] Also this provision was the result of amendments by Regulation 988/2009.
[16] The Member States listed in Annex V are Belgium, Germany Spain, France, Luxembourg, Austria and Portugal.

11.4.4. THE RELATION BETWEEN INDEPENDENT AND DERIVATIVE RIGHTS

If a member of the family is entitled to benefit in kind in his or her own right – e.g. since s/he starts to work as an employed person – this has priority to the right s/he derives as a member of the family. Article 32 gives a general rule: an independent right to benefits in kind based on the legislation of a Member State or on this Chapter of the Regulation has priority over a derivative right for members of the family.

However, a derivative right has priority over independent rights, where the independent right in the State of residence exists directly and solely on the basis of residence. So if, for instance, a country has a residence scheme under which all residents are insured, a child of a frontier worker would have a right of his or her own. However, as a result of the priority rule last mentioned the scheme applicable to the frontier worker has priority.

The frontier worker may, of course, have a spouse who has a right to benefit on his or her own right. The question arises how to apply the rule in that case. For this purpose, Article 32(2) provides that benefits in kind are provided to this spouse and the other members of the family by the State of residence if the spouse or the person caring for the children pursues an activity as an employed or self-employed person in that State. This is also the case if s/he receives a pension from that State on the basis of an activity as an employed or self-employed person. Thus if the spouse is an employed, self-employed person or pensioner and on the basis of this status entitled to sickness benefits in kind, this status has priority. If the spouse is entitled to benefits on the basis of residence only, the scheme of the frontier worker has priority to him or her.

11.4.5. PENSIONERS AND MEMBERS OF THEIR FAMILY

In Section 11.4.3 we discussed the retired frontier workers. This section will deal with pensioners in general, *i.e.* persons in receipt of or making an application for a pension.[17] The provisions on pensioners do, however, not apply if the pensioner or members of his or her family are entitled to benefits in kind under the legislation of a State on the basis of their quality of employed or self-employed person. So if a pensioner continues to work or resumes work and is insured on this basis, the rules apply which are relevant to employed and self-employed persons (Article 31).

---

[17]   Note that in Annex IX Member States can give special rules for the application of the Regulation to their own legislation. They may, for instance, assimilate non-statutory pensions, e.g. preretirement pensions, for the purpose of Article 23. Thus, these pensions are not within the scope of the Regulation, but persons receiving these pension can invoke Article 23.

A person who receives a pension or pensions under the legislation of two or more Member States, of which one is the Member State of residence, and who is entitled to benefits in kind under the legislation of that Member State, receives such benefits in kind from and at the expense of the institution of the place of residence, as though s/he were a pensioner whose pension was payable solely under the legislation of that Member State. This also applies to the members of his or her family.

So the basic rule is: pensioners receive benefits in the State of residence, provided they are entitled to benefits in kind under that legislation, even if they receive pension(s) also from another Member State (Article 23). In that case the sickness benefits are completely at the expense of the State of residence.

Example. A Swedish pensioner who is entitled to benefits in kind according to the sickness benefit insurance in Sweden moves to Spain. If this person is also entitled to a Spanish pension and if s/he is insured under the Spanish sickness benefits insurance, s/he receives Spanish sickness benefits and the costs are for Spain.

The Pensioner receives one or more Pensions and is not entitled to Benefits in Kind under the Legislation of the State of Residence

If a person receives one or more pensions from States and is *not* entitled to benefits in kind under the legislation of the State of residence, the following rule applies. S/he receives benefits in kind insofar as s/he would be entitled thereto under the legislation of the Member State or of least one of the Member States competent in respect of his or her pensions, if s/he resided in that State.

Example. If our Swedish pensioner would be entitled to sickness benefits in kind if she resided in Sweden, and s/he moves to Spain (where she is not entitled to a pension), she is entitled to benefits in kind under the Spanish legislation, but the costs are for Sweden.

A person may be entitled to more than one pension. The following priority rules apply to the division of costs in that case (which rule applies if s/he is entitled to pension from two countries, but not from the State of residence). If the pensioner is entitled to benefits in kind under the legislation of a single Member State, the cost is borne by the competent institution of that Member State. If the pensioner is entitled to benefits in kind under the legislation of two or more Member States, the costs are borne by the competent institution to whose legislation the person has been subject for the longest period of time. Should the application of this rule result in several institutions being responsible, the cost is borne by the institution applying the legislation to which the pensioner was last subject. The term legislation does not refer to sickness insurance specifically, but to the more general concept of legislation. Thus if a person was insured for an old age residence scheme for twenty years and insured for sickness benefit only for two years, s/he is considered to be under the legislation of this State for twenty years.

Summary

The general rule is that the pensioner is insured for sickness benefits in the State of residence, but only if the pensioner is entitled to a pension from the State of residence and entitled to medical care according to the legislation of that State. This is also the case if the pensioner receives pension from two or more other Member States: the State of residence is the State which has to provide medical care and which has to bear the costs if the pensioner is entitled to pension or medical care in that country. If s/he has no such rights in the State of residence, s/he is entitled to benefits in kind in the State of residence, but now for the account of the State from which s/he receives pension, provided s/he would be entitled to such benefits if s/he resided in that State. Consequently, the pensioner receives benefits in kind in the State of residence and the costs are reimbursed by the State where s/he is entitled to health care. The contents of the benefits are determined by the legislation of the State of residence.

If the Right to Benefits in Kind is not subject to Conditions of Insurance or Employment

Finally, there is a special rule for pensioners residing in the territory of a Member State under whose legislation the right to receive benefits in kind is not subject to conditions of insurance or employment and the person does not receive a pension from this country (Article 25). Without this rule, States with such systems are always responsible for the costs if persons move to this State and they could not have their costs reimbursed from the country from which the person concerned receives his or her pension, because s/he is entitled to medical care already on the basis of his or her residence. The Regulation provides that the costs of benefits in kind provided to this person and to the members of his or her family are in this case borne by the institution from which s/he receives the pension if s/he would have been entitled to benefits in kind from that country had s/he resided in that country. For this purpose the aforementioned *priority rules* apply.

Pensioners who go for Planned Care to the competent State

In the *Van der Duin* judgment the question was raised to what extent pensioners can ask for medical treatment in the State of origin.[18] The case concerned a Dutch person in receipt of disablement benefit, who resided in France. He was entitled to medical treatment in France. At a certain moment he went to the Netherlands to

---

[18]   Case 156/01, [2003] *ECR* I-7045.

be treated there. The Dutch sickness fund refused to bear the costs of the medical treatment.

The Court of Justice considered that allowing a socially insured person who benefits from the system for benefits in kind for pensioners to go at will to the pension State to receive medical treatment there, would imply that that Member State assumes a second time the burden of the care which it has already financed by means of the lump-sum payment to the Member State of residence. On the basis of the system of the Regulation the State of residence has become for pensioner, by reason of this legal fiction, the competent institution and the competent State as regards the granting of those benefits. This means that it is the State of residence which has the powers to grant authorisation to receive medical treatment in another State, including the State liable for pensions. So these persons are not at the charge of the competent State.

If Family Members do not Reside in the same Country as the Pensioner

If the family members do not reside in the same country as the pensioner, they receive benefits in kind from the institution of their place of residence in accordance with the provisions of the legislation administered by this institution insofar as the pensioner is entitled to benefits under the legislation of a Member State (Article 26). The costs are borne by the institution of the competent State responsible for the costs of the benefits in kind provided to the pensioner in his or her State of residence.

11.4.6. LEVYING CONTRIBUTIONS ON PENSIONERS

In respect of pensioners, there are special rules on their contributions, if they receive benefits at the costs of a State other than the State of residence. The institution of a Member State may deduct contributions for sickness, maternity and equivalent paternity benefits from the pension calculated in accordance with its legislation only to the extent that the costs of the benefits is to be borne by that State (Article 30).[19] This rule allows levying contributions on the whole income, including the pension paid by another Member State.

---

[19] The contributions concern benefits on the basis of Articles 23 to 26.

11.4.7. COORDINATION OF CARE INSURANCE BENEFITS IN CASE OF OVERLAPPING OF BENEFITS IN KIND AND BENEFITS IN CASH

In Section 11.2, we discussed the German care insurance; the benefits concerned were defined as sickness benefits in cash. This was done on the basis of the form of these benefits: a monthly allowance which was paid to the insured. It can happen, however, that another country has a scheme with comparable care provisions, which are not paid as a monthly allowance, but as benefits in kind. This may cause the risk of overlapping of benefits, for instance in the case of frontier workers. Such workers may receive benefits in cash from the State of employment and benefits in kind from the State of residence.

Regulation 883/2004 introduced coordination rules in order to prevent this overlapping (Article 34): if a recipient of long-term care benefits in cash which are provided by the Member State competent for cash benefits, is, at the same time and under the Chapter of sickness benefits, entitled to claim benefits in kind intended for the same purpose from the institution of the place of residence or stay in another Member State, and an institution in the first Member State is also required to reimburse the cost of these benefits in kind under Article 35, the general provision on prevention of overlapping of benefits laid down in Article 10 is applicable. Article 10 provides that unless otherwise specified, this Regulation shall neither confer nor maintain the right to several benefits of the same kind for one and the same period of compulsory insurance. There is only one restriction: if the person concerned claims and receives the benefit in kind, the amount of the benefit in cash shall be reduced by the amount of the benefit in kind which is or could be claimed from the institution of the first Member State required to reimburse the cost.

11.5. STAY OUTSIDE THE COMPETENT STATE: BENEFITS WHICH BECOME NECESSARY

In Section 11.4, we discussed the situation in which a person *resided* in a State other than the competent one. It may happen, of course, also that a person is *temporarily* ('stays') in another Member State and needs care.

In that case the insured person and the members of his or her family receive benefits in kind if they *become* necessary on medical grounds during their stay. Whether they become necessary has to be assessed, taking account of the nature of the benefits and the expected length of stay. These benefits are provided by the institution of the place of stay, in according to its legislation, on behalf of the competent State (Article 19). Thus, again, the institution has to apply its own legislation and the bill is for the competent institution.

If Article 19 applies, the person concerned receives the treatment without having to pay advances; his or her institution will pay the bill. For the purpose of letting these provisions work more smoothly, a European health insurance card was introduced. This card makes it easier to prove that one is covered by a particular national health scheme.

For example, if a person goes to a ski resort in another Member State and breaks a leg, this provision is applicable. Medical care in this situation becomes necessary on medical grounds during the stay. In case of the broken leg, medical care may mean transport to the hospital and applying gypsum. If this person suffers from a heart failure, the criteria to decide whether benefits become necessary – i.e. the nature of the benefits and expected length of stay – are in particular relevant. This may mean that in case of a very short stay, where there is no danger for the health of the person concerned, benefit is not provided and the person can upon return claim care in the State where s/he resides. It is up to the State of residence to decide whether care has become necessary.

All benefits in kind provided in conjunction with chronic or existing illnesses are covered by this provision. In the *Ioannidis* judgment,[20] the Court of Justice ruled that the concept of 'necessary treatment' cannot be interpreted as 'meaning that those benefits are limited solely to cases where the treatment provided has become necessary because of a sudden illness. In particular, the circumstance that a treatment necessitated by developments in the insured person's state of health during his temporary stay in another Member State may be linked to a pre-existed pathology of which s/he is aware, such as a chronic illness, does not mean that the conditions for the application of these provisions are not fulfilled'. Also benefits in kind provided in conjunction with pregnancy and childbirth are covered by this provision. However, this provision does not cover the situation where the aim of the temporary stay abroad is to give birth.[21]

The rule on medical care which becomes necessary also applies in the case of pensioners and the members of their families, on whom the provisions of the Regulation apply (discussed in Section 11.4.5) who stay in State other than the State of residence (Article 27(1)).

On the basis of Article 19(2) the Administrative Commission is instructed to draw up a list of benefits in kind which, in order to be provided during a stay in another Member State, require for practical reasons a prior agreement between the person concerned and the institution providing the care. For this list the essential criteria are the vital nature of the medical treatment and the fact that this treatment is accessible only in specialised medical units and/or by specialised staff or/and equipment. A non-exhaustive list based on these criteria is given in the Annex to Decision S3 (examples of this list are kidney dialysis and chemotherapy).

---

[20]   Case C-326/00, [2003] *ECR* I-1703.
[21]   *See* also Decision S3 of the AC, *OJ C* 106/40 of 2010.

11.6. PLANNED CARE

11.6.1. PLANNED CARE AND AUTHORISATION

A person may go to another Member State in order to receive a treatment there. This time it is not care which *becomes* necessary, but care which is planned to be obtained by the person concerned. The person may wish to receive treatment in another Member State, since s/he thinks the quality of health care is higher in that State or since there is a waiting list in his or her own country for the desired treatment.

Article 20 of the Regulation provides that an insured person travelling to another Member State with the purpose of receiving benefits in kind during the stay has to seek authorisation from the competent institution. If the authorisation is given, the benefits in kind are provided in accordance with the provisions of the legislation of the State of stay. In that case again the person concerned does not have to pay the care provider; the bill is settled by the institution where s/he is insured. Reimbursement of the costs is at the rate normally applicable in the Member State of treatment. Thus, if in the State of treatment patients have to pay part of the costs themselves, this also applies to persons from another Member State who invoke the coordination Regulation.

Article 20 mentions also situations in which authorisation for the treatment *has* to be provided. Authorisation has to be accorded where the treatment in question is among the benefits of the State of residence of the person concerned and where s/he cannot be given such treatment within a time-limit which is medically justifiable, taking into account his or her current state of health and the probable course of the illness. Thus, if there is a waiting-list and the person has to wait too long – in view of the just mentioned criteria – authorisation *has* to be given. In other situations the Member State can give authorisation, but is not, on the basis of the Regulation, obliged to do so.

Article 20 leaves it up to the Member States to determine whether and under which conditions treatment received in another Member State may be reimbursed to the competent institution. The Implementing Regulation gives several rules on the way they can organise reimbursement. Where a Member State provides for the possibility of reimbursement to individuals, Article 20 does not prevent it from making this conditional upon the person concerned having been authorised beforehand by the competent authority to receive treatment abroad.

A patient failing to obtain authorisation because the conditions of Article 20 have not been fulfilled is not eligible for reimbursement for treatment received in another Member State. If, however, a person has applied for permission to receive medical treatment in another Member State, but it has been wrongfully refused, a different rule applies, as was established in the case law. The Court found that this person is entitled to be reimbursed directly by the competent institution by an amount equivalent to that which it would ordinarily have borne if authorisation had been granted in the first place. This was the *Vanbraekel* judgment, which will be discussed in Section 11.6.2.[22]

The rule on planned medical care also applies in the case of pensioners and the members of their families, on whom the provisions of the Regulation apply (discussed in Section 11.4.6), who stay in a State other than the State of residence (Article 27(3)). This rule is the codification of the *Van der Duin* judgment, discussed in Section 11.4.5. Article 27(5) provides that the costs are in this case born by the institution of the place of residence if this State has opted for reimbursement on the basis of fixed amounts.

In the *Keller* case[23] the question was raised whether, if a person needs medical care which becomes necessary in another Member State, but the care providers of that State refer the patient to a third State, this has to be reimbursed on the basis of the Regulation. Ms Keller, of German nationality, was resident of Spain and insured under a Spanish general social security scheme. During her stay with her family in Germany, she was admitted to hospital and diagnosed with malignant tumours sufficiently serious to be likely to cause the patient's death at any time. In the initial period the care which had become necessary was provided. Subsequently, authorisation was asked for further treatment in the State of stay, since in view of the serious nature of her state of health, transfer to Spain was not advisable. The German doctors considered that the surgical operation which was immediately and vitally necessary for Ms Keller could only be performed in Switzerland. That private clinic was the only one in Europe which could treat with recognised scientific efficacy the condition Ms Keller was suffering from. Ms Keller paid the sum and then sought reimbursement. The question now was whether the competent (Spanish) institution was bound by the decision of the doctors in the State of stay to transfer the insured person to a hospital establishment in the territory of a non-member country on the ground that that establishment, according to current medical knowledge, is the only one to perform the kind of operation required with a real chance of success.

The Court ruled that once the competent institution has authorised the insured person to go to another Member State for medical purposes, the doctors authorised by the institution of the Member State of stay, acting within the scope of their office, who are called on to treat the insured person in the latter State, decide which treatment is necessary. The competent State is obliged to accept and recognise the findings and choices, subject to the existence of any abuse. Treatment can thus also take place in a non-Member State.

---

[22]   Case C-368/98 *Vanbraekel* [2001] *ECR* I-5363.
[23]   Case 145/03, *Heirs of Annette Keller,* [2005] *ECR* I-2529.

The Criterion of the Possibility to obtain Health Care within undue Delay

Authorisation may be refused only if the same or equally effective treatment can be obtained without undue delay. In the *Müller-Fauré and Van Riet* case,[24] the Court was asked what this term means. It replied that a refusal to grant prior authorisation which is based not on fear of wastage resulting from hospital overcapacity, but solely on the ground that there are waiting lists, is an unjustified restriction. Instead, it is essential that also account is taken of the specific circumstances attaching to the patient's medical condition. The national authorities are required to have regard to all the circumstances of each specific case. They have to take due account of the patient's medical condition at the time when authorisation is sought. They also have to take account, where appropriate, of the degree of pain or the nature of the patient's disability which might, for example, make it impossible or extremely difficult for him or her to carry out a professional activity. Finally, they have to take account of his or her medical history.

11.6.2. OBTAINING PLANNED CARE WITHOUT AUTHORISATION ON THE BASIS OF THE TREATY

The Kohll and Decker Case Law

In the previous section we saw that for obtaining care in another State authorisation is required. More precisely, authorisation is required for having the care financed by the health insurance in accordance with the coordination rules. In the *Kohll* and *Decker* judgments,[25] however, the Court ruled that the condition of authorisation is in some cases contrary to the Treaty. Mr Decker was a Luxembourg national, who bought a pair of spectacles in Belgium without authorisation. Therefore reimbursement was refused. Mr Decker contested that decision, relying, in particular, on the Treaty rules on the free movement of goods. In the other case, Mr Kohll, again a person of Luxembourg nationality, had his daughter treated by an orthodontist established in Germany, whereas no authorisation was obtained. The Court considered that the fact that a national measure may be consistent with a provision of secondary legislation, *i.e.* the Regulation, does not have the effect of removing that measure from the scope of the provisions of the Treaty. Article 22 of Regulation 1408/71, now Regulation 20 of Regulation 883/2004, does not prevent the reimbursement by Member States, at the tariffs in force in the competent State, of the costs of treatment provided in another Member State, even without prior authorisation.

---

[24]   Case C-385/99, *Müller-Fauré and Van Riet*, [2003] *ECR* I-4503.
[25]   Cases 120/95 and 158/96, [1998] *ECR* I-1935 and I-1871.

Subsequently, the Court discussed the compatibility of the disputed national rules (in the *Kohll* case) with the Treaty provisions on freedom to provide services according to Article 56 TFEU (at the time Article 49 EC) or (in the *Decker* case) the freedom of movement of goods according to Article 36 TFEU (at the time Article 30 EC). For this purpose, the Court examined whether the disputed rules constituted a restriction on freedom to provide services or goods and, if so, whether they were objectively justified. It considered that the disputed rules indeed constituted a restriction, as they deterred insured persons from approaching providers of medical services established in another Member State, as the costs incurred in that State were not reimbursed. The question was, therefore, whether the rule could be objectively justified. The Court argued that the risk that the financial balance of the social security system would be seriously undermined could constitute an overriding reason in the general interest capable of justifying a barrier of that kind. However, it is clear, the Court considered, that reimbursement of the costs of dental treatment provided in other Member States in accordance with the tariff of the State of insurance has no significant effect on the financing of the social security system. Hereupon the Court introduced the rule that the competent State did not have to reimburse a higher amount than it would have paid under its own system. Thus, suppose that Luxembourg pays 50 euro for glasses, and the ones bought by Mr Decker cost 200 euro, only 50 euro have to be reimbursed.

Also the fear that the quality of medical care could be in danger was not accepted as an objective justification: the Court referred to several EU directives concerning the mutual recognition of diplomas. It follows that doctors, opticians and dentists established in other Member States must be afforded all guarantees equivalent to those afforded to doctors, opticians and dentists established in national territory, for the purpose of freedom to provide services.

Thus, in both judgments the reimbursement had to be according to the tariffs of the State of insurance. Consequently, in this case the costs for Luxembourg were not higher than if the glasses and dental treatment were bought in that State.[26]

The rule that the compensation is limited to the rates which apply in the competent State was clarified in the *Vanbraekel* judgment,[27] which concerned the situation in which, according to the rules of the State of treatment, for a particular treatment a lower compensation was payable than in the competent State. The Court decided that in that case compensation at the level of the tariffs in the competent State was to be paid. Also this approach did not make the competent State worse off as a result of the freedom of movement of patients.[28]

---

[26] *See* also A.P. van der Mei, *Free Movement of Persons within the European Community. Cross-Border Access to Public Benefit.* Oxford 2003.

[27] Case 368/98, [2001] *ECR* I-5363.

[28] *See* Y. Jorens, 'Cross-Border Health Care in the European Union: Up to a Free Movement of Patients?', in: Gesellschaft für Versicherungswissenschaft und –gestaltung, *Social Security for Frontier Workers in Europe.* Berlin 2003, p. 90.

The *Kohll* and *Decker* judgments led to much discussion in the Member States, as they feared the effects of the judgments. In order to restrict the effects, they argued that the judgments did not apply to hospitals; they also argued that the case law applied in case of reimbursement systems only, so not where all care is provided in kind. We will discuss these questions below.

Applicability to Hospitals

Whether the case law was applicable to treatment in hospitals was the subject of the *Geraets-Smits and Peerbooms* judgment.[29] Mrs Geraets-Smits (insured in the Netherlands) suffered from Parkinson's disease and obtained a specific, multidisciplinary treatment of that disease in Germany. The sickness fund refused to refund the costs of the treatment on the grounds that satisfactory and adequate treatment for Parkinson's disease was available in the Netherlands. It added that the specific clinical treatment provided at the hospital provided no additional advantage and that there was therefore no medical necessity justifying treatment in that clinic. Her case was connected to that of Mr Peerbooms, who fell into a coma following a road accident. He was given no hope of recovery in the Netherlands, but an Austrian hospital gave Mr Peerbooms special intensive therapy, which particular technique was used in the Netherlands only experimentally at two medical centres, and not to patients over twenty-five. Mr Peerbooms had already exceeded this age limit. Also in this case the request for reimbursement was refused, since, owing to the experimental nature of the therapy concerned, that type of treatment was not regarded as normal within the professional circles concerned. Should that treatment nonetheless be held to be normal, the refusal was based, second, on the consideration that, since satisfactory and adequate treatment was available without undue delay in the Netherlands at an establishment with which the sickness insurance fund had contractual arrangements.

The Court had to examine whether, in so far as they concern medical services provided within a hospital infrastructure, such rules could be objectively justified. It argued that the possible risk of seriously undermining a social security system's financial balance may constitute an overriding reason in the general interest capable of justifying a barrier. Article 46 EC (now Article 52 TFEU) permits Member States to restrict the freedom to provide medical and hospital services in so far as the maintenance of treatment capacity or medical competence on national territory is essential for the public health and even the survival of the population. The objective of maintaining a balanced medical and hospital service open to all may fall within this derogation on grounds of public health, in so far as it contributes to the attainment of a high level of health protection.

---

[29]   Case 157/99, [2001] *ECR* I-5473.

As regards the prior authorisation requirement, the Court accepted that, by comparison with medical services provided by practitioners in their surgeries or at the patient's home, medical services provided in a hospital take place within an infrastructure with, undoubtedly, certain very distinct characteristics. This is because for determining the number of hospitals, their geographical distribution, the mode of their organisation and the equipment with which they are provided, and even the nature of the medical services which they are able to offer, a good planning system is necessary. This has to ensure that there is sufficient and permanent access to a balanced range of high-quality hospital treatment. It also assists in meeting a desire to control costs and to prevent, as far as possible, any wastage of financial, technical and human resources. If insured persons were at liberty to use the services of hospitals with which their sickness insurance fund had no contractual arrangements, whether they were situated in the Netherlands or in another Member State, all the planning which goes into such contractual system would be jeopardised at a stroke. The planning system was meant to guarantee a rationalised, stable, balanced and accessible supply of hospital services.

For these considerations, Community law does not in principle preclude a system of prior authorisation for this type of care. The conditions for such authorisation must nonetheless be justified with regard to the overriding considerations examined and must satisfy the requirement of proportionality. The Court considered that the disputed rules which required that the proposed medical or surgical treatment can be regarded as 'normal in the professional circles concerned' is not in principle incompatible with Community law to establish, with a view to achieving its aim of limiting costs, limitative lists excluding certain products from reimbursement under its social security scheme. Nonetheless, in exercising that power the Member State must not disregard Community law. This means that a prior administrative authorisation scheme must be based on a procedural system that is easily accessible and capable of ensuring that a request for authorisation will be dealt with objectively and impartially within a reasonable time and refusals to grant authorisation must also be capable of being challenged in judicial or quasi-judicial proceedings.

The problem with the Dutch Law was that the system was not based on a pre-established list of types of treatment, but on a general rule referring to what is 'normal in the professional circles concerned'. It has therefore left it to the sickness insurance funds to determine the types of treatment that actually satisfy that condition. The Court considered that only an interpretation on the basis of what is sufficiently tried and tested by international medical science can be regarded as satisfying the requirements following from the criterion of objective justification. To allow only treatment habitually carried out on national territory and scientific views prevailing in national medical circles to determine what is or is not normal will not offer those guarantees and will make it likely that Netherlands providers of treatment will always be preferred in practice.

Undue Delay

In the previous section, we discussed the case law on undue delay as a condition for the obligation to grant authorisation. The term was also subject of the case law on the Treaty provisions on planned health care, i.e. in the *Watts* case.[30] The referring court asked whether the criteria for the interpretation of the phrase 'within the time normally necessary for obtaining the treatment in question' in the coordination Regulation are the same as those used to define the term 'without undue delay' in the context of Article 49 EC, now Article 56 TFEU. The Court of Justice answered that it interpreted this term in the same way as it interpreted the term 'undue delay' in *Smits and Peerbooms* and *Müller-Fauré and Van Riet*.[31] There is no reason which seriously justifies different interpretations.[32]

Confirmation of the Case law on Non-hospital Care

In the *Müller-Fauré and Van Riet* case,[33] Mrs Müller-Fauré was a Dutch insured person, who underwent dental treatment in Germany; reimbursement was refused on the grounds that she had not obtained authorisation. Her case was combined with that of another Dutch person, Ms Van Riet, who suffered from pain in her wrist. She went for an operation in Belgium, since this could take place much sooner than in the Netherlands. Again no authorisation was obtained, thus reimbursement was refused.

The Court considered that the justification for the prior authorisation as provided by the Netherlands was meant to protect public health. However, no specific evidence was adduced for the argument that the actual competence of practitioners, working in surgeries or in a hospital environment, would be undermined because of numerous journeys abroad for medical purposes. In respect of the financial arguments, the Court made a distinction between hospital and non-hospital services, although it admitted that the distinction between these two forms might sometimes prove difficult to draw. In particular, certain services provided in a hospital environment but also capable of being provided by a practitioner in his or her surgery or in a health centre could for that reason be placed on the same footing as non-hospital services. Since the national court and the governments did not ask questions on this issue, the Court did not consider this issue in further detail.

In so far as the *hospital services* are concerned, the Court referred to the *Smits and Peerbooms* judgment, in which it ruled that for hospitals planning is essential

---

[30]   Case 372/04, [2006] *ECR* I-4325. *See*, on this case, also H.M. Stergiou, 'Op één been kan men niet lopen. Het arrest Watts een stap dichterbij de harmonisatie van patiëntenmobiliteit?', *NTER* 2006, p. 219.

[31]   Case C-385/99, *Müller-Fauré and Van Riet*, [2003] *ECR* I-4503.

[32]   *See* also Case C-56/01, *Inizan*, [2003] *ECR* I-12403.

[33]   Case C-385/99, *Müller-Fauré and Van Riet*, [2003] *ECR* I-4503.

and that the authorisation requirement is necessary and reasonable for this purpose. The *Müller-Fauré and Van Riet* case concerned, however, non-hospital services. The Court considered that no specific evidence has been produced to the Court, to support the assertion that, were insured persons at liberty to go without prior authorisation to Member State, that would be likely seriously to undermine the financial balance of the Netherlands social security system. The documents presented to the Court do not indicate that removal of the requirement for prior authorisation for that type of care would give rise to patients travelling to other countries in such large numbers, despite linguistic barriers, geographic distance, the cost of staying abroad and lack of information about the kind of care provided there, that the financial balance of the Netherlands social security system would be seriously upset and that, as a result, the overall level of public-health protection would be jeopardised. Use of foreign care will be made, in particular, in the border areas and exactly in these regions the Dutch funds have already made contracts with foreign care providers. Consequently, the effect of withdrawing the authorisation requirement is limited. In any event, it should be borne in mind that it is for the Member States alone to determine the extent of the sickness cover available to insured persons, so that, when the insured go without prior authorisation to a Member State other than that in which their sickness fund is established to receive treatment there, they can claim reimbursement of the cost of the treatment given to them only within the limits of the cover provided by the sickness insurance scheme in the Member State of affiliation.

In the *Watts* case[34] the Court added that refusals to grant authorisation, or the advice on which such refusals may be based, must refer to the specific provisions on which they are based. They must be properly reasoned in accordance with them. Likewise, courts or tribunals hearing actions against such refusals must be able, if they consider it necessary for the purpose of carrying out the review which it is incumbent on them to make, to seek the advice of wholly objective and impartial independent experts.

In relation to the dispute in the *Watts* case itself, the Court noted that the regulations on the National Health Service did not set out the criteria for the grant or refusal of the prior authorisation necessary for reimbursement of the cost of hospital treatment provided in another Member State. Therefore they did not circumscribe the exercise of the national competent authorities' discretionary power in that context. The lack of a legal framework in that regard also made it difficult to exercise judicial review of decisions refusing to grant authorisation.

Level of Reimbursement and Travel and Accommodation Costs

In the *Watts* case the applicant asked for reimbursement of the full costs of the treatment, and her travel and accommodation costs. The Court ruled that in

---

[34]   Case 372-04, [2006] *ECR* I-4325.

case of Article 49 EC (now Article 56 TFEU), it is for the Member States alone to determine the extent of the sickness cover available to insured persons. If an insured person goes without prior authorisation to another Member State for medical treatment, s/he can claim reimbursement of the cost of the treatment given to him or her only within the limits of the cover provided by the sickness insurance scheme in the Member State of affiliation. This means that s/he is only entitled to the amount which would be reimbursed if the treatment had been provided in the competent Member State.

Further, the question arose how the rules should be applied in a situation such as that of the United Kingdom's NHS which provides health care free at the point of delivery and does not provide for any system of reimbursement. No rates for reimbursement exist in that system. The Court replied that the absence of a system of rates or tariffs does not as such preclude the application of reimbursement rules. The final point is whether there is a right under Article 56 TFEU and Article 19 of Regulation 883/2004 to the reimbursement of travel and accommodation costs related to hospital treatment received in another Member State. The Court considered that the obligation of Article 19 of the Regulation relates exclusively to the expenditure connected with the healthcare received by the patient in the host Member State. These are the costs of hospital treatment, the cost of medical services strictly defined and the inextricably linked costs relating to the patient's stay in the hospital for the purposes of his or her treatment. The Regulation does not make provision for, but also does not prohibit, the reimbursement of such costs. Is there then an obligation to reimburse such costs under Article 56 TFEU? The Court added that the legislation of a Member State cannot, without infringing Article 56 TFEU, exclude reimbursement of the ancillary costs in another Member State whilst providing for the reimbursement of those costs where the treatment is provided in a hospital covered by the national system in question. By contrast, a Member State is not required to lay down a duty on its competent institutions to reimburse the ancillary costs where there is no such duty in case of movement within the Member State. It is for the referring court to determine which situation is the case.

Summary

In case of hospital care the possible risk of seriously undermining a social security system's financial balance may constitute an overriding reason in the general interest capable of justifying a barrier to the principle of freedom to provide services. Community law does not in principle preclude a system of prior authorisation for hospital care, in exercising that power the Member State must not disregard Community law. A prior administrative authorisation scheme must be based on a procedural system that is easily accessible and capable of ensuring that a request for authorisation will be dealt with objectively and impartially within a reasonable time and refusals to grant authorisation must also be capable of being challenged in judicial or quasi-judicial proceedings.

Refusals to grant authorisation, or the advice on which such refusals may be based, must refer to the specific provisions on which they are based and be properly reasoned in accordance with them. Likewise, courts or tribunals hearing actions against such refusals must be able, if they consider it necessary for the purpose of carrying out the review which it is incumbent on them to make, to seek the advice of wholly objective and impartial independent experts. The lack of a legal framework in that regard also makes it difficult to exercise judicial review of decisions refusing to grant authorisation.

A refusal to grant prior authorisation which is based not on fear of wastage resulting from hospital overcapacity but solely on the ground that there are waiting lists on national territory for the hospital treatment concerned, without account being taken of the specific circumstances attaching to the patient's medical condition, cannot amount to a properly justified restriction on freedom to provide services. Instead, the national authorities are required to have regard to all the circumstances of each specific case and to take due account not only of the patient's medical condition at the time when authorisation is sought and, where appropriate, of the degree of pain or the nature of the patient's disability which might, for example, make it impossible or extremely difficult for him to carry out a professional activity, but also of his or her medical history.

Overview of the different systems:[35]

| | EMERGENCY CARE | PLANNED CARE | PLANNED CARE |
	Coordination Regulation	Coordination Regulation	Directive
Legal basis	Article 48 free movement of workers)	Article 48 (free movement of workers)	Article 56 (free movement of services)
Prior authorisation for "hospital care"	No prior authorization	Obligatory	May be required by the Member States
Prior authorisation for "non-hospital care"	No prior authorization	Obligatory	Not needed
Means of payment	Benefits in kind provided according to the legislation of the Member State of treatment. Settlement of costs between the social security institutions of the two countries concerned.	Benefits in kind provided according to the legislation of the Member State of treatment (i.e. in some countries free of charge, in some countries out-of-pocket payment may be required). Settlement of costs between the social security institutions of the two countries concerned.	Out-of-pocket payment with subsequent reimbursement from the social security institution of the patient's home Member State.
Level of reimbursement	According to the rules of the MS of treatment.	According to the rules of the MS of treatment. If this is less than what a patient would receive in his or her home MS, the additional reimbursement covering that difference must be granted.	According to the rules of the patient's home MS. In any event, only actual costs of the treatment are reimbursed (i.e. a patient cannot make profit)

11.6.3. THE DRAFT DIRECTIVE ON PATIENTS' RIGHTS IN CROSS-BORDER HEALTHCARE

In 2008 the Commission made a proposal for a Patient mobility directive,[36] which was made in response to case law of the Court of Justice on the authorisation requirement for medical treatment. A main objective of the directive is to increase legal certainty in the field of cross-border care. Based on the case law just referred to, the new instrument aims at ensuring a clear and transparent framework for

---

[35]   This overview is based on a scheme included in the Commission's working document, p. 27 connected to the proposal for the Patient mobility directive, see next section.

[36]   Brussels, 2 July 2008, COM(2008) 414 final.

the provision of cross-border healthcare within the EU. The objective is also to avoid unjustified obstacles and to ensure that the care is safe and of good quality. In addition, it wishes to ensure that the procedures for reimbursement of costs are clear and transparent.

The system of the coordination Regulation will remain in place next to that of the Directive; if the coordination regulations have more beneficial rules, these have priority. Thus in case of care which becomes necessary, the Regulation is applied and the competent institutions make arrangements for the settlement of the costs; the patient does not have to pay the costs to the care provider. The Directive does not change anything in this regard; however, it has some requirements on providing information by the Member States, which may be helpful, as it appears that many care providers do not know these rules and in practice patients often have to pay the costs at the spot.

Secondly, it is provided that if the appropriate care for the patients' condition cannot be provided in their own country without undue delay, they will be authorised to go abroad. Any additional costs of treatment will be covered by public funds. This follows already from the Regulation and is not changed. This priority of the coordination Regulation is laid down in the draft directive.

In addition to this system of the Regulation, the draft directive puts in place an alternative mechanism, based on the Treaty provisions of free movement and the case law of the Court of Justice. This allows patients to seek healthcare in another Member State if they would have been entitled to this in their State of residence and be reimbursed up to the amount that would have been paid had they obtained that treatment at home. They bear the financial risk of any additional costs arising. Also here, however, for hospital care there is a separate rule.

Thus when the costs of healthcare are reimbursed according to the directive, the provisions of the directive apply, unless the patient is granted the authorisation pursuant to the coordination Regulation. Member States can, as under the present case law and system, define the benefits they choose to provide. Consequently, if a particular treatment is not included in a national system, e.g. forms of plastic surgery and hydro or balno-therapy, or spa cures, patients are not reimbursed if they make use of these in another Member State.

Reimbursement under the Directive

The Directive closely follows the approach of the Court of Justice. It leaves the different systems of reimbursement intact. In respect of this, the European Commission considered in its memorandum that patients might for two main reasons prefer healthcare abroad:
- the healthcare that they need is just not available in their own system, at least not within a reasonable time; or
- that healthcare is available at home, but it is more convenient for them to have it abroad – because it is closer, quicker, or better.

These are quite different reasons, the Commission argued; one is a matter of need, one is a matter of personal preference. Therefore, it continues, it seems reasonable they should be treated differently. If a patient has to go abroad to get the healthcare s/he needs because s/he cannot have it domestically, s/he should not lose out financially by doing so. But if s/he could stay at home and s/he just prefers to have the healthcare abroad, there is no reason why public funds should have to pay any additional costs as a result. On this distinction the dual system remains based.

Hospital Care and Non-Hospital Care

Like the Court of Justice, the Directive makes a distinction between non-hospital care and hospital care. The memorandum to the directive argues that it is not appropriate to establish or maintain the requirement of any prior authorisation for *non-hospital care* provided in another Member State. In so far as the reimbursement of such care remains within the limits of the cover guaranteed by the sickness insurance scheme of the Member State of affiliation, the absence of prior authorisation requirement will not undermine the financial equilibrium of social security systems. The memorandum further states that Member States may have limitations on the choice of provider or other domestic planning mechanisms which are applied domestically, including conditions, criteria of eligibility and regulatory and administrative formalities. These may also be applied to cross-border non-hospital healthcare, provided they respect internal market freedoms and any such restrictions on access to non-hospital healthcare abroad are necessary, proportionate and non-discriminatory.

At the moment of completing this book the directive was still under discussion and the proposal of the Commission was seriously amended. It is therefore not possible to describe the final version of the Directive yet.

11.7. REIMBURSEMENT RULES

Article 35 of Regulation 883/2004 provides that the benefits in kind provided by a Member State on behalf of the institution of another Member State under this Chapter have to be fully reimbursed. These reimbursements are determined and effected in accordance with the arrangements set out in the implementing Regulation. This can be done either on production of proof of actual expenditure, or on the basis of fixed amounts for Member States if the legal or administrative structures of these States are such that the use of reimbursement on the basis of actual expenditure is not appropriate. The Regulation gives the Member States the room to make the arrangements they prefer: two or more Member States may provide for other methods of reimbursement or waive all reimbursement.

CHAPTER 12
OLD-AGE AND SURVIVOR'S PENSIONS

12.1. INTRODUCTION

The coordination Regulation treats long-term benefits[1] – including old age, survivors and disability benefits – differently from short-term benefits. Short-term benefits, like unemployment benefits and sickness benefits, are coordinated according to the integration principle: only one benefit is awarded to a migrant worker and this is calculated in accordance with the legislation of one Member State only. For the long-term benefits we are dealing with here, it was found undesirable that the State in whose territory a person, who has worked in several countries, has become disabled or reaches pension age, is solely responsible for the costs of these benefits. Indeed, considerable costs can be involved in paying long-term benefits.

Therefore, for the coordination of old-age, disability and survivors' pensions, the *partial pensions method* is used. As a result, the total pension a person receives consists of a number of pensions, each based on the period of insurance completed in the Member States where s/he has been employed. The Member States where the person has been insured must each pay the costs of the pension related to the periods completed under their respective legislations. This does not mean that a pensioner has to apply for pensions in all these States and receives each month separate payments from each State where s/he has been insured. Instead, the State where s/he was last insured contacts the other Member States where the person was insured and pays the aggregated sum of these pensions to the pensioner.

The partial pension principle is laid down in Article 50 of Regulation 883/2004. This Article provides that the competent institution has to determine entitlement to benefit, under all the legislations of the Member States to which the person concerned has been subject, when a request for award has been submitted. Thus, if a person has been working in Spain, Lithuania and Germany successively, the competent German institution has to contact the two other Member States in order to have the pensions calculated which are due from these countries. This rule does not apply when the person concerned expressly requests deferment of

---

[1]   In some national systems the terms *pensions* and *benefits* have a difference in meaning. In the Regulation and in this book these terms have the same meaning.

the award of old-age benefits under the legislation of one or more Member States. Deferment is possible for old age pensions only.

It can happen that at a given moment the person concerned does not satisfy, or no longer satisfies, the conditions laid down by all the legislations of the Member States to which s/he has been subject. In that case the institutions of which the conditions are still satisfied must not take into account the periods completed under the legislations the conditions of which have not been satisfied, or are no longer satisfied, if this gives rise to a lower amount of benefit.

Furthermore, Article 50(4) provides that a new calculation has to be performed automatically as and when the conditions to be fulfilled under the other legislations are satisfied. A new calculation also has to be made when a person requests the award of an old-age benefit (e.g. if s/he deferred it earlier).

As was mentioned *supra*, the partial pension method means that the claimant must submit a claim to the institution of the Member State where s/he is insured or, if s/he is not insured anymore, to the institution of the last Member State whose legislation was applicable (this is called the contact institution). The date of submission of the claim applies in all the institutions concerned. The claimant has to submit the claim in accordance with the legislation of the contact institution and s/he has to supply all relevant information and supporting documents on the periods s/he fulfilled in other Member States (Article 46 of the Implementing Regulation). Article 47 of the Implementing Regulation provides that the contact institution has, with delay, to send claims for benefits to the other institutions in question, so that they can all start the investigation of the claim concurrently. These institutions have to inform the contact institution of the periods fulfilled under their legislation and make the calculations of their benefits (in accordance with the rules discussed below). Each institution has to notify the claimant of the decision it has taken and specify the remedies and periods allowed for appeal (Article 48 of the Implementing Regulation).

12.2. AGGREGATION OF PERIODS

Article 6 of the Regulation contains the general aggregation rules, which are also relevant to the long term benefits. For the long term benefits aggregation is relevant only to the acquisition, retention and recovery of the right to benefit, but not to the calculation of benefit. After all, the partial pension principle means that the benefits are calculated according to the period completed in each State where the person worked. Aggregation of periods for making the calculation would lead to having these periods counted twice. Thus the aggregation rules only help to fulfil the conditions for a waiting period, if any.

Example. A man has been insured in Luxemburg for 25 years for a survivors' pension. Then he moves to Germany, where he dies after three years. His widow would, under German law, not be entitled to a German pension, since for this pension a waiting-period of five years applies. The period fulfilled in Luxemburg can be used to satisfy the waiting period. The widow will then receive a pension based on the period fulfilled in Luxemburg and in Germany (see below for the calculation). If the situation was reversed, three years in Germany, twenty-five in Luxemburg, the same rules apply: also then Germany has to take account of the periods fulfilled in Luxemburg.

Article 51 gives a special provision on the aggregation of periods. If the legislation of a Member State makes the granting of certain benefits conditional upon the periods of insurance having been completed only in a specific activity as an employed or self-employed person, the competent institution of that Member State has to take into account periods completed under the legislation of other Member States only if completed under a corresponding scheme. If such a scheme fails, it is relevant whether the person was in the same occupation, or where appropriate, in the same activity as an employed or self-employed person. This rule means a limitation of the assimilation of periods of insurance. For instance, if a country has a scheme for pensions for civil servants or miners, only periods fulfilled in comparable schemes or jobs are relevant to the aggregation rules.

Some schemes require that a person has to be insured under the scheme concerned at the moment the risk materialises. For instance, a survivors scheme can contain the provision that a widow is entitled to survivors benefits only if the insured person (her husband) was insured under a scheme at the moment he dies. If the deceased person was insured in a scheme with such condition and then becomes insured in another State, s/he does not satisfy the condition of the previous scheme anymore that s/he was insured under that scheme at the moment the risk materialises. As a result, under the national rules no pension could be obtained even if it would follow from the partial pension approach of the Regulation. In order to solve this problem, the Regulation has a special rule: Article 51(3). This article provides that the condition that a claimant must be insured at the time of the materialisation of the risk is regarded as having been satisfied if that person has been previously insured under the legislation or specific scheme of that Member State and is, at the time of the materialisation of the risk, insured under the legislation of another Member State for the same risk or, failing that, if a benefit is due under the legislation of another Member State for the same risk. In this way a fictitious insurance is created for this type of schemes. This is also relevant to invalidity pensions; we will describe this system in more detail in the following Chapter.

12.3. CALCULATION OF THE AMOUNT OF BENEFITS

This section concerns the calculation of benefits. Every Member State where the person concerned has been insured must make in principle two calculations in accordance with Article 52.

12.3.1. CALCULATION OF THE INDEPENDENT BENEFIT

First, all Member States in whose territory a claimant has been insured must make a calculation of the pension a person would receive if the conditions for entitlement to benefits would have been satisfied exclusively under national law. The Regulation calls this the *independent* benefit. Thus the independent benefit is a pension acquired by virtue of the national legislation alone. In other words, a pension is an independent benefit, if it is not necessary to invoke the provisions of the Regulation for the purpose of acquiring a right to this pension and for the calculation of its amount.

Example 1. For a person who worked for three years in Germany, the independent pension would be zero, since the waiting period of five years required by German law is not satisfied.

Example 2. In a system where the amount of pension entitlement grows by two percent for each year of insurance, the independent pension is 20 per cent of the full national pension if a person was insured for 10 years in that country.

12.3.2. THE PRO-RATA BENEFIT

Second, the Member States have to calculate the *proportioned pension*, which is the pro-rata benefit due from their system. For the calculation of the proportioned pension, two steps have to be taken (Article 52(1)(b)). First, the so-called theoretical amount has to be calculated, and then a pro-rata calculation has to be made.

The Theoretical Amount

The theoretical amount has to be calculated for each Member State where the person concerned has been insured. The theoretical amount is equal to the benefit which the person concerned could claim if all the periods of insurance or residence would have been completed under the legislation of the State concerned on the date of award of the benefit. For the purpose of this calculation the State concerned has to apply the legislation which is in force at the moment of calculation. The number of theoretical pensions is the same as the number of Member States where the person concerned has been insured.

In the *Weber* judgment[2] the Court held that the competent State has to take the wages earned at the moment of the materialisation of the risk into account.

In some national systems the amount of the benefit does not depend on the duration of the periods completed. In that case that amount is considered the theoretical amount.

Example. Irma has been insured for forty years altogether in three different countries. She was insured for ten years in system A, where the growth of pension rights is two percent for each year of insurance. The theoretical amount of State A is (forty times two per cent), i.e. 80 per cent of the full national pension.

She worked also in country y; in this country the level of pension is 1.75% of the last income for each year of insurance. The theoretical amount is forty years (all her periods of work) times 1.75, which is 75 percent of the last earned income.

She was also insured in country w, which has a flat-rate pension of 1500 euro regardless of the period of insurance or residence. In that country 1500 euro is the theoretical amount. Thus for Irma these three theoretical amounts apply.

The Pro-Rata Benefit

The second step is that each Member State involved calculates the pro-rata benefit. This is calculated for each State by taking the ratio between the duration of periods completed before the materialisation of the risk under the legislation of that State and the total duration of the periods completed under the legislations of all the Member States concerned. In other words, the pro-rata benefit due by a State where a migrant worker was insured is to be calculated by multiplying the theoretical amount of that State by the result of the ratio of periods of insurance in that State to the full 'insurance career' of that person. In the calculation of these amounts the rules of overlapping, mentioned in Articles 53 to 55 are applied.

Example. Simon works from the age of 25 until the age of 65; he works ten years in country x. In country x pension rights increase by two per cent of the full pension for each year a person in insured in that country between 15 and 65. The full pension is 2000 euro. Suppose Simon's full career is forty years (ten years in State x, twenty years in State y and ten years in State w). For Simon the pro-rata pension is 10/40 * 2000 = 500.

In country y for each year of work 1.75 of the last income is acquired as pension right. Simon's theoretical amount is 40 years (all his periods of work) times 1.75: 75 percent of his last earned income. The pro-rata amount is (he worked twenty years in this country) 20/40 times 75% of his last earned wage.

Country w, where Simon reaches pension age, has a flat-rate pension of 1500 euro regardless of the period of insurance or residence if a person reaches 65 in

---

[2]   Case 181/183, [1984] *ECR* 4007.

this country. A condition to this pension is that one must be insured under this system when one reaches pension age. Thus 1500 is the theoretical amount for State w. Simon works twenty years in this country, the pro-rata amount is 10/40 of 1500.

12.3.3. COMPARISON OF THE INDEPENDENT AND PRO-RATA BENEFITS

The third step is to compare the independent benefit and the pro-rata benefit for each country. The highest amount resulting from this for each country is applied, *see* Article 52. Thus for each of the countries where the person worked this comparison has to be made. The comparison between the independent and the pro-rata amount is to be carried out to the amounts determined *after* the application of the national provisions against overlapping of benefits.

Example. In the last example, in the system of State w, the independent benefit is by definition the highest, since it is the same as the theoretical amount. The pro-rata benefit is by definition only part of this.

If we take this example, but assume a different order of countries where Simon was insured, e.g. State w, State x, and State y, the theoretical amount of State w is still 1500 euros. However, the independent benefit is this time zero, since he was not insured under that system at the moment he reaches pension age. Thus, the pro-rata pension is by definition higher for a country other than the last one. (Note that the independent benefit of the last country is not by definition higher than the pro-rata one; this is the case only if the level of benefit is independent of the period of insurance).

The pensioner receives the sum of the highest pensions which follow per country from this comparison. Suppose in x the independent pension is highest, in y the pro-rata pension and in w the independent pension; the pensioner receives the sum of these three pensions.

However, the sum of these pensions may be deemed too high as a result of the application of this rule. This is the case, for instance, if in one of the systems the level of pension does not depend on the period of insurance. In our last example, where the order of insurance was x, y, w, the last pension is not proportioned under national or EU law, so the sum of the pensions may be more than Simon earned as an income. In order to solve this problem, rules against overlapping of benefits are applied, which will be discussed in the following section.

In some systems the national benefit is always the same as the pro-rata benefit because of the structure of the scheme. A system like that of country x in our example could be such a scheme. In that case the calculation does not have to be made (Article 52(4)), for that purpose it is necessary that the scheme is mentioned in Annex VIII.

12.4. THE HISTORY OF THE COMMUNITY RULES TO PREVENT OVERLAPPING: THE PETRONI CASE LAW

In order to understand the present rules better and in order to introduce a doctrine which is relevant also to other categories of benefits, it is useful to discuss the history of the overlapping rules shortly.

Under Article 46(3) of Regulation 1408/71, a pensioner was entitled to the total sum of benefits calculated according to the rules mentioned in the preceding section, but this Article limited the outcome to *the highest theoretical amount of the benefits in question.*

When the sum of the benefits calculated for each country exceeds this highest theoretical amount, each institution which made the calculation had to adjust its benefit. Therefore, each State reduced benefit by an amount corresponding to the proportion which the amount of the benefit concerned bore to the total of the benefits determined in accordance with these provisions.

However, this Community rule to prevent overlapping of benefits was overruled by the *Petroni* judgment.[3] In this judgment the Court decided that Article 46(3) was partially void. The Court pointed out that the Regulations concerning the coordination of social security have as their basis, their framework and their bounds Article 48 to 51 EEC, now Article 45 to 48 TFEU. The aim of these Articles would not be attained if, as a consequence of the exercise of their right to freedom of movement, workers were to lose advantages in the field of social security guaranteed to them in any event by the laws of a single Member State. A limitation on the overlapping of benefits which would lead to a diminution of the rights which the persons concerned already enjoyed in a Member State by virtue of the application of the national legislation alone is incompatible with Article 51 EEC. Thus the ruling that the Community rule against overlapping was incompatible with Article 51 was based on the consideration of the Court that the legislative powers of the Council, as derived from this Article, are limited. The approach of the Court can be criticised, since the wording of Article 51 does not contain such a limitation. The enumeration of measures in this Article is likely to be an enunciative and not an exhaustive one.

The consequence of the *Petroni* judgment was that Article 46(3) was void, insofar as rights acquired on the basis of national law alone were infringed. Consequently, this Article could no longer preclude the application of national rules against overlapping which are (also) aimed at reducing the overlap with foreign benefits of the same kind. This conclusion was confirmed in the *Greco* judgment.[4]

---

[3]   Case 24/75, [1975] *ECR* 1149.
[4]   Case 37/77, [1977] *ECR* 1711.

It was now up to the national legislatures to give rules against overlapping. As such rules may give undesirable results, Regulation 1248/92 was adopted to regulate the application of national rules against the overlapping of benefits.[5] This Regulation introduced a new text of Article 46(3). This is now broadly followed in Article 53 of Regulation 883/2004, which will be discussed in the following section.

The *Petroni* judgment has often been referred to in later case law, also in respect of other types of benefits. It is sometimes called the *Petroni* principle, which is that Community law must not infringe rights acquired on the basis of national law alone.

12.5. THE PRESENT RULES TO PREVENT OVERLAPPING

12.5.1. INTRODUCTION

Article 53 of Regulation 883/2004 is meant to limit the application of national rules against overlapping of benefits. As we have already seen in Section 12.3.3, the comparison between the independent and the pro-rata amount is to be carried out to the amounts determined *after* the application of the national provisions against overlapping of benefits. The objective of the present Regulation is to restrict the application of national rules against the overlapping of benefits.

The Regulation makes a distinction between benefits of the same kind and benefits of a different kind. The definition of benefits of the same kind is important, since overlapping rules make distinctions depending on whether benefits are of the same kind or not. Article 53 defines what is meant by *overlapping of benefits of the same kind.* These are benefits which are calculated or provided on the basis of periods of insurance and/or residence completed by the same person. All overlapping of benefits that *do not* satisfy this definition is regarded as overlapping of benefits of a different kind. For instance, survivors' and disability pensions are not benefits of the same kind.

Example. Irina acquires an invalidity and an old age benefit on the basis of her own insurance periods; these are benefits of the same kind. If she acquires a right to a survivors pension on the basis of the insurance of her partner, this is a benefit of a different kind.

---

[5]   *OJ 1992 L 136*, p. 7.

12.5.2. GENERAL PRINCIPLES

In the case of overlapping of benefits of the *same* kind, or of a *different* kind or of *other income* (in other words, in all cases of overlapping of benefits), the following rules apply.

The competent institution has to take account of the benefits or incomes acquired in another Member State *only* where the legislation it applies provides for the taking into account of benefits or income acquired abroad. In other words, national rules against overlapping are only applicable to foreign benefits if they make an express reference to foreign benefits.

Furthermore, account has to be taken of the *gross* benefits, *i.e.* before the deduction of taxes, social security contributions and other individual levies or deductions (unless the legislation provides otherwise).

The third condition is that national rules against overlapping must not take account of benefits which are awarded on the basis of voluntary insurance or continued optional insurance.

If a single Member State applies rules to prevent overlapping because the person concerned receives benefits of the same kind or a different kind under the legislation of other Member States or income acquired in other Member States, the benefit due may be reduced solely by the amount of such benefit or such income. Thus, the effect of rules to prevent overlapping is limited to the amount of the foreign benefit or income and cannot exceed it.

12.5.3. OVERLAPPING OF BENEFITS OF THE SAME KIND

In case of benefits of the same kind, the following overlapping rules apply (Article 54). This Article provides that the rules against overlapping are not applicable to pro-rata benefits of the same kind. As a consequence, national rules against overlapping are applicable only to independent benefits. Furthermore the overlapping rules can apply to independent benefits only if the benefit concerned is:

– a benefit the amount of which does not depend on the duration of periods of insurance or residence; or
– a benefit the amount of which is determined on the basis of a credited period deemed to have been completed between the date on which the risk materialised and a later date which overlaps with
– a benefit of the same type (unless an agreement between two or more Member States to avoid the same credited period being taken into account more than once); or
– benefits the amount of which does not depend on the duration of periods of insurance or benefit.

Example. A person who has an independent old age pension in country w, the amount of which does not depend on the duration of periods of insurance or residence, receives also pensions from country x and y. Country w can, because the amount of the pension does not depend on the duration of periods of insurance or residence, deduct pensions x and y from its pension. Benefits may be reduced solely by the amount of such benefits of such income. If the sum of pensions from States x and y is higher than the pension from country w, the excess has to be paid, in addition to the pension from State w.[6]

12.5.4. OVERLAPPING OF BENEFITS OF A DIFFERENT KIND

Finally, Article 55 gives special provisions if the receipt of benefits of a different kind or other income requires the application of overlapping rules. This Article provides that if two or more independent benefits are concerned, the competent institution has to divide the amounts of the benefit(s) or other income by the number of benefits subject to the overlapping rules. In other words, this Article requires that where rules against overlapping are applied, the average of the various reductions resulting from the application of the rules against overlapping has to be taken.

Example. An employee is entitled to an old-age benefit of 1000 and a survivors' pension of 500. A national rule against overlapping requires that these benefits must not overlap with unemployment benefit, which is 800. If the rules of the Regulation did not apply, the amount of the old-age benefit would be reduced to 200 and that of the survivors' pension would be reduced to zero. The rules of the Regulation have as effect that the unemployment benefit is divided by the number of pensions (two) and that half the unemployment benefit is deducted from each pension. The old age pension is thus 600, the survivors' pension 100 and the unemployment benefit 80.

The second element of Article 55 concerns the concurrence of one or more pro-rata benefits. In that case the competent institution has to take into account the benefit(s) or other income and all the elements stipulated for applying the rules to prevent overlapping as a function of the ratio between the periods of insurance and/or residence for the calculation of the pro-rata benefit.

Example. A German widow receives a Belgian survivors' benefit and a German and Belgian old-age pension (based on insurance of ten years in Belgium and fifteen years in Germany). The pro rata part is 3/5 in Germany and 2/5 in Belgium. If this woman receives an income of 1,000 per month, a three-fifth's

---

[6]   Note that the overlapping rules cannot be applied on a pro-rata benefit (meaning that no other benefits can be deducted from such benefit), but a pro-rata benefit itself can be deducted from a benefit whose amount does not depend on duration of insurance.

part will be deducted from the German benefits and a two-fifth's part from the Belgian benefits.

The third element of Article 55 concerns the overlapping of one or more independent benefits and one or more pro-rata benefits. In that case the competent institutions have to apply the first method of Article 55 on the independent benefits, i.e. the amounts which would not be paid in the strict application of the national overlapping provisions are divided by the number of benefits subject to the overlapping rules. In other words, in this case the unpaid part is averaged by the States from which the person concerned receives benefits. The second method is to be applied to the pro-rata benefits, i.e. the rules against overlapping are taken into account only in proportion to the periods of insurance and/or residence which were taken into account to calculate the pro-rata benefit.[7]

12.6. RECALCULATION OF BENEFITS

Sometimes it is necessary to recalculate the amount of benefit, for instance in case of a rise of the costs of living or wages level. Another reason for recalculation of benefits is a change in exchange rates. Furthermore, the extent of disability can change, or it is possible that a person starts to gain income. The question arose when the recalculation has effect for foreign benefits, in other words when the calculation of Section 12.3 has to be done again.

Article 59(2) of the Regulation provides that if, by reason of an increase in the cost of living or changes in the level of income or other grounds for adjustment, the benefits of the State concerned are altered by a percentage or fixed amount, such percentage or fixed amount must be applied directly to the benefits determined under Article 52, without the need for a recalculation.

In other words, if the pensions are adjusted on the basis of social-economic factors, the percentage or amount does not lead to a recalculation. Thus, if the amount of a foreign pension is raised in order to take account of the costs of living, the other Member State cannot absorb this rise by recalculating its own benefit. If, however, the amount of the pension is changed because of changes in personal circumstances, such as the level of invalidity or the family situation, a recalculation on the basis of Article 52 is possible.

The limitation of Article 59 on the recalculation of pensions is mostly to the advantage of the beneficiaries.

The corresponding Article of Regulation 1408/71, Article 51 provided that this limitation applies only if pensions are determined according Article 46 (now

---

[7]   Article 55 provides that the competent institution shall not apply the division stipulated in respect of independent benefits, if the legislation it applies provides for account to be taken of benefits of a different kind and/or different income and all other benefits for calculating part of their amount determined as a function of the ratio between periods of insurance and/or residence.

Article 52). The Court ruled in the *Cassamali*[8] and the *Bogana* judgments[9] that this rule also applies to independent benefits. The present text of the Regulation does not refer to Article 52 anymore, so the case law can be deemed to be implemented and the limitation applies to both pro-rata and independent benefits.

Article 59(1) rules that if the national rules for determining benefits or calculating them are altered or if the personal situation of the person concerned undergoes a relevant change which would lead, under that legislation, to an adjustment of the amount of benefit, a recalculation has to be carried out, in accordance with Article 52.

12.7. REMOVING EFFECTS OF DIFFERING NATIONAL SCHEMES

A remarkable situation occurred in the *Van Munster* judgment[10] when a migrant worker received both a Belgian and a Netherlands old-age pension. Because of the different applicable national rules, the man received a lower pension when the wife retired. The Belgian Royal Decree no. 50 on retirement and survivors' pensions provides that persons are entitled to the family rate of an old-age pension only if the spouse is not entitled to an old-age pension in her own right. Under the Dutch Old Age benefit scheme both the man and the woman are entitled to a pension of their own after retirement at the age of 65. If one member of the couple is already over 65, and the other is below 65, the older one receives a supplement of 50% of the old-age benefit as the younger one is not entitled to benefit yet. If the other person also reaches the age of 65, this supplement is withdrawn and both persons receive their own benefit. The total amount granted under the Netherlands legislation does not change. The result is, however, that the man who first received a Belgian old-age pension at the family rate is now granted the rate for a single person only, as his spouse received a Dutch pension of her own when she became 65. The Court considered that if a national statutory scheme is applied on a migrant worker in the same way as on employees who remained in the same country, this can have unexpected consequences. These are hard to reconcile with the aim of Articles 45 to 48 TFEU. These consequences occur because the rights to a pension for migrant workers fall under two separate statutory schemes. The differences are the result of the fact that one of the two pension schemes grants a higher benefit to the employee whose spouse does not receive an old-age or comparable pension. Under the other scheme, each of the spouses receives, after reaching retirement age, half the pension of an equal part. This means the total family income does not rise.

---

[8]   Case 93/90, [1991] *ECR* I-1401.
[9]   Case 193/92, [1993] *ECR* I-755.
[10] Case 165/91, [1994] *ECR* I-4661.

The Court was not able to solve the problem. It considered that, taking account of the considerable difference between these statutory schemes, the principle laid down in the Treaty (Article 10 EC) of loyal cooperation between the competent authorities of the Member States requires that they apply all the available means in order to realize the aim of Article 45 TFEU.

Given this unsolved problem it is not surprising that the Court was asked in another case to answer questions concerning the meaning of the *Van Munster* judgment. This was the *Engelbrecht* decision.[11] The Court considered that some of the facts in the *Engelbrecht* case were almost identical to those in *Van Munster*, inasmuch as the amount of the pension previously awarded to Mr Engelbrecht under the Netherlands scheme is henceforth divided equally between Mr and Mrs Engelbrecht, but the couple's income has not been increased by this new award. The Belgian benefit awarded to Mr Engelbrecht was, however, reduced because of the application of the Dutch rules. The Court considered that the national court must, as far as it is possible, interpret it in a way which accords with the requirements of Community law, as the Court had already ruled in the *Van Munster* judgment. The Court, however, added a very important element: where application in accordance with these requirements is not possible, the national court must fully apply Community law and protect the rights conferred thereunder on individuals, if necessary by disapplying any provision in the measure which would, in the circumstances of the case, lead to a result contrary to Community law. In this context, the Court continued, the exercise of the right to free movement within the Community is impeded if a social advantage is lost or reduced simply because a benefit of the same kind is awarded to a worker's spouse under the legislation of another Member State if this is taken into account when, on the one hand, the grant of that latter benefit has not led to any increase in the couple's total income and, on the other, there has been a concomitant reduction of the same amount in the personal pension received by the worker under the legislation of that same State. Such a result might well discourage Community workers from exercising their right to free movement and would therefore constitute a barrier to that freedom enshrined in Article 39 EC.

Consequently, where the competent authorities of a Member State apply a provision of law:

– which fixes the amount of the retirement pension awarded to a married worker;

– which provides for that pension to be reduced by the amount of a pension awarded to the spouse under the scheme of another Member State, but;

– which provides for the application of a derogating clause in respect of overlapping where the pension paid elsewhere is less than a certain amount,

it is contrary to Article 45 TFEU for those authorities to reduce the amount of the pension awarded by the amount of a pension awarded to a person's spouse under

---

[11]   Case 262/97, [2000] *ECR* I-7321.

the scheme of another Member State, when the grant of that latter pension does not involve any increase in the couple's total income.

12.8. PERIODS COMPLETED BEFORE THE COMING INTO FORCE OF THE REGULATION

Article 87(2) provides that any period of insurance and, where appropriate, any period of employment, self-employment or residence completed under the legislation of a Member State prior to the date of application of this Regulation in the Member State concerned has to be taken into consideration for the determination of rights acquired under this Regulation. Consequently, if a person was insured in a Member State before the Regulation came into force for this Member State, also this period has to be taken into account for the calculation of benefit rights.

Thus, this rule is relevant to all present Member States for the periods fulfilled before the coming into force of Regulation 883/2004. It is also relevant for future new Member States, also for them the coordination rules have this retroactive effect.

12.9. THE RELATIONSHIP BETWEEN INTER-NATIONAL CONVENTIONS AND THE REGULATION

As we will see in Section 16.2, social security conventions between countries have been replaced by the Regulation, unless provided otherwise. The question arose as to whether this rule is consistent with Article 42 EC, now Article 48 TFEU, in particular in cases where the application of the other convention would be more favourable for the person concerned. We will discuss this issue in more detail in Chapter 18, but here some case law is already discussed. The *Rönfeldt* judgment[12] concerned Mr Rönfeldt. This was a German national and resident. From 1941 to 1951 he paid contributions for a German retirement pension. Subsequently, he worked in Denmark until 1971 and he paid contributions for a Danish old-age pension. After he returned to Germany, he had to pay German contributions again. The coordination Regulation requires only that periods of insurance have to be aggregated for the purpose of *acquiring* a right to benefit, not for the *calculation* of a right to benefit. The Convention concluded between Germany and Denmark of 1953, however, provided that periods of insurance completed under the legislation of Denmark had to be counted also for the calculation of the German pension.

---

[12]   Case 227/89, [1991] *ECR* I-323.

Article 6 of Regulation 1408/71 provided, like Article 8 of Regulation 883/2004, that the conventions concluded between Member States were replaced by the Regulation at the date it came into force.[13] This would have the effect that the Germany-Denmark convention was no longer applicable. The Court considered that because of Article 6 Mr Rönfeldt lost advantages which had been awarded to him by a bilateral convention. It ruled that this loss of benefit rights was not compatible with, what are now, Articles 45 and 48 TFEU. The Court had already pointed out in the *Petroni* judgment[14] that the purpose of these Articles would not be achieved if employed persons exercising their right to free movement lost advantages to which they would have been entitled by virtue of national law alone. This case law had to be interpreted, according to the Court, as meaning that benefits awarded by virtue of national law also comprise benefits to which one is entitled by virtue of international conventions which are in force between two or more Member States and which are integrated in their national legislation. The latter rules have to be applied if they are more advantageous than the application of Community law.

In the *Thévenon* judgment[15] the Court clarified the *Rönfeldt* ruling. It considered that the rule of the *Rönfeldt* judgment did not apply in the situation of Mr Thévenon, who had not exercised his right to free movement before the coming into force of Regulation 1408/71. This meant that at the time Mr Thévenon went to work abroad, the French-German Treaty, as far as its personal and material scope are concerned, was already replaced by Regulation 1408/71. He could not hold that he had lost social security advantages to which he would have been entitled on the basis of the French-German Treaty. As a result of this judgment, it is not necessary to investigate in all cases whether the application of the rules of a Treaty between two Member States leads to a more advantageous result than Regulation 1408/71. *See* further Chapter 16.

12.10. THE COORDINATION OF SUPPLEMENTARY PENSIONS

12.10.1. GENERAL

As we discussed in Chapter 5, non-statutory social security does not fall within the material scope of the coordination Regulation, unless a Member State has issued a declaration providing otherwise in respect of contractual arrangements which have been declared generally binding. France has issued such a declaration

---

[13]   *I.e.* 1 April 1973, when Denmark entered the European Community (note that Denmark entered the ec only after Mr Rönfeldt had returned to Germany).
[14]   Case 24/75, [1975] *ECR* 1149.
[15]   Case 475/93, [1995] *ECR* I-3813.

with respect to its unemployment benefits scheme and two supplementary old-age benefits schemes. Other Member States have not issued such declarations yet.

Although there has been considerable pressure to make coordination rules also for supplementary benefits, no much progress have been made so far.[16]

12.10.2. DIRECTIVE 98/49 ON SAFEGUARDING THE SUPPLEMENTARY PENSION RIGHTS OF EMPLOYED AND SELF-EMPLOYED PERSONS MOVING WITHIN THE COMMUNITY

One development was, however, that in 1998 the Council adopted Council Directive 98/49 on safeguarding the supplementary pension rights of employed and self-employed persons moving within the Community.[17] This Directive was based on Article 42 EC (now Article 48 TFEU).

The Directive defines a supplementary pension scheme as any occupational pension scheme established in conformity with national legislation and practice such as a group insurance contract or pay-as-you-go scheme agreed by one or more branches or sectors, a funded scheme or a pension promise backed by book reserves, or any collective or other comparable arrangement intended to provide a supplementary pension for employed or self-employed persons. Article 4 of the Directive entails that a person who leaves a pension scheme must not be confronted by a loss of vested pension rights when he moves to another Member State, if he would not have lost these rights had he started to work for another employer in the same Member State. Member States have to take the necessary measures to ensure the preservation of vested pension rights for members of a supplementary pension scheme in respect of whom contributions are no longer being made to that scheme, now that they have moved to another Member State. The protection must be to the same extent as for persons who remain within the same Member State. In other words, Article 4 is an equal treatment provision: those who leave the Member State and those who remain in that State have to be treated in the same way.

Article 5 provides that supplementary pensions also must be paid in another Member State. Consequently, payment can no longer be restricted to the territory of the competent State.

In general, it would often be preferable that an insured person could remain insured under the supplementary scheme in which s/he was already insured in the case that s/he moves to another Member State. The Directive requires this in

---

[16]   On these problems, see M.A.B.L Wienk, *Europese coördinatie van aanvullende pensioenen*, Deventer 1999; and E.A. Whiteford, *Adapting to Change: Occupational Pension Schemes, Women and Migrant Workers*, The Hague 1996.
[17]   Council Directive 98/49 of 29 June 1998, *OJ L* 209, p. 46.

exceptional cases only, *i.e.* in case of a posted worker who is a member of such a scheme during the period of his or her posting in another Member state. In this case, the posted worker and his or her employer are exempted from the obligation to pay contributions in another State (*i.e.* the State of employment). According to Article 3, 'posted worker' is the person who remains under the posting rules of the coordination Regulation subject to the legislation of the Member State of origin. Member States have to take measures to ensure that employers, trustees or others responsible for the management of supplementary pension schemes provide adequate information to scheme members when they move to another Member State, in relation to their pension rights and the choices which are available to them under the scheme.

12.10.3. PROPOSAL FOR A DIRECTIVE ON IMPROVING THE PORTABILITY OF SUPPLEMENTARY PENSION RIGHTS

In 2005 a proposal was made for a directive on improving the portability of supplementary pension rights. The objective of the directive was to take measures in order to take away the negative effects of the lack of coordination rules for supplementary pensions.[18] This was also based on Article 42 EC. However, this directive was not adopted by the Council. This draft directive proposed to cover all supplementary pension schemes, with the exception of the schemes covered by the coordination Regulation. The term portability used in the proposal referred to the right for an outgoing worker to acquire and retain supplementary pension rights.

The draft Directive provided that a worker who has not yet built up any acquired rights within the supplementary pension scheme, but who has already paid contributions, had to be reimbursed the contributions which were paid or these had to be transferred in full. A second element addressed by the proposal is high minimum ages for coverage. This is a major disincentive to the mobility of young workers if a departure before reaching this minimum age results in the loss of pension rights for the period worked before the minimum age. The proposal provided that a worker must start acquiring supplementary pension rights at the latest as of the age of twenty-one. Furthermore, the waiting period during which a worker cannot yet become a member of the scheme was reduced. According to the proposal this period should not exceed one year, unless the minimum age has not yet been reached.

In order to allow outgoing workers to build up sufficient supplementary pension rights during their career, particularly for those who have had a

---

[18] Proposal for a Directive of the European Parliament and of the Council on improving the portability of supplementary pension rights, COM(2005) 507 final.

succession of jobs, the possibility of applying qualifying periods, i.e. the period of membership to be completed before the worker obtains acquired rights, was limited. According to the proposal this period should not exceed two years.

Article 5 addressed the preservation of dormant pension rights. The objective of this Article was that a mobile worker should not have to suffer a considerable reduction in the acquired rights s/he has left within the supplementary pension scheme under his or her former employment relationship. The proposal takes account of the fact that Member States have different instruments for making this adjustment, depending in particular on how the rights of active members develop. The Article provides that Member States have to adopt the measures they deem necessary in order to ensure a fair adjustment of dormant pension rights so as to avoid that outgoing workers are penalised. In order to avoid excessive administrative costs stemming from the management of a high number of low-value dormant rights, the proposal provided also for the option not to preserve these pension rights, but to use a transfer or a payment of a capital sum representing the acquired rights when these do not exceed a threshold established by the Member State concerned.

Article 6 concerned the transferability of pensions. The outgoing worker should have the choice between maintaining his or her rights within the supplementary scheme of his or her former employment relationship and the transfer of his or her acquired rights, unless his or her new job is covered by the same supplementary pension scheme or unless the scheme makes a capital payment because of the low value of the rights acquired. The request has to be made within eighteen months after the termination of the employment. An outgoing worker opting for a transfer of his or her rights should not be penalised by calculations of the value of the rights transferred made by the two schemes involved in the transfer, or by excessive administrative charges.

In line with the spirit of the implementation of the internal market and the social provisions relating thereto, the proposal did not preclude any more advanced provisions on portability which Member States might take.

As was already mentioned, Member States did not accept the proposal (even though it was severely amended during the negotiations), among other reasons because of the requirement of a fair adjustment of dormant pension rights and the requirement of transferring pension rights. The rules of the directive could mean that the country to which rights were transferred had to pay higher rights than justified under its own rules. The directive did not give clear rules, but provided that workers should not be penalized, which could mean, in particular, that pensions had to be unconditionally indexed. Since pension funds may have conditions for indexation under their national rules, e.g. the state of the funds, this could cause important problems for these funds. Also the protection of dormant rights of mobile workers could be better than those staying in the Member State. Problematic was also the lack of rules on the fiscal effects of transferring pension rights.

12.10.4. CONCLUSION

The outcome of the discussions meant that coordination of supplementary benefits is still hardly possible. We saw that Directive 98/49 provides for an improvement of the legal position of persons who are subject to a supplementary pension scheme. The Directive gives the best protection to posted workers. Such protection is – given the limited applicability of the posting rules – for a temporary period only. For others, the Directive requires that vested rights are preserved and that pension rights are also paid upon retirement in another Member State. More protective rules are still lacking, e.g. on excessive waiting periods or aggregation rules which help to fulfil the waiting periods of a particular scheme. The general rules of the Treaty (Articles 45 and 48 TFEU – *see* the *Vougioukas* approach, Section 2.4) may be tried, although it is not sure where such attempts will be successful given the often very complicated nature of supplementary benefits.

CHAPTER 13

INVALIDITY PENSIONS

13.1. INTRODUCTION

In Chapter 12 we discussed the coordination of long term benefits, in which we focused on old-age and survivors' benefits. Although the coordination rules discussed are also applicable to disability benefits, this type of benefits has certain specific characteristics, which deserve particular attention. For this reason a separate chapter is dedicated to this type of benefit.

The coordination rules concerning long-term benefits involve, as we have seen in the previous chapter, that instead of the *integration principle* the pro-rata method is applied. As a result, the total pension a person receives consists of a number of pensions, based on the periods the person concerned has completed in the Member States where s/he has been employed. The Member States where the person has been insured must each pay the costs of the pension related to the periods completed under their respective legislations.

The reason for treating disability benefits differently from the other types in this Chapter is that coordination of disability benefits raises specific questions. For this reason the coordination Regulation dedicates a separate Chapter to invalidity benefits (Chapter 4).

These specific questions have to do, among other things, with the fact that there are two main different types of schemes.
1. The first type is the so-called Type B: the amount of benefit depends on the duration of periods of work or insurance completed by the insured person;
2. The second type is the so-called Type A scheme: the amount of benefit is not dependent on the duration of the insured periods[1] *and* the benefit is expressly mentioned in Annex VI.[2] The person receives a pension only if the risk materialises during insurance.

---

[1]   In some Type A schemes claimants have to serve waiting days before they are entitled to benefit. Such waiting days do not alter the character of the scheme as there is still no relationship between insured periods and the amount of benefit.

[2]   In some States the amount of benefit does not depend on the duration of insurance for survivors' benefits as well, but only for disability benefits there is a provision (Article 44) for persons who have been subject to Type A benefits only (to be discussed below).

Type B schemes generally lead to low benefits if the risk materialises after a short period of insurance. For instance, if a person requires two per cent of the standard benefit amount for each year of insurance, his or her benefit is fourteen per cent of this sum if the risk materialises after seven years.

Under Type B schemes a person can claim previously acquired rights under such a scheme even if s/he is not insured anymore under that scheme. For instance, a person is insured for twenty years under a Type B scheme. If his or her insurance ends, and the risk materialises, say, five years later, s/he can still claim benefit under this scheme. Under a Type A scheme a person is, in principle, entitled to benefit only if s/he is insured at the moment the risk materialises. In other words, if the insurance terminates and some time later the risk materialises, this person can no longer claim benefit under that scheme. Sometimes Type A schemes have some after-effect, to cover the period between two jobs, but this effect is limited in time (one or two months).

Type B schemes often have a waiting period; if a person becomes disabled during this period, s/he is not entitled to benefit at all. The coordination Regulation provides for some assistance by means of the aggregation rules: periods fulfilled in other Member States can be used to meet the waiting-period condition.

Under a Type A scheme a person receives the full benefit if s/he satisfies all conditions, even if the risk materialises at the very first day of insurance. Suppose that a scheme provides for a benefit of 70% of wage in case of full disability. If a person suffers an accident after seven days of work and becomes disabled, s/he is entitled to a benefit of 70 per cent of his or her wage.

The coordination rules have to solve two problems related to the characteristics of Type A schemes. The first problem concerns the interaction with Type B schemes. Suppose that a person who becomes disabled has been consecutively insured under a Type B scheme (of country x) and a Type A scheme (of country y). Without co-ordination rules, this person will receive a benefit under the Type A scheme and also under the Type B scheme, as the acquired pension rights under the Type B scheme are 'stored' and can be claimed at a later period. This leads to a too high benefit.

In the reversed situation, the person is first insured under a Type A scheme, and subsequently under a Type B scheme. If s/he becomes disabled, s/he is not entitled to benefit under the Type A scheme, since s/he is not insured under that scheme at the moment of materialisation of the risk. Consequently, this person will receive benefit under the Type B scheme only. As s/he has not completed a full career under that Type B scheme, his or her benefit will be lower than if s/he had not crossed the border.

The coordination rules have to solve both problems. They make a distinction between the situation in which a worker has been insured exclusively under Type A schemes (Section 13.2) and where s/he has been subject to at least one Type B scheme (Section 13.3).

13.2. AGGREGATION RULES

Some schemes make the right to invalidity benefit conditional upon the completion of periods of insurance or residence. To such schemes the aggregation rule of Article 6 is relevant: periods of employment, self-employment, insurance or residence completed in another Member State are taken into account as though they were periods completed under the legislation the competent State applies.[3] Like for old age and survivors benefits, the aggregation rules serve to satisfy waiting periods only; the amount of the pension is calculated according to the coordination rules described in Section 13.4.

Under Regulation 1408/71, the aggregation rules were interpreted by the Court as to avoid excluding persons whose risk had already materialised or which could be foreseen already at the start of the insurance in a particular Member State (the *Moscato* judgment).[4] The Court interpreted the aggregation rules of the Regulation as meaning that they have to ensure that the employee does not loose advantages in the area of social security to which s/he would have been entitled if s/he had spent his working life in one Member State only. Therefore, for the condition that at the time when the insurance became effective the claimant's state of health must not make it foreseeable that incapacity for work would shortly occur, the competent institution has to take account also of the periods of affiliation with the statutory scheme of another Member State. Under Regulation 883/2004 the assimilation rule of Article 6 covers this situation and has the same effect.[5]

13.3. A PERSON HAS BEEN EXCLUSIVELY SUBJECT TO TYPE A SCHEMES

A person who has been exclusively subject to Type A schemes is entitled to benefit only from the Member State whose legislation applies at the time when the incapacity for work occurs (Article 44(2)). Thus, if a person has been exclusively subject to Type A schemes, despite what was said before on the coordination of long term benefits, the integration principle is applied: a person receives benefit from one State only. This exception is not so strange, since also under national rules the person concerned would have received the full benefit from the country where s/he is insured at the moment of materialisation of the risk.

A difference between Regulation 883/2004 and Regulation 1408/71 is that under the latter Regulation *all* benefits whose amount did not depend on the

---

[3]   Furthermore Article 45 refers to Article 51 of the Regulation: these rules apply if the granting of benefits is conditional upon insurance in a particular activity or an occupation which is subject to a particular scheme (e.g. working in mines or as a teacher). In that case restrictions apply on the aggregation of periods, *see* Article 51.
[4]   Case 481/93, [1995] *ECR* I-3525.
[5]   *See* also the *Klaus* judgment, discussed in Section 11.3.1.

period of insurance were Type A benefits. Regulation 883/2004 has an additional condition for schemes to be of the A Type: the benefit has to be expressly included by the competent State in Annex VI. Otherwise it is treated as a Type B scheme, which requires the partial pension method (basically the same as for old-age benefits, discussed in the previous chapter). This means that a Member State may decide that a scheme, even if it does not relate the level of benefit to a period of insurance, is treated as a Type B scheme. The intended effect is that the benefits of the other State are taken into account, in other words the Member State (suppose it was the last where the person was insured) can deduct the benefit from the other country from its benefit.[6] Thus, Member States who consider that they are better off (since they are most often the last in a row of Type A schemes where a person has been insured) may decide not to list their scheme in the Annex.

Thus the Regulation provides that if a person has been insured under Type A schemes only, s/he has to rely on benefits from the State where s/he was lastly insured. If s/he is not entitled to benefits under this scheme s/he can claim benefits to which s/he is still entitled under the legislation of another Member State. This is possible, for instance, if, according to the provisions of the scheme, it has after-effect (e.g. for two or six months). For instance, a person may be covered by a scheme which does not consider him or her as disabled; if s/he is still within the period of after-effect of the preceding scheme, the person concerned may claim benefit under the latter scheme. In other situations it is not possible to claim benefits on the basis of the legislation of State other than the one the person is subject to, even if s/he would have satisfied the disability conditions of that scheme, apart from one exception. The integration principle may be applied also if a person has been insured under a Type B scheme for a very short period only before s/he was subject to a Type A scheme (Article 46(2)). This is the case if s/he satisfies the conditions for the right to benefit under the Type A scheme, without taking account of periods not completed under Type A schemes. The second condition is that s/he does not assert any claims to old-age benefits. This rule has to prevent persons who worked for a very short period under a Type B scheme from being affected by the negative consequences of that short period of insurance.

13.4. A PERSON HAS BEEN SUBJECT TO AT LEAST ONE TYPE B SCHEME

If a person has been subject to at least one Type B scheme, the *partial pension* method is applied (Article 46), which was discussed in Chapter 12. This rule also applies to schemes in which there is no relation between period of insurance and

---

6   If the other country has a Type B scheme there is already a division of costs, since the partial pension method is used.

the level of benefit which are not listed in the Annex. Article 46 provides that the coordination rules of Chapter 5 of the Regulation, the Chapter on old-age and survivors' benefits, are applied *mutatis mutandis* on invalidity benefits. This means that each Member State where the person concerned has been insured has to investigate whether s/he is entitled to benefit.

13.4.1. DETERMINING THE INCAPACITY FOR WORK

There can be large differences in the definition of disability between the schemes of the Member States. Thus it can happen that a person who has worked in various Member States is not entitled to benefit in all these States since s/he is not considered disabled by all these countries.

The assimilation rule of Article 5 does not have the effect that this person is considered incapacitated for work in all Member States. Instead, Article 46(3) gives a limited solution: a decision taken by an institution of a Member State concerning the degree of invalidity of a claimant shall be binding on the institution of any other Member State concerned, provided that the concordance between the legislations of these States on conditions relating to the degree of invalidity is acknowledged in Annex VII to the Regulation. However, in this Annex, only concordances between the legislation of some Member States are given. Belgium, France and Italy made such arrangements with each other. Thus, this possibility has not been used by many Member States so far.

In the other situations, each Member State has to apply its own legislation. Each institution has the possibility of having the claimant examined by a medical doctor or other expert of its own choice to determine the degree of invalidity (Article 49 of the implementing Regulation). For this purpose it has to take into consideration the documents etc. collected by the institution of any other Member State.

As we have already seen in Chapter 11, Article 87 of the Implementing Regulation concerns the right of a Member State to have a person medically examined. If a person is staying or residing within the territory of a Member State other than that of the debtor institution, the medical examination has to be carried out, at the request of that institution, by the institution of the beneficiary's place of residence. The institution of the place or stay has to forward a report to the debtor institution that requested the medical examination. This institution is bound by the findings of that report. The debtor institution has the right, however, to have the beneficiary examined by a doctor of its own choice. However, s/he can be asked to return to the Member State of the debtor institution only if s/he is able to make the journey without prejudice to his or her health and the cost of travel and accommodation is paid for by the debtor institution.

If a person is not considered disabled in one Member State and disabled in the other, the effects differ depending on whether Type B schemes are involved or Type A schemes. *See* for an example Section 13.4.3.

13.4.2. FICTION OF INSURANCE

Suppose that a person has been insured successively for ten years under a Type A scheme and 10 years under a Type B scheme and then s/he becomes disabled. In this case s/he does not satisfy the conditions of the Type A scheme that s/he is insured under this scheme when the risk materialises. This problem has to be dealt first, since a person can be entitled to a partial pension only under this scheme, if s/he is considered as insured under that scheme.

For this purpose the Regulation has a special rule: Article 51(3). This Article provides that the condition of being insured is regarded as having been satisfied if that person has been previously insured under the legislation or specific scheme of that Member State and is, at the time of the materialisation of the risk, insured under the legislation of another Member State for the same risk or, failing that, if a benefit is due under the legislation of another Member State for the same risk. The latter condition shall, however, be deemed to be fulfilled in the cases referred to in Article 57.

This rule does no longer refer to the Annex like was the case under Regulation 1408/71, but mentions two alternatives in which the fiction of insurance is assumed: either the person is insured under a scheme or receives benefit under that scheme.

This rule does not only apply to Type A schemes, but to all schemes which make the acquisition, retention or recovery of the right to benefits conditional upon the person concerned being insured at the time of the materialisation of the risk. For that reason we met the rule already in the previous chapter.

Example. An employee worked 5 years in Belgium, five years in the Netherlands (both having a scheme which requires that the person is insured at the moment of the materialisation of the risk) and then 10 years in Germany (Type B). If he resigns and is not insured, but becomes disabled after two years and is awarded German disability benefit, he is also satisfying the Belgian and Dutch conditions of being insured.

13.4.3. THE CALCULATION OF THE AMOUNT

Since we have already discussed the partial pension method for the old age pensions, we will go into this issue shortly only. As we saw, Chapter 5 of the Regulation is relevant to this calculation. Article 50 of Regulation 883/2004 provides that the competent institution has to determine entitlement to benefit under all the legislations of the Member States to which the person concerned has been subject, when a request for award has been submitted. Every Member State where the person concerned has been insured must make in principle two calculations in accordance with Article 52.

First, all Member States in whose territory a claimant has been insured must make a calculation of the pension a person would receive if the conditions for entitlement to benefits have been satisfied exclusively under national law. The Regulation calls this the *independent* benefit. Thus the independent benefit is a pension acquired by virtue of the national legislation alone. Second, the Member States have to calculate the pro-rata pension due from their system. For the calculation of the proportioned pension, two steps have to be taken (Article 52(1)(b)). First, the so-called theoretical amount has to be calculated and then a pro-rata calculation has to be made.

The *theoretical amount* has to be calculated for each Member State where the person concerned has been insured. It is equal to the benefit which the person concerned could claim if all his or her periods of insurance or residence were completed under its legislation. This provision means that each State where a person has been insured has to calculate the pension to which a person would be entitled if s/he had completed al the periods of insurance and of residence (until the award of benefit) under the legislation of that State. For the purpose of this calculation, the State concerned has to apply the legislation which is in force at the moment of calculation. This amount is calculated on the basis of all (both national and relevant foreign) periods of insurance in accordance with the national rules for calculation of the State making the calculation. The number of theoretical pensions is the same as the number of Member States where the person concerned has been insured.

The second step is that each Member State involved calculates the *pro-rata benefit*. This is calculated taking into account the ratio between the duration of periods completed before the materialisation of the risk under the legislation this State applies and the total duration of the periods completed before materialisation of the risk under the legislations of all the Member States concerned. In other words, the pro-rata benefit due by a State where a migrant worker was insured is to be calculated by multiplying the theoretical amount of that State by the result of the ratio of periods of insurance in that State to the full 'insurance career' of that person. The calculation of these amounts is with the application of the rules of overlapping, mentioned in Articles 53 to 55.

The third step is to compare the national benefit and the pro-rata benefit for each country. The highest amount for each country is applied, *see* Article 52. It may vary from country to country which amount is the highest.

In case of Type A schemes, the value of the independent pension depends on its place in the series of countries the person worked in. If the Type A scheme is the last scheme in which the person was insured (and s/he was insured under that scheme at the time of materialisation of the risk), the independent benefit is the full Type A pension. This benefit is the same as the theoretical amount, since this is the benefit the person would receive if she had fulfilled his or her whole insured life under that scheme. The pro-rata amount is thus, by definition, less than the independent amount.

If a Type A scheme is not the last scheme where a person was insured, e.g. s/he was first insured in Type A and then in Type B, the outcome is different. In that case the independent benefit is zero; since the pension has to be calculated according to national rules and since the person is not insured at the moment the risk materialises, s/he is not entitled to benefit. The theoretical amount is the same as the person would receive as if s/he had fulfilled his or her total career in this country, so that is the same as if the Type A benefit was the last one in the row. The pro-rata benefit is in this case always higher then the independent amount.

Example. Clara worked twenty years in Netherlands (Type A) and ten years in Germany (Type B). She becomes disabled in Germany. The theoretical amount of the Dutch pension is 75% of the last earned wages (suppose the wage was 3,000 euros, then the pension is 2250). The pro-rata fraction is two-thirds (twenty years out of thirty were spent in the Netherlands). The pro-rata amount for the Netherlands pension is, therefore, 2/3 of 2250, 1500. The national income would have been zero euro, as she was not insured at the moment of materialisation of the risk, i.e. under the national rules she would not have been entitled to benefit. For Germany, the pro-rata amount is one-third of the German theoretical amount.

The third step is to compare the national benefit and the pro rata benefit. The highest amount is applied. In the example of Clara the highest amount for the Netherlands is the pro-rata amount. Suppose that the situation was reversed: the first period was worked in Germany and the second in the Netherlands. In that case the national pension is highest. As we have already seen, this effect will always occur in the case of Type A schemes. When the Type A Scheme is the last scheme a person has been subject to, the national pension is always the highest.

The sum of the pensions calculated in the last mode is the German pro-rata pension plus the full Dutch benefit. This sum may even be higher than the previously earned income.

Therefore the rules against overlapping have to be applied. These were discussed in Chapter 12. As we have seen, the national rules against overlapping are only applicable if they make an express reference to foreign benefits. A second important rule is that the overlapping rules for benefits of the same kind are different from those for benefits of a different kind. Furthermore the overlapping rules can apply to independent benefits only if the benefit concerned is:

- a benefit the amount of which does not depend on the duration of periods of insurance or residence; or
- a benefit the amount of which is determined on the basis of a credited period deemed to have been completed between the date on which the risk materialised and a later date
  which overlaps with

- a benefit of the same type (unless an agreement between two or more Member States to avoid the same credited period being taken into account more than once); or
- benefits the amount of which does not depend on the duration of periods of insurance or benefit.

This means in Clara's example (last mode) that the Dutch pension is paid to her. The German pension is paid to the Dutch benefit administration. If the German pension exceeds the Dutch one, the excess is paid to Clara.

Example. Sarah has been insured by a German (Type B) and Dutch scheme (no relation between period of insurance and amount of benefit). She receives an independent benefit under the Dutch scheme since she was insured under this scheme when the risk materialises. Suppose that she is considered partially disabled and the amount of benefit is 800 euro. Suppose the German amount is 1000. The Dutch can deduct the German amount and have to pay the surplus: Sarah receives in total 1000 euro.

Article 50(2) provides that if at a given moment the person concerned does not satisfy, or no longer satisfies, the conditions laid down by all the legislations of the Member States to which he has been subject, the other Member States shall not take into account, when performing the calculation in accordance with Article 52(1) (a) or (b), the periods completed under the legislations the conditions of which have not been satisfied, or are no longer satisfied, where this gives rise to a lower amount of benefit.

Example 1. A person becomes disabled while insured under Type B schemes.

Peter has been insured in Italy (10 years) and Germany (5 years) successively. Suppose that for the Italian system he is not considered disabled and for the German scheme his disability is accepted. As a result he would receive only the pro-rata pension (5/15th of the German theoretical amount. Article 50(2) means that the Italian period is not taken into account.

Example 2. Type A is the last one.

If Peter has been insured in Italy (10 years) and Estonia (5 years) successively. Suppose, for the Italian system he is not considered disabled, whereas he is disabled for the Estonian one. Estonia has a Type A scheme. Even if he is not considered disabled under the Italian scheme, he receives the full Estonian benefit. This has to do with the *Petroni* principle. The only effect is that the benefit administration cannot deduct the Type B benefits under the rules of overlapping. This effect also occur if the scheme does not make is not mentioned in the Annex, e.g. if instead of under an Estonian scheme Peter became disabled under a Dutch scheme (no link between insurance period and benefit, but not listed in the Annex). Also here the *Petroni* principle leads to this outcome.

13.5. RECALCULATION OF BENEFITS

Article 59(2) provides that if, by reason of an increase in the cost of living or changes in the level of income or other grounds for adjustment, the benefits of the State concerned are altered by a percentage or fixed amount, such percentage or fixed amount must be applied directly to the benefits determined under Article 52, without the need for a recalculation.

In other words, if the pensions are adjusted on the basis of social-economic factors, the percentage or amount does not lead to a recalculation. Thus, if the amount of a foreign pension is raised in order to take account of the costs of living, the other Member State cannot absorb this rise by recalculating its own benefit. If, however, the amount of the pension is changed because of changes in personal circumstances, such as the level of invalidity or the family situation, a recalculation on the basis of Article 52 is possible.

The limitation of Article 59 on the recalculation of pensions is mostly to the advantage of the beneficiaries.

Article 59(1) rules that if the national rules for determining benefits or calculating them are altered or if the personal situation of the person concerned undergoes a relevant change which would lead, under that legislation, to an adjustment of the amount of benefit, a recalculation has to be carried out, in accordance with Article 52.

13.6. TRANSITION OF INVALIDITY BENEFITS TO OLD-AGE BENEFITS

The legislations of Member States vary in at which age persons are awarded old age benefit. Thus in some Member States persons retire at an earlier age than others. In order to avoid problems because of the differences in pension age, the Regulation has some coordination rules, found in Article 48. Article 48 makes a difference between Type A and Type B schemes.

If an old age or disability benefit is awarded on the basis of article 50 (a Type B benefit), the rules apply of Chapter 5. If a State terminates a disability benefit because the person concerned becomes entitled to an old age benefit, the other States have to continue to pay disability benefit until the person becomes entitled to old age benefit (or does no longer satisfy the conditions for disability benefit).

If a person has been awarded a disability benefit based on Article 44, the rules are more complicated. If such a disability benefit is replaced by an old age benefit and the other States where the person was not insured do not (yet) award an old age pension, these other Member States have to grant a disability benefit until the person concerned is entitled to an old age pension in these States. They must apply the fiction that the person became disabled under a Type B scheme and calculate their pensions on the basis of this fiction.

If, however, a Member State with a Type A scheme has awarded a disability benefit and the person concerned receives an old age benefit from another Member State, this would lead to an accumulation of benefits. Therefore the State with the Type A scheme has to recalculate benefits on the basis of the rules of Chapter 5.

13.7. THE PROBLEM OF DIFFERENCES IN WAITING PERIODS

Many Member States have a system in which a person who becomes incapacitated for work is first entitled to sickness benefit and then to disability benefit, provided s/he satisfies the conditions of these schemes. This may mean that a migrant is confronted with differences in waiting periods.

Example. Leonard is entitled to Dutch disability benefit after a period of twenty-four months. In Germany he receives sickness benefit during a period of 78 weeks before he is entitled to German disability benefit. Suppose that he first worked in the Netherlands and then in Germany. After 78 weeks he is entitled to a German disability benefit. For a Dutch pro-rata benefit he has to fulfil another 26 weeks of the waiting-period, since the Dutch waiting-period is twenty-four months. This is problematic for the person concerned in particular in the case when the period of insurance is Germany has been short compared to the Dutch one. In that case the German disability benefit is low and this person has a low income during the last part of the waiting period. Remember that this person is not entitled to a Dutch sickness benefit, since for this benefit the integration principle applies. In the reversed case, in which a person first is insured in Germany and then in the Netherlands, there is no problem with the waiting period. In this case rules against overlapping may apply (Dutch sickness and German disability benefits overlap).

The issue of differences in waiting periods was the topic of the *Leyman* judgment.[7] This judgment concerns a person who was first insured in Belgium and then in Luxembourg. According to the coordination and national rules, she was immediately (so without waiting period) awarded a Luxemburg invalidity benefit. This benefit was related to the duration of her insurance, which was low in this case. She was also entitled to a Belgian disability benefit, but this could be paid only after a waiting-period of one year. Since she was subject to the Luxembourg system, she had to rely on the small disability pension during the waiting period.

The Court considered that, as regards freedom of movement for workers, (what is now) Article 48 TFEU leaves in being differences between the Member States' social security systems. It follows that substantive and procedural differences between the social security systems of individual Member States are

---

[7]   Case C-3/08, not yet published.

unaffected by Article 48. It is not, however, in dispute that the aim of Article 45 TFEU would not be met if, through exercising their right to freedom of movement, migrant workers were to lose social security advantages guaranteed to them by the laws of a Member State, as this would negatively affect their right to freedom of movement. This would constitute an obstacle to that freedom. The law at stake caused a disadvantage during the first year of incapacity for workers as Ms Leyman compared with workers who are also definitively or permanently incapable of work but who have not exercised their right to freedom of movement. Workers who are in a situation such as that of Ms Leyman have paid social contributions on which there is no return so far as the first year of incapacity is concerned. The Treaty offers no guarantee to a worker that extending his or her activities into more than one Member State or transferring them to another Member State will be neutral as regards social security. Given the disparities in the social security legislation of the Member States, such an extension or transfer may be to the worker's advantage in terms of social security or not, according to circumstance. It follows that, even where its application is less favourable, such legislation is still compatible with Articles 45 if it does not place the worker at a disadvantage as compared with those who pursue all their activities in the Member State where it applies or as compared with those who were already subject to it and if it does not simply result in the payment of social security contributions on which there is no return.[8]

The application of the Belgian law in question is contrary to Community law, given that, firstly, it places that worker at a disadvantage in relation to those who are in the same situation of definitive incapacity to work but who have not exercised their right of freedom of movement and, secondly, it results in payment of social contributions on which there is no return. Where such a difference in legislation exists, the principle of cooperation in good faith laid down in Article 10 EC requires the competent authorities in the Member States to use all the means at their disposal to achieve the aim of Article 45 TFEU.

So, if persons are worse off as a result of cross border movement and they receive not benefit even if they paid contributions for it, this is inconsistent with the Treaty. It is up to the Member States to find a solution.

13.8. BENEFITS FOR ACCIDENTS AT WORK AND OCCUPATIONAL DISEASES

A special type of long term benefits concerns benefits for accidents at work and occupational diseases (Chapter 2 of the Regulation). When a person has been insured in more than one Member State, these benefits are not coordinated as partial pensions. Instead the integration principle applies, meaning, according to

---

[8] This was also decided in Cases C-393/99 and C-394/99 *Hervein and Others* [2002], *ECR* I-2829.

the provisions of the Regulation, that some of the coordination rules on sickness benefits apply (discussed in Chapter 11 *supra)* unless Chapter 2 of the Regulation gives more favourable rules (Article 36).

The coordination rules on sickness benefits which apply to this category are the following:

- Article 17, which provides that benefits in kind are provided according to the legislation of the State of residence.
- Article 18(1), which provides that benefits in kind can also be obtained in the competent State.
- Article 19(1), which provides that entitlement to benefits in kind in the State of stay if the benefits become necessary)
- Article 20(1), which concerns planned care.

Thus, if a person is insured in a country with a scheme for accidents at work and resides in another country, s/he is entitled to the benefits in kind available under the legislation of the State of residence; if s/he stays in the competent State, s/he can claim benefits in kind in that State.

The person who has sustained an accident at work or has contracted an occupational disease and who resides or stays in a Member State other than the competent Member State is entitled to the special benefits in kind of the scheme covering accidents at work and occupational diseases provided, on behalf of the competent institution, by the institution of the place of residence or stay in accordance with the legislation which it applies, as though s/he were insured under the said legislation.

For instance, if a person has been insured in a State without a scheme for occupational accidents and resides in a State having such scheme, s/he can claim benefits in kind under that scheme (e.g. for the rehabilitation of persons suffering from the effects of accidents at work).

Article 36 also provides that Article 21 – concerning the sickness benefits in cash – applies to the benefits for accidents at work and occupational diseases.

A special rule is that the competent institution of a Member State whose legislation provides for meeting the costs of transporting a person who has sustained an accident at work or is suffering from an occupational disease, either to his or her place of residence or to a hospital, has to meet such costs to the corresponding place in another Member State where the person resides, provided that that institution gives prior authorisation for such transport, duly taking into account the reasons justifying it. Such authorisation must not be required in the case of a frontier worker.

If a person suffers from an occupational disease has been exposed to the same risk in several Member States, the benefits that s/he or his or her survivors may claim have to be provided exclusively under the legislation of the last of those States whose conditions are satisfied. This makes it much easier for the person concerned to claim benefits.

If there is no insurance against accidents at work or occupational diseases in the Member State in which the person concerned resides or stays, or if such insurance exists but there is no institution responsible for providing benefits in kind, those benefits are provided by the institution of the place of residence or stay which is responsible for providing benefits in kind in the event of sickness. If there is no insurance against accidents at work or occupational diseases in the competent Member State, the provisions of this Chapter concerning benefits in kind shall nevertheless be applied to a person who is entitled to those benefits in the event of sickness, maternity or equivalent paternity under the legislation of that Member State if that person sustains an accident at work or suffers from an occupational disease during a residence or stay in another Member State. The costs have to be borne by the institution which is competent for the benefits in kind under the legislation of the competent Member State.

Article 35 (on the reimbursement of sickness benefits) applies also to the benefits of this section, reimbursement is made on the basis of actual costs (Article 41). However, two or more Member States, or their competent authorities, may provide for other methods of reimbursement or waive all reimbursement between the institutions under their jurisdiction.

13.9. SPECIAL NON-CONTRIBUTORY BENEFITS FOR INVALIDITY

As we have seen in Chapter 5, there are also special non contributory benefits for invalidity. For these benefits special coordination rules apply. Article 3(3) of Regulation 883/2004 provides that the Regulation applies to these special non-contributory benefits covered by Article 70. Article 70 reads that it applies to special non-contributory cash benefits which are provided under legislation which, because of its personal scope, objectives and/or conditions for entitlement, has characteristics both of the social security legislation referred to in Article 3(1) and of social assistance. For the purposes of this Chapter, Article 70 continues, special non-contributory cash benefits include those which provide solely specific protection for the disabled, closely linked to the said person's social environment in the Member State concerned, and where the financing exclusively derives from compulsory taxation.

For these benefits the export provision (Article 7) does not apply; neither do the other Chapters of Title III apply, i.e. the specific coordination rules for the benefits dealt with in this title. Therefore, these benefits are not calculated according to rules of Sections 12.2 and 12.3, but are coordination on the basis of the integration principle.

Article 70(4) provides that these benefits have to be provided exclusively in the Member State in which the persons concerned reside, in accordance with its legislation and they have to be provided by and at the expense of the institution of the place of residence. Consequently, the special non-contributory benefits are not exportable and the legislation of the State of residence determines whether one receives these benefits or not. This is a disadvantage for persons leaving a Member State having such type of benefit. It has also advantages for persons coming from outside, they become entitled to these benefits, even if the risk (e.g. disability) materialised already when they were outside the territory of the country where they wish to claim benefit.

CHAPTER 14

FAMILY BENEFITS

14.1. INTRODUCTION

Regulation 1408/71 made a distinction between family benefits and family allowances. Family benefits were all benefits in kind or in cash intended to meet family expenses; family allowances pertain to periodical cash benefits which are exclusively granted by reference to the number and, where appropriate, the age of the members of the family. The distinction in terms was relevant, as some provisions were relevant to family allowances only.

Fortunately, Regulation 883/2004 has simplified this Chapter and uses the term family benefits only. Article 1(z) defines family benefits as all benefits in kind or in cash intended to meet family expenses, excluding advances of maintenance payments and special childbirth and adoption allowances (as mentioned in Annex 1).

Note that as a result of this definition not all benefits payable to a member of the family are family benefits; they have to be intended to meet family expenses. Thus an invalidity benefit for the young handicapped paid to a child of a worker is not a family benefit or allowance, as it is paid to disabled persons only. The qualification of benefits is important, as this special benefit is not exportable, whereas family benefits have to be exported.

Another type of benefit which was subject of a dispute whether it was a family benefit or not was the child raising benefit. The case concerned child-raising allowance (*Erziehungsgeld*), a non-contributory benefit, discussed in the *Hoever and Zachow* judgment.[1] In order to be entitled to this benefit a person must be permanently or ordinarily resident in Germany. In addition s/he must bring up a dependent child in his or her household and must have no, at least no full-time, employment. The German government argued that the child-raising allowance was intended, by conferring a personal right, to remunerate the particular parent who both takes on the task of raising a child and personally fulfils the conditions for the granting of the allowance. Therefore the Government argued that it was not a family benefit.

The Court did not accept this argument. The aim of this type of benefit is, it argued, to meet family expenses, the same criterion as used in Regulation

---

[1]   Case 245/94, [1996] *ECR* I-4895.

883/2004. Child-raising allowance is paid only where the family of the person concerned contains one or more children. Furthermore, its amount varies partly according to the age and number of the children, and also according to the parents' income. Second, this type of benefit is intended to enable one of the parents to devote himself to the raising of a young child. Consequently, a benefit such as the child-raising allowance must be treated as a family benefit. We will further discuss this judgment in Section 14.3.

Also in the case of the Swedish parental benefit, it had to be investigated whether this was a type of family benefit; this lead to the *Kuusijärvi* judgment.[2] The Swedish government first argued that this was a maternity benefit; after the *Hoever and Zachow* judgment, the Government argued that the benefit at issue had to be regarded as a family benefit. It is paid for a maximum of 450 days by reason of the birth of a child and applies until the child reaches the age of eight, during which time one of the parents has the right not to work.

The Court concluded that these rules show that parental benefit is intended, on the one hand to enable the parents to devote themselves, in alternation, to the care of the young child until that child has started to attend school. On the other hand, it was intended to offset to some extent the loss of income entailed for the parent devoting himself to the care of the child in temporarily giving up his occupational activity. Therefore, it is indeed a family benefit.

In the *Humer* judgment the question was raised whether advances on the maintenance payments for children are within the scope of the Regulation.[3] The Court answered that the expression 'to meet family expenses' is to be interpreted as referring, in particular, to a public contribution to a family's budget to alleviate the financial burdens involved in the maintenance. The present advance was meant to ensure the maintenance of minor children in cases where their mothers are left alone with their children and, in addition to the heavy burden of raising their children, find themselves faced with the additional difficulty of obtaining maintenance for them from the father. Therefore this benefit constitutes a family benefit under this case law. However, the drafters of Regulation 883/2004 have departed from this case law by the definition of family benefits which was quoted supra. Advances of maintenance payments are thus no longer family benefits for the Regulation.

14.2. WHICH BENEFIT LEVEL: THAT OF THE STATE OF EMPLOYMENT OR RESIDENCE?

Family benefits constitute a special type of benefits. Unlike, for example, invalidity or unemployment benefits, it is not primarily the situation of the employed or

---

[2]   Case 275/96, [1998] *ECR* I-3443.
[3]   Case 255/99, [2002] *ECR* I-1205.

self-employed person himself which is relevant; benefit is paid for a third person. Consequently, the situation of family members has to be taken into account in deciding where benefit is to be paid. Family benefits are intended to meet family expenses and this is why the relationship between these benefits and the actual living standards and domestic situation of the claimant is much more relevant than in the case of other benefits.

This specific character is reflected in national conditions for entitlement to this kind of benefit: the majority of national schemes do not contain conditions as to the completion of periods of insurance in order for a person to be entitled to these benefits. If there are such conditions the general aggregation rule of the Regulation applies.

This type of benefit raises, however, another, more ideological, problem: is it to be paid at the rate of the State of residence or at that of the State of employment? In other words, should the amount of benefit be fixed at that payable in the State where the child resides or at that of the State where the employed person works? This question is not as easy to answer as it may seem. The application of the State of employment rate ensures equal treatment of workers who are employed in the same State. However, this equality exists to a relative extent only. If the differences between the living standards of the Member States are taken as a starting-point, on the basis of the equality principle one might as well argue for unequal treatment, that is for a calculation of child benefit in accordance with the rate of the State of residence.

The coordination Regulation does not, however, have the objective of creating equality in every respect – various examples of which we have seen in the previous chapters – but of creating equality of treatment between foreign workers and domestic workers in the State of employment. Article 48 TFEU, the legal basis of this Regulation, ensures the export of benefits rather than equal treatment in every situation. Consequently, the Regulation has opted for the level of the State of employment.

The Court decided in the *First Pinna* judgment,[4] discussed in Chapter 10, that the provision of the Regulation, which required that the State of residence benefit level be used in the case of French benefits, was contrary to the Treaty, now Article 45 TFEU. This case law prompted the Council to make a uniform regulation for all Member States which requires for all Member States the State of employment principle.[5]

---

[4]   Case 41/84, [1986] *ECR* 1.
[5]   Regulation 3427/89, *OJ L* 331/1.

14.3. COMPETENT STATE AND OVERRULING OF RESIDENCE REQUIREMENTS

Article 67 provides that a person is entitled to family benefits in accordance with the legislation of the competent Member State, including for his family members residing in another Member State, as if they are residing in the former Member State. With the phrase 'as if they were residing in that State', this Article overrules residence requirements in national schemes. This is a reminiscence of the export rule of Regulation 1408/71, since the general residence provision of the Regulation would already have this effect. Note that the competent State is determined on the basis in Articles 11-16.

For pensioners there is a separate rule, a pensioner is entitled to family benefits in accordance with the legislation of the Member State competent for his pension.

In Regulation 1408/71 this export rule was limited to employed and (since 1989) self-employed persons. The extension to all nationals, which is in line with the approach of the new Regulation, may have its largest effects in the area of family benefits.

In the *Humer* case,[6] discussed in Section 14.1, the question was raised, whether a minor child comes within the personal scope of the Regulation and can thus enforce a right to family benefits. The Court answered that at the material time the applicant was 'a member of the family' of each of her parents and thus comes within the personal scope of the Regulation. The purpose of (now) Article 67 is precisely to guarantee members of the family residing in a Member State other than the competent State the grant of the family benefits provided for by the applicable legislation. Admittedly, the Regulation does not expressly cover family situations following a divorce, but there is nothing to justify the exclusion of such situations from the scope of the Regulation. This interpretation is still relevant even now the material national benefit is no longer covered by the Regulation.

In the *Bronzino* judgment[7] the question was raised whether (what is now) Article 67 could overrule residence conditions in additional conditions for family benefits. The German law required that children between sixteen and twenty-one years of age be registered as unemployed persons in the territory to which the family benefits law is applicable (*i.e.* Germany). Mr Bronzino's children were registered with the Italian employment services. The Court ruled that Article 67 is intended to prevent a Member State from refusing family benefits on the grounds that the children of an employed person are residing in a Member State other than the competent State. If this was not the case, the employed person concerned would be impeded in his right to free movement. This is why it is to be assumed that the condition that a person must be available to the employment services of the State that grants the benefit is within the scope of Article 67. Consequently,

---

[6]   Case 255/99, [2002] *ECR* I-1205.
[7]   Case 228/88, [1990] *ECR* 531.

this condition is also fulfilled if the member of the family is available to the employment services of the State of residence.

In Section 14.1 we discussed the *Hoever and Zachow* judgment[8] and promised to come back to this judgment. The problem in this case was whether the claimants concerned were also entitled to the child-raising benefit outside the territory of Germany. In order to be entitled to this benefit it was required that the person resided in Germany or worked in Germany for at least fifteen hours a week. Mrs Hoever and Zachow did not satisfy this condition as they lived in the Netherlands and did not work or worked for less than fifteen hours a week. The Court considered that these conditions could deter a worker from exercising the right to freedom of movement. Consequently, it would be contrary to the purpose and spirit of (what is now) Article 67 of the Regulation to deprive a worker's spouse of a benefit to which he would have been entitled if the spouse had remained in the State providing that benefit. As a result, they could receive the child-raising allowance in the Netherlands.[9]

14.4. PRIORITY RULES

14.4.1. INTRODUCTION

One of the consequences of the specific character of family benefits, *i.e.* that these are granted on behalf of dependent persons, is the possibility of concurrence of entitlements to family benefit from two States when both parents are working. Article 68 gives priority rules to prevent the overlapping of benefits for the same child for the same periods.

The rule starts with the situation that benefits are paid by more than one Member State on different bases. The basis concerns the typology of the schemes: a scheme of country x may cover all workers, another scheme of country w may cover all residents. The order of priority is as follows. First rights available on the basis of an activity as an employed or self-employed person are paid. Secondly, the rights available on the basis of receipt of a pension are paid. Finally, rights obtained on the basis of residence are paid.

Decision F1 of the Administrative Commission provides that 'available on the basis of an activity as an employed or self-employed person' includes the period of temporary suspension of such an activity as an employed or self-employed person; and sickness, maternity, accident at work, occupational disease or unemployment, as long as wages or benefits, excluding pensions, are payable

---

8   Case 245/94, [1996] *ECR* I-4895.
9   As was apparent in the *Martínez Sala* case (Section 10.6), Germany appeared to be unhappy with this judgment and it tried to convince the Court to come back from its case law. The Court refused to do so as this request was not based on any arguments.

in respect of these contingencies; or (ii) during paid leave, strike or lock-out; or (iii) during unpaid leave for the purpose of child-raising, as long as this leave is deemed equivalent to such an activity as an employed or self-employed person in accordance with the relevant legislation.[10]

Example. The father works in country x where the scheme awards benefits on the basis of an employees' scheme to those who are employed. The mother does not work and lives in country y with a scheme where family benefits are paid to all residents. Family benefits from country x have priority.

Article 68(1)(b) concerns the situation that benefits are payable by more than one Member State on the same basis. Thus, for instance, two countries are involved which have both schemes which cover employed persons only. Or there are two countries both having residence schemes.

The order of priority is then established by referring to the following criteria. In the case of rights available on the basis of an activity as an employed or self-employed person, the place of residence of the children is relevant, provided that there is such activity. So if country x has an employees scheme and country y as well, and the children live in country x and one of the parents works in that country this country has priority. If this is not the case the State with the highest amount of benefits has to pay these. In the latter case, the cost of benefits is shared in accordance with criteria laid down in the Implementing Regulation.[11]

If family benefits are available on the basis of receipt of pensions, the place of residence of the children is decisive, provided that a pension is payable under its legislation. Otherwise it is the State in which the longest period of insurance or residence under the conflicting legislations was spent. In the case of rights available on the basis of residence, the place of residence of the children is decisive.

Example. The father works in Member State *A* and the mother works in Member State *B*, the family also lives in B. Both schemes have a right to family benefit on the basis of employment. Member State B (the place of residence of the children) has priority.

Suppose the father lives in Member State *A* and the mother lives in Member State *B, and* the children also live in B, and both States have a residence scheme. Priority is given to Member State *B,* the State of residence of the children.

In the *Dammer* judgment[12] a lacuna was discovered in the provisions of Regulation 1408/71. It appeared that the Regulation did not contain provisions for a situation in which the child resides in a State other than the States where the parents work. Mr Dammer worked in Belgium and Mrs Dammer worked in Germany whereas they both lived with their child in the Netherlands.

---

[10]   OJ C 106/12 of 2010.
[11]   See for a 'provocative' interpretation of these rules, S. Devetzi, 'The Coordination of Family Benefits by Regulation 883/2004', *EJSS* 2009, p. 205.
[12]   Case 168/88, [1989] *ECR* 4553.

Mr Dammer applied for family benefits in Belgium. The Court considered that as the provisions of the Regulation did not give any guidance as to where benefit could be claimed, the principles underlying Article 42 EC, what is now Article 48 TFEU, were to be considered. It referred to the *Petroni* judgment,[13] in which it held that the objectives of Articles 45 to 48 TFEU would not be attained if employed persons, as a result of exercising their right to free movement, would be deprived of advantages in the field of social security, which are guaranteed by the legislation of the Member State where they reside. In the present case, the Court sought an analogous solution. It decided that the employed person is entitled to a supplement amounting to the difference between the two benefits at the expense of the competent institution of the Member State which was the first to award a right to benefit. In the Member State where the person at a later date acquired a right to benefit, benefit is thus suspended, insofar as the amount of that benefit is higher than the amount in the first State. The result of this case law is that the costs of child benefit (apart from a supplement) are borne by the Member State which is the first to award benefit.Subsequently, the Regulation was amended.[14] The approach of Regulation 1408/71 (the highest amount is paid, with a cost sharing provision) is followed in Regulation 883/2004, as we saw above.

In order to (try to) ensure a smooth functioning of the rules, Article 68(3) provides that if a claim is submitted to the competent institution of a Member State whose legislation does not have priority that institution has to forward the application without delay to the competent institution of the Member State whose legislation is applicable by priority. It also has to inform the person concerned and to provide, if necessary, the differential supplement mentioned in the following section.

The Relationship between the Rules for Determining the Legislation applicable and the Export Rules

The relationship between the rules for determining the legislation applicable and the export rules was discussed in the *Una McMenamin* judgment.[15] Mrs Una McMenamin was a frontier worker who worked as a teacher in Northern Ireland (UK) and resided with her husband and her children in Ireland. Her husband was employed in Ireland. The Irish legislation confers entitlement to child allowance on the person with whom the child normally lives. If the child lives with its father and its mother, the law provides that it is the child's mother who is entitled to

---

13 Case 24/75, [1975] *ECR* 1149.

14 A new Article 10(3) of Regulation 574/72 provided that, the Member State whose legislation grants the highest benefit pays the full amount, whereas the other Member State refunds, within the limits of the amounts provided for in that legislation, half this amount. The new article was inserted by Regulation 1945/93, *OJ L* 181/1. This is a better rule than the one designed by the Court, as in the approach of the Court the State which was the first to pay had to bear the highest charges. The new rule gives a better division of costs.

15 Case 119/91, [1992] *ECR* I-6393.

the allowance. When Mrs McMenamin applied for benefit, the adjudication officer decided that she was entitled only to a supplement, namely the amount necessary to bring the family allowances payable to her under the corresponding Irish legislation up to the level of child benefit under the United Kingdom law. The Court ruled that the provision that a person is subject to the legislation of one Member State only, as laid down in (what is now)Article 11, does not prevent particular benefits from being governed by more specific rules of the Regulation, in this case (what is now) Article 67 of the Regulation. Consequently, in this case the right to child benefit of the mother from United Kingdom is suspended, and the latter State has to pay a supplement if the Irish benefit is lower than the British benefit.

In the *Huijbrechts* judgment,[16] the Court decided that the rules of Title III (to which Article 67 belongs) do not determine which State is the competent one; the rules of Title II only determine/ the competent State which is, in general, the State of employment. The rules of Title III are supplementary rules.

14.4.2. DIFFERENTIAL SUPPLEMENTS

In the preceding section we discussed the priority rules. The effect of these rules is that the right under a scheme which does not have priority is suspended. It may happen, however, that the suspended benefit is higher than the scheme which has priority. Already under Regulation 1408/71 the Court decided that this was contrary to the Treaty, as we will discuss below. Regulation 1408/71 was amended in order to supplement the difference. Also Regulation 883/2004 has such rules. Article 68(2) provides that if entitlements to family benefits by virtue of other conflicting legislation or legislations are suspended up to the amount provided for by the first legislation, a differential supplement is provided, if necessary, for the sum which exceeds this amount. As a result the family receives family benefits from two countries.

Example. The father works in country x and the children live with the mother in country y, whereas both are employees schemes. Suppose that family benefits are 300 in x and 200 in y. In this example, 200 euro are paid by y and a supplement of 100 is due from x.

However, a differential supplement does not need to be provided for children residing in another Member State when entitlement to the benefit in question is based on residence only.

The requirement that a supplement has to be paid is based on earlier case law of the Court, *i.e.* the *Ferraioli* judgment.[17] The Court considered that as a general

---

[16]   Case 131/95, [1997] *ECR* I-1418.
[17]   Case 153/84, [1986] *ECR* 1401.

rule migrant workers may not lose benefit rights acquired on the basis of national legislation alone. The rules against overlapping of benefits form an exception to this principle, but the reduction of benefits must not be more than what the beneficiary actually receives.

Benefits must also be supplemented when the right to child benefit is not based on national law alone, but if the Regulation has to be invoked as well, *e.g.* for allowing export, if this is not possible under national rules. This was decided in the *Beeck* judgment.[18] In this case German family benefits were suspended, since Mr Beeck's wife received child benefit on the basis of Danish Law. The German benefit was higher than the Danish child benefit. Therefore, Mr Beeck applied for a supplement. The German benefit was, however, not a benefit Mr Beeck would have received on the basis of national law alone, as the German law did not provide for benefits outside the territory of Germany. Consequently, he needed to rely on the export rule for family benefits. The Court decided that a supplement has to be paid, even though no national benefits *stricto sensu* were involved.

A broad interpretation of 'rights acquired under national legislation' can be found in the *Athanasopoulos* judgment.[19] One of the questions raised was whether a supplement also had to be granted for a child born after the return of the pensioner to the State of origin. The Court replied in the affirmative to this question. Again it referred to the objective of the coordination Regulation, namely the free movement of workers. If workers had to keep their residence in a Member State in order not to lose part of the amount of the benefits to which they would be entitled to in that State, the free movement of workers would be impeded.

A further problem emerged because national legislation provided that the amount of benefit could be reduced in accordance with the *national* income of the beneficiary and of the members of the family. The Court considered that if the legislation of the Member State which has to pay the benefits contains a possibility of reduction, such a reduction is also possible when the beneficiary resides in a State other than that Member State. If it is the legislation of the Member State from which the *supplement* is claimed which contains such a provision, this provision may also be applied. The amount of benefits actually received from the new State of residence has then to be compared to the amount of benefits which would have been received if the beneficiary had not transferred his residence. The Member State which has to pay the benefits or the supplements has to apply the national rules as if the beneficiary and the members of his family reside in its territory.

As was mentioned *supra*, according to the case law of the Court, the supplement has to be paid if family allowances are due according to the national law alone. In the *Bastos Moriana* judgment[20] the Court clarified this rule. The

---

[18]   Case 104/80, [1981] *ECR* 503.
[19]   Case 251/89, [1991] *ECR* I-2797.
[20]   Case 59/95, [1997] *ECR* I-1096.

applicants, of Spanish nationality, worked for various periods in Germany, where they paid compulsory contributions to the workers' pension scheme. Several years after returning to Spain, they became incapacitated for working. They were awarded a German invalidity pension, following the aggregation of the periods of insurance completed in Germany and in other Member States. The German family allowances were suspended. They applied for a supplement from the German benefit agency inasmuch the suspended German benefit was higher than the Spanish one. The Court considered that its case law concerning supplements was based on the principle that the objective of Articles 39 to 42 EC would not be achieved if, as a consequence of the exercise of their right to freedom of movement, workers were to lose social security advantages guaranteed to them in any event by the laws of a single Member State (this case law is in accordance with, in particular, the *Petroni* judgment, *see* Chapter 12 of this book). Consequently, the Articles concerned were interpreted as meaning that the principle of a single State responsible for payment is subject, as regards family benefits, to an exception requiring the other Member State to grant a supplement.[21] Having regard to the reasoning underlying that exception, the Court continued, its scope cannot be widened in such a way that a supplement must be also granted where the entitlement of the pensioner or orphan exists only by virtue of the application of the aggregation rules of the Regulation. In that situation, the application of the Articles does not deprive the persons concerned of the benefits granted under the laws of another Member State alone. Consequently, the competent institution of a Member State is not bound to grant a supplement to pensioners or orphans residing in another Member State where the amount of family benefits is lower, if entitlement to the pension has not been acquired solely by virtue of insurance periods completed in that State. The Court added that this decision is consistent with the *Athanasopoulos* decision, discussed *supra*, in which it argued that the supplement also has to be paid when the children where born after transfer of residence. This decision does not affect the case law that entitlement to a supplement presupposes entitlement to a pension acquired solely under national legislation.

---

[21]   This was established in the *Laterza* judgment, Case 733/79, [1980] *ECR* 1915.

CHAPTER 15

UNEMPLOYMENT BENEFITS

15.1. THE TERM UNEMPLOYMENT BENEFITS

Article 1 of the Regulation gives a definition of some types of benefit, including pre-retirement benefit and family benefit. Unemployment benefit is, however, not defined. This is regrettable, since it is not always clear when a benefit does or does not qualify as unemployment benefit. At first sight one may be inclined to say that this is a quite easy matter: unemployment benefit is a benefit payable to persons who have reduced, ceased or suspended their remunerative activities and are available to the labour market. In the *Acciardi* judgment[1] the Court mentioned these characteristics to conclude that the benefit concerned was an unemployment benefit. The Court decided that it was relevant that the right to benefit was restricted to unemployed persons; that it ended as soon as the beneficiary reached the statutory retirement age; that one became entitled to this benefit immediately upon expiration of the right to unemployment benefit under the Unemployment Benefits Act; and that the law imposed several conditions on the beneficiary which ensured that he was available for work. All these circumstances were relevant to this decision.

From later case law it appears, however, that the availability condition is not always decisive. Some unemployment benefit schemes exempt particular categories of beneficiaries from the obligation to seek work, such as persons over a particular age. It can then be disputed that the benefit in question is unemployment benefit. In answer to this, the Court decided in the *De Cuyper* case[2] that also such type of benefit can be unemployment benefit. The case concerned Mr De Cuyper who had obtained dispensation from the obligation to submit to the local control procedures imposed on unemployed persons. He wished to have the benefit exported, but export of unemployment benefits was limited in time. For this reason he argued that the benefit in question was not an unemployment benefit, but rather a preretirement benefit. The Court disagreed: the benefit was aimed at enabling the workers concerned to provide for themselves following an involuntary loss of employment when they still had the capacity for work. It added to this, that in order to distinguish between different categories of

---

[1]   Case 66/92, [1993] *ECR* I-4567.
[2]   Case 406/04, [2006] *ECR* I-6947.

social security benefits, the risk covered by each benefit must also be taken into consideration. Thus, an unemployment benefit covers the risk associated with the loss of revenue suffered by a worker following the loss of his employment when he is still able to work. A benefit granted if that risk materialises, namely loss of employment, and which is no longer payable if that situation ceases to exist as a result of the claimant engaging in paid employment, must be regarded as constituting an unemployment benefit. The benefit paid to Mr De Cuyper was calculated in the same way as for all unemployed persons, and had the same conditions on past employment as in the case of other recipients of the benefit. The benefit was subject to the Belgian statutory unemployment benefits scheme, and even if Mr De Cuyper did not have to register as a job-seeker or accept any suitable employment, he still had to remain available to those services so that his employment and family situation could be monitored. For all these reasons, the Court held that it was an unemployment benefit.

It follows from the *De Cuyper* judgment that a main criterion in labelling a benefit as unemployment benefit is whether benefit is part of a scheme for unemployment benefits and whether the person concerned has to be subject to monitoring by the employment services.[3] However, these criteria are not always helpful, for example, in cases in which partly different conditions apply for categories exempted from the condition to seek work. Furthermore, sometimes benefits require availability for work but are part of a disability benefit scheme. Disputes may arise easily on the qualification of such benefits.

In the *Meints* judgment[4] the question was whether a compensation benefit for redundant agricultural workers was an unemployment benefit. The Court considered, in deciding that this was not an unemployment benefit, that the recipient of the benefit at issue must repay it if he is reemployed by his former employer within twelve months following the termination of his contract of employment. Secondly, neither entitlement to the benefit nor the amount of this benefit is related to the length of the period of unemployment, since entitlement arises simply where the former contract of employment has been terminated and the recipient is unemployed when he receives the benefit. Thirdly, the benefit at issue is not a recurrent payment but is paid as a single fixed sum varying only in relation to the age of the applicant. It was clear, moreover, that the main purpose of this benefit was to provide support with regard to the social consequences

---

[3] The definition in Regulation 883/2004 of preretirement benefits may cause problems in this respect: preretirement benefits are all cash benefits, other than unemployment benefit or an early old age benefit, provided from a certain age to workers who have reduced, ceased or suspended their remunerative activities until the age at which they qualify for an old-age benefit or an early retirement benefit, the receipt of which is not conditional upon the person concerned being available to the employment services of the competent State (Article 1). This definition presupposes that we know what is meant by unemployment benefit, but it will be hard to distinguish between unemployment benefits, payable to those who do not have to be available for work, and preretirement benefits.

[4] Case 57/96, [1997] *ECR* I-6708.

of the structural reorganisation of the agricultural sector. It was thus intended as a redundancy payment.[5] As a result the benefit could not be refused, since it was an advantage under Regulation 1612/68 (see Chapter 9). If it were an unemployment benefit, it could have been refused since Mr Meints did not reside in the Netherlands (see below, on the frontier workers rule).

Not all elements which are part of an Unemployment Benefits Act fall under the term unemployment benefits in the Regulation. The Court considered in the *Mouthaan* judgment,[6] that benefits in case of insolvency of the employer are not unemployment benefits, because these do not have the character of compensating loss of wages after the start of the unemployment period.

A further category in which problems of qualification can occur is that of *reintegration schemes* for unemployed persons, for example schemes that provide training or allow unemployed persons to work while remaining in receipt of benefit. In the *Knoch* judgment the Court considered that unemployment benefits are those benefits that replace wages lost by unemployment, the objective of which is to provide an income for the costs of living of the employee.[7] It appears from the *Campana* judgment that these benefits comprise not only benefits in cash after the start of a period of unemployment, but also training benefits in the case of imminent unemployment.[8] The Court considered that the relevant articles have to be interpreted in the light of Article 51 EEC (now Article 48 TFEU), which is to establish the most favourable conditions for achieving freedom of movement and employment for Community workers within the territory of each Member State. In the light of the present economic situation, the Court added, the Member States have established assistance for vocational training intended both to enable persons in employment to improve their qualifications to avoid the threat of unemployment and to enable unemployed persons to retrain and find new employment. Both types of benefit are intended to combat unemployment. Consequently, it would be contrary to the aim of Article 48 TFEU to exclude from the scope of (what is now) Article 3 and Article 61 of the coordination Regulation, as a matter of principle, benefits intended to prevent future unemployment. However, the Court, added, Germany has rightly pointed out that benefits intended to encourage vocational training may also be directed at objectives other than the fight against unemployment, such as improving the personal circumstances of recipients or satisfying certain special needs of the economy. Consequently, the expression unemployment benefits must be restricted to assistance for vocational training which concerns either persons who are already unemployed or persons who are still in employment but are actually threatened by unemployment. The national authorities have to assess in each individual case whether a person in

---

[5]   *See* also Chapter 9, where we saw that Article 7(2) of Regulation 1612/58 is relevant to this payment.
[6]   Case 39/76, [1976] *ECR* 1901.
[7]   Case C-102/91, [1992] *ECR* I-4341.
[8]   Case 375/85, [1987] *ECR* 2387.

employment who applies for assistance for vocational training may be deemed to be actually threatened by unemployment.

Reintegration measures can thus be covered by the term unemployment benefits, but it remains unclear which measures are included and which are not. Whether they are covered by the Regulation may be relevant, for instance, if reintegration schemes require periods of insurance or employment for admittance; when reintegration measures are denied to, for instance, frontier workers; and when export of a reintegration provision to another Member State is sought.

The case law we have discussed in this section shows that there have been disputes on the term unemployment benefit. We may expect further cases on this issue, now that new types of benefits are being developed and the scope of the Chapter on unemployment benefits has been extended to schemes for the self-employed. It is therefore regrettable that no definition of unemployment benefits is included in the new Regulation.

15.2. OVERVIEW OF THE SYSTEM OF COORDINATION OF UNEMPLOYMENT BENEFITS

One important difference between the Unemployment Chapters of Regulation 883/2004 and Regulation 1408/71 concerns the personal scope of this chapter. When in 1989 the personal scope of Regulation 1408/71 was extended to self-employed persons, this extension did, with one exception (i.e. the export of unemployment benefit), not include unemployment benefits. As a result, a self-employed person, who consecutively worked in two Member States, could not aggregate periods of insurance or employment if s/he claimed benefit in the country of last employment[9] (suppose that State had a scheme for the self-employed). A self-employed who became entitled to unemployment benefit in a Member State could export this benefit in accordance with the export rules of the then Regulation (Article 69).

In Regulation 883/2004, all articles of the Unemployment Chapter are applicable to self-employed persons.

In view of the characteristics of unemployment benefits three articles of Regulation 883/2004, which lay down important general coordination principles, are not applicable to unemployment benefits. These are the following:
- Article 5: this Article requires, among other things, that if legislation of a Member State attributes legal effects to the occurrence of certain facts or

---

[9] By State of last employment is meant the State where the unemployed person last performed activities as an employed or self-employed person before becoming unemployed.

events, facts or events occurring in any Member State, these have to be treated in the same way;

- Article 6: this Article gives a general provision on the aggregation of periods; a State which makes the right to benefit conditional upon completion of periods of insurance, employment, self-employment or residence shall also take these periods into account when completed in another Member State;
- Article 7: this Article gives a general waiver of residence rules.

These articles all start with the phrase 'unless provided otherwise by this Regulation' and the Chapter on unemployment benefit makes use of this possibility to deviate from the main rules, as we will see below.

With respect to the coordination rules of unemployment benefits, three types of situations can be distinguished:

1. A person resides in the competent State. In other words, the State where he resides is the same as the competent State. For the rules in this situation, *see* Section 15.3;
2. A person works in one State and resides in another State, while he returns at least once a week to the State of residence, in other words, he is a frontier worker. This situation is dealt with in Section 15.4;
3. A third situation concerns a person for whom the competent State and the State of residence are not the same, and where the person concerned is not a frontier worker. For this situation, *see* Section 15.5.

15.3. THE UNEMPLOYED PERSON RESIDES IN THE COMPETENT STATE

The first situation which may occur is that the unemployed person resides in the competent State; as we have seen before, the competent State is the country which is assigned by the rules for determining the legislation applicable. This will often be the State where the person concerned has lately been employed, but that need not always be the case: posting or an Article 16 agreement may determine that a legislation other than that of the State of employment applies.

If the employee becomes unemployed in the competent State, and if s/he resides in that State, s/he will be paid only the unemployment benefits payable under the legislation of that State. Thus the integration principle applies to unemployment benefits and the person concerned cannot apply for benefits from States where s/he worked before.

Article 61 gives special rules on aggregation of periods of insurance, employment or self-employment which may be necessary in order to satisfy the conditions of the legislation of the competent State.

For the application of these aggregation rules, it is required that the person concerned has most recently completed periods of insurance, employment or self-employment in the State where s/he claims benefit, depending on which type the legislation requires. This rule is laid down in Article 61(2) of the Regulation, which corresponds to Article 67(3) of Regulation 1408/71. The unemployed person, therefore, cannot use the Regulation to apply for benefits from States in which he worked previously.[10]

Article 61 makes a distinction according to whether a national scheme requires periods of insurance, employment, or self-employment. It deviates therefore from the general aggregation rule of Article 6, discussed in Chapter 3. Instead, Article 61(1), sentence 2, reads that when the applicable legislation makes the right to benefits conditional upon the completion of periods of insurance, periods of employment or periods of self-employment completed under the legislation of another Member State, these shall not be taken into account unless such periods would have been considered to be periods of insurance had they been completed in accordance with the applicable legislation.

In the *Warmerdam* case[11] the question arose what is meant by the term periods of insurance. The problem arose since the Netherlands Unemployment Benefits Act requires that claimants must have worked at least one day in a number of weeks during the period of reference (at present at least one day in the 26 weeks lying in the 36 weeks before the start of the unemployment period). These days have to be fulfilled in an employment relationship, but the Dutch law does not specify whether these periods are to be called periods of insurance or periods of work. Thus, the question arose as to whether the Dutch system requires periods of insurance.

The Court answered that the term periods of work refers only to periods in which work was done which, under the system under which they are performed, are not considered as periods which give the right to affiliation with a system of unemployment insurance. In other words, periods of insurance are all periods which are relevant to acquiring a right under the unemployment benefit scheme.

Periods of work completed in another Member State are relevant to the claim in a State which requires periods of insurance, on condition that these periods are considered in the latter State as periods of insurance.

Example. A person works under an unemployment benefit scheme for the self-employed in State x. In State y he adopts work as an employed person and is insured under an employees' unemployment benefit scheme. The periods fulfilled in State x are relevant to the qualifying conditions of State y if he does not work long enough in this State to fulfil the conditions in State y.

According to the *Frangiamore* judgment[12] also in the reversed situation the aggregation rules are applicable: a person works in a scheme in country x, where

---

[10] The requirement that unemployed person last worked or was insured in the State where s/he claims benefit does not apply in the case of persons who do not reside in the competent State (frontier workers and non frontiers not residing in the competent State, see next section).

[11] Case 388/87, [1989] *ECR* 1203.

[12] Case 126/77, [1978] *ECR* 724.

he is not insured, and then moves to country y and works there, where the same type of work is insured. The new Regulation Article 61(2) provides, however, that periods of employment or self-employment completed under the legislation of another Member State are only taken into account if such periods would have been considered insurance under the legislation of the competent State. The *Frangiamore* judgment is thus overruled by the new Regulation.

Example: jobs of less than fifteen hours a week are not insured in Germany for unemployment insurance. In the Netherlands there are no thresholds for insurance. If a person has first worked in Germany and then starts to work in the Netherlands, and needs the aggregation of periods in Germany for his claim in the Netherlands, the periods in Germany count for this purpose since they are considered as insured periods in this country; the fact that they are not insured in Germany is irrelevant.

Article 1(t) of Regulation 883/2004[13] defines the term periods of insurance in the same way as Regulation 1408/71.[14] Therefore the *Frangiamore* and *Warmerdam* case law applies also under the new Regulation.[15] An additional effect of the interpretation of these rules is that a period of insurance for a scheme for the self-employed counts as a period of insurance for a scheme for the employed and vice versa. Note that a person can, however, claim unemployment benefit under an employees' scheme only if he has been lastly insured under such scheme. This does not prevent aggregation of other types of insurance before this last period. The same is mutatis mutandis true for the other schemes.

---

[13] According to Article 1(t) the term period of insurance means periods of contribution, employment or self-employment as defined or recognised as periods of insurance by the legislation under which they were completed or considered as completed, and all periods treated as such, where they are regarded by the said legislation as equivalent to periods of insurance. According to Article 1(u) the term period of employment or period of self-employment mean periods so defined or recognised by the legislation under which they were completed, and all periods treated as such, where they are regarded by the said legislation as equivalent to periods of employment or to periods of self-employment.

[14] For the same conclusion, *see* R. Cornelissen, 'The New EU Coordination System for Workers who become Unemployed', *European Journal of Social Security*, 2007, p. 218.

[15] Thus, a country without an insurance for the self-employed, which requires periods of insurance for entitlement under its employees benefits scheme, has to take the periods of self-employment into account of a system under which these count towards the unemployment insurance. For instance: a person who worked in State B with a self-employed person's insurance scheme, and who moves to State A with an unemployment benefits scheme for employed persons, can, after a period of insurance as an employed person in State A (see next section for this condition), have these periods in State B aggregated when he applies for benefit under the employed person's unemployment insurance scheme in State A.

Overview of aggregation possibilities

Periods of insurance in State A count as such in State B	these periods are aggregated for the claim in B
Periods which are not periods of insurance in State A, but are such periods in State B	these periods are aggregated for the claim in B
Periods of insurance according to the law of State A, but not according to the law of State B	these periods are not aggregated for the claim in B

If periods count neither according to the legislation of State A nor to that of State B, they cannot be aggregated. So if in State A jobs of less than 15 hours are not insured and in State B jobs of less than 20 hours are not insured, periods completed in such jobs are not aggregated.

A second question which arose is whether periods of employment can be taken into account if these are fulfilled under any branch of social security, or that they count only when they are fulfilled under an unemployment insurance scheme, *i.e.* in *the same branch* of social security. This question was raised in the *Warmerdam* case.[16] Mrs Warmerdam, a woman of Dutch nationality, worked in Scotland as a potter under a contract of employment. The only contingency she was insured for was accidents at work. Before she went to Scotland to accompany her husband who went for a training period in this country, she worked in the Netherlands and qualified for unemployment benefit. After her husband completed his training, she returned to the Netherlands and applied for unemployment benefit. She was refused this benefit on the grounds that she had not been insured for unemployment benefit in Great Britain.

The Court of Justice considered that the aggregation rule does not require that periods have to be completed as periods of insurance for the same branch of social security. As a consequence, the Netherlands had to take into account the periods completed in the UK, even though these were not periods of insurance under the UK legislation, as these periods would have been periods of insurance if they had been completed in the Netherlands.

The Claimant must have lastly completed Periods of Insurance or Periods of Work in Accordance with the Provisions of the Legislation under which the Benefits are claimed

The aggregation rules are subject to an important restriction. Article 61(3) provides that, in order to have periods aggregated, the person concerned must have lastly completed periods of insurance or periods of employment in accordance with the provisions of the legislation under which the benefits are claimed. There are no conditions on the duration of periods completed in the competent State

---

[16]   Case 388/87, [1989] *ECR* 1203.

before one can ask to have the aggregation rules applied. This interpretation was confirmed in the *Van Noorden* judgment.[17]

Example. An employee who worked a few years in the Netherlands and who, after he became unemployed, went to the United Kingdom, cannot claim British unemployment benefit.

A person who has been insured under a scheme for the self-employed and who moves to a country without a scheme for the self-employed, is not entitled to unemployment benefit if s/he continues to work as self-employed in that country and then loses this work. If this person is insured, however, even for a short period, in a scheme for the employed, s/he is entitled to benefit under that scheme if s/he can, if necessary with the help of the aggregation rules, satisfy the conditions.

Article 61 is not applicable to frontier workers who are completely unemployed nor to employed persons, other than frontier workers, who make themselves available for work in the State where they reside or who return to that territory; a special rule applies to them which will be discussed in the following sections (Sections 15.4 and 15.5).

As was discussed above, apart from some exceptions discussed below, under Community law an unemployed person is not entitled to unemployment benefits on the basis of the national legislation of a State other than the one in whose territory s/he became unemployed.[18] In the *Gray* case the Court was asked whether this rule was compatible with Article 42 EC, now Article 48 TFEU.[19] It was argued that the contested rule constitutes an impediment to the free movement of employed persons because it leads to a financial disadvantage for employed persons who have been engaged in one Member State and who immediately after they have become unemployed start to seek work in another Member State. The Court considered that Article 42 EC does not prohibit the Community legislature from imposing conditions to the rules which it establishes in order to ensure freedom of movement. As regards unemployment benefits, the Community legislature found it necessary to impose some conditions to guarantee that unemployed persons seek work in the State where they last worked (which means that the expenses for these unemployment benefits are to be born by that State). These conditions have to ensure that benefit is paid only to persons actually seeking work. The Court concluded that by making these conditions, the Council correctly exercised its powers of discretion. Consequently, these provisions were upheld.

---

[17]   Case 272/90, [1991] *ECR* 2543. Until July 1986, France aggregated all periods in other Member States (even when such an aggregation was not required by the Regulation). However, from this date it changed its policy.

[18]   Case 20/75, *D'Amico*, [1975] *ECR* 891.

[19]   Case 62/91, [1992] *ECR* 2039.

15.4. FRONTIER WORKERS

15.4.1. INTRODUCTION

The rules on persons who do not reside in the competent State affect mostly frontier workers. For this reason we will call these rules as the frontier workers rules. As was the case in Regulation 1408/71, Regulation 883/2004 provides that wholly unemployed frontier workers have to rely on the unemployment benefits in the State of residence (Section 15.4.3). For partially unemployed frontier workers a different system applies (Section 15.4.4).

15.4.2. THE DEFINITION OF FRONTIER WORKERS

Article 1(f) defines frontier workers as persons who pursue their occupation in the territory of a Member State which is different than their State of residence to which they return as a rule daily or at least once a week.

The meaning of this term was subject of the *Bergemann* case.[20] Mrs Bergemann worked and resided in the Netherlands before she married a German man. She resigned and moved to Germany during her maternity leave. In Germany she applied for German unemployment benefit. However, she was refused the right to benefit as she did not satisfy the benefit conditions and she was not able to rely on Article 67 of Regulation 1408/71 (now Article 61), since her last employment was not in Germany. Consequently, she wished to rely on the frontier workers rule. The Court considered that the term frontier worker presupposes a regular movement across the border. Consequently, an employee who moves to another Member State, but who does not return to the prior State (like Mrs Bergemann), is not a frontier worker.[21]

As was mentioned *supra*, in Regulation 883/2004 the Chapter on unemployment benefit was extended to the self-employed. This is also relevant to the provisions on the frontier workers. If a self-employed person, being a frontier worker, resides in a country with a scheme for the self-employed, s/he can claim such benefit in case of unemployment, even if s/he worked in another country before becoming unemployed. Under the rules of Regulation 1408/71 s/he could not rely on the frontier workers rule, since that did not include frontier workers, and therefore this self-employed person did not have a right to unemployment benefit.

---

[20] Case 236/87, [1988] *ECR* 5125.
[21] Whether or not a person is a frontier worker is to be decided by the national court, Case 227/81, *Aubin*, [1982] *ECR* 1991.

15.4.3. THE WHOLLY UNEMPLOYED FRONTIER WORKERS

Article 65(2) provides that a wholly unemployed person who, during his last activity as an employed or self-employed person, resided in a Member State other than the competent State, and who continues to reside in that Member State or returns to that State, has to make himself or herself available to the employment services in the State of residence. This Article contains – compared with Regulation 1408/71 – also a new element: a wholly unemployed person may, as a supplementary step, make himself or herself available to the employment services of the Member State in which he pursued his last activity as an employed or self-employed person.

Article 65 thus gives priority to defining where the unemployed person has to seek work. Note that the unemployed person does not have a choice between States where s/he can make himself available for the employment services; s/he has to be available in the State of residence in any case.

Article 65(5)(a) concerns the right to unemployment benefit in this case: the person concerned can claim benefit in accordance with the legislation of the State of residence, as if s/he had been subject to that legislation during his or her last activity as an employed or self-employed person. Benefits are provided by and at the expense of the institution of the place of residence. Thus wholly unemployed frontier workers are paid unemployment benefits in the State of residence.

Is the Wholly Unemployed Frontier Workers' Rule consistent with the Treaty?

As follows from Article 65(2), wholly unemployed frontier workers are subject to the legislation on unemployment benefits in their country of residence, even if they seek work in the country of last employment (in addition to seeking work in the State of residence). The conditions and the level of benefit are set according to the legislation of the State from which the benefits are due.

For frontier workers, this rule may be disadvantageous, as they are deprived of the rights they acquired by virtue of the legislation of the State of employment. These benefits might be higher and/or longer than those of the State of residence (although also the reverse may be true). This rule is also unattractive to the State of residence, as no contributions for this benefit were paid in this State, whereas it is now confronted with the expenses for this benefit. This rule is problematic, in particular, for less prosperous countries when their inhabitants go to work as frontier workers in rich neighbouring countries.

The rule that wholly unemployed frontier workers receive unemployment benefits in accordance with the legislation of the State of residence was challenged before the Court of Justice. The first time was in the *Mouthaan* judgment.[22] In this judgment the Court held that the frontier workers rule was not inconsistent with

---

[22]   Case 39/76, [1976] *ECR* 1901.

the Treaty. The Court argued that according to the ninth recital of Regulation 1408/71, this Article serves to ensure that a worker placed in one of the situations set out therein may receive unemployment benefits in conditions most favourable to the search for new employment.

This is a remarkable consideration, given that the ninth recital of Regulation 1408/71 does not refer to the frontier workers' rule (Article 71) at all. Instead, it mentions the objective 'to secure mobility of labour under improved conditions' and mentions the provision of Article 69 (the export provision of Regulation 1408/71, now Article 64).[23] The argument developed in *Mouthaan* was that for frontier workers the State of residence is the place where the conditions are most favourable to the search for new work, and therefore it was justified that also unemployment benefits are to be paid by this State. The Court's decision was based on Recital 9 only and therefore there is only a very small basis for justifying the disputed rule against the alleged indirect discrimination which is the effect of this rule.

In his conclusion to the *Mouthaan* case, the Advocate General mentioned the *Petroni* principle (discussed in Section 12.4). as 'a question that obviously suggests itself',[24] but he did not discuss this any further. Since the referring judge did not raise the question on compatibility with 'Petroni', the Court of Justice did not discuss this issue.

An explanation for the approach of the Court may be that for Mr Mouthaan the outcome of his case was favourable. He worked in Germany, where he was not insured, and lived in the Netherlands where he wished to claim benefit. For this it was necessary that the frontier workers rule was considered valid. Indirect discrimination and the *Petroni* principle were not relevant to this applicant. However, the justification given in this judgment was also used in later cases.

---

[23]   The full text of the recital reads: 'Whereas, in order to secure mobility of labour under improved conditions, it is necessary to ensure closer co-ordination between the unemployment insurance schemes and the unemployment assistance schemes of all the Member States, whereas it is therefore particularly appropriate, in order to facilitate search for employment in the various Member States, to grant to an unemployed worker, for a limited period, unemployment benefits provide for by the legislation of the Member State to which he was last subject.' The unemployment assistance schemes mentioned here are schemes to help the unemployed back into work (reintegration schemes). The recital quoted is also included in Regulation 883/2004, now Recital 32, where the term 'unemployment assistance schemes' is replaced by 'employment services'.

[24]   The *Petroni* principle states that coordination rules of the Regulation must not infringe upon benefit rights derived from the application of national law alone One could argue that frontier workers are not entitled to unemployment benefit from the State of employment on the basis of national law alone, if that State does not allow for payment of benefit outside its territory and that it is therefore not a benefit right based on national law alone. However, in the case of family benefits, the Court ruled that infringements of national benefits rights, which require the Regulation for export, are still contrary to the *Petroni* principle (*Beeck* judgment, Case 104/80, [1981] *ECR* 503).

In the *Aubin* judgment, the *Mouthaan* judgment was confirmed.[25] In this case also the outcome was desired by the applicant, i.e. that he was entitled to benefit in the State of residence.

The justification for the frontier workers' rule is that people have the best chances of finding work in the countries in which they live. There are no preparatory documents of the Regulation which mention this rationale for the frontier workers' rule. Thus it was the Court of Justice itself which construed this argument.

Although there is no research I know of which shows that the assumption underlying the rule is correct, it has a high common sense attractiveness. For instance, education systems, languages and cultures differ from State to State. For these reasons it is very likely that a person will find it more difficult to find work in a State where he does not live. There are, however, exceptions to this assumption, such as when a person has worked for twenty years in five different jobs in a neighbouring State.

Even if the assumption is true, it does not explain why frontier workers cannot receive benefits from the State of employment, i.e. the State where they were insured before becoming unemployed. Even if a frontier worker has to seek work or is allowed to seek work in the State of residence, his or her work seeking activities could be supervised either by the competent State in the State in which s/he lives, or by the State of residence on behalf of the competent State. In practice, however, supervising beneficiaries in another Member State is neither easy nor efficient and there may also be legal limitations to a State in obtaining information in another State without permission. Therefore it is more logical that the State of residence supervises the obligations of the benefit recipient. The problem then is that States do not really trust other Member States to take their supervision tasks seriously. This very lack of trust explains the coordination rules on unemployment benefit.[26] States find it hard to leave the supervision of the obligations to find work to other Member States, despite duties placed on Member States under the EC Treaty, to cooperate to realise the obligations flowing from the Treaty, and despite employment strategies that have been developed within the EU framework in the past decade. Nor does the cooperation article (Article 76) of the Regulation itself give them much faith in one other. This Article concerns the exchange of information between the Member States. In fact, neither of these provisions provides Member States with serious legal remedies they can use against one another if they do not fulfil their obligations correctly. It is understandable that Member States are suspicious of each other's willingness

---

[25]   Case 227/81, [1982] *ECR* 1991.

[26]   The general feeling of mistrust was worded explicitly during the Council meetings on the Chapter on unemployment benefits, as reported by Mr Rob Cornelissen, one of the attendants: 'In fact, most Member States feared that the employment services of the state of residence would not at all be motivated to find a job for workers for whom they were not financially responsible', EJSS, 2007, p. 218.

and capability to supervise persons for whom they are not financially responsible: often their own employment offices focus their reintegration activities on recipients of unemployment benefit instead of those without benefit. The net gains of investing in finding people jobs are much higher if this leads to termination of benefit entitlement.

As a result of this reality, the assumption that persons have the best chance of finding work in the State of residence lead to the rule that this State has to pay the unemployment benefits to the frontier workers. This system of Regulation 1408/71 is continued in Regulation 883/2004.

Although the steps followed in this argument are understandable, we must bear in mind that this is not the only possible approach. After all, the rule is quite problematic, since it deprives an unemployed person of benefits for which s/he has paid contributions. S/he receives benefits from a different system with different conditions, possibly even lower benefits. Since workers often go to work in countries with better labour conditions and better social security systems, we can expect that most workers are worse off as a result of this rule.[27]

15.4.4. PARTIALLY UNEMPLOYED FRONTIER WORKERS

Article 65(1) concerns *partially unemployed* persons who reside in a State other than the competent State. This provision reads that a person who is partially or intermittently unemployed and who, during his last activity as an employed or self-employed person, resided in a Member State other than the competent Member State has to make himself or herself available to his or her employer or to the employment services in the competent Member State.

This person receives unemployment benefits in accordance with the legislation of the competent Member State as if s/he were residing in that Member State. S/he receives these benefits from the institution of the competent Member State.

Although it is crucial whether a person is partially or wholly unemployed, the Regulation does not define what is meant by these terms. The Court was asked to give an interpretation of these terms in the *De Laat* judgment.[28] Mr De Laat worked full-time for a Belgian employer until his contract was terminated and replaced by a new, part-time contract. The question was whether or not this was a form of partial unemployment. The Court considered that by laying down the rule that a wholly unemployed frontier worker is entitled to benefits solely in the Member State in which s/he resides, Article 71(1)(a)(ii) was based on the assumption that such a worker would find in that State the conditions most favourable to the search for new employment. However, the protection of

---

[27] For further discussion, see F. Pennings, Coordination of Unemployment Benefits under Regulation 883/2004', *EJSS* 2009, p. 177.

[28] Case 444/98, [2001] ECR I-2229.

workers would be weakened if a worker who, in a Member State other than the State of residence, remained employed in the same undertaking, but part-time, while remaining available for work on a full-time basis, was obliged to apply to an institution in his place of residence for help in finding additional work. The fact that he has gone from full-time employment to part-time employment by virtue of a new contract is, in this respect, irrelevant. More specifically, the employment office of the place of residence would be considerably less well placed – when compared with its counterpart in the competent State – to assist the worker in finding additional employment on terms and conditions compatible with his part-time job since, in all likelihood, such employment would have to be in the territory of the competent Member State. It is only when a worker no longer has any link with the competent Member State and is wholly unemployed that he must apply to the institution of his place of residence for assistance in finding employment. Consequently, the Court decided that in the case of Mr De Laat, he could claim unemployment benefit in the State of employment.[29]

This judgment caused some problems for the benefit administration. Some States applied the judgment only in cases identical to the *De Laat* case, i.e. a worker continuing to work for his or her employer in a part-time job. This restrictive approach clearly did not fit with the criteria developed by the Court. In order to try to solve such problems, in 2005 the Administrative Commission made a decision in which a definition of partial unemployment is given,[30] which was replaced by Decision U3 in 2009.[31] It provides that determination of the nature of partial or wholly unemployment depends on whether or not any *contractual* employment link exists or is maintained between the parties, and not on the duration of any temporary suspension of the workers activity.

Thus, the criterion is now whether or not there is a contractual link; if there is none, the person is wholly unemployed. This criterion is more strict than the *De Laat* judgment, that requires 'any link with the State of employment'. Under that criterion also prospects for further work are relevant. The new criterion is more precise, so it easier to apply to the benefit administration; we may assume that the Court finds this precision acceptable.

However, there are also problems with the interpretation of the AC's criterion. Suppose, for example, that a person has two part-time jobs and loses one, or that he has a full-time job and this is succeeded by a job with a new employer. Some benefit administrations assume wholly unemployment in this case, as there is no longer a contractual link between the employer *of the lost job* and the employee. Indeed, close reading of the text of the decision can lead to such an interpretation, since it says 'whether or not there is any contractual link between *the parties*' (my

---

[29]   It seems, however, that he would not be successful in this since the Belgian system does not provide unemployment benefits for the partially unemployed (whereas the Dutch system would have); this does, of course, not alter the outcome of the case.

[30]   O.J. 30 of 18 May 2006, p. 37.

[31]   Decision U3, OJ C 106/45 of 2010.

italics). However, it is also obvious that this interpretation departs fundamentally from the *De Laat* judgment, in which the Court said that there must not be any link *with the country of* employment. Moreover, such interpretation does not fit either with the rationale of the *De Laat* criterion that was based on where the best chances of finding work existed. It is therefore very unlikely that this interpretation is correct: relevant is instead whether an employee has a contractual link with any employer in the State of employment,

15.4.5. THE FRONTIER WORKER MOVES TO THE STATE OF LAST EMPLOYMENT

An issue raised in the case law was what happened if a frontier worker, who became entitled to unemployment benefit, moved to the former State of employment. Would this move affect his benefit position and could s/he thus influence his benefit position? The Court considered in the *Huijbrechts* judgment[32] that wholly unemployed frontier workers can claim, on the basis of a legal fiction, benefits in the State of residence as though it were the State where they were last employed. This legal fiction suspends the obligations of the latter State but does not extinguish them. Therefore, where an unemployed frontier worker, after receiving unemployment benefit in the State of residence settles in the Member State in which he was last employed, the derogation ceases to apply. The State in which he was last employed must begin to assume its obligations under the Regulation in relation to unemployment benefits.

The question arises whether this case law also applies under Regulation 883/2004. Article 11 provides that a person receiving unemployment benefits in accordance with Article 65 under the legislation of the Member State of residence shall be subject to the legislation of that Member State. In this view we cannot consider this as a suspension of the main rules.

This means that it is relevant to know whether Article 65 still applies to a person who goes to live in a State where s/he previously worked. On the basis of close reading of Article 65 one could argue that a person who is frontier worker at the moment when he became unemployed is subject to Article 65 and cannot be considered anymore as a non-frontier worker when he goes to live in the State of employment. However, given that this approach is a deviation from the State of employment principle and constitutes discrimination on grounds of residence, there is a sound reason to doubt whether this outcome is consistent with the principle of free movement of workers. Only the Court of Justice will be able to give the final answer this question.

---

[32]   Case 131/95, [1997] *ECR* I-1418.

15.5.   PERSONS OTHER THAN FRONTIER WORKERS WHO DO NOT RESIDE IN THE COMPETENT STATE

15.5.1.   THE CRITERIA FOR QUALIFICATION AS NON-FRONTIER WORKER

There is another category which falls within the category referred to by Article 65(2), *i.e.* a wholly unemployed person who resided in a Member State other than the competent State and who is *not* a frontier worker (hereafter: the non-frontier worker rule).

Most often non-frontier workers who do not reside in the competent State are persons whose State of residence is so far away from the State of employment that they cannot return to the former at least once a week. They will have a place of stay in the State of employment, but this is not considered as their residence. In other words, the ties with the State of origin are strong enough to call that State the State of residence. An example is a seasonal worker who works in a State far away from the State of origin. Another example is that of a worker from one of the new Member States who does all kinds of construction or maintenance work in another Member State, who lives in temporary accommodation (caravan, camp site, rented apartment) and has maintained his residence in the State of origin.

The Court argued that for non-frontier workers the State of residence is the State where the worker, although occupied in another Member State, continues habitually to reside and where the habitual centre of his interests is also situated (the *Di Paolo* judgment).[33] The duration and the durability of the place of residence of the person concerned before his departure to the State of employment, the duration and objective of his absence, the nature of the activities performed in the other Member State, and the intention of the person concerned, as appears from all circumstances, are relevant in defining his centre of interests. The Court argued that the transfer of liability for payment of unemployment benefits from the Member State of last employment to the Member State of residence is justified for certain categories of workers who retain close ties with the country where they have settled and habitually reside. It would, however, no longer be justified if by an excessively wide interpretation of the concept of residence the point were to be reached where all migrant workers who pursue an activity in one Member State, while their families continue habitually to reside in another Member State, were given the benefit of the exception of the non-frontier worker rule. It follows from these considerations, the Court continued, that the provisions of Article 71(1)(b)(ii) must be interpreted strictly. This is also true, we can expect, for Article 65(5)(b) of Regulation 883/2004.

---

[33]   Case 76/76, [1977] *ECR* 315.

An example of the application of these criteria can be seen in the *Reibold* judgment.[34] It concerned an employed person who for the duration of two academic years worked in another Member State; the job was part of an exchange programme of universities. The Court decided that the non-frontiers rule is applicable as from the outset it was clear that the duration of this job was to be limited within the habitual framework of the exchange programme, and that the activities of the person concerned were interrupted every three months by lengthy holiday periods during which he stayed in the accommodation which he had kept in the State of origin.

As was said in the beginning, most often non-frontier workers who do not reside in the competent State are persons whose State of residence is so far away from the State of employment that they cannot return at least once a week to the State of residence. This is, however, not always the case. The competent State can also be the State assigned by an Article 16 Agreement or the State which issued a posting certificate. This was confirmed in the *Van Gestel* judgment.[35] Mr van Gestel was employed in the Netherlands where he also resided. With a view to his temporary transfer to an affiliated company in Belgium, Mr Van Gestel moved to Belgium and an agreement was made on the basis of (what is now) Article 16 of the coordination Regulation that he remained subject to the Netherlands social security legislation. When he was dismissed he applied for Belgian unemployment benefit but his claim was rejected, on the ground that he was not insured in this country. The Court answered that the non-frontier workers rule was applicable: it is decisive for the application of this provision that the person concerned has his residence in a State other than the one where he was subject to the legislation during his last activities.

15.5.2. THE APPLICABLE UNEMPLOYMENT BENEFITS SCHEME FOR NON-FRONTIER WORKERS

The third sentence of Article 65(2) provides that this person, if s/he does not return to his State of residence has to make himself or herself available to the employment services in the Member State to whose legislation s/he was last subject.[36] In this case the person receives, following the main rules, benefits from the State of employment.

---

[34]   Case 216/89, [1990] *ECR* 4163.
[35]   Case 454/93, [1995] *ECR* I-1707.
[36]   What is meant by availability under Article 71 was dealt with in the *Naruschawicus* judgment (Case 308/94, [1996] *ECR* I-207). Mrs Naruschawicus, of Belgian nationality, worked until 20 April 1991 under a contract of employment for the Belgian army in Germany. During this period she lived in Germany but because of her status as civil servant she kept her legal place of residence in Belgium. When she became unemployed she remained living in Germany but applied for unemployment benefit from Belgium. She was subject to the employment office and travelled regularly from Germany to Liège. After benefit was initially awarded it

However, if the person returns to the State of residence, s/he first receives, on the return to the State of residence, benefits in accordance with Article 64. Thus s/he continues to receive benefits from the State of employment during three months (see Section 15.9). Subsequently, s/he receives benefits in accordance with the legislation of the State of residence.

Consequently, these persons have the right to choose: either they remain in the State of last employment and are entitled to benefit from that State; or they return to the State of residence and are entitled to benefit under that State. Regulation 883/2004 makes a stricter link between the applicability of unemployment benefit and the State where the person concerned stays or resides than Regulation 1408/71. The choice is only whether s/he stays or resides in the State of employment or the State of residence. Benefit entitlement follows the choice. It seems that it is no longer possible to claim benefit from the State where one does not reside merely by being available for the employment services of that State.

A non-frontier worker can thus return to the State of residence *after* s/he has already received unemployment benefit in the State of employment for some period. In the *Knoch* judgment[37] the question was raised how the remaining benefit in the State of residence has to be calculated now this person has already received unemployment benefit for some time. There are considerable differences between the regime of United Kingdom unemployment benefit scheme and the German regime: United Kingdom benefits are flat rate and are paid during the same period for all claimants; the German benefits are wage-related and the duration of payments depends on the employment record of the claimant. The Court reasoned that the German benefit administration should take account of the periods of insurance during which Mrs Knoch had been subject to the British legislation. The periods during which benefits were paid could be deducted from the total number of benefit days she would have been entitled to under German law. The competent organisation of a Member State whose legislation makes the acquisition and the duration of unemployment benefits dependent on the completion of periods of insurance has to deduct the number of *days* during which benefits were actually paid (*i.e.* the period during which she was in the United Kingdom) from the number of days acquired under the other regime.

---

was refused retroactively. The question was whether an employee can receive benefit on the basis of Article 71(b)(ii) when he registers as seeking work at the employment offices of that State, even if he is, because of distance, available to a lesser extent than normal for applying for vacancies offered by that office. The Court ruled that such an employed person remains available for the employment services in the territory of the competent State when he registers as a person seeking work at the employment services of that country and when he is subject to the supervision of the competent services of that State.

[37]   Case 102/91, [1992] *ECR* I-4341.

15.6. ATYPICAL FRONTIER WORKERS

15.6.1. THE MIETHE JUDGMENT

In the *Miethe* case[38] the wholly unemployed frontier workers' rule of Regulation 1408/71 was disputed. Mr Miethe, of German nationality, moved in 1976 to Belgium, but he remained at work as a salesman in Germany. In Germany he could stay with his mother-in-law, which he regularly did, and which he continued to do when he became unemployed in 1979 and started seeking work in Germany. In Germany he applied for unemployment benefit, but his application was unsuccessful. The relevant question in this case was whether the rule that determined the applicable unemployment legislation for wholly unemployed frontier workers had exclusive effect. Does this rule, which meant that the State of residence was the competent State, really mean that it is not possible for the persons concerned to obtain benefit from the State of employment, even if the person concerned satisfies the benefit conditions of the latter State?

The Court of Justice replied that the frontier workers' rule is an exception to the general rule of Article 13 of the Regulation, Article 11 of the new Regulation, which is that employed persons are subject to the legislation of the State of employment. For the wholly unemployed frontier worker there is no right to choose between the law of the State of residence and the State of employment. A wholly unemployed frontier worker cannot receive benefit from the legislation of the State of employment as this would mean that such an employed person would have the right to choose. A different interpretation of this Article would, according to the Court, ignore the objective of coordination.

Thus, if Mr Miethe were a frontier worker, the legislation to be applied was that of the State of residence and no other. Subsequently, however, the Court discussed the question whether Mr Miethe was really a frontier worker. It recalled that the objective of the frontier workers' rule was to ensure that a migrant worker could receive unemployment benefits under those conditions which were most favourable to his search for a new job. This includes assistance to his efforts to be re-integrated into the labour market. Thus, it is tacitly assumed in this Article that those conditions are most favourable in the State of residence. A problem arises, however, if a wholly unemployed person, although satisfying the criteria as a frontier worker, has such connections in the State of employment, both personally and professionally, that s/he will have the best chance of finding work again in that State. Such a person is not a frontier worker within the meaning of the frontier workers' rule. The Court decided that it is for the national court to decide whether an employed person who resides in another State than one in whose territory s/he is employed has nevertheless the best chance of reintegration in the State of employment. In the case of an affirmative answer to this question,

---

[38]   Case 1/85, [1986] *ECR* 1837.

the person is to be treated as a non-frontier worker not residing in the competent State.

The Court mentions 'personal and professional connections' with the State of employment which mean that the unemployed person has the best chance of finding employment in that State. In fact Mr Miethe's family resided in Belgium so he had personal connections with the State of residence. However, it appeared that he lived in Belgium only because he could find a house in this country which was closer to the school of the children so that they could return home every day. Aside from this, the personal connections of the family were in Germany.

The Court may have underestimated the number of situations in which the *Miethe* rule can apply. Sometimes large groups of persons cross the border, for instance, since housing is cheaper at that side of the border.

The *Miethe* judgment also leads to interpretation problems. For instance, the Netherlands benefit administration decided that atypical frontier workers have better chances on the labour market of the country of work (Germany) and they were refused Dutch unemployment benefit. The Dutch Central Appeals Court accepted this approach.[39] There is some sense in this approach, as the question arises why the State of residence, where no contributions were paid, has to pay unemployment benefit to persons who have better chances on the labour market in the country where they were previously employed. Still, it is questionable whether this interpretation of the *Miethe* judgment was consistent with the Court's approach, whereas atypical frontier workers belong to the category of Article 71(1)(b) of Regulation 1408/71, and that meant that they had the right to choose.

15.6.2. IS THE MIETHE JUDGMENT STILL RELEVANT UNDER REGULATION 883/2004?

Whether the *Miethe* judgment is still relevant under Regulation 883/2004 was one of the 'hot' issues during the drafting process of Regulation 883/2004. Relevant to this discussion was the difference in texts of the two Regulations. Under the new Regulation unemployed frontier workers may make themselves available, in addition to the State of employment, to the State of last employment. Does the difference in approach between the regulations, as discussed in the previous sections, mean that the *Miethe* judgment can no longer be applied?[40]

---

[39]   CRvB 25 June 1997, *RSV* 1998/58.

[40]   Rob Cornelissen, former head of the Free Movement of Workers and Coordination of Social Security Schemes unit of DG Employment of the European Commission, argued that the *Miethe* case law is still in force (R. Cornelissen, 'The New EU Coordination System for Workers who become Unemployed', *European Journal of Social Security*, 2007, p. 211). Cees Van den Berg, retired head of the Department of International Treaties of the Dutch Ministry of Social Affairs and Employment, argues that the *Miethe* case law will lose its meaning once the new Regulation comes into force. His main point is that the drafters of the new text have included

A textual argument could be that, in the *Miethe* judgment, the Court put the atypical frontier worker on a par with the non-frontier worker, and that means application of the rules of Article 71(1)(b) of Regulation 1408/71. According to the first indent of that provision, the non-frontier worker is entitled to unemployment benefit from the State of last employment if he is available to its employment services. The second indent concerns the situation in which the non-frontier has returned to the State of residence or is available to the employment services of that country. Regulation 883/2004 provides that the non-frontier worker who has not returned to the State of residence has to be available to the employment services of the State of employment. From the system of the Regulation and the national law in question, it follows that s/he is entitled to benefit from the competent State. Unlike Regulation 1408/71, the new Regulation does not contain the rule that the non-frontier worker, who is available to the employment services of the competent State, is entitled to benefit in that State as if s/he resided in that State. In other words, returning to the State of residence excludes him or her from receiving benefit from the competent State. Article 65(5)(b) of the new Regulation provides that a non-frontier worker who returns to the State of residence is entitled to unemployment benefit from that State. So if we take the *Miethe* rule, which refers to Article 71(1)(b), the problem is that the rule corresponding to the latter provision is missing in the new Regulation.

In other words, it can be argued that though, under the new Regulation, there are still *Miethe* cases – atypical frontier workers -, the new rules mean that even if they are treated as non-frontier workers, this would always mean that they are paid unemployment benefit according to the rules of the State of residence, since the they have 'returned' to the State of residence.

However, this interpretation does not acknowledge that Article 71(1)(b)(ii) of the old Regulation provided that the non-frontier worker, who makes himself available for work to the services of employment of the State of residence, or who returned to the State of residence, is entitled to benefit from that State. In case of the atypical frontier workers, it could also then be said that they 'returned' to the State of residence, so that is the State where they are entitled to benefit. Still, Article 71(b) was interpreted thus that despite their 'return' to the State of residence, the atypical frontier workers could claim benefit in the State of employment. Therefore, the *Miethe* case law was not based on the literal text of

---

all existing case law in the new text; thus, if the *Miethe* law is not implemented, it follows that it is not part of the new Regulation. From a legal point, Van den Berg's argument is not valid. One cannot hold that if a rule of the case law is not implemented, it is no longer valid. On the contrary, where the texts of two successive regulations are materially the same and where the text does not explicitly make clear that a particular rule or interpretation does not exist anymore, the old case law remains valid. Since the rules on unemployment benefits for frontier workers in Regulation 883/2004 remain a deviation from the main rule that benefits are paid by the State of employment and this may constitute indirect discrimination, and the *Miethe* case law is not referred to, the conclusion is that, without further indications, the old case law remains relevant whatever the alleged intention of the legislature.

the old Regulation and it is therefore questionable whether the new text does not leave room for choice.

The text of the new Regulation leaves us with another problem. Article 65(2) does not provide that the non-frontier workers who are available to the State of employment are entitled to benefit from this State as if they reside in the State. So, unlike Article 71(1)(b)(1), this provision does not waive the residence conditions of national legislation for this category. Also Article 11, giving the rules for determining the legislation applicable, does, unlike Article 13 of Regulation 1408/71, not waive residence conditions. The question remains therefore whether the *Miethe* case law can be maintained as that would mean that the residence conditions of Article 65 have to be waived.

There are arguments in favour of an affirmative answer. It has to be kept in mind that frontier workers are deprived of unemployment benefit of the country of last employment, whereas the *lex loci laboris* is the main principle of the Regulation. If there is no justification for this deviation, it is a case of indirect discrimination. In the *Miethe* judgment the Court found a solution to solve this problem in a case, in which the objective justification was not valid, by calling persons as Mr Miethe 'non-frontier workers'. This meant that the Court had to depart from the literal text of the Regulation.

The problem of indirect discrimination remains under the new Regulation. Even if it is accepted that the new Regulation contains provisions that make the application of the *Miethe* rule difficult, this problem remains. One solution may be that the Court does not apply Article 65 to atypical frontier workers and waives the residence provisions on the basis of Article 45 TFEU because of the indirect discrimination they cause.

On 9 July 2008, the European Parliament adopted the following amendment, which proposed a new recital, which became Recital 13 of Regulation 987/2004: 'This Regulation provides for measures and procedures to promote the mobility of employees and the unemployed. Frontier workers who have become completely unemployed may make themselves available to the employment services in both their country of residence and the Member State where they were last employed. However, they should be entitled to benefits only from their Member State of residence'.[41] In the report by Jean Lambert, who proposed the amendment, the following justification was mentioned: 'With the inclusion of this text there can no longer be any misunderstanding about whether the Miethe judgment is still to be applied or not.' This is a somewhat remarkable wording, since it suggests that it is a misunderstanding, instead of uncertainty. In fact, nor in the amendment nor in the justification the rapporteur made clear whether or not the *Miethe* judgment is still to be applied. We may assume that she meant to answer this question negatively. However, the European Parliament did not adopt an amendment to exclude a *Miethe* interpretation. Since Article 13 refers to frontier workers and

---

[41]   P6_TA(2008)0348.

the Court considered cases as Mr Miethe as non-frontier workers, it is a miracle why the Parliament thought that the question could be solved by this amendment. Although the administrations will most probably not continue the *Miethe* case law anymore, one can expect that there will be court cases on this issue. These will have to make clear what the fate of *Miethe* is.

15.6.3. THE PROPOSAL FOR MODERNISATION

The Proposal for Simplification of the Coordination Regulation of 1998 gave a uniform coordination rule on unemployed persons who, during their last employment, resided in a Member State other than the competent State. If they reside in the territory other than the competent State and make themselves available to the employment services of the State of residence, they receive benefit from the competent State (Article 51 of the Proposal). Thus, this provision treats the wholly unemployed, the partially unemployed persons and persons who are unemployed because of unforeseen circumstances in the same way: they are entitled to receive unemployment benefit in the State of employment. This provision would take away a series of interpretation problems of the Regulation, such as what is meant by 'partially unemployed' or 'wholly unemployed'. The distinction between frontier worker and non-frontier worker who returns to his State of residence and the *Miethe* cases would disappear. The Proposal also removed the problem of indirect discrimination against frontier workers which underlies the present rules. Another advantage is that the charges for the benefits are where they should be: in the country where contributions were paid. However, the Proposal was not accepted, as we have seen in the preceding sections.

15.7. REIMBURSEMENT RULES

It is not only the unemployed persons themselves, but also some Member States that were not happy with the rule for the wholly unemployed frontier workers, since they have to bear the cost. An innovation of Regulation 883/2004 is the reimbursement rule. This involves that the benefits provided by the State of residence under Article 65(5) – thus including both the frontier workers and the non-frontier workers not residing in the competent State who have returned to the State of residence – remain at the expense of the State of residence (Article 65(6)). However, the competent institution of the State, to whose legislation the person was last subject, has to reimburse the State of residence with the full amount of benefits paid for the first three months. The reimbursement is no more than the value of benefits of the competent State. Therefore it may not be a full reimbursement, but, in any case, the competent State is not 'better off' as a result of the coordination rules.

The reimbursement period is extended to five months when the person concerned has, during the preceding 24 months, completed periods of employment or self-employment of at least twelve months in the country of last employment.

It follows from this new rule that the problems for the Member States have, for a large part, been solved as a result of this compromise: the link between the supervision and payment of benefits is maintained, while reimbursement rules reduce the costs for the States in which many frontier workers live. For the frontier workers there are no improvements, aside from their right to seek work in two States. This raises the question why it was not provided that frontier workers should receive a supplement to their unemployment benefit, if it is lower than they would have received in the competent State, to make their benefits equal to those provided in the competent State. After all, the competent State has to reimburse the costs, so the frontier worker could benefit from such a solution whereas the State of residence would not be worse off.

15.8. THE CALCULATION OF UNEMPLOYMENT BENEFIT

Article 62 provides how the level of wage-related unemployment benefits has to be calculated. The principle expressed in this Article is that the benefit administration has to take account exclusively the wages or professional income received by the unemployed person during his activity in the State where this was performed.

This applies also where the legislation of the competent State provides for a specific reference period for the determination of the salary which serves as a basis for the calculation of benefits and where, for all or part of this period, the person concerned was subject to the legislation of another Member State.

There is, however, one category of workers which cannot satisfy the conditions of this Article: frontier workers. In their case, the competent State is not the State of last employment but the State of residence. In the *Grisvard and Kreitz* judgment concerning French frontier workers in Germany the Court had to give a solution for this.[42] The Court considered that the general situation will be that the level of remuneration in the State of employment is often higher than in the State of residence. As a result, the rule that unemployment benefit payable to frontier workers could never be calculated on the basis of the remuneration in the State of employment would discourage frontier work and would violate the principles underlying the coordination regulation. The provision of Article 68 of Regulation 1408/71 must therefore be interpreted as follows: in the case of a wholly unemployed frontier worker, the competent institution of the State of residence, of which the national legislation provides that the calculation of benefit depends on earlier earned wages, must calculate this benefit by taking account of

---

[42]   Case 201/91, [1992] *ECR* I-5009.

the wages received by the unemployed person in the last employment in which he worked in the State of employment.

Regulation 883/2004 takes account of this case law (Article 62(3)): it rules (after amendment by Regulation 988/2009) that as far as unemployed persons covered by Article 65(5)(a) are concerned, the institution of the place of residence has to take into account the salary or professional income received by the person concerned in the Member State to whose legislation he was subject during his last activity as an employed or self-employed person, in accordance with the Implementing Regulation.

In the *Stallone* judgment[43] the Court was asked to clarify the meaning of Article 68(2) of Regulation 1408/71, which is relevant to a Member States whose legislation provides that the amount of benefits varies with the number of family members. This article prescribes that the competent institutions of that Member State must take into account family members residing in the territory of another Member State, as though they were residing in the territory of the competent State. Such obligation does not exist if, in the Member State where the family members reside, another person is entitled to unemployment benefits for the calculation of which family members are taken into consideration. The Court was asked whether Article 68(2) precludes application of a Belgian rule according to which unemployed persons are only entitled to unemployment benefit at the higher 'head of household rate' conditional on the requirement that family members live together with the unemployed person. Mr Stallone, an unemployed Italian national living in Belgium, was refused such higher rate benefit on the ground that his family members had returned to Italy. The Court considered that the Belgian rule was incompatible with Article 68(2) of the Regulation. The Belgian rule does not explicitly require that family members live in Belgian territory, but it was clear that the condition that they live together with the unemployed person implicitly and necessarily implied that family members reside on Belgian territory. The Court did not agree with the argument that the disputed Belgian rule falls outside the scope of Article 68(2) because the Belgian rule merely demands that an unemployed person lives with one of his family members and that, once that condition is satisfied, the amount of an unemployment benefit does not vary according to the number of members of the family. The Court held that such a restrictive interpretation would be incompatible with the aim of Article 68(2) to avoid indirect discrimination on grounds of nationality and did not accept the argument that the rule in question could be justified by the need to check that family members are really dependent on the unemployed person.

---

43   Case 212/00 [2001] *ECR* I-7625.

15.9. EXPORT OF UNEMPLOYMENT BENEFITS

15.9.1. THE CONDITIONS FOR EXPORT

Unemployment benefits are a complicated type of benefit because of their close link with the obligation to seek work. Beneficiaries of unemployment benefit are required to keep their unemployment as short as possible by actively seeking work. For this purpose, supervision by the employment office is essential; this supervision can mostly, although not always, be best given in the State where benefit is paid. The possibilities of receiving unemployment benefits in another Member State are therefore more restricted than in the case of other types of benefits.

Article 48 TFEU provides that the Council has to take measures to guarantee the payment of social security benefits in another Member State. This principle is laid down in the general waiving of residence conditions (Article 7 of the Regulation). However, this Article does not apply to unemployment benefits, as we have already seen. Instead Article 64 of Regulation 883/2004 governs the export of unemployment benefits. The opportunity to export unemployment benefit exists to a limited extent only.

In the Proposal for Simplification of Regulation 1408/71 the Commission proposed to extend the period a person can seek work from three months to six months.[44] The Council, however, did not accept this proposal. During the Council discussions it appeared that many Member States were afraid that an extended research period would be abused, and therefore the Commission proposal was not adopted.[45] Consequently, like Regulation 1408/71, Article 64 mentions three months as a maximum period for export of unemployment benefits.

In order to invoke Article 64, the employed person must have been registered as a person seeking work and have remained available to the employment services of the competent State for at least four weeks after becoming unemployed. The competent services or institution may authorise his departure before such time has expired. Furthermore, he must register as a person seeking work with the employment services of the Member State to which he has gone and must be subject to the control procedure of that State and adhere to the conditions laid down under the legislation of that State. This condition is satisfied if s/he registers within seven days of the date s/he was no longer available for the employment services of the competent State. Thus, if s/he was not available for work during these seven days, this does not affect his or her right to unemployment benefit.

---

[44] COM (1998) 779.
[45] R. Cornelissen, 'The New EU Coordination System for Workers who become Unemployed', *European Journal of Social Security,* 2007, p. 204.

Entitlement to benefit is retained for a period of three months[46] from the date when the person ceased to be available to the employment services of the State which he left.

The competent services may extend the export period to a maximum of six months. Benefits are provided by the competent institution in accordance with the legislation it applies and at its own expense. In addition, Regulation 883/2004 provides, like Regulation 1408/71, that in exceptional cases the competent institutions may allow the person concerned to return at a later date without loss of entitlement. A difference exists in the number of times the claimant can make use of the rule. Under Regulation 1408/71, the possibility offered by Article 69 could be invoked only once between two periods of unemployment. The provisions of Regulation 883/04 are more flexible: between two periods of employment the unemployed person can make use of Article 64 several times, as long as he respects the overall maximum period of three months (or six months, if extended by the competent institution).

The person concerned must return to the competent State before the expiry of the period during which benefit is retained (Article 64(2)). He loses, however, as provided by this Article, all entitlement to benefits of the competent State if he does not return in time, unless the provisions if the competent State are more favourable (see also Section 15.9.3). In exceptional cases, the time limit for return may be extended by the competent services without loss of entitlement.[47]

15.9.2. THE POWERS TO EXTEND THE EXPORT PERIOD

The *Coccioli* case concerned this extension possibility under Regulation 1408/71. The Court was asked about the position of a person who, being ill, did not apply for an extension until the three month period had expired.[48] Can extension also be given retroactively? The Court replied that the Regulation does not provide that a request for extension must necessarily be made before the expiration of the period. In fact, amongst the 'exceptional cases' may be cases which prevent not only the return of the unemployed person to the competent State within the period prescribed, but also prevent the lodging of a request for extension before the expiration of that period. The freedom of the competent services of the Member States is not restricted to take into consideration all factors which they regard as relevant and which are inherent both in the individual situation of the

---

[46] The total duration of his benefit must not be longer than if s/he had stayed in the competent State.
[47] Article 69(2), last sentence.
[48] Case 139/78, [1979] *ECR* 991.

workers concerned and in the exercise of effective control. This means that benefit services have a broad discretion in applying this rule.

15.9.3. THE LOSS OF REMAINING BENEFIT RIGHTS IN CASE OF A LATE RETURN

The effects of a late return are harsh and have been subject of disputes for some decades. It is possible that an unemployed person was entitled to a long benefit period (four or five years or even longer) but loses all rights because of his late return. One might have expected that the Court of Justice would not have accepted this provision on grounds of the *Petroni* principle. In the *Petroni* judgment[49] the Court established the principle that benefit rights acquired by virtue of national law alone must not be infringed on the basis of the Regulation. The question of whether this case law applied also in respect of the loss of unemployment benefits was answered in the *Testa* judgment.[50] Mr Testa, of Italian nationality, received German unemployment benefit and was allowed to seek employment in Italy. He returned one day late and was refused the remaining period of benefit. The Court considered that the export rule (Article 69 of Regulation 1408/71) was not simply a measure to coordinate national law on social security, but established an independent body of rules in favour of workers claiming the benefit which constitute an exception to national legal rules and which must be interpreted uniformly in all the Member States. The migrant worker has an advantage as Article 69 frees him for a period of three months of the duty to keep himself available to the employment services of the competent State. As part of a special system of rules which gives rights to workers which they would not otherwise have, Article 69(2) cannot therefore be equated with the provisions held invalid by the Court in the *Petroni* judgment.

The Court also discussed – in answer to the national court's questions – whether Article 69(2) infringed the fundamental rights guaranteed in this manner by Community law The Court argued that consideration should first be given to the fact that the system set up by Article 69 is an optional system. The system applies only to the extent to which such application is requested by a worker, who thereby foregoes his right of recourse to the general system applicable to workers in the State in which he became unemployed. The consequences laid down by Article 69 of failing to return in good time are made known to the worker, in particular by means of an explanatory sheet (E 303/5) written in his own language which is handed to him by the competent employment services. His decision to opt for the system under Article 69 is therefore made freely and with full knowledge of the consequences.

---

[49]   Case 24/75, [1975] *ECR* 1149. See also Section 12.4.
[50]   The *Testa, Maggio and Viale* judgment, Cases 41/79, 121/79 and 796/79, [1980] *ECR* 1979.

Finally, it must be emphasised that the second sentence of Article 69(2), which provides that in exceptional cases the three-month period laid down by Article 69 may be extended, ensures that the application of Article 69(2) does not give rise to disproportionate results. Whilst the competent services of the States enjoy a wide discretion in deciding whether to extend the period laid down by the Regulation, in exercising that discretionary power they must take account of the principle of proportionality which is a general principle of Community law. In order to apply this principle correctly in cases such as this, in each individual case the competent services and institutions must take into consideration the extent to which the period in question has been exceeded, the reason for the delay in returning and the seriousness of the legal consequences arising from this delay. The Court concluded that even supposing that the entitlement to the social security benefits in question may be held to be covered by the protection of the right to property as it is guaranteed by Community law – an issue which it did not seem necessary to settle in the context of these proceedings – the rules laid down by Article 69 did not involve any undue restriction on the retention of entitlement to the benefits in question. As a result, Article 69(2) was upheld.

In 1980 the European Commission issued a proposal in order to soften the effects of a late return, but this was not adopted.[51] According to the proposal unemployed persons would retain their right to unemployment benefits in accordance with the national legislation of the competent State, provided that they return to the territory of that State either within *i.e.* three months, or, after the expiry of this period, but before the expiry of the period during which, under the legislation of that Member State, the worker may leave the territory of the said State without thereby forfeiting his right to benefits.

15.9.4. THE PRESENT RULES

Regulation 883/2004 has a novelty: the person who returns too late loses all entitlement to benefit, unless the provisions of that legislation are mover favourable. Indeed, Member States may have their own rules on the period after which benefits are lost after a late return. These are applicable, if favourable for the person concerned.

Example. The legislation of a Member State provides that if a person goes abroad, the right relives after the moment the right ends, if the period is no longer than six months. Peter stays eight months abroad. His benefit is exported on the basis of the Regulation for three months, then the right is terminated. Since the right to benefit ended only after the three months of export, Peter would have lost his right only after 9 months of staying abroad. As he returns earlier, the right relives after his return.

---

[51]   Com. (80) 312 final, *see also OJ* 9 July 1980, 169/22.

There is an important difference in the rules concerning the export of benefit: Under Regulation 1408/71, the State in which the person is seeking work pays the benefit and it is reimbursed by the competent State. It appeared in recent years that some Member States had financial problems in paying the benefits, as the reimbursements often came much later. The new Regulation provides that the competent institution has to pay the benefits. This is an improvement for poorer Member States, which have sometimes difficulties in financing the benefits they have to pay to persons from other countries when they are reimbursed much later.

15.9.5. FRONTIER WORKERS AND EXPORT OF BENEFIT

The question arose whether also frontier workers can invoke the export provision, to look for work in a third State. This question was raised before the Dutch Central Appeals Court in a case of a German frontier worker residing in the Netherlands, but seeking work in France. From the *Huijbrechts* judgment the Central Appeals Court inferred that he could not invoke the export provision, Article 69.[52] The European Commission started an infringement procedure against the Netherlands, which lead to the *Commission versus the Netherlands* judgment.[53]

In this judgment the Court ruled that Article 69 of Regulation 1408/71 must be interpreted as applying to wholly unemployed frontier workers, so that the Member State in which such workers reside is obliged to ensure, under the conditions laid down by Article 69, that their right to unemployment benefits is retained.

Since Article 11 of the Regulation provides that unemployed persons to whom Article 65 applies are subject to the legislation of the State of residence, it follows already from this provision that this State has to apply the export provision of the Regulation.

---

[52] Central Appeals Court 23 May 1998, *USZ* 1998, 134.
[53] Case 311/01, *European Commission v. the Netherlands*, [2003] *ECR* I-3103.

CHAPTER 16

THE RELATION BETWEEN REGULATION 883/2004 AND BILATERAL TREATIES

16.1. INTRODUCTION

Before Regulation 3 came into force there were already several bilateral agreements between countries that would later become Member States. Also Member States who accessed the Union later had already bilateral agreements with coordinating provisions. In addition, there are multilateral treaties that bind Member States. Consequently, the Regulation has to provide which rules have priority in case of concurring rules.

Article 8 of the Regulation gives a general priority to the Regulation itself. This Article provides that the Regulation replaces any social security convention applicable between Member States falling under its scope. Certain provisions of social security conventions entered into by the Member States before the date if application of this Regulation shall, however, continue to apply, provided that they are more favourable to the beneficiaries or if they arise from specific historical circumstances and their effects are limited in time. These provisions are included in Annex II.

The application of provisions of treaties which have priority over Regulation 883/2004 can lead to differences in treatment depending on whether a person falls under a convention or not. As the Regulation requires equal treatment, Article 8 provides that if, on objective grounds, it is not possible to extend some of these provisions to all persons to whom the Regulation applies this shall be specified.

Article 8 enables two or more Member States to conclude, as the need arises, conventions with each other based on the principles and in the spirit of the Regulation. Such agreements may be useful in facilitating the application of the Regulation. Examples are the agreements on the basis of Article 16 which can deviate from the general rules for determining the legislation applicable or agreements on the (non-)reimbursement of medical expenses (*see* Chapter 11).

16.2. INFRINGEMENT ON SOCIAL SECURITY ADVANTAGES ACQUIRED ON THE BASIS OF INTERNATIONAL TREATIES

As we saw in Section 16.1, social security conventions are replaced by the Regulation unless otherwise provided. The question arose as to whether this rule is consistent with Article 42 EC, now Article 48 TFEU, in particular in cases where the application of the other convention would be more favourable for the person concerned.

The first time the Court had to answer this question was in the *Walder* case.[1] In that judgment the Court held that it was clear from Article 5 of Regulation 3 (Article 6 of Regulation 1408/71 and Article 8 of Regulation 883/2004) that the principle that the provisions of social security conventions concluded between Member States were replaced by Regulation 3 was mandatory in nature. This principle did not allow for exceptions save for the cases expressly stipulated in the Regulation. The Court added that the fact that social security conventions concluded between Member States were more advantageous to persons covered by Regulation 3 was therefore insufficient to justify an exception to this principle, unless such conventions were expressly preserved by the Regulation.

This *Walder* judgment led to much criticism and the *Rönfeldt* judgment[2] was therefore welcomed, as for a long time several authors thought that the Court had departed from the *Walder* approach in this judgment. Mr Rönfeldt was a German national and resident. From 1941 to 1951 he paid contributions for a German retirement pension. Subsequently, he worked in Denmark until 1971 and he paid contributions for a Danish old-age pension. After he returned to Germany, he had to pay German contributions again. The problem in Mr Rönfeldt's case was that the ages for retirement pension entitlement were different between Germany and Denmark. In Denmark, the retirement age was sixty-seven and in Germany this age was sixty-five. In addition, under the German scheme an early retirement pension could be claimed at the age of sixty-three, but for that pension it was required that one had completed thirty-five years of insurance. Therefore, he was refused early retirement benefit.

Regulation 1408/71 required only that periods of insurance have to be aggregated for the purpose of *acquiring* a right to benefit but not for the *calculation* of a right to benefit. The Convention concluded between Germany and Denmark of 1953, however, provided that periods of insurance completed under the legislation of Denmark had to be counted not only for the establishment of a right but also for the calculation of the German pension.

Article 6 of Regulation 1408/71 provides, as we have seen, that the conventions concluded between Member States were replaced by the Regulation at the

---

[1]   Case 82/72, [1973] *ECR* 599.
[2]   Case 227/89, [1991] *ECR* I-323.

date it came into force.[3] This would have the effect that the Germany-Denmark convention, which provided that the Danish periods would be counted for the calculation of the pension, was no longer applicable. The Court considered that because of Article 6 Mr Rönfeldt lost advantages which had been awarded to him by a bilateral convention. It ruled that this loss of benefit rights was not compatible with Articles 39 and 42 EC, now Articles 45 to 48. The Court had already pointed out in the *Petroni*[4] and *Dammer* judgments[5] that the purpose of these Articles would not be achieved if employed persons exercising their right to free movement lost advantages to which they would have been entitled by virtue of national law alone. This case law had to be interpreted, according to the Court, as meaning that benefits awarded by virtue of national law also comprise benefits to which one is entitled by virtue of international conventions which are in force between two or more Member States and which are integrated in their national legislation. The latter rules have to be applied if they are more advantageous than the application of Community law. A different interpretation would involve a substantial restriction on Articles 39 and 42 EC as it would place a person who exercises the right to free movement in a less advantageous position.

Also on this judgment a lot of criticism was given, as it was feared that the *Rönfeldt* judgment would apply in all cases where bilateral Conventions were involved and that this would lead to complicated situations. Bilateral and multi-lateral agreements are so numerous, so complicated and so varied that it would be unrealistic to require social security bodies to calculate for each migrant worker not only his benefit rights in accordance with national law and Community law, but also in accordance with international conventions.

In the *Thévenon* judgment[6] the Court clarified the *Rönfeldt* ruling. Mr Thévenon was a French national who had been compulsorily insured as an employee, first from 1964 to 1977 in France and subsequently in Germany. The German social assistance agency considered that the periods of insurance completed by Mr Thévenon in France had to be taken into account for the calculation of the German pension, in accordance with the rules of the General Treatment on social security between France and Germany (1950).

The Court remarked that according to Article 9 of this Treaty the periods completed under both schemes have to be taken into account for the calculation of the amount of benefit if a German or French employee had worked in both countries under one or more schemes of invalidity insurance. Regulation 1408/71 did not take periods abroad into account for the calculation of the amount of benefit. The Treaty thus provided for a more attractive result than the Regulation. The Court considered that it had already ruled in the *Walder* judgment that from

---

[3]   *I.e.* 1 April 1973, when Denmark entered the European Community (note that Denmark entered the EC only after Rönfeldt had returned to Germany).

[4]   Case 24/75, [1975] *ECR* 1149.

[5]   Case 168/88, [1989] *ECR* 4553.

[6]   Case 475/93, [1995] *ECR* I-3813.

Article 6 and 7 of the Regulation it follows that Community regulations replace the provisions of treaties concluded between Member States. These provisions have a compulsory character and do not allow for exceptions apart from those explicitly mentioned in the Regulation. Nor do exceptions apply if these treaties would lead to higher benefits than on the basis of the Regulation.

The *Rönfeldt* judgment concerned, according to the Court, a situation in which at the moment when Mr Rönfeldt returned to Germany, Denmark had not yet entered the EU. The Treaty between these two countries had not yet been replaced by Regulation 1408/71. Therefore, it had to be investigated if the periods completed in Denmark before Regulation 1408/71 applied to Denmark, and if so, how these should be taken into account for the calculation of the pension in the other Member State.

The answer given to this question in the *Rönfeldt* judgment did not apply in the situation of Mr Thévenon, who had not exercised his right to free movement before the coming into force of Regulation 1408/71. This meant that at the time Mr Thévenon went to work abroad, the French-German Treaty, as far as its personal and material scope are concerned, was already replaced by Regulation 1408/71. This employee cannot hold that he had lost social security advantages to which he would have been entitled on the basis of the French-German Treaty.

As a result of this judgment, it is not necessary to investigate in all cases whether the application of the rules of a Treaty between two Member States leads to a more advantageous result than the coordination Regulation.

In the *Gómez Rodríguez* judgment[7] the question was raised how the *Rönfeldt* judgment (which requires comparison of the Treaty and the Regulation) has to be applied; the question was, in particular, when the comparison was to be made. Only once, or every time when there were differences in effect? The case concerned the orphans of a worker, a Spanish national, who had been insured as an employed person in Germany and Spain. In 1985 he died in Spain without having drawn a pension. The German benefit agency granted the sons orphans' pension on the basis of the Convention on social security between Germany and Spain. When Spain acceded to the EC the Spanish pension insurance institution had sole competency to grant orphans' benefits from 1 January 1986 (as provided by Article 78(2)) until they reached the age of 18 (the maximum age under Spanish law). The sons then applied to the German agency for orphans' pensions under German law, which are payable for students up to the age of 25.

The national court asked whether, in such a situation, Articles 39 and 42 ec preclude the loss of social security advantages for workers which would result from the inapplicability, following the entry into force of the Regulation, of a bilateral social security convention. In this situation, the appellants' father completed his periods of insurance in Spain and Germany before the accession of Spain to the ec. Consequently, the rule identified in *Rönfeldt* applies. It follows that the persons

---

[7]   Case 113/96, [1998] *ECR* I-2482.

concerned cannot lose the social security advantage which they were guaranteed by the bilateral convention in question. In this case, however, a comparison had already been made between the advantages resulting from the Convention and those resulting from the Regulation. The outcome was that the arrangements under the Regulation were more favourable for the appellants, and therefore the principle identified in *Rönfeldt* cannot be applied. If it were otherwise, every migrant worker in the same position as the appellants could at any time ask for either arrangements under the Regulation or those under the Convention to be applied, depending on the most advantageous outcome for him at the time. Such a comparison of the advantages, made on a regular basis whenever there is a change in the personal circumstances of the persons concerned, throughout the period during which the benefits are granted, would cause considerable administrative difficulties for the competent authorities of the Member States despite there being no basis for the comparison in the Regulation.

Consequently, Articles 39 and 42 EC preclude the loss of social security advantages for workers only at the first determination of benefit on the basis of the Regulation. Only at that time a comparison has to be made between the rights to be derived from either instrument and, consequently, not again at a later moment. Following this approach, the main problem with the *Rönfeldt* approach, the administrative charges for the administration, has been taken away considerably.

In the *Thelen* case[8] a convention relating to unemployment insurance concluded between Germany and Austria was involved. Mr Thelen was a German national who lived from 1986 to 1996 in Austria and, during that period, had pursued various jobs which were subject to compulsory unemployment insurance contributions. Having moved to Trier (Germany), Mr Thelen applied for unemployment there in 1996. His claim was rejected on the ground that he had not completed the qualifying period. Mr Thelen had not fulfilled insurance periods in Germany and thus he did not fulfil the requirement laid down in Article 67(3) of Regulation 1408/71 of having completed lastly periods of insurance or employment in Germany. However, that condition was not contained in the Austro-German convention on unemployment insurance. The question thus arose whether Mr Thelen could rely on this convention. Regulation 1408/71 entered into force in Austria on 1 January 1994.

The Court observed that Mr Thelen was already employed in Austria prior to the date Regulation 1408/71 came into force. From the principles developed in the *Rönfeldt* and *Thevenon* judgments, it follows that the substitution of the Convention by the Regulation could not deprive Mr Thelen of the rights and advantages accruing to him from the Convention. That conclusion was not altered by the fact that the case under consideration involved unemployment benefits and not, as in previous cases, retirement or invalidity pensions.

---

[8]   Case 75/99, [2000] *ECR* I-9399.

In the *Kaske* judgment[9] the same Austro-German convention on unemployment insurance was involved, now in a case before a court in Austria. Ms Kaske, who held both German and Austrian nationality, worked between 1972 and 1982 in Austria during which period she was subject to compulsory unemployment insurance. From 1983 until 1995 she worked and paid unemployment contributions in Germany. In 1995 and 1996 she received unemployment benefit in that Member State. After a brief period of employment in 1996, she returned to Austria where she immediately applied for unemployment benefit. Prior to her application, however, she had not completed any periods of insurance or employment, as required by Article 67(3) of Regulation 1408/71. Accordingly, the aggregation rules of Article 67 could not be applied with the result that the competent Austrian institution rejected her application for unemployment benefit. Ms Kaske invoked the Austro-German convention on unemployment insurance which does not contain a condition comparable to Article 67(3) of the regulation.

A first question was whether the *Rönfeldt* and *Thevenon* case law also applies where a worker has exercised the right to freedom of movement prior to the entry into force in his or her Member State of origin of Regulation 1408/71 and the Treaty. The Court held that the sole purpose of these principles is to perpetuate entitlement to an established social right not enshrined in EC law at the time when the national of a Member State relying on it enjoyed that right. The *Rönfeldt* judgment derived from the notion of a legitimate expectation that rights previously accrued under a convention are respected. Accordingly, this case law also applies to workers who moved to other Member States prior to the entry into force of the Treaty.

---

[9]   Case 277/99, [2000] Ecr I-1261.

CHAPTER 17

EU AGREEMENTS WITH THIRD COUNTRIES CONTAINING COORDINATION PROVISIONS

17.1. THE EURO-MEDITERRANEAN ASSOCIATION AGREEMENTS

The EU can conclude treaties with States not belonging to the European Union. Some of these are relevant to the coordination of social security. Examples of such treaties are the agreements with Egypt, Israel, Jordan, Lebanon, Morocco, Tunisia and Algeria. In some of these treaties – with Morocco and Algeria – provisions are included which aim to achieve the principle of equal treatment on the basis of nationality. These treaties also include some provisions on the aggregation of periods of insurance or residence and on the payment of benefits.[1] In the case law discussed here Article 41 of the Treaty EC-Morocco is relevant, which is now replaced by Article 65 of the Euro Mediterranean Agreement with this country.

Article 41 of the Treaty EC-Morocco provides: that '1. Subject to the provisions of the following paragraphs, workers of Moroccan nationality and any members of their family living with them shall enjoy, in the field of social security, treatment free from any discrimination based on nationality in relation to nationals of the Member States in which they are employed. (..)'

In the *Kziber* judgment the corresponding provision of the predecessor, the EC-Morocco Treaty, was invoked.[2] The Belgian National Employment Agency refused to grant unemployment allowances to Miss Bahia Kziber, a Moroccan national, as she did not possess Belgian nationality. She lived with her father, a Moroccan national, who was a pensioner residing in Belgium where he had worked as a wage-earner.

The first question was whether Article 41(1) of the Agreement has direct effect. The Court considered that a provision of an agreement concluded by the Community with non-Member countries must be regarded as being directly applicable when, regard being had to its wording and to the purpose and nature of the agreement itself, the provision contains a clear and precise obligation which

---

[1]   OJ 2000, L 70.
[2]   Case 18/90, [1991] *ECR* 199.

is not subject, in its implementation or effects, to the adoption of any subsequent measure.

Article 41(1) of the Agreement satisfies those criteria, the Court considered, as it lays down in clear, precise and unconditional terms a prohibition of discrimination, based on nationality, against workers of Moroccan nationality and the members of their families living with them in the field of social security. The fact that Article 41(1) states that the prohibition of discrimination applies only subject to the provisions of the following paragraphs may not be interpreted as divesting the prohibition of discrimination of its unconditional character in respect of any other question which arises in the field of social security.

Subsequently, the Court had to decide what was meant by the term 'social security' in Article 41. The Court answered this question saying that this term must be understood by means of analogy with the identical concept in Regulation 1408/71. Article 4 of that Regulation lists unemployment benefits among the branches of social security. As regards the concept of 'worker' in Article 41(1) of the Agreement, it encompasses both active workers and those who have left the labour market, *inter alia*, after reaching the age required for the receipt of an old-age pension. The Court concluded that Article 41(1) precludes a Member State from refusing to grant unemployment benefit provided by its legislation in favour of young persons in search of employment, to a member of the family of a worker of Moroccan nationality living with him, on the grounds that the person in search of employment is of Moroccan nationality.[3]

The *Krid* judgment[4] concerned discrimination against an Algerian widow in France. The Court decided that Article 39 of the Agreement with Algeria prohibited this discrimination.

It has not yet been decided whether the provisions other than the non-discrimination clause in the Agreements also have direct effect. Some of these provisions, such as the aggregation of periods of work or insurance, are in principle applicable as they need no technical implementing provisions. We have seen an example of the application of the rules on the aggregation of periods on the basis of Article 42 EC, now Article 48 TFEU, even though there was no regulation governing this issue in the *Vougioukas* judgment[5] which concerned the special schemes for civil servants (Chapter 2). It is not yet clear whether the Court will also follow this approach with respect to these agreements, but it is likely that it will in the case where no implementing rules are necessary. Other parts of the Agreement cannot be applied without implementing rules.

Because of the case law mentioned above, in the newer Euro Mediterranean Agreements the equal treatment provisions for workers are no longer inserted.

---

[3]   *See*, for a comparable approach, the *Yousfi* judgment (Case 58/93, [1994] *ECR* I-1353).
[4]   Case 103/94, [1995] *ECR* I-719.
[5]   Case 443/93, [1995] *ECR* I-4033.

17.2. DECISION 3/80 OF THE ASSOCIATION COUNCIL EC-TURKEY

Some Association Treaties give the Community and the cooperating country the possibility of making coordination rules. So far only Decision 3/80 on the application of social security schemes of the Member States of the European Community to Turkish workers and members of their families has been adopted.[6] This decision has not been implemented by the contracting parties. Its purpose is the coordination of the social security schemes of the Member States for Turkish nationals and not the coordination of the Turkish social security scheme with the coordination rules of the EU.

In Article 1 of the Decision it is provided that terms as 'member of the family', 'place of residence', and 'family benefits' mean the same as in Article 1 of Regulation 1408/71. Consequently, the personal and material scope of the Decision are the same as that of Regulation 1408/71; Article 3(1) of both instruments – containing a non-discrimination clause – also has the same meaning.

In the *Taflan-Met* judgment[7] the question arose as to whether widows who wished to claim the Netherlands survivors' benefit in Turkey could rely on this decision. Ms Taflan-Met was a Turkish national, residing in Turkey, and the widow of a Turkish worker who was employed in various Member States, including the Netherlands. After her husband's death, she applied for a widows' pension in the Member States where her husband had worked. The application was rejected by the Netherlands authorities on the grounds that her husband had died in Turkey, whereas, under the Netherlands legislation, the insured person or his successors are entitled to claim benefit only if the insured risk materialises at a time when the person concerned is covered by that legislation. Decision 3/80 could be helpful to her, as this contains rules analogous to Regulation 1408/71. These rules would create the fiction that her husband was insured at the time of materialisation of the risk (for the corresponding provisions of Regulation 1408/71, *see* Chapter 13).

The Court first had to answer the question of whether Decision 3/80 has entered into force. This Decision contains no provision on its entry into force. The Court referred to the Agreement on which that decision is based. This Agreement provided that the Contracting Parties are bound by the measures they take. Now that they had adopted Decision 3/80, the Court decided it had entered into force on the date on which it was adopted, that is to say, 19 September 1980.

The second question was, whether the provisions of Decision 3/80, and more specifically Articles 12 and 13, have direct effect in the territory of the Member States. The Court followed its general case law on when a provision of the Treaty is directly applicable (*see* previous section): the provisions must contain a clear

---

[6]   *OJ* 1983 *C* 110, p. 60.

[7]   Case 277/94, [1996] *ECR* I-4085. *See* also H. Verschueren, "Na het arrest Taflan-Met: is er leven na de dood?', *Migrantenrecht* 1997, p. 29.

and precise obligation which is not subject, in its implementation or effects, to the adoption of any subsequent measures. Decision 3/80 does not satisfy these criteria. Comparison of Regulations 1408/71 and 574/72, on the one hand, and Decision 3/80, on the other, shows that the latter does not contain a large number of precise, detailed provisions, even though such were deemed indispensable for the purpose of implementing Regulation 1408/71 within the Community. Consequently, it must be held, according to the Court, that by its nature Decision 3/80 is intended to be supplemented and implemented in the Community by a subsequent act of the Council. On 8 February 1983 the Commission submitted a proposal for a regulation implementing Decision 3/80.[8] However, that proposal has not yet been adopted by the Council. It follows from these considerations, the Court ruled, that even though some of its provisions are clear and precise, Decision 3/80 cannot be applied so long as supplementary implementing measures have not been adopted by the Council.

From this consideration it could be concluded that the clear and precise provisions of the Decision, like the non-discrimination clause, could also not be applied. In the *Sürül* judgment the Court did not follow this interpretation.[9] This case concerned a Turkish employed person, Mr Sürül, who resided legally with his wife in Germany; they were, for the purpose of study and family reunion respectively, given an accessory residence authorisation. In 1992, Mrs Sürül gave birth within German territory to a child whom she cared for and brought up. She was granted family allowances. However, with effect from 1 January 1994, the Federal Child Benefit Law provided that in order to be entitled to benefit a residence entitlement or residence permit was required and consequently the benefit agency refused to continue payment of benefit. The accessory residence authorisation did not qualify as a residence permit or entitlement.

The question was whether Decision 3/80 could be invoked in order to remove the requirements on the residence permit. The German government submitted that following the *Taflan-Met* judgment Article 3(1) has no direct effect. The Court considered, however, that in this case the disputed provision does not, unlike Articles 12 and 13, require implementing measures. Mrs Sürül relied solely on the principle of non-discrimination on the grounds of nationality. The Court considered that its reasoning in *Taflan-Met*, that Articles 12 and 13 do not have direct effect, must apply by analogy to all the other provisions of that decision which require additional measures for their application in practice. However, that reasoning cannot be transposed to the principle of equal treatment in the field of social security, embodied in Articled 3(1). Article 3 is suitable for direct

---

8   *OJ* 1983 *C* 110, p. 1.
9   Case 262/96, [1999] *ECR* I-2685. *See* also H. Verschueren, 'The *Sürül* Judgment: Equal Treatment for Turkish Workers in Matters of Social Security', *European Journal of Migration and Law*, 1999, p. 371.

application, as this provision lays down in clear, precise and unconditional terms a prohibition of discrimination based on nationality.

Finally, the Court had to answer the question of whether Article 3(1) must be interpreted as precluding the application of legislation of a Member State which requires that a Turkish national, who has been authorised to reside in its territory and is lawfully resident there, hold a certain type of residence document in order to receive family allowances. The answer was in the affirmative, as the Turkish national in this situation has to be treated in the same way as nationals of the host Member State. The requirement to hold a particular type of residence document does not apply for nationals of Germany and the condition applicable to Turkish nationals was therefore as being discriminatory incompatible with Decision 3/80.

CHAPTER 18

SOME CONCLUSIONS ON THE DEVELOPMENT OF COORDINATION LAW

18.1. THE IMPACT OF THE COORDINATION REGULATION

The conclusion that the coordination regulations have so far had an important impact on the social security position of persons, that is, employed persons and self-employed persons, moving within the European Union, is not exaggerated. The objective of coordination laid down in Article 51 EEC, later Article 42 EC, and now Article 48 TFEU, that measures should be taken which are necessary for free movement, appears to have been very important for the development of the regulations. The Court of Justice constantly refers to this objective and uses it as a fundament for its interpretations. The case law of the Court of Justice has largely contributed to the impact of the coordination rules; the Court often gave provisions of the Regulation a broad interpretation (or narrow, if necessary)[1] in order to promote free movement. In this respect there are important differences with other coordination instruments, including bilateral treaties and the coordination treaties of other international organisations, such as the ILO and Council of Europe, which are interpreted by their supervisory bodies in a much more technical way. A second important difference with other coordination instruments is that the provisions of the Regulations are binding and overrule national law that is contrary to them; this effect is all the more strengthened by the existence of a Court supervising the regulation. As Member States have always been reluctant to have their social security systems affected by international organisations, this strong enforcement system has been of paramount importance.

In the course of time the provisions of the Treaty have received increasing importance, including the one on free movement of workers and the one on European citizenship. These have already had an important impact on the development of coordination law and are expected to have further effects in the future. An example is the *Hendrix* judgment,[2] discussed in Chapter 5. The loss of

---

[1]   For instance of the meaning of social assistance benefit, which is excluded from the scope of the Regulation.

[2]   Case C-287/05, [2007] *ECR* I-6909.

benefits caused by moving from one Member State to another is in the first place seen as an obstacle to free movement. Member States are therefore forced, by Community law and case law, to make exceptions to their territorial view on the scope of these welfare schemes. This impact is important to interpretation of the Regulation provisions and has therefore always be kept in mind when applying the Regulation.

Some of the problems with the coordination of social security have remained unsolved through the years and a solution in the future is still very far away. Even though Article 42 EC (now Article 48 TFEU) has been the basis for a dynamic coordination Regulation, the limits embedded in this provision clearly affect the possibilities for taking away all problems for migrants. The limited legal basis enshrined in Article 48 TFEU means that regulations based on it can only coordinate social security schemes, but do not and cannot take away the disparities between the various schemes. This is a deliberate choice of the legislature, but the effects of these disparities can sometimes drive people to despair.

These polar sides of the playing field for coordination – on the one side the dynamic possibilities created by the Treaty and on the other side the inherent limits to the competence of coordination rules – also framed the possibilities for the present Regulation.

18.2. SIMPLIFICATION AND MODERNISATION

It is interesting to view the Regulation from the point of view of the modernisation and simplification process with which it all started. Modernisation is a complex concept in general, since it suggests a neutral phenomenon, hiding the fact that particular choices underlie it. The concept of the modernisation of social security is, however, not so complex as such, as the choice to be made within the EU framework is already clear: promotion of free movement. From this point of view the direction for modernisation is clear: to extend of the scope, both personal and material, of the Regulation, since if, for instance, a particular benefit is not covered, migrant persons could be hindered as a result. Another dimension of modernisation is the adaptation of the Regulation to the case law of the Court of Justice. If the Court has given a particular interpretation to a provision of the Regulation, or to an article of the Treaty which seriously affects the Regulation, it may be desirable to incorporate this new approach. Such modernisation may, however, affect national social security systems in such a way as to make Member States reluctant to agree with such proposals. Their reluctance is often understandable, but progress can also be blocked by a single Member State which can make use of its veto right.

There is more support for simplification. It is clear that a complex rule is problematic both for administrative bodies and for migrant persons. A complication to achieving simplification is that proposals for modernisation and simplification do not necessarily overlap, at least not if we take the position of anxious Member States into account.

Sometimes there is concurrence however between the goals of modernisation and simplification, as can be seen with respect to the extension of the personal scope of the regulation. The restricted personal scope of Regulation 1408/71 has often been criticised: it included employed and self-employed persons only. The new Regulation covers all persons subject to social security schemes covered by the Regulation. The new text is thus both simple and modern. We have to acknowledge that in some countries the effects will be limited, as only employed persons are covered by the social security schemes covered by the Regulation. In other countries the effects may be larger, in the case of residence schemes for instance, but the case law of the Court regarding members of the family and Article 18 EC (Article 21 TFEU) had determined already that some coordination rules applied to them.

Simplification and modernisation can therefore take place at the same time. The simplification is clear: the Regulation needs fewer rules to determine the personal scope and define various categories. Modernisation is also at stake: in the Europe of the migrant person, the European citizen, it is obvious that coordination must not be limited to economically active persons. An important ongoing limitation of regulation is the position of third country nationals. Following the *Khalil* judgment, it was determined that Article 42 EC did not cover them. Regulation 859/2003 partially solved the issue, however a problem still is the requirement that the facts concerned must involve at least two Member States. The new Regulation involves new negotiations on a third country Regulation and this seems to be a very difficult process.[3] Attempts of the author to obtain documents of the negotiations from the Council were not successful.

For the material scope too, modernisation is important.[4] The 1998 Proposal of the Commission was a real modernisation of material scope of the co-ordination regime, since it was no longer to be limited only to specified risks. Article 2 of the Proposal provided that 'this Regulation shall apply to all social security legislation concerning the following, in particular.' This approach did not survive the discussions in the Council and is not reflected in the material scope as described in Article 3 of Regulation 883/2004. The 1998 Proposal further provided that agreements declared generally binding would fall within the material scope of the coordination regime; a declaration from the Member State concerned that the scheme is within the material scope would no longer have been required. This extension did not reach the final version of Regulation 883/2004 either.

---

[3]   See R. Cornelissen, 'Third-Country Nationals and the European Coordination of Social Security', *European Journal of Social Security,* 10(4) 2008, p. 374.

[4]   See F. Pennings, 'The European Commission Proposal to Simplify Regulation 1408/71', *European Journal of Social Security,* 3(1) 2001, p. 45-60.

The new Regulation is therefore criticised because of the limited list of benefits covered and the limitation only to statutory schemes. Simplification was not really needed here, but modernisation is urgently required, since migrant persons may be confronted by gaps in their social protection when they cross borders.

It can also be seen that if there were to have been modernisation, it would not have been by means of simple rules. For instance, the effects of extending the coordination rules to collective agreements and other contractual schemes, while desirable, would be hard to oversee, since all kinds of provisions can be found in collective agreements. Holiday pay, study and training grants, sabbatical leave, loyalty stamps and bad weather stamps are common examples of such supplementary social security provisions.

Sometimes collective agreements provide for supplements to statutory social security (increases to the benefit rates) or replace statutory protection which was withdrawn (privatisation). Some coordination rules, such as the non-discrimination clause and the provision on the export of benefits, would apply very well to the benefits mentioned in collective agreements. In fact, non-discrimination rules are already applicable to collective agreements, such as Article 7(2) of Regulation 1612/68. Other co-ordination rules can lead to problems if they are applied without restrictions to these benefits. One example is a sabbatical leave provision with an eligibility requirement of seven years of work accrued with the same employer. An employer cannot be expected to allow an employee to aggregate periods of work for other employers for the purpose of satisfying this condition, since this employer has to pay the full costs of the sabbatical. Problems arise also in the case of employees working in two countries. If the rules for determining the legislation applicable apply to these agreements as well, the employee concerned falls under one collective agreement only, insofar as its social security provisions are considered. The effects are hard to manage and some of the effects are undesirable. Member States could prevent these problems by no longer extending collective agreements, but that would be an unattractive option. Thus, this modernisation would require more rules and could lead to more complications.

The almost complete lack of progress in this area is deplorable, especially because, as a result of the privatisation of social security, more and more schemes are becoming non-statutory and thus excluded. Moreover, new types of benefits are being created all the time and their non-coverage is problematic. An example is the non-coverage of study grants. In the *Bosmann* case, Ms Bosmann could not receive family benefits for her children over 18 from the Netherlands. For children of this age study grants are the appropriate form of subsistence, but these grants are not exportable, meaning that she did not have these benefits for her children. The Court solved this problem by allowing the national court to decide that she could claim family benefits from Germany, but this also creates a complication for the coordination rules, which can now affect the systems of two countries. Extension of the material scope of the Regulation would have been a more appropriate solution, but that is possible only by the legislator.

Even though it is difficult to include all forms of social security in the material scope at once, it should be possible to investigate options in this area at a quicker pace. One possibility could be that Member States would have to give good arguments as to why a particular scheme could not be included in the material scope of the Regulation. Another possibility is to apply only part of the coordination techniques to non-statutory schemes, such as the non-discrimination rule and the rule on the export of benefits.

A third area of changes to the Regulation concerns the rules for determining the legislation applicable. These have been seriously simplified and reordered and require much less space in the text of the regulation than under Regulation 1408/71. The principle of exclusive effect has also been strengthened, which also simplifies the application of the rules. If undesirable effects at the national level from these changes have been foreseen, then they have been accepted, or at any rate Member States will now have to solve any that arise.

The addition of the requirement to consider 'substantial activities' in the rules covering simultaneous activities in two Member States may be called a modernisation. It is not a simplification, since it is now more difficult to know whether the conditions are satisfied and disputes can arise from this. Also other rules for determining the legislation have become more difficult, to the sense that it is necessary to know where the employer is established or whether a person has the status of civil servant or worker. The wording of the rules has, however, been importantly simplified.

The rules on posting are not simplified, but maybe the problem here is that they are at present *too* simple and that further conditions are necessary. Here we can see that the contrary interests of Member States made it difficult to agree on such a more elaborate system. Some of the disputes and uncertainties on these rules are already quite old, but the legislature has so far been unable to realise a more elaborate system.

In respect of the Chapters on the specific benefits it can be said that the new provisions for family benefits definitely contribute to the simplification of coordination law: they are much shorter and clearer when compared to the complicated 'Family Benefits' chapter of the old Regulation.

It is hard to call Regulation 883/2004 a simplification with respect to unemployment benefits, as the deviations from the *lex loci laboris* for frontier workers and non-frontier workers not residing in the competent State still involve special, complicated rules. The 1998 proposal for simplification was indeed a simplification, as it made the competent State responsible for the payment of benefits in all cases. It was also a modernisation, as it involved a division of tasks: the payment of benefits by the competent State, and the supervision of obligations by the State of residence. This modernisation was clearly too radical for the Member States. At the end of the day, the new Regulation still has most of the same main rules as the old one. That means that it has inherited several of the problems of the old one, such as the unsatisfactory rules for frontier workers, possibly the *Miethe* case law, the special position of non-frontier workers not residing in the competent State, and the limited possibility to seek work in another Member State.

The changes in the Chapter on unemployment benefits were made for the benefit of the Member States rather than for the unemployed. The new reimbursement rules for the States of residence of frontier workers, and payment rules in cases of the export of benefits for persons seeking work, are clear examples of improvements for the States. For the frontier workers there are few improvements. Another lack of modernisation is that little attention is paid to reintegration measures.

In the sickness benefits chapter it is remarkable that the relationship between the freedom of services and the coordination of social security is till unsolved. This is a problematic issue. Thus the Regulation cannot be called a real modernisation with respect to this chapter.

18.3. CONCLUSIONS

Regulation 883/2004 seems to be successful if we consider it from the point of view of simplification. It has considerably fewer rules and some are drafted in a simpler way. This has been a huge process which could not have been done just with a Regulation amending Regulation 1408/71. Moreover, even small changes nowadays require a lot of discussion and the project of developing a new text is a better framework for such discussions than a proposal for an amending regulation.

From the point of view of modernisation the assessment is more critical. Even some almost unavoidable steps are not taken, such as the extension of the material scope and the elaboration of the relationship between the mobility of patients and the coordination rules.

The European Commission and the Council have not made clear how discussions towards further modernisation should take place. The Preamble refers to issues where there has been serious pressure (among others from the European Parliament) and where some cautious steps are mentioned. Still, there is little consensus on such areas among the Member States.

CHAPTER 19

A BRIEF OVERVIEW OF NON-EU COORDINATION INSTRUMENTS

19.1. CONVENTIONS OF THE INTERNATIONAL LABOUR ORGANISATION

Aside from the EU co-ordination Regulation, there are other supranational coordination schemes. These are discussed in this chapter.

An organisation which has made a global coordination scheme is the International Labour Organisation (ILO). Among other things, the ILO, which was created after the First World War, is responsible for preparing and adopting treaties and recommendations as well as supervising the observance of existing international labour standards. Besides representatives of the governments of Member States, representatives from employers' organisations and trade unions sit on every board. The creation of this organisation brought about an institutional framework which has the powers and the authority to draw up coordination and harmonisation treaties.[1]

A limited number of ILO Treaties is devoted to the *coordination* of the social security schemes of signatory States. Furthermore, a number of ILO Conventions contain coordination rules alongside other provisions. Coordination under the ILO progresses with difficulty and, as a result, it is still in a rudimentary stage. The reason is that world-wide conventions with extensive coordination rules run the risk of being ratified by only a small number of countries. Hence it is natural that the Convention holding the largest number of ratifications (Convention 118) is very specific, prohibiting discrimination on the ground of nationality and requiring export of benefits. Conventions which require high standards are, of course, more problematic for many Member States.

---

[1]   For a historical overview of the ILO, *see* G. Tamburi, 'L'Organisation internationale du Travail et l'évolution des assurances sociales dans le monde', in: P. Köhler en H. Zacher, *Beiträge zu Geschichte und aktueller Situation der Sozialversicherung,* Berlin 1983, p. 647; G. Perrin, 'De aktie van de internationale arbeidsorganisatie ten gunste van de coördinering en van de harmonisering van de wetgevingen betreffende de sociale zekerheid" *BTSZ* 1969, p. 1165-1253. For the texts of ILO Treaties can be found on the web site of the ILO, *see* webfusion.ilo.org/public/db/standards/normes/index.cfm?lang=EN.

ILO Convention 48 is specifically devoted to coordination. This Convention provides extensive rules for the maintenance of rights in the course of acquisition and acquired rights under invalidity, old-age and widows' and orphans' insurance schemes.[2] This Convention has a limited significance, however, as it has been ratified by only a small number of States.[3] Generally, the Convention was considered to be too detailed and too inflexible. Therefore, negotiations were opened for a new Convention, Convention 157, which has so far attracted only a few ratifications.[4]

Now that the EU coordination rules have gained in importance (being binding on all Member States and some associated States), the ILO coordination rules have faded to the background. Yet, the ILO was able to offer considerable technical support in drawing up EU coordination rules.[5]

19.2. CONVENTIONS OF THE COUNCIL OF EUROPE

While the First World War led to the foundation of the ILO, the Second World War resulted in the Congress of Europe, organised in The Hague in May 1948. During this Congress, propositions were made for a Unified Europe with freedom of movement of persons, of opinions and of goods, as well as a Human Rights Convention and a Court of Justice for Human Rights. This resulted in the Statute of the Council of Europe, which was signed on 5 May 1949. Currently, all West European States and some Central and East European States are members of this organisation. The aim of the Council of Europe, as laid down in its Statute, is to achieve greater unity between its members for the purpose of safeguarding and realising the ideals and principles which form their 'common heritage' and of facilitating their economic and social progress. This includes social justice and the promotion of the freedom of movement of workers.[6]

From an institutional point of view, the Council of Europe is not strong. The Council of Europe is an organisation of a purely intergovernmental character, based on voluntary cooperation between States unwilling to give up their sovereign power.[7] These characteristics of the Council of Europe place it in a

---

[2]   Convention of 22 June 1935.

[3]   After cancellation by the Netherlands, Hungary, Spain, Poland and Czechoslovakia, this Treaty holds for Bosnia and Herzegovina, Croatia, Israel, Italy, The former Yugoslav Republic of Macedonia. Montenegro, Serbia, Slovenia and Spain.

[4]   Convention of 23 June 1982. It has so far been ratified by Spain, Sweden, the Philippines and Kyrgyzstan.

[5]   *See* G. Perrin, 'De aktie van de internationale arbeidsorganisatie ten gunste van de coördinering en van de harmonisering van de wetgevingen betreffende de sociale zekerheid', BTSZ 1969, p. 1165-1253.

[6]   For the case law of the court, *see* http://www.echr.coe.int and for the web site of the Council of Europe, http://www.coe.fr/index.asp.

[7]   *See*, for the Council of Europe, H. Wiebringhaus, 'Die Sozialversicherung im Rahmen der Funktionen, der Möglichkeiten und der sozialpolitischen Vorhaben des Europarats', in: Köhler

position somewhere between the EU and the ILO and its importance with respect to international social policy initiatives has decreased in the past decades.

The current low-key position in the field of social security contrasts with the early days of the Council of Europe. During this stage, the Council started with great élan to prepare conventions to promote social progress. These activities fitted in well with the above mentioned general objectives of the Council; these objectives implied the task and objective of coordination and harmonisation of social security law of the Member States. In order to encourage the freedom of movement of workers, two Interim Agreements on social security were signed in 1953.[8] These agreements were meant to be a temporary provision for the period until the European Convention on Social Security of the Council of Europe had been signed and ratified by the Member States. The latter Convention was signed in 1972.[9] This Convention was aimed at the multilateral coordination of the social security systems of the Member States. Due to the small number of ratifications of this Convention, however, this objective was not achieved.[10]

In addition to the Interim Agreements, the European Convention on Social and Medical Assistance was signed in Paris on 11 December 1953. This is the only multilateral Convention on *public assistance* and this Convention received much ratification, viz. sixteen Member States of the Council of Europe. It has taken over the role of the earlier bilateral treaties on public assistance.

Article 1 of this Convention provides that the contracting parties undertake to ensure that nationals of the other signatory States who are lawfully resident in the territory of one of the States, and who are without sufficient resources, are entitled like the own nationals to social and medical assistance, and on the same conditions as those provided by the legislation in force in that part of the territory. The Convention provides that the costs of assistance to a national of a contracting party are borne by the State that has granted the assistance.[11] It can be seen that this Convention does not require States to refund the costs to the State where the benefit has been granted to their nationals, as is the case in some other bilateral agreements. The second basic principle of this Convention is that a national of a signatory State who is lawfully resident in the territory of another signatory State, shall not be repatriated on the sole ground that he is in need of assistance.[12]

---

en Zacher 1983, p. 507. The Council of Europe also established the European Convention for the Protection of Human Rights and Fundamental Freedoms, which is relevant to social security (as Article 6 requires due process, which is relevant to social security adjudication).

[8]   European Interim Agreement on social security schemes relating to old age, invalidity and survivors; European Interim Agreement on social security other than schemes for old age, invalidity and survivors; signed at Paris, 11 December 1953.

[9]   Convention on Social Security of 14 December 1972.

[10] *See*, for the coordination rules of this Convention, H. Urbanetz, 'Modaliteiten voor het behoud van de rechten en de berekening van de prestaties in het Europees Verdrag inzake sociale zekerheid en andere samenordeningsinstrumenten', *BTSZ* 1991, p. 359.

[11] *See* Article 4 of this Convention.

[12] Article 6 of the Convention. More extensively on this Convention, G. Vonk, *De coördinatie van bestaansminimumuitkeringen in de Europese Gemeenschap*, Deventer 1991.

In Chapter 20 we shall discuss some of the harmonisation instruments of the European Union.

PART II
SOCIAL POLICY

CHAPTER 20

SOCIAL POLICY INSTRUMENTS
OF THE EUROPEAN UNION

20.1. GENERAL: THE POWERS OF THE EU TO TAKE SOCIAL POLICY INITIATIVES

The Provisions of the Treaty concerning social policy can be found in Articles 151-161 TFEU. Article 151 reads: 'The Union and the Member States, having in mind fundamental social rights such as those set out in the European Social Charter signed at Turin on 18 October 1961 and in the 1989 Community Charter of the Fundamental Social Rights of Workers, shall have as their objectives the promotion of employment, improved living and working conditions, so as to make possible their harmonisation while the improvement is being maintained, proper social protection, dialogue between management and labour, the development of human resources with a view to lasting high employment and the combating of exclusion. To this end the Union and the Member States shall implement measures which take account of the diverse forms of national practices, in particular in the field of contractual relations, and the need to maintain the competitiveness of the Union economy.

They believe that such a development will ensue not only from the functioning of the internal market, which will favour *the harmonisation of social systems*, but also from the procedures provided for in the Treaties and from the approximation of provisions laid down by law, regulation or administrative action'. (italics added)

The EEA Agreement also contains provisions in the area of social policy. Articles 66 to Article 72 EEA are analogous to Articles 151 to 161 TFEU.

Article 151 refers to the 'harmonisation of social systems', but in fact it does not provide anything else than the point of view that harmonisation will automatically take place as a result of the functioning of the market. The reason for this obscure text can be explained by the drafting process of the earliest version of this Article, i.e. Article 117 EC Treaty. During the negotiations on the draft EC Treaty, France strongly pleaded for a provision in favour of the harmonisation of social security in the Treaty. France considered this to be essential since French enterprises in a unified market would suffer too much from the large financial charges imposed by French social security on these enterprises. Germany opposed this point of view, on the grounds that social security costs are but one of many factors relevant to the competitive position of enterprises in a single market. In other words, the costs for social security per worker constitute only one element of all expenses related to labour. Differences in social security expenses between Member States would, for example, be compensated for by the differences in the level of wages and taxes. Elements such as infrastructure, the social climate and the tax regime are also relevant to the competitive position of an enterprise. All these factors together determine the competitive position of enterprises. If solely social security were harmonised, competitive relationships would deteriorate rather than improve. Thus the ambiguous text of Article 117 EC Treaty is a compromise between these different opinions.

Article 117 EC Treaty did not grant any powers to the Community legislator to realise the objectives of this Article. However, for this purpose Article 352 TFEU can be used (ex Articles 94 EEC and 308 EC): 1. If action by the Union should prove necessary, within the framework of the policies defined in the Treaties, to attain one of the objectives set out in the Treaties, and the Treaties have not provided the necessary powers, the Council, acting unanimously on a proposal from the Commission and after obtaining the consent of the European Parliament, shall adopt the appropriate measures. Where the measures in question are adopted by the Council in accordance with a special legislative procedure, it shall also act unanimously on a proposal from the Commission and after obtaining the consent of the European Parliament.

When the Treaty of Amsterdam came into force, Article 137 was inserted, now Article 153 TFEU, which provides for the instruments to realise the objective of Article 136 EC (now Article 151 TFEU). This will be discussed in more detail in Section 20.3.

20.2. THE SUBSIDIARITY PRINCIPLE

For the application of what are now Articles 352 TFEU and Article 153 TFEU, the principle of subsidiarity is important. Article 5(1) TEU provides that the use of Union competences is governed by the principles of subsidiarity and proportionality. Para. 3 of this Article provides that under the principle of subsidiarity, in areas which do not fall within its exclusive competence, the Union shall act only if and in so far as the objectives of the proposed action cannot be sufficiently achieved by the Member States, either at central level or at regional and local level, but can rather, by reason of the scale or effects of the proposed action, be better achieved at Union level.

This Article does not provide criteria for the application of the subsidiarity principle either. After all, when can we say that measures 'cannot be sufficiently' achieved and can, therefore, 'by reason of the scale or effects', be better achieved by the Community? Is it sufficient that the internal market brings about social disruption which is difficult to solve by the Member States themselves, in view of the competitive aspects of social measures? Does this mean that, in view of the poverty in many areas of Europe, the Member States are not capable of solving these problems by themselves? It is clear that the positions taken by the parties concerned before entering negotiations on possible measures has not been altered on the basis of this Article.

The principle of subsidiarity has several dimensions.[1] On the one hand it may mean that higher bodies must not execute tasks which can be done by lower bodies in the hierarchy (*vertical subsidiarity*). In accordance with this principle, a decision is to be made at an hierarchic level which is as low as possible. However, this does not provide criteria for its application. Is a relevant criterion for selecting a level that a measure can be implemented most effectively and/or efficiently on that level? If so, what do 'efficiency' and 'effectiveness' mean in this context?

A different dimension of the principle of subsidiarity concerns the relationships between the social partners (*horizontal subsidiarity*). This concept requires that the Community legislature does not take measures that can also be taken by the social partners. This type of subsidiarity is an answer to the objections that may exist to vertical subsidiarity. After all, with vertical subsidiarity there is the problem that, although it might be understandable that Member States wish to rely on the principle of subsidiarity to keep as much autonomous powers as possible, this impedes the establishment of a clear social policy. In the case of social security there is no driving force for such a policy. This is why solutions to adjustment problems (competitive problems) and a possible redistribution of means by a social policy are not, or are only slowly, being developed.

Horizontal subsidiarity includes initiatives by the social partners at a Community level as well as on a national level. The first type of action is based on a central perspective and this may result in advantages compared to the principle of vertical subsidiarity. However, to achieve this, strong organisation of social partners on a European level will be necessary. Moreover, once these organisations have gained more influence, they still have a long way to go to free themselves from the inevitable national interests and perspectives of the participating organisations. Therefore, the principle of subsidiarity appears to be a serious impediment to developing a social Europe at sufficient speed. The Treaty of Amsterdam provides a basis for the involvement of the social partners, *i.e* Article 152. We will discuss this Article in the following section.

---

[1] Cf. *Subsidiarity: the Challenge of Change*, Maastricht 1991, which contains a collection of articles on this principle.

20.3. THE INSTRUMENTS OF TITLE X TO TAKE SOCIAL POLICY MEASURES

Article 153(1) provides that with a view to achieving the objectives of Article 151, the Union shall support and complement the activities of the Member States in a couple of fields. One of them is the improvement of the working environment in order to protect the health and the safety of the workers. Other fields concern the integration of persons excluded from the labour market, social security and social protection of workers, the combating of social exclusion and the modernisation of social protection systems without prejudice to the rules on migrants. This means that at present the Union has the powers to take also initiatives on social security beyond the protection of the migrants. However, Article 153(2)(a) also provides that the Council must not take any measure which brings about harmonisation of the laws and regulations of the Member States. Consequently, though the scope of operation of the Council is extended, there are still no powers for harmonisation initiatives. Instead they may adopt, in the fields referred to in paragraph 1(a) to (i), – i.e. *not* in the area of (j) the combating of social exclusion and (k) the modernisation of social protection systems – by means of directives, minimum requirements for gradual implementation, having regard to the conditions and technical rules obtaining in each of the Member States.

However, for a number of issues, unanimity of votes is required (Article 153(3)), *e.g.* in the field of social security and social protection of workers, the protection of workers where their employment contract is terminated and financial contributions for the promotion of employment and job-creation. Consequently, for the main part of our subject, unanimity of votes is required for a proposal from the Commission.

Article 153 provides explicitly that the provisions adopted pursuant to this Article do not prevent any Member State from maintaining or introducing more stringent protective measures compatible with the Treaty. Provisions pursuant to Article 153 shall not affect the right of Member States to define the fundamental principles of their social security systems and must not significantly affect the financial equilibrium thereof. This text shows that the Member States are still very afraid to give the Council the power to make harmonising measures in the area of social security.

Article 154 concerns the role of the social partners at Union level. According to this provision, the European Commission has the task of promoting consultation between the social partners at the Community level and has to take any relevant measure to facilitate their dialogue by ensuring balanced support for the parties.

To this end, before submitting proposals in the social policy field, the Commission has to consult the social partners on the possible direction of Union action. If, after such consultation, the Commission considers Union Community action advisable, it has to consult management and labour on the content of the envisaged proposal. Management and labour shall forward to the Commission an opinion or, where appropriate, a recommendation.

On the occasion of such consultation, the social partners may inform the Commission of their wish to initiate the process provided for in Article 155. The duration of this procedure must not exceed nine months, unless the social partners and the Commission decide to extend this period.[2]

Article 155 provides that should the social partners so desire, the dialogue between them at Union level may lead to contractual relations, including agreements. These agreements can be implemented in two ways. Agreements concluded at Union level can be implemented in accordance with the procedures and practices specific to the social partners and the Member States. Implementation can also be realized by means of a joint request for a Council decision on a proposal from the Commission. In the case of social security, unanimity in the Council is necessary for such a Council decision.

20.4. THE OPEN METHOD OF COORDINATION

As we saw in the previous section, the powers to take social policy measures are limited; moreover, there is little enthusiasm to take such measures, even where there are powers to do so. Since binding rules in this area are seen as too threatening to the powers of the Member State to define their own social policy, a new instrument was developed, the Open Method of Coordination (OMC).[3] This instrument is meant to influence the policies of the Member States in a 'soft' way. The Open Method of Coordination must not be confused with the type of coordination of social security schemes in favour of migrants, which was discussed in the first part of this book.

The purpose of the Open Method of Coordination is to generate systematically information on best practices, which is useful for Member States to realise important objectives of the Treaty, whereas they can take account of the relevant national circumstances.

Within the framework of the Open Method of Coordination Member States must make national action plans in which they make clear how they aim to realise the objective of combating social exclusion.[4]

---

[2] On the role of the social partners *see* L. Betten, 'The Role of the Social Partners in the Community's Social Policy making: Participatory Democracy of Furthering the Interests of Small Elites', in: C. Engels and M. Weiss, *Labour Law and Industrial relations at the Turn of the Century*, The Hague 1998, p. 239.

[3] *See*, on the Open Co-ordination Method, B. Schulte, 'The new European 'Buzzword': Open Method of Co-ordination', *European Journal of Social Security* 2002, p. 343 ff.; J. Berghman and K. Okma, 'The Method of Open co-ordination: Open procedures or closed circuit? Social policy making between science and politics', *European Journal of Social Security* 2002, p. 331 ff.

[4] See the progress report on combating social exclusion, European Commission, *Joint Report on Social Inclusion*, Luxembourg, 2002.

The Open Method of Coordination was developed in the 1990s in the area of employment policy. Employment policy is an important policy area for the EU, since it is part of the European Employment Strategy (EES). The EES, which was initiated in the 1990s, was initially solely part of the EMU instruments. It made use of mid-term objectives, indicators and convergence aims. In 1997 the EES was made part of the Treaty of Amsterdam (Article 125 EC, now Article 145 TFEU). Later the OMC was also applied in other areas: social inclusion; pensions; immigration; education and culture; and asylum. More recently its use has been suggested for other areas as well, including health care, environmental affairs and the promotion of mobility of researchers.

In short, the OMC is an instrument meant to meet certain objectives defined by the Council of Ministers. It requires Member States to submit reports on the national state of affairs in the policy area concerned, and on the basis of discussions within the Council on these reports, Member States are given guidelines which require them to take measures to reach the set objectives. Subsequently the Member States have to report the results of their policies.

A major aim of the employment strategy was to increase the employment rate in the Member States and to improve the overall economic situation. The European Union was not, however, given the competence to make binding rules on the employment policies of the Member States. The OMC can be seen then as an instrument for realising the objectives of the employment strategy, thus compensating for the lack of EU competence in this area. Article 145 TFEU does not give the powers to EU institutions to make rules which bind the Member States. Instead, according to this Article, Member States and the Community shall, in accordance with this title of the Treaty, work towards developing a coordinated strategy for employment. This strategy must be particularly aimed at promoting a skilled, trained and adaptable workforce, and labour markets responsive to economic change, with a view to achieving the objectives defined in Article 3 TFEU.

Article 146 mentions the obligations for the Member States, which create the OMC framework: Member States, through their employment policies, shall contribute to the achievement of the objectives referred to in Article 145 in a way consistent with the broad guidelines of the economic policies of the Member States and of the Community adopted pursuant to Article 121(2). In addition, the Member States, having regard to national practices related to the responsibilities of management and labour, have to regard promoting employment as a matter of common concern, and shall coordinate their action in this respect within the Council.

These provisions, together with Article 147, constitute the legal basis for the OMC in employment policy. In Article 148 the procedure is described in more detail. Note that the Treaty does not use the term 'Open Method of Coordination' to describe the procedure.

The OMC procedure as described in Article 148 TFEU is as follows. First, each year the European Council has to consider the employment situation in the Community. On the basis of a joint annual report by the Council and the Commission, the Council adopts conclusions on this employment situation. On the basis of these conclusions, the Council, acting by a qualified majority on, inter alia, a proposal from the Commission, has, each year, to draw up guidelines which the Member States have to take into account in their employment policies. Subsequently, each Member State has to write an annual report on the principal measures taken to implement its employment policy in the light of these guidelines; these reports are sent to the Council and the Commission. The Council examines these reports – i.e. on the employment policies of the Member States – in the light of the employment guidelines.

The Council can, if it considers it appropriate in the light of that examination, make recommendations to Member States on a proposal from the Commission. Finally, on the basis of the results of the reports, the Council and the Commission have to make a joint annual report to the European Council on the employment situation in the Community and on the implementation of the guidelines for employment.

Thus, the OMC is a cycle of guidelines, recommendations and reports:
- a report and conclusions are made by the Council on the employment situation; these set objectives, and in order to be able to measure the extent to which these are reached, common indicators are used (e.g. reaching an employment level of 70 per cent);
- guidelines are made by the Council for Member States;
- annual reports of the Member States on the measures they have taken in light of guidelines with action plans;
- an examination by the Council of the reports (peer reviewing);
- recommendations by Council to Member States; and
- an annual report by Council and Commission on the employment situation.

Initially, it was feared that the OMC would not have much effect. However, the Council issued detailed and specific recommendations. These recommendations are to be taken into account for the next reports Member States have to write. Thus, Member States have to consider these recommendations when developing their policies, making them quite influential.

The analysis of the reports, the comparison of the results reached in the Member States, and the description of best practices of other Member States, constitute pressure on the Member States to continue to aim for the formulated objectives. We can conclude that, while having formally kept the freedom to choose the national instruments to meet the objectives of the employment strategy, Member States have to take the recommendations into account, in any case if they do not succeed in meeting the objectives of the employment strategy with their own instruments. The OMC has thus become a way to set Member

States in motion without hard law at the EU level. It is an instrument which leaves the powers to develop a policy basically at the national level, but still has serious effects on national employment policy. In other words, the OMC is an instrument which deals in a very specific way with the subsidiarity principle.

As, from this point of view the OMC in employment was seen as successful, the Method was introduced in other areas as well.[5]

The first 'new' area where the OMC was introduced was social inclusion. Social inclusion – or 'combating social exclusion' – is important from a political point of view, as the EU is often criticised for being an economic organisation only, which aims at promoting and enforcing more competition and demands the abolition of social protection rules if these impede competition. In order to mitigate these effects, the EU has to take action in the area of social policy.

The Treaty gives, in Article 3 TFEU, the obligation to the Community to promote, *inter alia*, a high level of employment and of social protection, a high level of protection and improvement of the quality of the environment, the raising of the standard of living and quality of life, and economic and social cohesion and solidarity among Member States. This Article shows that social objectives constitute a very important part of the obligations of the EU, but EU institutions have very few powers to realise these objectives.

Combating social exclusion is a main objective of European social policy.[6] However, the term 'social inclusion' is far from clear.[7]

The European Commission mentioned the following objectives for combating social exclusion:

– the promotion of participation in work and the promotion of access to all sources, rights, goods and services;
– measures to prevent the risk of social exclusion;
– measures to help the most vulnerable groups to re-integrate into society ('social inclusion');
– mobilisation of all the bodies concerned to combat social exclusion.[8]

For our purpose it suffices that social exclusion is more than poverty, since poverty does not necessarily mean that one cannot or does not participate in social

---

[5]   E. Szyszczak, 'Experimental Governance: the Open Method of Coordination', *European Law Journal*, 2004, p. 489 ff.

[6]   See, on this topic, D.G. Mayes, J. Berghman and R. Salais, *Social Exclusion and European Policy*, Cheltenham and Northampton, 2001; E. Aposapori and J. Millar, *The Dynamics of Social Exclusion in Europe*, Cheltenham and Northampton 2003.

[7]   See, for a thorough analysis, K. Vlemminckx and J. Berghman, 'Social Exclusion and the Welfare State', in D.G. Mayes, J. Berghman and R. Salais, *Social Exclusion and European Policy*, Cheltenham and Northampton, 2001, p. 34 ff; and P. Schoukens, 'How the European Union Keeps the Social Welfare Debate on Track: 'A Lawyer's View on the EU Instruments Aimed at Combating Social Exclusion', EJSS 2002, 117 ff.

[8]   Communication of the Council of 17 October 2000, *OJ* 13 March 2001, 82/4.

activities or benefit from these. Also, persons with an income above subsistence level can sometimes be excluded from particular activities or benefits.

The OMC inclusion was elaborated by a request to each Member State in 2001 to benchmark the state of social inclusion in its country by producing a two-year national action plan. Member States also had to present national level strategies for improving the situation. In 2003 the European Commission published a joint report on social inclusion in which the approaches of the Member States were compared and contrasted and recommendations were given.

In order to win the fight against social exclusion, the national measures and results were compared on the basis of so-called social inclusion indicators. These indicators are still subject to further development, but already show what results have been achieved in the Member States. The idea behind these indicators is that social exclusion is a relative concept: relevant is whether citizens have access to, among other things, work, housing and health care. The indicators have to show whether national measures are effective in ensuring access to these elements.

The OMC on social inclusion has no basis in the Treaty, as is the case with OMC on employment. Instead, the procedure can be based on Article 153(2)(a) TFEU, which provides that the Council can take measures in order to encourage Member States to cooperate by means of initiatives which increase knowledge, exchange information, and give information on examples of good results ('best practice'). Since this procedure does not provide for the power or the obligation to give recommendations and guidelines, as is the case with the OMC on employment, the OMC on social inclusion (and other OMCs in areas other than employment) are sometimes called OMC *light*.

CHAPTER 21

EQUAL PAY FOR MEN AND WOMEN: ARTICLE 157 TFEU

21.1. INTRODUCTION

Article 157 TFEU (previously Article 119 EC Treaty and 141 EC) sets out the principle of equal pay for men and women. This Article provides: '1. Each Member State shall ensure that the principle of equal pay for male and female workers for equal work or work of equal value is applied. 2. For the purpose of this Article, 'pay' means the ordinary basic or minimum wage or salary and any other consideration, whether in cash or in kind, which the worker receives directly or indirectly, in respect of his employment, from his employer. (..)'

It was France which took the initiative to insert Article 119 EC Treaty in the draft Treaty of 1957. For the convenience of the reader we will refer to this article by the current reference, Article 157 TFEU.

At the time of making the EC Treaty, some future Member States had already ratified ILO Convention No. 100 concerning equal remuneration for men and women for work of equal value. Three of the future Member States had, however, not ratified this Convention. Therefore, the fear existed that the latter States could have a competitive advantage by employing women as a cheaper source of labour. This would amount to distortion of competition. Such distortion was not acceptable from the point of view of social policy and, therefore, Article 157 was inserted into the Treaty. Despite this history, Article 157 proved to be important for the development of a specific part of European social security law.

In the interpretation of this article, three judgments concerning Mrs Defrenne have been of pioneering importance. Mrs Defrenne was employed as an air hostess by Belgian Sabena (an airline company). She gave up her duties in 1968 in pursuance of a provision of her contract of employment which stated that contracts held by women members of the crew shall terminate on the day on which the employee in question reaches the age of forty years. She started three actions on the basis of (what is now) Article 157 TFEU which led to three Court of Justice judgments.

The First *Defrenne* judgment concerned the Royal Decree which laid down special rules governing *pensions* for the air crew of Sabena.[1] It had to answer the question of whether the exclusion of female air hostesses from the Sabena pension was contrary to the principle of equal pay laid down by Article 157. In answer to this question, the Court referred to the second paragraph of Article 157 which extends the concept of pay to any other consideration, whether in cash or in kind, whether immediate or future provided that the worker receives it, albeit indirectly, in respect of his employment from his employer. The Court concluded that although consideration of the nature of social security benefits is not, therefore, in principle alien to the concept of pay, social security schemes or benefits, in particular retirement benefits, directly governed by legislation without any element of agreement within the undertaking or the occupational branch concerned, which are obligatorily applicable to general categories of workers, cannot be brought within this concept, as defined in Article 157. The payment due from the employers in the financing of such schemes does not constitute a direct or indirect payment to the worker.

Consequently, the pension for Sabena crew which was established by legislation (a special Royal Decree for Sabena) did not form 'pay' in the sense of Article 157. Therefore, Mrs Defrenne could not rely on this Article.

The *Second Defrenne* judgment[2] concerned the calculation method of her *allowance on termination of service*. The Court first considered the question of whether Article 157 had direct effect. It argued that Article 157 pursues a double aim. Firstly, in the light of the different stages of the development of social legislation in the various Member States, the aim of Article 157 is to avoid a situation where undertakings established in Member States which have actually implemented the principle of equal pay suffer a competitive disadvantage in intra-Community competition as compared to undertakings established in States which have not yet eliminated discrimination against women with regard to pay. Secondly, as is emphasised in the Preamble of the Treaty, this provision is part of the social objectives of the Community, which is not merely an economic union but which is at the same time intended, by common action, to ensure social progress and seek the constant improvement of the living and working conditions of its peoples. This double aim, which is at once economic and social, shows that the principle of equal pay forms part of the foundations of the Community. This explains why this principle has to be fully secured.

Another question raised in this case was whether Article 157 forbids a distinction being made between men and women in the calculation of the allowance at the end of the contract. The Court makes a distinction between, firstly, direct and overt discrimination, which may be identified solely with the aid of the criteria referred to in Article 157 based on equal work and equal pay and,

---

[1]   Case 80/70, [1971] *ECR* 446.
[2]   Case 43/75, [1976] *ECR* 455.

secondly, indirect and disguised discrimination, which can only be identified by reference to more explicit implementing provisions of a Community or national character.

The forms of direct discrimination which may be identified solely by reference to the criteria laid down by Article 157 include, particularly, those, the Court considered, which have their origin in legislative provisions or in collective labour agreements and which may be detected on the basis of a purely legal analysis of the situation. This applies even more in cases where men and women receive unequal pay for equal work carried out in the same establishment, whether public or private. In such a situation, the Court is in a position to establish all the facts which enable it to decide whether a female worker is receiving lower pay than a male worker performing the same tasks. In such a situation, at least, Article 157 is directly applicable and may thus give rise to individual rights which the courts must protect.

The Court made here a rather confusing distinction between direct (overt) and indirect (disguised) discrimination. Indirect discrimination in this case did not have the meaning it usually has, of making a distinction on seemingly neutral criteria, which has different effects for some categories. In case of indirect discrimination in the latter sense, Article 157 is directly applicable. This can be seen in the *Jenkins* judgment[3] and also in the *Bilka* judgment, to be discussed in Section 21.2.

Another question raised was whether, given the possible economic consequences of attributing direct effect to Article 157, the retroactive effect of this judgment has to be limited. The judgment which gives direct effect to Article 157 might have financial consequences in many branches of economic life if it were to have retroactive effect from the date the Treaty came into force. The Court decided that although the practical consequences of any judicial decision must be carefully taken into account, it would be impossible to go so far as to diminish the objectivity of the law and compromise its future application on the grounds of the possible repercussions which might result, as regards the past, from such a judicial decision. However, in the light of the conduct of several of the Member States, and the views adopted by the Commission and repeatedly brought to the notice of the circles concerned, it was appropriate to take exceptionally account of the fact that, over a prolonged period, the parties concerned have been led to continue with practices which were contrary to Article 157, although not yet prohibited under their national law. In these circumstances, the Court concluded, it was appropriate to determine that as the general level at which pay would have been fixed cannot be known, important considerations of legal certainty affecting all the interests involved, both public and private, made it impossible in principle to reopen the question as regards the past. Therefore, the direct effect of Article 157 cannot be relied on in order to support claims concerning pay periods prior

---

[3]   Case 96/80, [1981] *ECR* 911.

to the date of this judgment, except in the case of those workers who had already brought legal proceedings or made an equivalent claim.

As we have seen, Mrs Defrenne was dismissed on the basis of a clause in her contract of employment providing that contracts of female cabin crew members terminate when they reach the age of forty. The *Third Defrenne* case[4] concerned the question of whether this clause was allowed. Mrs Defrenne established that no such limit was attached to the contract of male cabin attendants who were assumed to do the same work. Article 157 itself did not preclude such a rule; the Directives which would do so were not yet in force at the time.[5] Therefore, Mrs Defrenne had to establish a link between her dismissal and `pay'. She claimed that the disputed clause was contrary to Article 157 because she could only be remunerated in the same way as men on the condition that she has the same working conditions. Moreover, the age-limit had disadvantageous pecuniary consequences for her end of contract allowance and pension.

The Court answered that the field of application of Article 157 had to be determined within the context of the system of the social provisions of the Treaty, which were set out in the chapter formed by Article 117 EC Treaty (now Article 352 TFEU, *see* previous chapter). The general features of the conditions of employment and working conditions are considered in Articles 151 and following TFEU from the point of view of the harmonisation of the social systems of the Member States and the approximation of their laws in that field. There was no doubt, according to the Court, that the elimination of discrimination based on the sex of workers was part of the programme for social and legislative policy which was clarified in certain respects in a Council Regulation and a directive.[6] In contrast to the provisions of (what are now) Articles 151 and following, which are essentially in the nature of a programme, Article 157, which is limited to the question of pay discrimination between men and women workers, constitutes a special rule, whose application is linked to precise factors. In these circumstances the Court considered it impossible to extend the scope of that Article to elements of the employment relationship other than those expressly referred to. It was, therefore, the Court decided, impossible to widen the terms of Article 157 to the point of, firstly, jeopardising the direct applicability which that provision must be acknowledged to have in its own sphere and, secondly, intervening in an area reserved by Articles 151 and following to the discretion of the authorities referred to therein. As a result Mrs Defrenne was not successful in this case.

---

[4]   Case 149/77, [1978] *ECR* 1365.
[5]   Regulation of 21 January 1974, *OJ* 1974 *C* 13, p. 1, and Directive 76/207, *OJ* 1976 *L* 39, p. 1.
[6]   *See* previous note.

21.2. ARTICLE 157 AND OCCUPATIONAL PENSIONS

In the *First Defrenne* judgment the Court pointed out that a consideration of the nature of social security benefits is not, in principle, alien to the concept of pay. In this decision the Court decided, however, that pensions which were established by legislation were not within the scope of Article 157 TFEU. In the *Bilka* judgment[7] the Court confirmed that other types of pensions fall under this Article. Bilka Kaufhaus, a department store, had for several years had a supplementary pension scheme (an occupational pension) for its employees. According to this scheme part-time employees qualified under the scheme only if they had been in full-time employment for fifteen years out of a total of twenty. Mrs Weber did not satisfy this requirement as she worked full-time for only eleven years.

The Court considered that the occupational scheme in question was indeed within the ambit of Article 157 TFEU. The occupational pension scheme in question, although adopted in accordance with German legislation for schemes of this type, originated from an agreement made between Bilka and the works council representing its employees. This agreement supplemented the social security benefits payable under national legislation with benefits financed solely by the employer. Therefore, the benefits paid to employees under the disputed scheme constituted consideration paid by the employer to the employee in respect of his employment within the meaning of Article 157. Consequently, statutory social security such as in the *Defrenne* case does not fall within the scope of Article 157, whereas a scheme based on an agreement does.

The following question was whether the scheme disputed in the *Bilka* case, with special conditions for part-time workers, was contrary to Article 157, as these conditions were applicable to both men and women. The Court argued that if the number of female part-time workers was disproportionate compared to the number of male part-timers, the rule on part-timers could constitute indirect discrimination against women, unless it could be justified by objective reasons. Bilka (the employer) maintained that the exclusion of part-time workers was based on objectively justified economic grounds. It emphasised that the employment of full-time workers, in comparison with part-time workers, involves fewer ancillary costs and permits staff to be used for the whole period during which stores are open. The Court ruled that it fell to the national court to decide whether, and if so to what extent, the grounds put forward by an employer to explain the adoption of a pay practice which in fact affects more women than men, could be considered to be objectively justified for economic reasons. For this purpose the national court has to investigate whether the means found for achieving the objective of the firm (reducing the number of part-timers) correspond to a real need on the part of the firm, are appropriate with a view to achieving the objective in question and are necessary to that end.

---

[7]   Case 170/84, [1986] *ECR* 1607.

From this judgment it can be derived that to answer the question of whether a specific rule is indirectly discriminatory, the following steps have to be followed.

First, it is important whether a scheme, although using neutral criteria, affects in a significant way men rather than women (or vice versa).

If the answer is positive, it has to be decided whether the scheme is justified by objective factors that are not related to discrimination (grounds of justification).

If this question is also answered positively, the court has to investigate whether the objective is necessary and whether the means chosen by the legislator are appropriate and necessary in order to reach the objective of the scheme. In the *Bilka* judgment, the question of applicability of Article 157 arose with respect to the exclusion of part-timers from occupational schemes. Another issue which can arise with respect to occupational schemes is the difference in retirement age for men and women respectively. For women this age was often lower than for men. As men can also invoke Article 157, this issue was brought before the Court in the *Barber* judgment.[8] Mr Barber was a member of a pension scheme established by his employer (an assurance firm). The scheme was financed wholly by the employer. It was a 'contracted out' scheme, which is a scheme which is allowed, after approval by the authorities, to replace statutory social security provisions, *i.e.* the earnings-related part of the State pension scheme.

Under this pension scheme, the normal pension age was fixed for the category of employees to which Mr Barber belonged at sixty-two for men and at fifty-seven for women. The age difference was equivalent to that which exists under the State social security scheme where the normal pension age is sixty-five for men and sixty for women.

The scheme provided that, in the case of redundancy, members of the pension fund were entitled to an immediate pension subject to having attained the age of fifty-five for men or fifty for women. Mr Barber was made redundant when he was aged fifty-two. It is not disputed that a woman in the same position as Mr Barber would have received an immediate retirement pension as well as the statutory redundancy payment and that the total value of these benefits would have been greater than the amount paid to Mr Barber.

The Court first had to consider whether the benefits paid by an employer to a worker in connection with the latter's compulsory redundancy fell within the scope of Article 157. The Court pointed out that as regards, in particular, the compensation granted to a worker in connection with his redundancy, it must be stated that such compensation constitutes a form of pay to which the worker is entitled in respect of his employment. It is paid to him upon termination of the employment relationship, which makes it possible to facilitate his adjustment to the new circumstances resulting from the loss of his employment and which provides him with a source of income during the period in which he is seeking new employment. It falls within the scope of Article 157.

---

[8]   Case 262/88, [1990] *ECR* 1990.

The following question was whether a retirement pension paid under a 'contracted-out' private occupational scheme falls within the scope of Article 157. The Court referred to the *First Defrenne* judgment where it had stated that social security schemes or benefits, in particular retirement pensions, directly governed by legislation without any element of agreement within the undertaking or the occupational branch concerned, which are compulsorily applicable to general categories of workers, do not fall under Article 157. The schemes in question in this case, however, were the result either of an agreement between workers and employers or of a unilateral decision taken by the employer. They were wholly financed by the employer or by both the employer and the workers without any contribution being made by the public authorities in any circumstances. Accordingly, such schemes form part of the consideration offered to workers by the employer. Secondly, such schemes are not compulsorily applicable to general categories of workers. On the contrary, they apply only to workers employed by certain undertakings, with the result that affiliation to those schemes derived out of necessity from the employment relationship with a given employer. Thirdly, even if the contributions paid to those schemes and the benefits which they provide were partly a substitute for those of the general statutory scheme, that fact could not preclude the application of Article 157. It is apparent that occupational schemes such as those referred to in this case may grant to their members a higher amount of benefit than the amount which would be paid by the statutory scheme, with the result that their economic function is similar to that of the supplementary schemes which exist in certain Member States, where affiliation and contribution to the statutory scheme is compulsory and no derogation is allowed. Consequently, the pension paid under a contracted-out private occupational scheme falls within the scope of Article 157.

The Court concluded that it is contrary to Article 157 TFEU for a man who is made compulsorily redundant to be entitled to claim only a deferred pension payable at the normal pensionable age, whereas a woman in the same position is entitled to an immediate retirement pension as a result of the application of an age condition that varies according to sex in the same way as is provided for by the national statutory pension scheme.

21.3. LIMITATION OF THE TEMPORAL EFFECT OF THE BARBER JUDGMENT

The last subject of the *Barber* judgment concerned the effects of the judgment *ratione temporis* because of the serious financial consequences of the interpretation of Article 157 given in this judgment. The Court considered that it could, as it had done in the *Second Defrenne* case as an exception, and taking account of the serious difficulties which might be created by its judgment as regards events in the past, restrict the possibility of all persons concerned relying on this interpretation. In the *Barber* case, it was relevant that Article 7(1) of Directive 79/7 (as we will see in Section 22.5.6) authorised the Member States to defer the compulsory implementation of the principle of equal treatment with regard to the determination of pensionable age for the purposes of granting old-age pensions. That exception had also been incorporated in Article 9(a) of Directive 86/378 on the implementation of the principle of equal treatment for men and women in occupational schemes, which was to apply to contracted-out schemes such as the one at issue in this case (*see* Section 23.2.5 below). The Court considered that in the light of those provisions, the Member States and the parties concerned were reasonably entitled to consider that Article 157 did not apply to pensions paid under contracted-out schemes. In these circumstances, the overriding considerations of legal certainty precluded legal situations, which had exhausted all their effects in the past, from being called into question where that might retroactively upset the financial balance of many contracted-out pension schemes.

Therefore, the Court ruled, the direct effect of Article 157 may not be relied upon in order to claim entitlement to a pension with effect from a date prior to this judgment, except in the case of workers who before that date had initiated legal proceedings or made an equivalent claim under the applicable law.

The judgment led in turn to many new questions. The main question was whether this judgment meant that a claimant of an occupational pension could, on the basis of Article 157, claim an *equal amount of benefit* from the date of the ruling (17 May 1990), or if it meant that only the acquisition rules for pensions had to be the same for men and women from this day. The first interpretation had important financial consequences because in the past the application of the principle of equal treatment in respect of pensions was not foreseen when calculating contribution rates; the result of the alternative interpretation would be that the effects of unequal treatment in the past would still be felt for many years. A protocol was annexed to the Treaty of Maastricht with regard to this question.[9] It reads as follows: 'For the purposes of Article 119 EC Treaty [now Article 157 TFEU, benefits under occupational social security schemes shall not be considered as remuneration if and in so far as they are attributable to periods of employment prior to 17 May 1990, except in the case of workers or those claiming under them who have before that date initiated legal proceedings or introduced an equivalent claim under the applicable national law.'

This Protocol is a statement by the Council which fits in with the second interpretation of the *Barber* judgment. In the following sections, we will discuss which interpretation is followed by the Court.

---

[9]   *OJ* 1992 C 229/104.

21.4. LIMITATION IN TIME IN THE CASE OF WIDOWERS' PENSIONS AND AGE DISCRIMINATION

In 1993, the Court issued the *Ten Oever* ruling, in which the temporal effects of the *Barber* judgment were clarified.[10] In this case Mr Ten Oever wished to claim a survivor's pension from the occupational pension scheme to which his deceased spouse was affiliated. His wife died on 13 October 1988. The scheme was funded by employers and employees. At the date of her death, under the provisions of the scheme, only a widows' pension was payable. Pensions for widowers were only made payable after 1 January 1989. Consequently, Mr Ten Oever was refused benefit. Mr Ten Oever claimed, on the basis of the *Barber* judgment, that his pension had to be considered as pay within the meaning of Article 157 TFEU and that, therefore, no discrimination in the pension scheme was allowed.

The Court answered that the pension scheme did indeed fall within the scope of 'pay' within the meaning of Article 157. The second question to be answered concerning the temporal effect of the *Barber* judgment was more difficult. The Court reasoned that it is a characteristic of this form of pay that there is a time lag between the accrual of entitlement to a pension, which occurs gradually throughout the employee's working life, and the actual payment, which is deferred until a particular age. The Court also took into consideration the way in which occupational pension funds are financed and thus of the accounting links in each individual case between the periodic contributions and the future amounts to be paid. On the basis of this statement, the Court ruled that equal treatment of men and women can be claimed, in the matter of occupational pensions, only in respect of benefits payable for periods of employment subsequent to 17 May 1990, the date of the *Barber* judgment. The Court opted, as can be seen in this judgment, for the second interpretation of the *Barber* judgment which corresponds with the Protocol. As a result, Mr Ten Oever was refused benefit as his wife had died during a period which lay before the *Barber* judgment.

The subject of the *Advel Systems* judgment[11] concerned age differences for pension schemes. The question was how a transitory scheme, which has to correct previous unequal treatment of men and women, should be drafted. The scheme in question was financed by both employers' and employees' contributions. Until 1 July 1991 the pension scheme provided that the normal pensionable age was 65 years for men and 60 for women. With effect from 1 July 1991 the normal pensionable age was to be 65 for both men and women. The amendment applied both to benefits earned in respect of years of service after 1 July 1991 and to benefits earned in respect of years of service prior to 1 July 1991. The increase of the retirement age for women meant that their pensions were decreased

---

[10]   Case 109/91, [1993] *ECR* I-4879.
[11]   Case 408/92, [1994] *ECR* I-4435.

significantly after 1 July 1991, the date of equalisation. The national court wanted to know what scope the employer had to take measures to realise equal treatment for men and women in the past as well as for the future.

The Court answered that it was in order to comply with the *Barber* judgment that the occupational scheme concerned adopted the measure now in dispute. In order to do so, it opted for one of the two possible ways of achieving equal treatment: instead of granting men the same advantage as that enjoyed by women, and thus lowering their retirement age to that for women, the scheme raised the retirement age for women to that for men. This included the period prior to the *Barber* judgment and, as a result, the position of women was made less favourable. In the *Second Defrenne* judgment the Court already ruled that members of the disadvantaged group were to be given the same arrangements as those enjoyed by other workers, arrangements which, failing correct implementation of Article 157 TFEU in national law, remain the only valid point of reference. The national court must set aside any discriminatory provision of national law, without having to request or await its prior removal by collective bargaining or by any other constitutional procedure. Application of this principle to the present case means that, as regards the period between 17 May 1990 (the date of the *Barber* judgment) and 1 July 1991 (the date on which the scheme adopted uses to achieve equality), the pension rights of men must be calculated on the basis of the same retirement age as that for women. As regards periods of service prior to 17 May 1990, the *Barber* judgment excluded application of Article 157 TFEU to pension benefits payable in respect of those periods, so that employers and trustees are not required to ensure equal treatment as far as those benefits are concerned. It follows that as far as those latter periods are concerned, Community law established no rule which would prevent retroactive reduction of the advantages which women enjoyed.

As regards periods of service completed after the entry into force of the rules designed to eliminate discrimination (in this case, 1 July 1991), Article 157 does not preclude measures which achieve equal treatment by reducing the advantages of the persons previously favoured. Article 157 merely requires that men and women should receive the same pay for the same work without imposing any specific level of pay.[12] The decision can be represented in the following scheme:

	17 May 1990	July 1991
unequal treatment is allowed	equal pension age	new retirement age (65)
before 17 May 1990	for men and women (60)	

---

[12] This judgment was followed by the *Van den Akker* judgment, Case 28/93, [1994] *ECR* I-4527.

21.5. RETROACTIVE EFFECT IN OTHER CASES OF UNEQUAL TREATMENT

In the previous section we discussed judgments of the Court on widowers' pensions and differences in pension age. In these judgments the Court took account of the gradual implementation of the principle of equal treatment of men and women and consequently it limited the retroactive effect of the *Barber* judgment. This limitation does not, however, apply in the case of the exclusion of part-time workers; as appears from the *Vroege* judgment[13] in their cases the effects of their exclusion have to be taken away completely and this includes retroactive effects. Since 1975 Mrs Vroege has been employed on a part-time basis. Before 1 January 1991, the pension scheme rules of her employer provided that only men and unmarried women employed for an indeterminate period and working at least 80% of the normal full day could be members of the scheme. Since Mrs Vroege never worked for more than 80% of the full day she was not allowed to pay contributions into the scheme and was therefore unable to acquire pension rights. On 1 January 1991 new pension scheme rules came into force, providing that employees of both sexes who have reached 25 years of age and who work at least 25% of normal working hours can join the scheme. The pension scheme rules also provided that women who were not members before 1 January 1991 can purchase additional years of membership, provided, however, that they had reached the age of 50 on 31 December 1990. Since she had not reached the age of 50 on 31 December 1990, Mrs Vroege could not rely on that transitional provision and therefore she could begin to accrue pension rights only as from 1 January 1991. Consequently, she challenged the new pension scheme rules on the grounds that since they did not give her the right to be a member of the pension scheme in respect of periods of service prior to 1 January 1991, they involved discrimination which was incompatible with Article 157.

The question to be answered by the Court was whether the limitation in time of the effects of the *Barber* judgment also applied to part-time workers who were excluded from occupational pension schemes. The Court answered that it is important to remember the context in which it was decided to limit the retroactive effects of the *Barber* judgment. It considered that according to its established case law, it may exceptionally, having regard to the general principle of legal certainty inherent in the Community legal order and the serious difficulties which its judgment may create as regards the past for legal relations established in good faith, find it necessary to limit the possibility for interested parties, relying on the Court's interpretation of a provision to call into question those legal relations. The Court therefore established two essential criteria for deciding to impose such a limitation, namely that those concerned should have acted in good faith and that there should be a risk of serious difficulties if retroactive effect is used.

---

[13]   Case 57/93, [1994] *ECR* I-4541.

As regards the first criterion, the Court first of all found that Article 9(a) of Directive 86/378 provided for the possibility of deferring the compulsory implementation of the principle of equal treatment with regard to the determination of pensionable age, as did the exception provided for in Article 7(1)(a) of Directive 79/7. In the light of those provisions, the Member States and the parties concerned were reasonably entitled to consider that Article 157 did not apply to pensions paid under contracted-out schemes and that derogations from the principle of equality between men and women were still permitted in that sphere.

As regards the criterion of serious difficulties, the Court also held in the *Barber* judgment that if any male worker concerned could, like Mr Barber, retroactively assert the right to equal treatment in cases of discrimination which, until then, could have been considered permissible in view of the exceptions provided for in Directive 86/378, the financial balance of many occupational schemes might be upset retroactively. These criteria were applied in the *Ten Oever* case which confirmed the limitation of the retroactive effect of the *Barber* judgment.

It follows, in particular, from the foregoing that the limitation of the effects in time of the *Barber* judgment concerns only those kinds of discrimination which employers and pension schemes could reasonable have considered to be permissible owing to the transitional derogations for which Community law provided and which were capable of being applied to occupational pensions.

As far as the right to join an occupational scheme is concerned, there is no reason to suppose that the groups concerned could have been mistaken about the applicability of Article 157 TFEU. According to the Court, it has indeed been clear since the judgment in the *Bilka* case that a breach of the rule of equal treatment committed through not recognising such a right is caught by Article 157. Since the *Bilka* judgment included no limitation in time, the direct effect of Article 157 can be relied upon in order to retroactively claim equal treatment in relation to the right to join an occupational pension scheme. This may be done as from 8 April 1976, the date of the *Defrenne* judgment in which the Court held for the first time that Article 157 has direct effect (and which also contained a limitation of the effect of the judgment in time).

The *Fisscher* judgment[14] concerned a case comparable to the *Vroege* case, discussed above, but in this case *married women* were excluded from the pension fund. The Court reproduced most of the considerations from the *Vroege* judgment and reached the same conclusion. Thus, in the case of married women there is also no limitation in time of the effect of *Barber*. An additional question which was raised in this case was, however, whether the fact that a worker can claim to join an occupational pension scheme retroactively allows the worker to avoid paying the contributions relating to the period of membership concerned. The Court answered that where discrimination has been suffered, equal treatment is

---

[14]   Case 128/93, [1994] *ECR* I-4583.

to be achieved by placing the worker discriminated against in the same situation as that of workers of the other sex. It follows that the worker cannot claim more favourable treatment, particularly in financial terms, than he would have had if he had been duly accepted as a member. This means that contributions can be required retroactively.

In the *Moroni* judgment[15] the question was raised whether Article 8(1) Directive 86/378 – which provided that equal treatment did not have to be realised before 1 January 1993 – meant that claimants could not invoke the directive in a claim based on Article 157 with respect to the payment of pensions before 1 January 1993. The Court answered that Article 157 is directly applicable to each form of discrimination which can be shown with the sole criteria of equality of work and equality of payment, the criteria which form part of this Article. As pension ages can be determined directly with the help of the criteria of Article 157, it is no longer necessary to look at the effects of the Directive. Equality of treatment with respect to occupational pensions can, however, as we can see in the *Ten Oever* judgment, only be invoked with respect to benefits due on the basis of periods of work lying after 19 May 1990.

Conclusion: With respect to those issues where it could not be clear to the pension funds that equal treatment was required from 1976, the *Barber* judgment does not have retroactive effect. This implies that with respect to survivors' pensions and unequal pension ages equal treatment cannot be invoked with retroactive effect. In other instances, such as the exclusion of part-timers and married women, it could have been clear from the *Bilka* judgment that the funds had to realise equal treatment. Therefore, in these instances the effect of the *Barber* judgment are not limited in time.

21.6. THE MEANING OF THE TERM 'PAY'

In the *Neath* case the Court was asked whether an employer is allowed to distinguish between employers' contributions for male and female employees.[16] Mr Neath was employed under a *contracted-out* scheme until 27 June 1990, the date on which he was made redundant. At that time he was fifty-four years and eleven months old. According to the rules of that contracted-out scheme, male employees may not claim a full company pension until they are sixty-five years of age while female employees may receive a full pension at sixty years of age. Mr Neath's financial position would be more favourable if the interpretation of the *Barber* judgment were that any male employee retiring after 17 May 1990 is entitled to have his pension recalculated on the same basis as his female counterpart in relation to the entire period of service.

---

[15]   Case 110/91, [1993] *ECR* I-6591.
[16]   Case 152/91, [1993] *ECR* I-6935.

The Court considered that the *employees'* contributions correspond to a percentage of the employees' salary which is identical for men and women. The *employer's* contributions, however, vary over time, so as to cover the balance of the cost of the pensions promised. They are higher for female employees than for male employees. This variability and inequality are due to the use of actuarial factors in the mechanism for funding the scheme. In the case of the transfer of acquired rights, and in the case where part of a pension is converted into capital, the fact that account is taken of different actuarial factors has the result that male employees are entitled to sums lower than those to which female employees are entitled. Essentially, the national court wanted to know whether such differences are compatible with Article 157. The Court ruled that contributions paid by employees are an element of their pay since they are deducted directly from their salary. The amount of those contributions must therefore be the same for all employees, male and female. This is not so in the case of the employer's contributions which ensure the adequacy of the funds necessary to cover the cost of the pension promised and in doing so securing their payment in the future, that being the substance of the employer's commitment. Employees' contributions, therefore, are 'pay' in the sense of Article 157, while employers' contributions are not.

CHAPTER 22

EQUAL TREATMENT OF MEN AND WOMEN IN STATUTORY SOCIAL SECURITY: DIRECTIVE 79/7

22.1. INTRODUCTION

Article 157 TFEU concerns pay alone and not statutory social security. In order to ensure that there is equal treatment in the area of statutory social security also, the Council has made a directive. The character of a directive differs from that of a regulation. The directive is binding as to the result to be achieved, upon each Member State to which it is addressed. However, the national authorities retain the freedom of the choice of forms and methods to achieve this result. This does not mean that a directive is less binding than a regulation. After all, Member States are obliged to adjust national rules which are not in accordance with a specific directive. Provisions of a directive may sometimes offer little discretion to the Member States as to how the rules are to be executed; if, for instance, the directive requires equal treatment of men and women in relation to social security, national provisions contrary to this rule have to be repealed. Furthermore, the Court of Justice has consistently held that if a Member State does not implement a directive within the period prescribed by that directive, the directive has, under certain conditions, direct effect and individuals can rely on it before a national court.

These conditions are:
- the provision contains an explicit obligation on the Member States;
- the provision is unconditional and sufficiently precise;
- additional implementation rules are not required; and
- the provision is meant to restrict the discretionary power of the Member State.[1]

If these conditions are satisfied, individuals can rely on a directive before the national court. The directive then has direct effect; examples of direct effect of a directive are given below. Directives do not have a horizontal effect. It is the State which has to guarantee that individuals can realise the rights awarded to them in the directive.

---

[1]   Case 8/81, Becker [1982] *ECR* 53.

Directive 79/7 concerns the progressive implementation of the principle of equal treatment for men and women in matters of social security.[2] This Directive applies to *statutory social security* schemes.

In addition, Directive 86/378 concerns the implementation of the principle of equal treatment for men and women in occupational social security schemes.[3] This Directive concerns non-statutory schemes and has already been mentioned in the previous chapter.

Directive 86/613 concerns the application of the principle of equal treatment for men and women engaged in an activity, including agriculture, in a self-employed capacity, as well as the protection of self-employed women during pregnancy and motherhood.[4] This Directive concerns the self-employed.

Finally, the Commission issued a proposal for a directive completing the principle of equal treatment of men and women in statutory social security and occupational schemes; this has not been adopted yet.[5] Given the important effects of Directive 79/7 on social security, the Member States were not enthusiastic to adopt further measures, as we will see in this chapter. Directive 79/7 will be discussed in this chapter. The other Directives are considered in Chapter 23.

Directive 79/7 requires the progressive implementation of the principle of equal treatment for men and women in matters of social security. The term *progressive* expresses the idea that the Directive does not apply to all parts of social security. Only statutory schemes are covered by this Directive and some exceptions apply (survivors' benefits and family benefits are not within the material scope). Furthermore, the period of implementation of this Directive was six years; this period expired on 23 December 1984. Finally, Article 7 of the Directive allows Member States to exclude some areas of statutory social security from the Directive's scope.

22.2. THE PERSONAL SCOPE OF DIRECTIVE 79/7

Directive 79/7 applies to the working population, including self-employed persons; workers and self-employed persons whose activity is interrupted by illness, accident or involuntary unemployment; as well as to persons seeking employment, retired and invalid workers; and self-employed persons (Article 2).

The working population in this Directive thus covers more than just persons actually engaged in work, civil servants included. Persons who worked in the past and those who will work in the (near) future (*i.e.* who are seeking work) are also

---

[2]   Directive of 19 December 1978, *OJ* 1979 *L* 6, p. 24.
[3]   Directive of 24 July 1986, *OJ* 1986 *L* 225.
[4]   Directive of 11 December 1986, *OJ* 1986 *L* 359.
[5]   *OJ* 1987 *C* 309.

covered. Only persons with no link with economic life (such as housewives) do not fall within the scope of this Directive.

The term *working population* in Article 2 of the Directive was discussed in the *Drake* judgment.[6] Mrs Drake was married and lived with her husband. In June 1984, her mother, a severely disabled person who received an *attendance allowance*, came to live with her. Mrs Drake gave up her work in order to look after her mother. Under British law an invalid care allowance was payable to persons who (among other things) were regularly and substantially engaged in caring for a severely disabled person. This allowance was not paid to married women living with their husbands. Could Mrs Drake rely on the Directive in order to remove this discriminatory clause? This question was raised, as it was uncertain whether she fell under the personal scope of the Directive, because she did not suffer from disability herself.

The Court pointed out that persons like Mrs Drake whose activity is interrupted by one of the contingencies mentioned in Article 3 – *i.e.* illness, accident, involuntary unemployment, old age or disability – belong to the working population. Consequently, she can invoke the Directive. Persons 'indirectly' affected by a risk which is mentioned in Article 3 such as Mrs Drake also belong to the field of application of this Directive.

From the *Zürchner* judgment[7] it appears that only a person who terminated occupational activities in order to care for another person, can – by means of the *Drake* approach – invoke the Directive. A housewife who starts to care for another person does not fall under the personal scope of the Directive.

Mrs Zürchner wished to rely on a legal aid scheme for the purpose of bringing a claim against the sickness benefit administration of her spouse because it refused to pay for her care for her spouse. Mrs Zürchner's spouse, who was in gainful employment before suffering from an accident, was not able to walk. His situation required the help of a third person for his household and medical care. His spouse had taken on these tasks. The German administration refused to pay for this, as the German Law provided: 'One is entitled to care only if a person, who does not form part of the household, cannot care for the sick person to an adequate extent.' According to Mrs Zürchner this provision is contrary to the Directive.

The Court was asked whether a person in the situation of Mrs Zürchner as a spouse of an invalid person also falls under 'working population' in the sense of Article 2. At the time when her spouse was affected by the accident, she was not employed in gainful employment, and in this respect she was in a situation different to Mrs Drake's. It could be argued, however, that her work done for her husband, which could also have been done in a remunerated form, implies that she was part of the working population. This was a difficult question for the Court, as it would mean that housewives should be seen as part of the working

---

[6]   Case 150/85, [1986] *ECR* 1995.
[7]   Case 77/95, [1996] *ECR* I-5689.

population, especially if they had to perform heavy tasks. Mrs Zürchner argued that she had to follow training for the care she provided to her husband and that this work should by its nature and extent be assimilated with occupational work. If she did not do this work, a remunerated person would have to do it. The Court considered, however, that the Directive does not apply to persons who are not in gainful employment, or who are not seeking work or whose work or seeking work has not been interrupted by one of the risks mentioned in Article 3 of the Directive. From these considerations it follows that the term 'occupational activity', which is implied in the term 'working population' in Article 2 of the Directive, must be interpreted as requiring an economic activity, *i.e.* an activity which is done for remuneration in a broad sense. The Court argued that it has to be acknowledged that a person can be obliged to rely on a third person when he is not, or is no longer, able to do specific activities himself such as caring for the children or domestic work. These activities require certain capabilities and would have to be done on a remunerated basis if a person, whether a family member or not, could not do them on a voluntary basis. The Court did not, however, go so far as to accept that housewife's activities indeed constitute occupational activities: an interpretation of the term 'working population' which would include members of the family who perform an unremunerated activity which would be done by a third person if the family member could not do it, would extend the scope of the Directives without any restrictions, whereas, according to the Court, Article 2 aims to restrict the personal scope.

The approach of the Court is arguably not a very principled one: it does not make clear why the personal scope of the Directive has to be restricted. In fact, the Directive has no other effect than removing discrimination and there is no good reason to allow discrimination in the case of housewives. Moreover, whether a person falls under the Directive or not depends on accidental circumstances: if Mrs Zürchner had a job (even a small one) or was registered at the employment office as seeking work when her husband was affected by the accident, she would have been within the personal scope.

Persons who interrupted their occupational activities in order to dedicate themselves to the care of their children are usually *not* within the personal scope of the Directive. This reason for the interruption of their occupational activities is not mentioned in the list of contingencies in Article 3. This was shown by the *Johnson* judgment.[8]

This judgment concerned a woman who stopped working in 1970 in order to care for her then six year old daughter. In 1980 she wanted to start working again but because of a back ache she was unable to do so. Therefore in 1981, when she was living alone, she was awarded a non-contributory invalidity benefit. In 1982 she started to cohabit with a man. Payment of her benefit was terminated, because at that time a woman, cohabiting with a man, who claimed disability

---

[8]   Case 31/90, [1991] *ECR* 3723.

benefit, had to show that she was incapable of doing normal household activities. This condition did not apply to men. Mrs Johnson did not satisfy this condition.

One way to fall under the Directive is to be a person seeking employment whose search is made impossible by the materialisation of one of the risks listed in Article 3. In this case it is not relevant why the person concerned left previous employment or even whether or not that person previously carried out an occupational activity. However, a person in these circumstances must prove that he was seeking employment when one of the risks specified in Article 3 materialised and it is for the national court to answer the question whether this is the case. For this purpose, it is particularly relevant of whether that person was registered with an employment organisation responsible for dealing with offers of employment or assisting persons seeking employment. It is, furthermore, relevant whether he had sent job applications to employers and whether certificates were available from firms stating that he had attended interviews. These criteria opened the possibility for Mrs Johnson to fall under the personal scope of the Directive.

A judgment in which it appeared clearly that persons who were not working or who interrupted their occupational activities for a reason other than the ones mentioned in Article 3 are not within the personal scope of the Directive, was the *Achterberg-Te Riele* judgment.[9]

This judgment concerned three joined cases of women who felt discriminated again by a provision in the Dutch Law on General Old-Age Insurance, to be discussed in Section 22.5.3. One of the three applicants worked as an employed earner and terminated her activities when she married. The second had never been engaged in occupational activities and the third had worked as an employed earner, had become unemployed (and received unemployment benefit for some time) but had never sought work again.

The Court held that Article 2 in conjunction with Article 3 of the Directive means that the Directive only covers persons who are working at the time when they become entitled to claim an old-age pension or whose occupational activity was previously interrupted by one of the risks set out in Article 3(1)(a). It follows from this analysis that the Directive does not apply to persons who had never been available for employment or who had ceased to be available for a reason other than the materialisation of one of the risks referred to in the Directive itself. This reply was not affected if the person concerned stopped working and was not available for employment before the last date for transposing the Directive.

In the *Verholen* judgment[10] as well, the consequences of the limited personal scope of the Directive were apparent. The question was raised whether a person who is not covered by the personal scope, but who is insured under a national scheme falling within the material scope of the Directive, can rely on the Directive. The Court answered this question negatively. A second question in this case was

---

9   Joined Cases 48, 106 and 107/88, [1989] *ECR* 1963.
10   Joined cases 87/90, 88/90 and 89/90, [1991] *ECR* 3757.

whether the spouse of a person suffering from discrimination at a national level could rely on the Directive. The spouse had been an employee and therefore fell within the personal scope. As he would receive a supplement for his wife if the discriminatory rule were overruled, he was an interested party. The Court answered that persons who do not fall within the personal scope of the Directive are not prevented from invoking it when they have a direct interest in the Directive being respected with regard to the persons protected by it. In the present case, however, the applicant was only allowed to invoke a provision applicable to his wife if she effectively fell within the personal scope of this Directive.

In the *Megner and Scheffer* case[11] the question was raised of whether persons working in small part-time jobs fall within the personal scope of the Directive.

Under the German legislation persons working less than 18 hours a week were not insured for unemployment insurance. The case concerned two female cleaners whose normal working time was a maximum of ten hours per week. They applied for admission to this insurance scheme but were refused on the basis of their small number of working hours. They claimed that this was contrary to Article 4(1) of Directive 79/7.

Do persons working in small jobs fall within the scope of the Directive? The Court considered that Article 2 implies that the definition of the working population is very broad since it covers any worker including persons who are merely seeking employment. The German Government and the employer had argued that persons in subsidiary employment are not part of the working population within the meaning of Article 2, because the small earnings which they receive from such employment are not sufficient to satisfy their needs. The Court did not accept this argument. The fact that a worker's earnings do not cover all his needs cannot prevent him from being a member of the working population.

In the *Nolte* judgment[12] the approach from the *Megner* judgment was followed. According to the German social security law, a disabled person is entitled to a disability benefit if he can show that he has been subject to liability for compulsory contribution payments during at least three out of the last five years. Small jobs are exempted from compulsory insurance. Mrs Nolte had worked in a small job as a cleaner from 1977 until March 1987 when she terminated her activities. Since June 1988 she was seriously ill and was no longer capable of performing remunerated work. On 28 November 1988 Mrs Nolte applied for a disability benefit. This was refused on the grounds that she had not worked during the required period.

The only point in which the considerations in the present judgment deviated from the *Megner and Scheffel* judgment is that the German Government had argued that Mrs Nolte could not rely on the Directive for a different reason. This was that she had terminated employment more than one year before the start of

---

[11]   Case 444/93, [1995] *ECR* I-4741.
[12]   Case 317/93, [1995] *ECR* I-4625.

her disability and there were no indications that she was at work at that moment. The Court remarked, however, that Mrs Nolte could claim, according to German law, a disability benefit if the periods during which she had been working in her small job were considered as periods of compulsory insurance. For this reason the Court decided that she fell within the personal scope of the Directive.

22.3. THE MATERIAL SCOPE OF DIRECTIVE 79/7

The material scope of Directive 79/7 is defined in Article 3: Article 3(1) provides that the Directive concerns:
a. statutory schemes which provide protection against the following risks: sickness, invalidity, old age, accidents of work and occupational diseases, unemployment;
b. social assistance, in so far as it is intended to supplement or replace the schemes referred to in (a).

Article 3(2) provides that the Directive shall not apply to the provisions concerning survivors' benefits nor to those concerning family benefits, except in the case of family benefits granted by way of increases of benefits falling under a.

In the *Drake* judgment,[13] the Court ruled that a benefit for persons caring for an invalid person also fell within the scope of the Directive. The Court considered that protection against the consequences of the risk of invalidity can be given in various ways. One way is that an allowance is payable to the disabled person himself and another allowance is paid to a person who provides care (the UK has such a system). Another Member State might arrive at the same result by paying an allowance to the disabled person at a rate equivalent to the sum of those two benefits. In order to ensure a progressive implementation of the Directive in a harmonious manner throughout the Community, Article 3(1) must be interpreted as including any benefit which in a broad sense forms part of one of the statutory schemes referred to as well as social assistance provisions intended to supplement or replace such a scheme. If this was not the case, it would be possible to remove existing benefits covered by the Directive from its scope by making formal changes to such benefits.

As can be seen from this decision, the Court does not pay too much attention to the formal aspects of a scheme. This was also apparent in the *Richardson* judgment.[14] In the United Kingdom the Secretary of State is authorised to exempt certain categories of persons from prescription charges (medical costs). Relevant criteria are the age, the type of condition and the resources available to these categories. The Secretary of State had provided exemptions for, among other persons, a man who has attained the age of 65 years and a woman who has

---

[13]   Case 150/85, [1986] *ECR* 1995.
[14]   Case 137/94, [1995] *ECR* I-3407.

attained the age of 60 years. The preliminary question was whether the scheme was within the scope of the Directive, now that it was not part of the statute itself and now that it concerns contributions.

The Court stated that in order to fall within the scope of Directive 79/7, a benefit must constitute the whole or part of a statutory scheme providing protection against one of the specified risks, or a form of social assistance having the same objective. Although the way in which a benefit is granted is not decisive for the purposes of Directive 79/7, in order to fall within its scope the benefit must be directly and effectively linked to the protection provided against one of the risks specified in Article 3(1) of the Directive. A benefit such as that provided for in the British regulations concerned fulfils those conditions.

Not all types of benefit fall under the material scope of the Directive. An example can be seen in the *Jackson and Cresswell* judgment.[15]

This case concerned British *income support*. This benefit was granted to anyone aged at least eighteen whose income did not exceed a specified amount and who was engaged in no more than 24 hours a week. The applicants were single mothers with small children. One of them started vocational training, in respect of which she received a weekly allowance: the other started to perform part-time work. In order to stay below the relevant amounts of income which made them eligible for income support, they wished to deduct from their income the child-minding expenses which they incurred during the period in training. The applicants argued that the refusal to take child-minding costs into account was indirectly discriminating against women.

Whether these benefits were within the material scope of the Directive was of relevance. The Court answered that if a benefit to fall within the scope of Directive 79/7, it must constitute the whole or part of a statutory scheme providing protection against one of the specified risks or must be a form of social assistance with the same objective. Income support does not satisfy these conditions. The fact that the recipients of the disputed benefit are in fact in one of the situations covered by Article 3(1) of the Directive (the applicants were considered unemployed) was not relevant. Exclusion from the scope of Directive 79/7 is justified where the law sets the amount of the benefits in question independently of any consideration relating to the existence of any of the risks listed in Article 3(1). The fact that the national schemes at issue exempt claimants from the obligation to be available for work shows that the benefits in question cannot be regarded as being directly and effectively linked to protection against the risk of unemployment. Consequently, the applicants could not invoke the Directive.

In the *Smithson* judgment[16] another type of benefit did not fall within the material scope of the Directive. The contested scheme in this case was British housing benefit. This was payable to persons whose actual income was below a

---

15   Cases 63/91 and 64/91, [1992] *ECR* I-4973.
16   Case 243/90, [1992] *ECR* I-467.

theoretical amount as defined in the scheme. One of the factors relevant to the increase of this benefit was that one is a single person and is between sixty and eighty years of age. Furthermore, one must be in receipt of one or more social security benefits including in the invalidity pension. This pension is payable until pension age (which is sixty for women and sixty-five for men).

The Court argued that a benefit can fall under the scope of the Directive if it is directly and effectively linked to protection against one the risks listed in Article 3. Article 3 does not, however, concern housing costs. Age and invalidity of the claimant are just two of the criteria to determine the financial needs of the applicant. Even if these criteria are decisive for the increase of the benefit this is not sufficient to bring this benefit within the material scope of this Directive.

22.4. THE RELATIONSHIP OF DIRECTIVE 79/7 TO ARTICLE 157 TFEU

Now that the material scope of both Article 157 TFEU and the Directive have been described, it can be understood that there are some borderline cases in which it is not clear which instrument applies. An example of such a borderline case is the *Beune* judgment.[17] The case concerned the Dutch Public Servants Superannuation Fund (ABP), which provides supplementary pensions for civil servants and those assimilated with them. These pensions supplement the Law on general old-age insurance benefits (AOW). The level of benefit depends on the periods of insurance. They were governed by a statute (meanwhile they are privatised)

The pensions had elements of supplementary occupational pensions. Do they fall under Article 157 TFEU or Directive 79/7?

The Court considered that in order to determine whether a pension scheme such as the ABP scheme falls within the scope of Directive 79/7 or of Article 57 TFEU, the following criteria may be relevant: is the pension scheme of a statutory nature?; is it based on negotiations between employers' and employees' representatives?; does it supplement statutory social security benefits?; how is the pension scheme financed?; is it applicable to general categories of employees?; and, finally, what is the relationship between the benefit and the employee's employment? In its case law the Court considered the criterion of whether the scheme has a contractual basis as decisive. The criterion of whether there is an agreement has therefore precedence to the criterion of statutory origin. In the *Bilka* judgment (*see* Section 21.2), for instance, the Court stated that even if it is adopted in accordance with legislation, a pension scheme based on an agreement between an employer and staff representatives with the effect of supplementing social benefits paid under generally applicable national legislation with benefits

---

[17]   Case 7/93, [1994] *ECR* I-4471.

financed entirely by the employer, is not a social security scheme, and that such a scheme provides benefits constituting consideration received by the worker from the employer in respect of his employment within the meaning of the second paragraph of Article 157 TFEU. A pension scheme set up by negotiation between both sides of the industry and funded wholly by the employees and employers in that industry, to the exclusion of any financial contribution from the public purse, falls within the scope of Article 157 TFEU, even when the public authorities, at the request of the employers' and trade union organisations concerned, declare the scheme compulsory for the whole of the industry concerned. However, the Court continued, the negotiation between the employers and employees' representatives must be such that it results in a formal agreement.

Conclusion: A pension scheme which is the result of negotiations between the social partners, which result in an agreement, falls within the scope of Article 157 TFEU.

22.5. THE EQUAL TREATMENT RULE OF DIRECTIVE 79/7

22.5.1. INTRODUCTION

Article 4 reads:
1. The principle of equal treatment means that there shall be no discrimination whatsoever on ground of sex either directly, or indirectly by reference in particular to marital or family status, in particular as concerns:
   - the scope of the schemes and the conditions of access thereto;
   - the obligation to contribute and the calculation of contributions;
   - the calculation of benefits including increases due in respect of a spouse and for dependants and the conditions governing the duration and retention of entitlement to benefits.

Consequently, Article 4 forbids direct and indirect discrimination. Article 4(2) provides that the principle of equal treatment is without prejudice to the provisions relating to the protection of women on the grounds of maternity.

22.5.2. THE DIRECT EFFECT OF DIRECTIVE 79/7

As directives are addressed to the Member States, it was not clear at first sight whether individuals could rely on a directive. In Section 1 of this chapter, we saw that this is indeed possible where provisions of a directive appear, as far as their subject matter is concerned, to be unconditional and sufficiently precise. Such circumstances occur where a Member State does not implement provisions of a directive within the time-limit mentioned in that directive. In that case individuals can rely on the directive against any national provision which is incompatible with the directive, or insofar as the provisions of the directive define rights which individuals are able to assert against the State.

The question of whether the equal treatment provision of Directive 79/7 has direct effect was answered in the *FNV* judgment.[18]

Article 13(1)(l) of the Dutch Earnings-related Unemployment Assistance Scheme (WWV) excluded workers who, being married women, were not described as main wage-earners in a family, under the rules adopted by the competent minister, from the right to benefit. The Federatie Nederlandse Vakbeweging (Netherlands Trades Union Federation) started a legal action in order to obtain a decision that the Netherlands acted unlawfully by maintaining in force or refusing to cease to apply this Article after 23 December 1984.

The question was whether Article 4 had direct effect as from 23 December 1984. The Court answered that Article 4 is unconditional and sufficiently precise as it precludes, generally and unequivocally, all discrimination on the grounds of sex. Secondly, the question arose whether the prohibition of discrimination which it contains may be regarded as unconditional having regard to the exceptions provided for in Article 7. Article 7 merely reserved to Member States the right to exclude certain clearly defined areas from the scope of the Directive. The disputed provision does not fall under these exceptions. Therefore, Article 7 is not relevant in this case. As for Article 5, which obliges Member States to take the measures necessary to ensure that any laws, regulations and administrative provisions contrary to the principle of equal treatment are abolished, it cannot be inferred that it lays down conditions to which the prohibition of discrimination is subject. Consequently, Article 4(1) of the Directive does not confer on Member States the power to make conditional or to limit the application of the principle of equal treatment within its field of application. Consequently, individuals can rely on this Article before the national courts as from 23 December 1984.

Now the direct effect was established, the question arose of what the consequences for individuals were. Article 4 precludes any form of discrimination but what does this mean for national provisions inconsistent with this Article? Are in the *FNV* case married women, not being main wage-earners in a family, entitled to the disputed benefit? Or are, from now on, male married persons, not being main wage-earners, no longer entitled to this benefit? The Court answered that in the absence of measures implementing the Directive, women are entitled to be treated in the same manner and to have the same rules applied to them as men who are in the same situation, since, where the said Directive has not been implemented, those rules remain the only valid point of reference (*see*, for the

---

[18]   Case 71/85, [1986] *ECR* 3855.

same approach, the *Defrenne* judgment in the previous Chapter).[19] Therefore, married women who are not the main wage-earner were no longer excluded from entitlement to the disputed benefit.

The *FNV* judgment concerned a case of direct discrimination which was not removed before the end of the implementation period of the Directive. A comparable situation was disputed in the *McDermott and Cotter* judgment.[20]

The case concerned married women whose unemployment benefit was terminated after one year on the grounds that a married woman could receive unemployment benefit for a maximum of 312 days. A married man, a single man or a single woman would have received benefit for seventy-eight days more. The applicants required the annulment of the termination of their benefit after the 312 benefit days, on the grounds that from 23 December 1984 they were entitled to benefit at the same rate and for the same period as married men.

The Court agreed with this view: the national rule was incompatible with the Directive. Until the moment that the national government adopted the necessary implementing measures, women were entitled to have the same rules applied to them as were applied to men in the same situation.

22.5.3. PROHIBITION OF THE EFFECTS OF A FORMER DISCRIMINATORY RULE

Most of the cases brought before the Court which concerned direct discrimination concerned transitory rules that were related to prior discriminatory rules or situations, and in these transitory rules the effects of the prior discrimination could still be seen. As a result of such a transitory rule Mrs McDermott and Cotter, whose first judgment was discussed in the previous section, had a new case. This was because the subsequent law adopted by the Irish legislator still had a directly discriminatory effect. This led to a second preliminary reference and to the *Cotter and McDermott* judgment.[21]

Under the British Social Welfare Act 1981, a married man was automatically entitled to increases in his social security benefits in respect of a spouse and children without having to prove that they were actually dependent on him, whereas married women were required to fulfil additional conditions.

That position was altered by the Social Welfare Act 1985 which confined the payment of an increase in respect of an adult dependant to a situation where actual dependency can be shown, irrespective of the sex of the claimant. A transitional rule provided that claimants who did not have a spouse actually dependent on

---

[19]   The approach of the FNV judgment is followed in the judgments of the Court, Case 31/90, *Johnson*, [1991] *ECR* 3723; Case 286/85, *McDermott and Cotter*, [1987] *ECR* 1453; Case 102/88, *Ruzius-Wilbrink*, [1989] *ECR* 4311, discussed in the following section.
[20]   Case 286/85, [1987] *ECR* 1453.
[21]   Case 377/89, [1991] *ECR* 1155.

them, and therefore ceased to be entitled to an increase, became eligible for a compensatory allowance. It was common ground that those provisions covered only married men who previously received automatic increases even if they had no actual dependants.

The Irish government argued that the prohibition of discrimination laid down in Article 4(1) of the Directive applied only to circumstances in which the person in respect of whom an increase has been granted was financially dependent. The Court decided that this argument could not be upheld. Article 4 of the Directive applied, in particular, to the calculation of benefits, including increases for spouses and dependants. From this it is clear that the Article also applies to increases for non-dependent spouses. The determination of the conditions for increases of social security benefits is left, according to the Court, entirely to the Member States, with the restriction that the principle of equal treatment has to be taken fully into account. As long as the necessary implementation measures for the Directive are not adopted, the application of the rules which apply to men who are in the same situation remains the only valid point of reference. Therefore, if men did not have to show after 23 December 1984 that their spouses were actually dependent on them, and if they received the increases automatically, women have the same automatic right to increases if they are in the same circumstances as these men. Specific additional conditions are not allowed.

The Irish government further argued that the Directive should not be interpreted in such a way that it would lead to an 'unjust enrichment'. This principle of national law means that payment to an applicant, even if it would be according to the law, does not have to take place if that payment would lead to unjust enrichment of the person concerned to the detriment effect of the defendant. A radical interpretation of the equal treatment principle could have the effect that one family received the same increase twice, *i.e.* when both partners receive social security benefits in the same period. The Court rejected this argument. If such an application of the principle of unjust enrichment was accepted, the national authorities could use their own illegal behaviour as an argument to deprive Article 4 of its full meaning.[22]

In the *Dik* case as well,[23] the contested regulation concerned the effects of older discriminatory rules, this time again the Dutch Earnings-related Unemployment Assistance Scheme (WWV), already the subject of the *FNV* judgment in the previous section.

The disputed WWV provision was repealed with retroactive effect as from 23 December 1984. A transitional measure, however, provided that the repeal of that Article was not to apply to workers whose unemployment commenced before 23 December 1984, unless they were in receipt of the benefit under the

---

[22] On the effects of discriminatory rules from the past, *see* also the *Borrie Clarke* judgment, Case 384/85, [1987] *ECR* 2865.
[23] Case 80/87, [1988] *ECR* 1601.

Werkloosheidswet (Unemployment Insurance Act – WW) on that date. This meant that the discriminatory provision still applied for existing cases.

The Court considered that the Directive does not provide for any derogation from the principle of equal treatment laid down in Article 4(1) in order to authorise the extension of the discriminatory effects of earlier provisions of national law. That is so notwithstanding the fact that those inequalities are the result of transitional provisions. If a man who lost his employment and his right to benefit under the WW before 23 December 1984, and who did not obtain benefit under the WWV before that date, was entitled to benefit under the WWV after that date, a woman in the same position would also be entitled to such benefit without having to satisfy any additional condition applicable exclusively to married women before that date.

The *Verholen* judgment[24] also concerned the effect of previous discriminatory rules.

The contested regulation was the Dutch General Old-age Pension Law (AOW) which provided until 1 April 1985 that married women were not insured under this act during the periods that their husbands were not insured because they were employed in another State. Although under the general rules of this residence-based scheme residents of the Netherlands were insured, the category just described was excluded. The opposite was not the case: a married man, resident of the Netherlands, whose wife was insured abroad, remained insured. The effects of the exclusion from insurance was a reduced old-age benefit when the woman reached pension age.

The Court considered that it had already ruled in the *Dik* judgment that the Directive does not contain exceptions to the equal treatment principle. Consequently, older national provisions must not have discriminatory effects after 23 December 1984, even if these are the effect of benefit conditions in force before this date.

Women falling under the Directive are therefore entitled to an unreduced benefit. Thus the approach of the Court with respect to *statutory* old-age pensions is different from that regarding occupational pensions, for the approach with respect to the latter type, *see* the *Ten Oever* judgment (discussed in Section 21.3 above). Directive 79/7 is a different scheme than Article 157 TFEU, with a different history and, therefore, the Court did not allow the effects of previous discriminatory rules to continue to have an impact.

Consequently, a reduction of the pension because of non-insured years cannot be applied to these Dutch old-age benefits payable after 23 December 1984, even if the person concerned was not insured on grounds of the rule that the spouse of the employer working abroad was not insured during these periods. In order to invoke this rule, one must fall under the personal scope of the Directive

---

[24] Cases 87/90, 88/90 and 89/90, [1991] *ECR* 3757.

at the moment one applies for this benefit. For this reason Mrs Achterberg (*see* Section 22.2) could not rely on the Directive, whereas Mrs Verholen could.

In the *Van Gemert-Derks* case[25] the question was raised whether the withdrawal of disability benefit was acceptable in the case of persons who received a widows' pension.

The Dutch General Law on Disability Benefits provided that the right to a disability benefit was to be withdrawn as soon as a woman became entitled to a widows' pension. A widows' pension is granted after an application for this benefit is made or it may be granted *ex officio* by the benefit administration. The replacement of a disability benefit by a widows' pension meant that the woman concerned received a lower benefit. As widows' pensions were by virtue of the text of this Law payable to women only, this rule affected only women; the disability benefit of male beneficiaries could not be withdrawn when they became a widower. However, the Dutch Court of Appeal ruled in 1988 that by virtue of Article 26 of the International Convention on Civil and Political Rights, widowers were also entitled to benefit under the General Law on widows' benefits. Consequently, the question arose as to how to interpret the disputed provision of the General Law on Disability Benefits.

The first question was whether Directive 79/7 still allowed national courts to apply Article 26 of the Convention. This question was raised as application of the latter Article could lead to different situations in the Member States. Some Member States had ratified this Convention while others had not. The Court replied that as regards benefits which are not within the material scope of Directive 79/7, these benefits are governed by national and international law. A decision of a national court based on Article 26 of the Convention mentioned above does not affect the implementation of the principle of equal treatment.

The second question of the national court was whether the rule of the General Law on Disability Benefits mentioned above was contrary to Article 4 of Directive 79/7. The Directive does not apply to survivors' benefits, so the question arose whether this issue could be solved by interpretation of the Directive. The Court considered that the disputed provision concerned the withdrawal of disability benefit. Consequently, Directive 79/7 was applicable. The next question was whether the disputed rule involves discrimination. The Court considered that a provision of national legislation, which deprived women of benefit, whereas men in the same situation were not deprived of this benefit, constituted discrimination within the meaning of Directive 79/7. The Dutch benefit administration had argued that at present widows' benefits were granted only after an application had been received. From 1989, all beneficiaries of a general disability benefit who became widows were informed of the consequences of claiming for the widows' benefit. The Court considered this procedure acceptable; it could not be said that the Directive is infringed upon if a widow renounced her right to a

---

[25]   Case 337/91, [1993] *ECR* I-5943.

general disability benefit, on condition that she has been informed accurately and comprehensibly of the financial effects of substitution of this benefit by a widows' benefit. It is up to the national court to decide whether the widow concerned had indeed renounced her entitlement to benefit after she had been informed in this way.

22.5.4. PROCEDURAL LIMITATIONS FOR REALISING EQUAL TREATMENT

National law often restricts the periods for which benefit can be claimed with retroactive effect. As some Member States were late in removing discriminatory rules from their national law, the question arose as to what extent national rules of procedure are contrary to the Directive. This matter was dealt with in the *Emmott* judgment.[26]

Mrs Emmott's situation closely resembled that as described in the (first) *McDermott and Cotter* judgment (*see* Section 22.5.2) and concerned the same national scheme. In 1987 Mrs Emmott had written a letter to the Minister in order to obtain benefit. The Minister answered that no decision could be taken as there was still a case pending on this issue (*i.e.* the *McDermott and Cotter* judgment). When this judgment was delivered (1987) Mrs Emmott applied to receive as from 23 December 1984 the same amount of benefits as are paid to a married man in a situation identical to hers. The national authorities, however, argued that the time-limit for initiating proceedings was not observed and this constituted a bar to her claim.

The Court of Justice was asked whether the ruling in *McDermott and Cotter* must be understood as meaning that in respect to a claim on Article 4, general principles of Community law precluded the authorities of a Member State from relying upon national procedural rules, in particular rules relating to time-limits. The Court held that in the absence of Community rules on the subject it is for the domestic legal system of each Member State to determine the procedural conditions and also in respect of claims concerning protection of the rights which individuals derive from the direct effect of Community law. Such conditions must not be less favourable than those relating to similar actions of a domestic nature nor can they be framed so as to render virtually impossible the exercise of rights conferred by Community law. Whilst the laying down of reasonable time-limits which, if unobserved, bar proceedings satisfies in principle the two conditions mentioned above, account must nevertheless be taken of the particular nature of directives. It must be borne in mind that the Member States are required to ensure the full application of directives in a sufficiently and precise manner so that, where directives are intended to create rights for individuals, they can

---

[26]   Case 208/90, [1991] *ECR* 4269.

ascertain the full extent of those rights and, where necessary, rely on them before the national courts. Only in specific circumstances, in particular where a Member State has failed to take the implementation measures required or has adopted measures which are not in conformity with a directive, has the Court recognised the right of persons affected to rely, in judicial proceedings, on a directive against a defaulting Member State. Therefore, the Court argued, this is a minimum guarantee, arising from the binding nature of the obligation imposed on the Member States by the effect of directives, which cannot justify a Member State absolving itself from taking implementation measures appropriate to the purpose of each directive in due time. This is because as long as a directive has not been properly transposed into national law, individuals are unable to ascertain the full extent of their rights. That state of uncertainty for individuals subsists even after the Court has delivered a judgment finding that the Member State in question has not fulfilled its obligations under the directive. This is also the case if the Court has held that a particular provision or provisions of the directive are sufficiently precise and unconditional to be relied upon before a national court. Only the proper transposition of the directive will bring that state of uncertainty to an end and it is only upon that transposition that the legal certainty which must exist if individuals are to be required to assert their rights is created. It follows that until such time as a directive has been properly transposed, a defaulting Member State may not rely on an individual's delay in initiating proceedings against it in order to protect rights conferred upon him by the provisions of the directive. A period laid down by national law, within which proceedings must be initiated, cannot begin to run before that time.

In the *Steenhorst-Neerings* case[27] the Court was asked whether the *Emmott* ruling was also relevant to legislation limiting the possibility of claiming benefit with retroactive effect. This question, unlike in *Emmott*, did not concern procedural rules.

Initially, the Dutch General disability benefit was not payable to married women. By a law of 1979, married women also became eligible for this benefit, but an exception was made in respect of women who had begun to suffer incapacity for work before 1975. The Dutch court of appeal, however, decided in 1988 that this was contrary to Article 26 of the International Convention on Civil and Political Rights. This meant that married women whose incapacity materialised before 1975 could receive disability benefit as from 1980, the date on which the 1979 Act came into force. The General Disability Law provided that one could not receive benefit with retroactive effect for more than one year from the date of application.

The Court was asked whether the latter rule was compatible with Community law. It considered that the conditions for this benefit must be the same for men and women. Moreover, the conditions for entitlement to benefit were to be governed

---

[27]   Case 338/91, [1993] *ECR* I-5475.

by national law, must not be less favourable then those generally applicable for this type of benefit and must not make the exercise of rights which were derived from Community law impossible. The national court had asked this question with the *Emmott* judgment in mind. The Court replied that a rule of national law which limits the retroactive effect of a claim is different from the rule which was disputed in the *Emmott* case. The loss of rights following from a delay in initiating procedures before a court corresponds to the need to prevent administrative decisions from being liable to dispute in proceedings outside a restricted time period. The provision in the legislation which limits the retroactive effect of applications for disability benefit serves an objective which is totally different from time limits for initiating a procedure before a court. The legislative provision is needed to satisfy the requirements of proper administration and, in particular, to maintain the financial balances of a pay-as-you-go system. As a result, the disputed national rule was not contrary to the Directive.[28]

22.5.5. INDIRECT DISCRIMINATION

Article 4 of the Directive also precludes indirect discrimination. It is much more difficult to decide whether a rule is indirectly discriminatory than when direct discrimination is in dispute. A rule is indirectly discriminatory, if its effects are different for either of the sexes even though it does not itself contain criteria directly related to sex. In such a case it is not relevant whether the person or body who made this rule had the intention of discriminating on the basis of sex.

From the judgments of the Court it appears that many cases of alleged indirect discrimination concern supplements for dependants. The first such case was the *Teuling-Worms* judgment.[29]

According to the Dutch Law on Insurance against Incapacity for Work (WAO), benefit could be increased by means of supplements for dependent family members. Mrs Teuling was not entitled to benefit supplements because of the income arising from or in connection with her husband's work. Mrs Teuling claimed that the system of supplements constituted indirect discrimination against women.

The Court pointed out that the disputed supplements were not directly based on the sex of beneficiaries but took account of their marital status or family situation. It emerged that a considerably smaller proportion of women than of men were entitled to such supplements. This would be contrary to Article 4(1) of the Directive if that system of benefits could not be justified by reasons which exclude discrimination on the grounds of sex. According to statistics provided to the Commission by the Netherlands Government, a significantly greater

---

[28]   For a comparable case, *see* the *Second Johnson* judgment, Case 410/92, [1994] *ECR* I-5483.
[29]   Case 30/85, [1987] *ECR* 2497.

number of married men than married women receive a supplement linked to family responsibilities. This results from the fact that in the Netherlands there are at present considerably more married men than married women who carry out occupational activities, and therefore considerably fewer women who have a dependent spouse. Therefore the question of objective justification arose. According to the Netherlands Government, the Disability Benefits Act sought to provide a minimum subsistence income to persons with no income from work. The Court considered that if supplements to a minimum social security benefit are intended, where beneficiaries have no income from work, to prevent the benefit from falling below the minimum subsistence level for persons who, by virtue of the fact that they have a dependent spouse or children, bear heavier burdens than single persons, such supplements may be justified under the Directive. The Court left the final answer to whether this is the case to the national court: if the national court determines that the disputed supplements correspond to the greater burden which beneficiaries having a dependent spouse or children must bear in comparison with persons living alone, and serve to ensure an adequate minimum subsistence income for those beneficiaries and are necessary for that purpose, the grant of such supplements is not contrary to the Directive.

Thus, three steps have to be taken in the case of discrimination: first, one must examine whether the regulation has different effects for women and men; then one must consider whether there are objective reasons for the contested regulation; and, finally, it has to be examined whether the regulation is necessary and adequate to achieve these aims.

The criteria to assess objective justification in the *Teuling* case, in particular, appeared to be problematic to apply. The Dutch court of the first instance[30] considered the disputed increases not necessary and adequate, as in some cases supplements were paid even if beneficiaries achieved an income above the minimum income. The scheme was therefore considered indirectly discriminatory. On appeal, the Central Appeals Court[31] followed a different approach. It considered that all categories of income, which were not taken into account by the means test, concerned disability benefits. Therefore, the court considered that it had obviously been the intention of the legislator that the means test should not affect those disability benefits; in other words, the contested benefits were to be a basic benefit and this should not be reduced to the detrimental effect of those other specific benefits. This ancillary objective is acceptable and the effects of this are not such that it cannot be said that the increases are not necessary or inadequate.

Other types of benefit conditions can also raise the question of alleged indirect discrimination. A second case before the Court, the *Ruzius-Wilbrink* case,[32] concerned, again, the Dutch General Disability Benefit Law (AAW).

---

30   RvB Amsterdam 29 December 1987, *RSV* 1988/173.
31   CRvB 19 April 1990, *RSV* 1990/323.
32   Case 102/88, [1989] *ECR* 4311.

Benefits on the basis of this law are, as a rule, flat rate, *i.e.* related to the minimum wage. However, for persons who earned *less* than the minimum wage before they suffered incapacity for work, benefit was calculated on a lower individual basis. As this calculation method applies only where one earned less than the minimum wage, this rule is relevant only for (low paid) part-time workers. Women are more likely to work in such jobs.

The Court considered that such a provision led, in principle, to discrimination against female workers in relation to male workers and must be regarded as contrary to the objective pursued by Article 4(1) of Directive 79/7, unless the difference of treatment between the two categories of workers is justified by objective factors unrelated to any discrimination on the grounds of sex. The only reason put forward by the Netherlands government to justify the difference of treatment was that it would be unjust to grant part-timers an allowance higher than the income previously received. This could not objectively justify that difference of treatment since, in a substantial number of other cases, the amount of the allowance granted under the 1975 Law was higher than the previous income. The national courts had to decide whether there were other objective justifications for this rule.

In later judgments, the Court of Justice followed an approach in which it became clear that the disputed supplements and calculation rules were accepted. The first judgment is the result of an infringement procedure, the *Commission* v. *Belgium* judgment.[33] Under Belgian law, the benefit rate for unemployed persons who were financially responsible for a partner was higher than for persons who were not responsible for a partner. The benefits concerned were earnings-related.

The Court considered that a system with increases, which takes account of the marital and family situation and which has the effect that fewer women than men can apply for such a benefit, is potentially indirectly discriminatory. This is, however, not the case if objective factors upon which the differentiation is based. The Belgian government had argued that the reason that more men were eligible for an increase was due to the fact that more men were employed in occupational activities and that this constituted such an objective factor. The Court replied that this reason was insufficient to decide that this provision is not discriminatory.

In order to be objectively justified, the regulation in question has to correspond to a necessary objective of the social policy of a State and has to be appropriate and necessary to attain that objective. The Belgian government responded that the objective of the national scheme was to grant, within the limits of its funds, a minimum replacement income, taking account of the family situation of the claimant. Secondly, the Belgium scheme aimed to avoid an overly large drop in income in the first year and also to provide for a special provision for the long-term unemployed who had dependants. The Court considered that these principles of the national system were part of its social policy and that Member States are allowed a reasonable margin of discretion in relation to their social

---

[33] Case 229/89, [1991] *ECR* I-2205.

policy. The maximum level for the earnings-related benefit and the increase for long-term unemployed persons whose incomes were below a specified minimum constituted elements which meant that the national scheme has the character of a social minimum scheme. In respect of a social minimum scheme, Community law does not prevent a Member State from taking account of the relatively higher needs of beneficiaries with dependants.

As we can see, in this judgment the Court of Justice leaves considerable room for discretion to the Member States in respect of social minimum schemes. The Court also followed this approach in the *Molenbroek* case[34] that concerned increases to Dutch old-age pensions.

The Dutch General Old Age Pension Law provided for an increase for the partner of a retired person who had not yet reached pension age, if this partner had insufficient means. Income, if any, of the partner was deducted from the increase. It was not disputed that under this scheme men were more likely to receive an increase for a dependant partner. This was due to the fact that, in a couple, the man is often older than his spouse. Even if the man is younger than his wife, he will often have income from occupational activity which will mean that his wife will not qualify for the increase.

The conditions under which the increase were payable were far more generous than the contested regulation in the *Teuling-Worms* case As for the old-age benefit supplements, the income of the pensioner himself was not taken into account. The scheme was, therefore, not strictly appropriate or necessary to guarantee a minimum income. The Court pointed out that factors constitute objective justification, if the scheme corresponds with a justified objective of the social policy of the Member State whose regulation was contested. The means used by a Member State had to be appropriate to attain the objective of the social policy and had to be necessary. The Dutch old-age pension had the characteristics of a basic income payment, in the sense that it aimed to guarantee a minimum income to the persons concerned irrespective of other income. Thus, the income of the pensioner was not taken into account in calculating the increase for the dependant. The reason for this was, the Court considered, that the objective of the national legislation was to provide a couple with an income which they would have received if they had both reached retirement age. The increases were therefore necessary to maintain the character of a basic income payment in the Dutch Old-age Benefit Law. Under these circumstances, the fact that in some situations an increase is also paid to persons for whom the increase is, because of their other income, not necessary to guarantee a subsistence minimum does not mean that the means chosen by the Member State are not necessary. From these considerations, it followed that the national legislation fitted in with a legitimate objective of social policy and that the increases were considered appropriate to

---

[34]   Case 226/91, [1992] *ECR* I-5943.

attain this objective and were necessary. They were justified by factors not linked to discrimination on the grounds of sex.

This time the Court itself answered the question of whether the Dutch scheme is discriminatory and did not leave this question, as it has done, for instance, in the *Bilka* judgment, to the national court.

The approach of the *Molenbroek* judgment was continued in the *Megner and Scheffel* judgment.[35]

The main question in this case was whether the exclusion of persons working in part-time jobs with a low number of working hours from social security protection was compatible with Article 4 of Directive 79/7. The case concerned two women who were employed as cleaners by a firm. Their normal working time was a maximum of two hours per working day, five days a week. They were excluded from the compulsory insurance under the statutory sickness and old-age scheme and also from the insurance for unemployment benefit. They had filed a request to the competent German benefit administrations to be covered by these acts but this request was refused.

This judgment has already been discussed supra, where the Court had to answer the question of whether they fell under the personal scope of the Directive. The second question was whether the exclusion of subsidiary employment from the social insurance was forbidden by Article 4 of the Directive. The Court considered that indirect discrimination was involved, which is forbidden unless the measures chosen reflect a legitimate social policy aim of the Member State whose legislation is at issue and are appropriate to achieve that aim and are necessary in order to do so.

The German government explained that there is a social demand for subsidiary employment. In order to respond to that demand they fostered the existence and supply of such employment. The only means of doing this within the structural framework of the German social security scheme was to exclude subsidiary employment from compulsory insurance. The jobs lost would not be replaced by full or part-time jobs subject to compulsory insurance. On the contrary, there would be an increase in unlawful employment and a rise in circumventing devices (for instance, false self-employment) in view of the social demand for subsidiary employment.

The Court observed that in the current state of Community law social policy is a matter for the Member States; it is for the Member States to choose the measures capable of achieving the aim of their social and employment policy. In exercising that competence, the Member States have a broad margin of discretion. The social and employment policy aim relied on by the German government is objectively unrelated to any discrimination on the grounds of sex and, in exercising its competence, the national legislature was reasonably entitled to consider that the

---

[35]   Case 444/93, [1995] *ECR* I-4741.

legislation in question was necessary in order to achieve that aim. Consequently, the legislation in question could not be described as indirect discrimination.[36]

We can see in these judgments that the Court applies a less strict test on objective grounds for justification than it had done in its earliest judgments on this issue, such as in the *Teuling* ruling. In that ruling the Court considered that a scheme must be appropriate, necessary and proportional to its objectives in order to be objectively justified in the case of a suspicion of indirect discrimination. In the *Commission v. Belgium* judgment, the Member States were given the room within their social policy objectives to decide the provisions concerning minimum benefits to some extent themselves. But the latter judgment still concerned benefits which provided for a minimum income in households. In the *Megner and Scheffel* judgment, the room for discretion became larger: the social policy concerning wage related benefits was now also considered as belonging to the discretionary room of the Member States, at least in so far as part-time employment is concerned.[37]

Conclusion: Questions of indirect discrimination appeared not to be easy to deal with. If the criteria for objective justifications are strict, many national schemes may be contrary to the Directive. This will be the case, in particular, with schemes which provide a minimum income for families. A radical application of the equal treatment rule would impede social policy measures: Member States cannot expect to pay a supplement to every beneficiary regardless of his need, so the only solution is to abolish the schemes which, in turn, leaves the problem of poverty. This is, of course, a consequence the Court did not want to be responsible for. Consequently, the Court has left it to national legislators to make their instruments of social policy and does not, in the case of alleged indirect discrimination, investigate the reasons given as objective justification when measures of social policy are concerned, in any case not when social policy measures are aimed at guaranteeing a subsistence income. It is regrettable, however, that the Court also followed this approach in the *Megner and Scheffel* judgment, as this does not concern minimum benefits but earnings-related (insurance) benefits. In fact, a scheme in which jobs of less than fifteen hours are uninsured does not respond to new developments in the labour market, where such jobs are not exceptional anymore, and affects women predominantly.

---

[36]   In the *Nolte* judgment (Case 317/93, [1995] *ECR* I-4625) the problem raised and the answer given by the Court resembled that of the *Megner and Scheffel* judgment to a large extent.

[37]   *See,* for comparable cases, the *Roks-de Weerd* judgment (Case 343/92, [1994] *ECR* I-571) and the *Posthuma-van Damme and Öztürk* judgment (Case 280/94, [1996] *ECR* I-179).

22.5.6. THE ARTICLE 7 EXCEPTION

Article 7 of Directive 79/7 reads: 'This Directive shall be without prejudice to the right of Member States to exclude from its scope:

a. the determination of pensionable age for the purposes of granting old-age and retirement pensions and the possible consequences thereof for other benefits;
b. advantages in respect of old-age pension schemes granted to persons who have brought up children; the acquisition of benefit entitlements following periods of interruption of employment due to the bringing up of children;
c. the granting of old-age or invalidity benefit entitlement by virtue of the derived entitlements of a wife;
d. the granting of increases of long-term invalidity, old-age, accidents at work and occupational disease benefits for a dependent wife;
e. the consequences of the exercise, before the adoption of this Directive, of a right of option not to acquire rights or incur obligations under a statutory scheme.'

This provision led to a number of rulings in which the differences in pension age between men and women were disputed. The cases concerned, in particular, situations in which the earlier distinction in pension age was repealed but the effects of that distinction were still felt. In the *Van Cant* judgment[38] the question of the extent of the exceptions was discussed.

The Belgian Royal Decree of 24 October 1967 provided that the normal pension age for men was sixty-five and for women sixty. The amount of pension was calculated over forty-five years of work in the case of men, and forty years of work in the case of women. The income earned in each of these years was divided by forty-five (men) or forty (women); the pension was the aggregated sum of these calculations. In 1990, the eligible pension ages were revised and pension age was set at sixty for men and women. The amount of the pension was, however, still calculated in accordance with the rules of the Decree of 1967 and, as this method was less attractive to men than to women, Mr Van Cant disputed this rule.

The Court considered that this law was of a discriminatory nature and was prohibited by the Directive. This could only not be the case if Article 7(1)(a) of the Directive was applicable. This Article authorises the Member States to defer implementation of equal treatment with regard to pensionable age in old-age pensions. Once the differences in national law concerning pension age were repealed, the exception in Article 7 could no longer be invoked to justify differences in the calculation of old age pensions which had been connected with

---

[38]   Case 154/92, [1993] *ECR* I-3811.

the difference in pension age. The *De Vriendt* judgment[39] can be seen as a follow-up to the *Van Cant* decision.

In decisions made between 18 December 1990 and 16 December 1994, the Pensions Office awarded the plaintiffs, all of them male employees, retirement pensions on the basis of their employment record, calculated in forty-fifths. On 16 June 1996, while the proceedings were still pending, the Belgian Parliament enacted a law interpreting the 1990 Law, hereafter 'the interpretative law'. This Law provides that the term 'retirement pension' is defined as the replacement income granted to a beneficiary who is deemed to have become unfit for work by reason of old age, this event being deemed to occur at the age of 65 for male beneficiaries and 60 for female beneficiaries. Hence this Law reintroduced a difference in pension age which was meant to allow again differences in the calculation of the amount of pension. The objective of the Law was to gradually fix the pension age at the age of 65 for both men and women.

The Court considered that the possibility of derogation provided for in Article 7(1)(a) must be construed strictly. It follows from the nature of the exceptions contained in Article 7 that the Community legislature intended to allow Member States to maintain temporarily the advantages accorded to women to enable them progressively to adapt their pension systems without disrupting the complex equilibrium of those systems. It is therefore necessary to determine whether in this case the discrimination relating to the method of calculating retirement pensions is necessarily and objectively linked to the maintenance of national provisions which prescribe different pensionable ages for men and women. Whether the national legislation has maintained different pensionable ages for men and women is a question of fact which it is for the national court to determine. If such a difference has been maintained, the calculating methods are necessarily and objectively linked to the difference in pension ages and are therefore acceptable. This approach was confirmed in the *Wolfs* judgment.[40]

In the *Richardson* judgment[41] the disputed regulation was a British one, already referred to in Section 22.3. The Secretary of State is authorised to exempt specific categories from payment of prescription charges. The Secretary of State had provided exemptions for, among others, men who reached the age of 65 years or women who reached the age of 60. The question was raised whether Article 7 authorises a Member State which, pursuant to that provision, has maintained different pension ages for men and women, to also provide that women are to be exempt from prescription charges at the age of 60 whilst for men the age is 65.

The Court stated that where, pursuant to Article 7(1)(a) of Directive 79/7, a Member State prescribes different retirement ages for men and women for the purposes of granting old-age and retirement pensions, the scope of the permitted

---

[39] Cases 377/96 to 384/96, [1998] *ECR* I-2105.

[40] Case 154/96, [1998] *ECR* I-6173.

[41] Case 137/94, [1995] *ECR* I-3407.

derogation, defined by the words 'possible consequences thereof for other benefits' contained in Article 7, is limited to forms of discrimination existing under the other benefit schemes which are necessarily and objectively linked to the difference in retirement age. That is so where the discrimination in question is objectively necessary in order to avoid disturbing the financial equilibrium of the social security system or to ensure coherence between the retirement pension scheme and other benefit schemes. The granting of benefits under non-contributory schemes to persons in respect of whom certain risks have materialised, where this occurs without reference to their entitlement to an old-age pension by virtue of contribution periods completed by them, has no direct influence on the financial equilibrium of contributory pension schemes. There is here an inverse relationship between entitlement to the benefit, constituted by exemption from prescription charges as provided for in the British regulations, and the payment of contributions, inasmuch as it is only once a person has reached pensionable age and is no longer liable to pay National Insurance contributions that he is exempt from prescription charges under that provision. That being so, the Court argued, it must be accepted that the removal of the discrimination would not affect the financial equilibrium of the pension system. That conclusion cannot in any way be affected by the mere fact that extending entitlement to exemption from prescription charges to men who have reached the age of sixty would increase the financial burden borne by the State in the funding of its national health system. Therefore, the discrimination at issue is not objectively necessary to ensure coherence between the retirement pension system and the British regulations on prescription charges. Although the fact that the elderly will generally incur more prescription charges than younger people at a time when they will normally have less disposable income may provide some justification for exempting them from prescription charges above a certain age, that consideration does not require this benefit to be granted at the statutory pensionable age and, therefore, at different ages for men and women.

In the *Richardson* judgment, discussed above, a non-contributory benefit was involved. In the *Graham* judgment[42] the questions concerned contributory benefits. The approach of the Court led to a different result in this case. The disputed British scheme provided that where a person has received sickness benefit for a period of 168 days due to incapacity for work, he is entitled to invalidity pension for each subsequent day of incapacity for work if he is under the pensionable age, set at 65 for men and 60 for women. The Court noted that such legislation is discriminatory. First, the rate of invalidity pension for women is limited to the rate of the retirement pension to which they would have been entitled had they not opted to defer payment of that pension from the age of 60. This is true for men only when they become 65. The Court considered that the scope of the derogation to the principle of equal treatment permitted by Article 7(1) is limited to the forms

---

[42]   Case 92/94, [1995] *ECR* I-2521.

of discrimination which are necessarily and objectively linked to the difference in pensionable age. As regards the forms of discrimination in the present case, the Court found that they are objectively linked to different pensionable ages: they arise directly from the fact that that age is fixed at 60 for women and 65 for men. Since invalidity benefit is designed to replace income from occupational activity, there is nothing to prevent a Member State from providing for its cessation and replacement by a retirement pension when they have reached pensionable age. Consequently, this scheme was allowed.

22.6. CONCLUSION

In general, it can be said that the Court followed a radical approach by giving broad interpretations to the personal and material scope of the Directive and by ruling that old schemes must not continue to have discriminatory effects. However, a notorious lack of protection stems from the fact that women do not fall under the Directive if they stopped working in order to raise children.

With respect to the case law on indirect discrimination, we can see that the Court has changed its case law through time: initially it appeared to be rather tight on the nature and content of grounds for objective justification. If one reconsiders the old criteria, the present approach is not completely contrary to those criteria. The present case law does not leave many possibilities to fight situations of alleged indirect discrimination.

CHAPTER 23

EQUAL TREATMENT OF MEN AND WOMEN: THE OTHER DIRECTIVES

23.1. DIRECTIVE 86/378

23.1.1. INTRODUCTION

Directive 86/378 was adopted by the Council on 24 July 1986.[1] It aims to ensure the implementation of the principle of equal treatment for men and women in occupational social security schemes and this directive is an important complement to Directive 79/7 because the latter concerns statutory social security only.

The implementation period of this Directive expired on 1 January 1993, but Member States were allowed to defer some parts of the Directive. In Chapter 21 we discussed the *Bilka* and *Barber* judgments which interfered with these exceptions. In 1997, Directive 86/378 was amended by Directive 96/97[2] in order to make the former Directive consistent with the case law on Article 157 TFEU.

23.1.2. THE PERSONAL SCOPE OF DIRECTIVE 86/378

The personal scope of this Directive is defined in approximately the same way as for Directive 79/7. This means that the Directive applies to members of the working population including self-employed persons, persons whose activity is interrupted by illness, maternity, accident or involuntary unemployment and persons seeking employment, and to retired and disabled workers (Article 3). It is plausible that the case law of the Court on the personal scope of the Directive 79/7 is also relevant to questions concerning the personal scope of this Directive. Directive 96/97 added the persons claiming under the persons mentioned above to the personal scope.

---

[1]   *OJ* 1986 *L* 225.
[2]   *OJ* 1997 *L* 46/20.

23.1.3. THE MATERIAL SCOPE OF DIRECTIVE 86/378

The object of the Directive is to implement, in occupational social security schemes, the principle of equal treatment. Article 2 defines *occupational social security schemes*: these are schemes not governed by Directive 79/7 whose purpose is to provide workers, whether employees or self-employed, in an undertaking or a group of undertakings, an area of economic activity or occupational sector or group of such sectors, with benefits intended to supplement the benefits provided by statutory social security schemes or to replace them. It is not decisive whether membership of such schemes is compulsory or optional.

Some types of schemes are excluded from the scope of this Directive. These are individual contracts of self-employed persons and schemes for self-employed persons with only one member. Nor does the Directive apply, in the case of employed person, to insurance contracts to which the employer is not a party. Optional provisions of occupational schemes offered to participants individually in order to guarantee them additional benefits, a choice of date on which the normal benefits will start, or a choice between several benefits are also excluded.

The Directive does not preclude an employer granting to persons who have already reached the occupational pension retirement age, but who have not yet reached retirement age for the statutory retirement pension, a pension supplement until the persons benefiting from the supplement reach the statutory retirement age. The aim of this is to make equal, or more equal, the overall amount of benefit paid to these persons in relation to the amount paid to persons of the other sex who are in the same situation and who have already reached the statutory retirement age.

The Directive applies to occupational schemes which provide protection against the following risks: sickness, invalidity, old age (including early retirement) industrial accidents and occupational diseases and unemployment. In addition to the contingencies mentioned in Directive 79/7, Directive 86/378 also applies to early retirement schemes.

The Directive also applies, according to Article 4(b), to occupational schemes which provide for other social benefits, in cash or in kind, and in particular to survivors' benefits and family allowances if such benefits are accorded to employed persons and thus constitute a consideration paid by the employer to the worker by reason of the latter's employment.

23.1.4. THE PRINCIPLE OF EQUAL TREATMENT

According to Article 5 of this Directive, the principle of equal treatment requires that there shall be no discrimination on the basis of sex, either directly or indirectly. The Directive mentions in particular discrimination by means of reference to marital or family status, especially as regards the scope of the scheme and the conditions of access to the scheme; the obligation to contribute and the calculation of contributions; the calculation of benefits, including supplementary benefits due in respect of a spouse or dependants; and the conditions governing the duration and retention of entitlement to benefits.

In the Directive, a list of areas is given where provisions are supposed to be contrary to the principle of equal treatment. These include provisions based on sex, either directly or indirectly, in particular by reference to marital or family status for determining the persons who may participate in an occupational scheme. In addition provisions based on sex for fixing the compulsory or optional nature of participation in an occupational scheme are contrary to the Directive. They include provisions based on sex for laying down different rules as regards the age of entry into the scheme. The minimum period of employment or membership of the scheme required to obtain the benefits thereof and provisions based on sex laying down different rules, except as provided for in Article 6(h) and Article 6 (i) – discussed below – for the reimbursement of contributions where an insured person leaves a scheme without having fulfilled the conditions guaranteeing him a deferred right to long-term benefits. They also include provisions based on sex for setting different conditions for the granting of benefits or of restricting such benefits to workers of one or other of the sexes. Provisions based on sex for fixing different ages and for suspending the retention or acquisition of rights during periods of maternity leave or leave for family reasons, which are granted by law or agreement and are paid by the employer are also included.

Article 6(h) provides that criteria which set different levels of benefit for the different sexes are provisions which are supposed to be contrary to the equal treatment provision. An exception applies, however, insofar as it may be necessary to take account of actuarial calculation factors which differ according to sex in the case of benefits designated as defined contribution. Directive 96/97 adds to this: in the case of funded defined-benefit schemes, certain elements may be unequal where the inequality of the amount results from the effects of the use of actuarial factors differing according to sex at the time when the scheme's funding is implemented. In the annex to the Directive, examples of such elements can be found. The annex mentions:

– conversion into a capital sum of part of a periodic pension;
– transfer of pension rights;
– a reversionary pension payable to a dependant in return for the surrender of part of a pension;
– a reduced pension where the worker opts to take early retirement.

This subparagraph concerns schemes in which a certain pension is proposed. An example is a scheme which guarantees that a person receives eighty per cent of the last earned wages at pension age. In this case, different benefits may not be defined for men or women, except insofar as it is necessary to take account of actuarial factors which differ for the sexes. This provision applies for benefits paid from contributions. In particular, if the life expectancy for men and women differs, a difference is allowed in benefits.

Article 6(i) concerns the criteria for setting different levels of worker contribution and for setting different levels of employer contribution in the case of benefits designated as defined contribution (sometimes these schemes are called money purchase schemes).

Article 6(j) mentions different standards or standards applicable only to workers of a specified sex as considered contrary to equal treatment, except in the cases provided for in Article 6(h) and Article 6(i); *i.e.* the guarantee or retention of entitlement to deferred benefits when a worker leaves a scheme. Thus, different standards can also continue to be applied in the case of the transfer of pensions, insofar as actuarial elements referred to in Article 6(h) and Article 6(i) are concerned.

According to the obligations of the Directive, Member States shall take all necessary steps to ensure that provisions contrary to the principle of equal treatment in legally compulsory collective agreements, staff rules of undertakings or any other arrangements relating to occupational schemes are null and void or may be declared null and void or are amended. Schemes containing such provisions may not be approved or extended by administrative measures.

The Directive imposes the obligation on Member States to introduce into their national legal systems such measures as are necessary to enable all persons who consider themselves injured by the failure to apply the principle of equal treatment to pursue their claims before the courts, possibly after bringing the matters before other competent authorities.

This is an important rule, also found in the Directive 79/7, as the Directive concerns schemes established by employers or independent organisations which have to administer the occupational schemes. For individuals, this Article is necessary as otherwise there would be no way for them to ensure their rights with regard to these schemes; this is due to the fact that directives do not have horizontal effect.

The *Ten Oever* case law (*see* Section 21.4) has been inserted into the Directive. It now reads that any measure implementing this Directive, as regards paid workers, must cover all benefits derived from periods of employment subsequent to 17 May 1990 and shall apply retroactively to that date (with an exception for those who have already started proceedings prior to that date). For Member States entering the Union at a later date, the relevant moment is the day of accession to the Union.[3]

---

[3]   Transitional Provisions of Directive 96/97 (*OJ L* 20 December 1996, L 46).

23.1.5. THE EXCEPTIONS TO THE PRINCIPLE OF EQUAL TREATMENT

The Directive contained some exceptions where equal treatment could be deferred. Following the *Barber* judgment these exceptions could no longer be upheld. At present, they apply to schemes for the self-employed only, as is defined in Directive 96/97.

Under the present rules, Member States may defer compulsory application of the principle of equal treatment with regard to the self-employed (article 9):

(a) determination of pensionable age for the granting of old-age or retirement pensions, and the possible implications for other benefits in the case of schemes for self-employed persons:
 – either until the date on which such equality is achieved in statutory schemes;
 – or, at the latest, until such equality is prescribed by a directive;
(b) survivors' pensions until Community law establishes the principle of equal treatment in statutory social security schemes in that regard;
(c) the application of the first subparagraph of point (i) of Article 6(1) to take account of the different actuarial calculation factors, at the latest until 1 January 1999.

23.2. DIRECTIVE 86/613: EQUAL TREATMENT OF THE SELF-EMPLOYED

23.2.1. INTRODUCTION

Directive 86/613 concerns the application of the principle of equal treatment between men and women engaged in an activity, including agriculture, in a self-employed capacity, as well as the protection of self-employed women during pregnancy and motherhood.[4]

The purpose of this Directive is to ensure the application in the Member States of the principle of equal treatment between men and women engaged in an activity in a self-employed capacity, or contributing to the pursuit of such an activity, as regards those aspects not covered by Directive 79/7. The period of implementation is up to 30 June 1989.

---

[4]   Directive of 11 December 1986, *OJ* 1986 *L* 359.

23.2.2. THE PERSONAL SCOPE OF DIRECTIVE 86/613

The Directive covers self-employed workers. This term includes all persons pursuing a gainful activity on their own account, under the conditions laid down by national law, including farmers and members of the liberal professions.

Secondly, the Directive covers the spouses of the self-employed workers, not being employees or partners, where they habitually, under the conditions laid down by national law, participate in the activities of the self-employed worker and perform the same tasks or ancillary tasks.

23.2.3. THE MATERIAL SCOPE OF DIRECTIVE 86/613

There are, as yet, few social security schemes for self-employed workers. The Directive states in view of this that if a contributory social security system for self-employed workers exists in a Member State, that Member has to take the necessary measures to enable the spouses of self-employed workers, who are not protected under the self-employed worker's social security scheme, to join a contributory social security scheme voluntarily.

A further, weak obligation on Member States is to undertake to examine whether, and under what conditions, female self-employed workers and the wives of self-employed workers may, during interruption in their occupational activity owing to pregnancy or motherhood, have access to services supplying temporary replacements or existing social services. They also have to examine whether women in these circumstances may be entitled to cash benefits under a social security scheme or under any other public social protection system.

23.2.4. THE PRINCIPLE OF EQUAL TREATMENT

For the purposes of this Directive, the principle of equal treatment implies the absence of all discrimination on the grounds of sex, either directly or indirectly, by reference in particular to marital or family status (Article 3).

23.3. PROPOSAL FOR A DIRECTIVE COMPLETING THE PRINCIPLE OF EQUAL TREATMENT

23.3.1. INTRODUCTION

The Proposal for a Directive Completing the Principle of Equal Treatment[5] aims to complete the principle of equal treatment in areas of social security that were excluded from Directives 79/7 and 86/378. The objective of this draft Directive is to extend the principle of equal treatment to the provisions of statutory schemes concerning survivors' benefits and family benefits. It also intends to extend the principle to the corresponding provisions of occupational schemes (including those concerning the family benefits of occupational schemes for self-employed earners). Thirdly, its objective is the extension of the equal treatment principle to the areas excluded or deferred pursuant to Article 7(1)(a) to (d) of Directive 79/7 and Article 9(a) of Directive 86/378. The Council has not yet adopted this Directive.

23.3.2. THE PERSONAL SCOPE OF THE DRAFT DIRECTIVE

The proposed Directive will apply to the working population (including self-employed persons, workers whose activity is interrupted by illness, maternity, accident or involuntary unemployment and persons seeking employment). The Directive will also apply to retired workers and disabled workers and to members of the family, survivors and other persons dependent on those referred to under the three categories mentioned above, these categories of dependents to be defined by the Member States' national legislation.

23.3.3. THE MATERIAL SCOPE OF THE DRAFT DIRECTIVE

Under the conditions laid down by the Directive, the principle of equal treatment would be extended to the provisions of statutory schemes concerning survivors' benefits and family benefits. The extension would also apply to the corresponding provisions of occupational schemes (including those concerning family benefits or occupational schemes for self-employed earners). The third object of extension concerns the areas in which the implementation of the principle of equal treatment was excluded or deferred pursuant to Article 7 of Directive 79/7 and Article 9 of Directive 86/378. The last category is that of provisions concerning social assistance, where they are intended to supplement the benefits referred to

---

[5]   COM (87) 494, *OJ* 1987 C 309/11.

under the provisions of statutory schemes concerning survivors' benefits and family benefits and the parts excluded from Directive 79/7.

23.3.4. THE PRINCIPLE OF EQUAL TREATMENT

This draft Directive gives several definitions of how equal treatment is to be implemented for the various types of benefit excluded so far. For this purpose, the Directive is subdivided into various sections.

As regards *surviving spouses' benefits*, the principle of equal treatment means that there shall be no discrimination on the grounds of sex. To this end, Member States can either grant entitlement to widows' pensions on the same terms for widowers or replace widows' benefits by the creation or extension of a system of individual rights open to all surviving spouses regardless of sex.

With regard to *orphans' benefits and other survivors' benefits* the principle of equal treatment means that there shall be no discrimination on the grounds of the sex of the deceased parent or of the orphan.

The second chapter of the Directive contains provisions on *family benefits*. Article 7 provides that the principle of equal treatment means that there shall be no discrimination on the grounds of sex with regard to child benefit and benefits introduced to assist parents to assume their parental responsibilities. The principle of equal treatment thus completed in this area applies both to natural parents and other persons responsible for a child and thus meets the conditions (other than those which are incompatible with this principle) laid down for the granting of benefits referred to in paragraph 1 of Article 7.

A special chapter is dedicated to *retirement pensions*. This chapter provides for the extension of the principle of equal treatment to areas where its implementation might be excluded or deferred under Article 7 of Directive 79/7 and Article 9 of Directive 86/378. When a pension age is determined for the purpose of granting old age and retirement pensions, it shall be identical for both sexes.

Fixing an identical age can also lead to a reduction or increase in that age for workers of a given sex. If women can retire at the age of sixty and men at the age of sixty-five, equal treatment may mean that the women may not in the future retire before the age of sixty-five. In respect of such effect, Article 9 provides that provision shall be made for gradual implementation and for temporary safeguards for workers who have reached the specified age, enabling them, if they wish, to claim their pension at the age previously prescribed.

The Directive also forbids discrimination with respect to the advantages of old age pension schemes granted to persons who have brought up children, or regarding the acquisition of benefit entitlements following periods of interruption of employment due to the bringing-up of children. The granting of old age or invalidity benefit entitlements by virtue of the derived entitlements of a spouse, or the granting of increases in long-term benefits in respect of invalidity, old age, accidents at work and occupational disease for a dependent spouse, shall be authorised solely in the case of those spouses who on the date when this Directive comes into effect have not established their own personal entitlement to these benefits.

CHAPTER 24

TOWARDS A SOCIAL EUROPE?

The case law of the Court of Justice had a central place in this study. We focused, in particular, on how the Court interpreted the principles underlying the coordination Regulation and Directive 79/7. We saw that the Court followed an approach in which the principles of freedom of movement and equal treatment were given a meaning which left no room for any Community and national legislation inconsistent with these principles. In this, the Court followed a radical approach. It frequently explicitly pointed out that this Community legislation required a uniform interpretation which must not allow the Member States to escape their responsibilities under Community law. By this case law, the Court has made an immense contribution to the development of a Social Europe.

Also the limits of the possibilities of the Court of Justice became clear in this study. These limits appeared especially with respect to those subjects where the differences between the Member States are very large. Thus, the Court regularly deviated from its earlier case law and developed a new approach in order to respond to problems raised by the Member States. This can be seen in the *Newton* judgment[1] (which restricted the overruling of residence requirements with respect to hybrid benefits-Chapter 5), and the *Lenoir* judgment[2] (which did not go into the question of indirect discrimination – Chapter 10). Furthermore, the consequences of the *Ten Holder* judgment,[3] which was considered as being problematic, were mitigated by the *Daalmeijer* judgment.[4] Examples from equal treatment law are the *Ten Oever* judgment[5] (in which a less wide-reaching interpretation of the *Barber* judgment[6] was given – Chapter 21), and the *Commission* v. *Belgium* and *Molenbroek* judgments[7] (Chapter 22), where the Court gave a much softer application of the prohibition of indirect discrimination in Directive 79/7 in the cases where minimum benefits are concerned.

It can be said that the influence of the governments of the Member States and of the Commission on the proceedings before the Court in respect to such

---

[1]   Case 356/89, [1991] *ECR* 3017.
[2]   Case 313/86, [1988] *ECR* 5391.
[3]   Case 302/84, [1986] *ECR* 1821.
[4]   Case 245/88, [1991] *ECR* 555.
[5]   Case 109/91, [1993] *ECR* I-4879.
[6]   Case 262/88, [1990] *ECR* 1990.
[7]   Case 229/89, *Commission* v. *Belgium* [1991] *ECR* 2205; Case 226/91, *Molenbroek* [1992] *ECR* I-5943.

subjects is greater than is usual in national proceedings. This influence has been given an institutionalised form in the possibility for the Commission and the Member States to express their views to the Court. Indeed, there are additional (more indirect) methods for influencing the Court, of which the Protocol to the Treaty of Maastricht on (what is now) Article 157 TFEU (the Barber Protocol – *see* Section 22.3) is an example.

These ways of influencing the case law of the Court do not make a common policy more easy; nor do they facilitate consistent case law from the Court of Justice.

The judgments of the Court mentioned above concern, in particular, areas of Community law in respect of which the Court had given earlier rulings which led to significantly higher expenses for the Member States. More specifically, the judgments often concerned *non-contributory* benefits.[8] The objections of the Member States to the possibility of exporting these benefits, as long as such benefits do not guarantee a minimum income for comparable risks in all Member States, is quite understandable. Some writers explain problems with the harmonisation of social security systems by referring to differences in traditions.[9] In my view, the problems with these judgments are not, primarily, due to discrepancies arising from different traditions in the social security systems of the Member States. The judgments mentioned concerned problems which can be regarded as being due to the transitional stage of development of systems. An example concerns the supplements payable to persons who have dependents. These aroused the suspicion of indirect discrimination (the *Teuling-Worms* judgment[10]); these may also be expected to be of a temporary nature. After all, many organisations and authors have pointed to the need for an individual system of social security and the labour force participation rate of women is currently increasing.

These remarks are not meant to suggest that all problems will be solved overnight. The developments mentioned above do, in their turn, provoke critical remarks, for example, concerning the type of employment in which the growing participation rate of women is realised. This is often precarious employment. Nor can one expect that the internal single market will lead to a satisfactory social protection system in all Member States. Consequently, the hypothesis that the problems with Community action, which were analysed in this book, are mainly due to transitional stages in social protection, does not mean that no initiatives are needed to attain a Social Europe. The hypothesis is, however, useful to indicate which measures are appropriate. This is because coordination problems appear, in particular, to be related to differences in the levels of protection. These differences will not disappear if the Community legislator does not take action.

---

[8]   *E.g.* the *mobility allowance* in the United Kingdom, Dutch General Disability benefits at a minimum level, the transitory advantages of the Dutch (flat-rate) old-age benefits, the French school benefits in the *Lenoir* judgment.

[9]   Pieters 1989a.

[10] Case 30/85, [1987] *ECR* 2497.

Nor can it be expected that the Court will be able to solve the problems arising from the differences between the Member States without such initiatives. One might argue that the Court should not have altered its case law on political or financial grounds. This would, however, not work well, as the resistance of the Member States to such an approach would become too great. Moreover, such an approach would also lead to undesirable results.

The conclusion that initiatives of the Community legislator are needed in the field of subsistence benefits, accentuates, on the other hand, the criticism of the weak instruments on minimum protection described in Chapter 20. In my view, there is a need for stronger instruments. The lack of enthusiasm of the Member States to establish a European social policy is mainly at the level of principle. Most systems of the Member States reach higher standards than those contained in the international standards applicable. ILO Convention no. 102, for instance, has been ratified by a considerable number of the Member States.[11] The resistance to higher and binding standards seems to be mainly due to the present feelings in the Member States regarding to the 'powers' of the Community bodies rather than to hard arguments. The United Kingdom, for instance, which has so far been the most important adversary of a European social policy, has a comprehensive social security system. An increase in Community standards would – in the present state of affairs – not lead to a radical change in the United Kingdom system. Moreover, the United Kingdom scheme is at present affected more than others by the discrepancy between its traditional nature, on the one hand, and the system of Regulation 883/2004 on the other, as can be seen from the predominance of United Kingdom cases (child benefit, sickness benefit, mobility allowances).

Consequently, a first step in the process of harmonisation and improvement of co-ordination could be to develop a stronger Community instrument (such as a directive) to improve the protection provided by subsistence benefits. This should establish standards that are no lower than those already reached by the Member States at present. To this end, the Commission should make a study of the present state of affairs. A new element would be that the Commission should undertake this study in relation to the benefits which proved problematic for coordination.

This would lead to the following steps. The European Commission would, following ILO Convention no. 102, and having in mind the problems in protection levels which caused practical problems for co-ordination initiatives, would undertake an analysis of the present situation. This would analyse to what extent Member States already satisfy the standards of the ILO Convention mentioned. Subsequently, the measures necessary to satisfy these conditions completely should be studied. With the transitional nature of several national benefits in mind, it could be argued that there should be (financial) support from the EU for those systems in which the standards have not yet been reached. Finally, one should study the type of additional protection needed to find solutions in

---

[11]   For the ratifications of ILO Conventions, *see* the website of the ILO, www.ilo.org.

those areas where the realisation of comprehensive co-ordination has proved problematic. This last question would lead to long-term objectives.

This approach would be useful as proposals for harmonisation initiatives would be, as a result of the steps described above, suggested by the need for a solution in relation to co-ordination. The solutions would not be done on the basis of the objective of establishing a EU social policy as such, which is resisted by some Member States. Consequently, this approach, in which a link is made between the problems existing for harmonisation and co-ordination respectively, would be in line with the subsidiarity principle, discussed in Chapter 20 of this book.

TABLE OF CASES

ECJ 4 December 1986, Case 71/85, FNV *v.* the Netherlands, [1986] *ECR* 3855
ECJ 24 February 1987, Cases 379-381/85 and 93/86, Giletti et al., [1987] *ECR* 955
ECJ 12 March 1987, Case 22/86, Rindone, [1987] *ECR* 1339
ECJ 24 March 1987, Case 286/85, McDermott and Cotter, [1987] *ECR* 1453
ECJ 11 June 1987, Case 30/85, Teuling-Worms, [1987] *ECR* 2497
ECJ 18 June 1987, Case 316/85, Lebon, [1987] *ECR* 2811
ECJ 24 June 1987, Case 384/85, Borrie Clarke, [1987] *ECR* 2865
ECJ 9 July 1987, Case 377/85, Burchell, [1987] *ECR* 3329
ECJ 24 September 1987, Case 43/86, De Rijke-van Gent, [1987] *ECR* 3611
ECJ 29 September 1987, Case 126/86, Zaera, [1987] *ECR* 3697
ECJ 17 December 1987, Case 323/86, Collini, [1987] *ECR* 5489
ECJ 17 December 1987, Case 147/87, Zaoui, [1987] *ECR* 5551
ECJ 8 March 1988, Case 80/87, Dik, [1988] *ECR* 1601
ECJ 7 June 1988, Case 20/85, Roviello, [1988] *ECR* 2805
ECJ 21 June 1988, Case 39/86, Lair, [1988] *ECR* 3161
ECJ 21 June 1988, Case 197/85, Brown, [1988] *ECR* 3205
ECJ 29 June 1988, Case 58/87, Rebmann, [1988] *ECR* 3467
ECJ 22 September 1988, Case 236/87, Bergemann, [1988] *ECR* 5125
ECJ 27 September 1988, Case 313/86, Lenoir, [1988] *ECR* 5391
ECJ 28 February 1989, Case 29/88, Schmitt, [1989] *ECR* 581
ECJ 2 March 1989, Case 359/87, Second Pinna judgment, [1989] *ECR* 585
ECJ 14 March 1989, Case 1/88, Baldi, [1989] *ECR* 667
ECJ 12 May 1989, Case 388/87, Warmerdam, [1989] *ECR* 1203
ECJ 27 June 1989, Cases 48/88, 106/88, 107/88, Achterberg, [1989] *ECR* 1963
ECJ 27 June 1989, Case 24/88, Georges, [1989] *ECR* 1905
ECJ 5 December 1989, Case 114/88, Delbar, [1989] *ECR* 4067
ECJ 14 December 1989, Case 168/88, Dammer, [1989] *ECR* 4553
ECJ 13 December 1989, Case 322/88, Grimaldi, [1989] *ECR* 4407
ECJ 13 December 1989, Case 102/88, Ruzius-Wilbrink, [1989] *ECR* 4311
ECJ 22 February 1990, Case 228/88, Bronzino, [1990] *ECR* 531
ECJ 21 March 1990, Case 199/88, Cabras, [1990] *ECR* 1023
ECJ 2 May 1990, Case 293/88, Winter-Lutzins, [1990] *ECR* 1623
ECJ 3 May 1990, Case 2/89, Kits van Heijningen, [1990] *ECR* 1755
ECJ 8 May 1990, Case 175/88, Biehl, [1990] *ECR* 1779
ECJ 27 May 1990, Case 262/88, Barber, [1990] *ECR* 1990
ECJ 14 October 1990, Case 105/89, Buhari Haji, [1990] *ECR* 4211
ECJ 8 November 1990, Case 177/88, Dekker *v.* VJV, [1990] *ECR* 3941
ECJ 13 November 1990, Case 216/89, Reibold, [1990] *ECR* 4163
ECJ 13 November 1990, Case 308/89, Di Leo, [1990] *ECR* 4185
ECJ 13 November 1990, Case 106/89, Marleasing, [1990] *ECR* 4135
ECJ 7 February 1991, Case 227/89, Rönfeldt, [1991] *ECR* 323
ECJ 21 February 1991, Case 140/88, Noij, [1991] *ECR* 387
ECJ 21 February 1991, Case 245/88, Daalmeijer, [1991] *ECR* 555

ECJ 26 February 1991, Case 292/89, Antonissen, [1991] *ECR* 745

ECJ 7 March 1991, Case 10/90, Masgio, [1991] *ECR* 1119

ECJ 13 March 1991, Case 377/89, Cotter and McDermott, [1991] *ECR* 1155

ECJ 20 MARCH 1991, Case 93/90, Cassamaili, [1991] *ECR* I-1401

ECJ 7 May 1991, Case 229/89, Commission *v.* Belgium, [1991] *ECR* 2205

ECJ 16 May 1991, Case 272/90, Van Noorden, [1991] *ECR* 2543

ECJ 11 June 1991, Case 307/89, Commission v. France, [1991] *ECR* 2903

ECJ 11 June 1991, Case 251/90, Athanasopoulos, [1991] *ECR* 2797

ECJ 20 June 1991, Case 356/89, Newton, [1991] *ECR* 3017

ECJ 27 June 1991, Case 344/89, Vidal, [1991] *ECR* 3245

ECJ 11 July 1991, Case 31/90, Johnson, [1991] *ECR* 3723

ECJ 11 July 1991, Cases 87/90, 88/90 and 89/90, Verholen, [1991] *ECR* 3757

ECJ 25 July 1991, Case 208/90, Emmott, [1991] *ECR* 4269

ECJ 4 October 1991, Case 196/90, Madelein de Paep, [1991] *ECR* 4815

ECJ 4 October 1991, Case 15/90, Middleburgh, [1991] *ECR* 4655

ECJ 19 November 1991, Case 6/90, Francovich, [1991] *ECR* 5357

ECJ 28 November 1991, Case 198/90, Comm. v. Netherlands [1991], *ECR* 5799

ECJ 28 November 1991, Case 186/90, Durighiello, [1991] *ECR* 5773

ECJ 16 January 1992, Case 57/90, Commission v. France, [1992] *ECR* I-75

ECJ 28 January 1992, Case 204/90, Bachmann v. Belgium, [1992] *ECR* I-249

ECJ 4 February 1992, Case 243/90, Smithson, [1992] *ECR* I-467

ECJ 5 February 1992, Case 253/90, Commission v. Belgium, [1992] *ECR* I-531

ECJ 10 March 1992, Case 215/90, Twomey, [1992] *ECR* I-1823

ECJ 19 March 1992, Case 188/90, Doriguzzi, [1992] *ECR* I-2039

ECJ 8 April 1992, Case 62/91, Gray, [1992] *ECR* I-2737

ECJ 3 June 1992, Case 45/90, Paletta v. Brennet, [1992] *ECR* I-3423

ECJ 11 June 1992, Case 90/91, Di Crescenzo, [1992] *ECR* I-3851

ECJ 8 July 1992, Case 243/91, Taghavi, [1992] *ECR* I-4401

ECJ 8 July 1992, Case 102/91, Knoch, [1992] *ECR* I-4341

ECJ 16 July 1992, Cases 63/91 and 64/91, Jackson and Cresswell, [1992] *ECR* I-4973

ECJ 16 July 1992, Case 78/91, Hughes, [1992] *ECR* I-4839

ECJ 22 September 1992, Case 153/91, Petit, [1992] ECR I-4973

ECJ 1 October 1992, Case 201/91, Grisvard and Kreitz, [1992] *ECR* I-5009

ECJ 10 November 1992, Case 326/90, Commission v. Belgium, [1992] *ECR* I-5517

ECJ 19 November 1992, Case 226/91, Molenbroek, [1992] *ECR* I-5943

ECJ 9 December 1992, Case 119/91, Una McMenamin, [1992] *ECR* I-6393

ECJ 17 February 1993, Cases 159/91 and 160/91, Poucet, [1993] *ECR* I-637

ECJ 18 February 1993, Case 193/92, Bogana, [1993] *ECR* I-755

ECJ 30 March 1993, Case 282/91, De Wit, [1993] *ECR* I-1221

ECJ 30 March 1993, Case 328/91, Thomas et.al., [1993] *ECR* I-1247

ECJ 26 May 1993, Case 310/91, Schmid, [1993] *ECR* I-3011.

ECJ 2 August 1993, Case 66/92, Acciardi, [1993] *ECR* I-4567

ECJ 1 July 1993, Case 154/92, Remi van Cant, [1993] *ECR* I-3811

ECJ 1 February 1996, Case 280/94, Posthuma and Özturk, [1996] *ECR* I-179
ECJ 1 February 1996, Case 308/94, Naruschawicus, [1996] *ECR* I-207
ECJ 8 February 1996, Case 8/94, Laperre, [1996] *ECR* I-273
ECJ 15 February 1996, Case 53/95, Kemmler, [1996] *ECR* I-703
ECJ 28 March 1996, Case 272/94, Guiot, [1996] *ECR* I-1905
ECJ 28 March 1996, Case 243/94, Rincón Moreno, [1996] *ECR* I-1887
ECJ 30 April 1996, Case 308/93, Cabanis, [1996] *ECR* I-2097.
ECJ 2 May 1996, Case 206/94, Second Paletta judgment, [1996] *ECR* I-2357
SAECJ 13 June 1996, Case 170/95, Sparato, [1996] *ECR* I-2921
ECJ 11 July 1996, Case 25/95, S. Otte, [1996] *ECR* I-3745
ECJ 10 September 1996, Case 277/94, Taflan-Met et al., [1996] *ECR* I-4085
ECJ 12 September 1996, Case 251/94, Lafuente Nieto, [1996] *ECR* I-4187
ECJ 12 September 1996, Case 278/94, Comm. v. Belgium, [1996] *ECR* I-4307
ECJ 10 October 1996, Cases 245/94, 312/94, Hoever and Zachow, [1996] *ECR* I-4895
ECJ 24 October 1996, Case 335/95, Picard, [1996] *ECR* I-5625
ECJ 24 October 1996, Case 435/93, Dietz, [1996] *ECR* I-5223
ECJ 7 November 1996, Case 77/95, Züchner, [1996] *ECR* I-5689
ECJ 30 January 1997, Case 340/94, De Jaeck, [1997] *ECR* I-461
ECJ 30 January 1997, Cases 4/95 en 5/95, Stöber and Pereira, [1997] *ECR* I-531
ECJ 30 January 1997, Case 221/95, Hervein, [1997] *ECR* I-635
ECJ 20 February 1997, Case 88/95, Martínez Losada, [1997] *ECR* I-895
ECJ 27 February 1997, Case 59/95, Bastos Moriana, [1997] *ECR* I-1096
ECJ 13 March 1997, Case 131/95, Huijbrechts, [1997] *ECR* I-1418
ECJ 12 June 1997, Case 266/95, Merino García, [1997] *ECR* I-3301
ECJ 25 June 1997, Case 131/96, Mora Romero, [1997] *ECR* I-3676
ECJ 17 September 1997, Case 322/95, Iurlano, [1997] *ECR* I-4897
ECJ 25 September 1997, Case 307/96, Baldone, [1997] *ECR* I-5133
ECJ 2 October 1997, Case 144/96, Cirotti, [1997] *ECR* I-5360
ECJ 9 October 1997, Case 31/96, Naranjo Arjona, [1997] *ECR* I-5517
ECJ 4 November 1997, Case 20/96, Snares, [1997] *ECR* I-895
ECJ 13 November 1997, Case 248/96, Grahame and Hollanders, [1997] *ECR* I-6427
ECJ 27 November 1997, Case 57/96, Meints, [1997] *ECR* I-6708
ECJ 15 January 1998, Case 113/97, Babahenini, [1998] *ECR* I-188
ECJ 12 February 1998, Case 366/96, Cordelle, [1998] *ECR* I-594
ECJ 5 March 1998, Case 160/96, Molenaar, [1998] *ECR* I-880
ECJ 5 March 1988, Case 194/96, Kulzer, [1998] *ECR* I-921
ECJ 12 March 1998, Case 314/96, Djabali, [1998] *ECR* I-1157
ECJ 28 April 1998, Case 158/96, Kohll, [1998] *ECR* I-1935
ECJ 28 April 1998, Case 120/95, Decker, [1998] *ECR* I-1871
ECJ 30 April 1998, Case 377/96, De Vriendt, [1998] *ECR* I-2119
ECJ 7 May 1998, Case 113/96, Gómez Rodríguez, [1998] *ECR* I-2482
ECJ 12 MAY 1998, Case 85/96, Martínez Sala, [1998] *ECR* I-2691

ECJ 11 June 1998, Case 275/96, Kuusijärvi, [1998] *ECR* I-3443
ECJ 11 June 1998, Case 297/96, Partridge, [1998] *ECR* I-3477
ECJ 24 September 1998, Case 35/97, Commission *v.* France, [1998] *ECR* I-5325
ECJ 24 September 1998, Case 132/96, Stinco and Panfilo, [1998] *ECR* I-5246
ECJ 22 October 1998, Case 143/97, Conti, [1998] *ECR* I-6365
ECJ 22 October 1998, Case 154/96, Wolfs, [1998] *ECR* I-6173
ECJ 10 December 1998, Case 279/97, Voeten and Beckers, [1998] *ECR* I-8293
ECJ 17 December 1998, Case 153/97, Grajera Rodríguez, [1998] *ECR* I-8645
ECJ 26 January 1999, Case 18/95, Terhoeve, [1999] *ECR* I-345
ECJ 25 February 1999, Case 90/97, Swaddling, [1999] *ECR* I-1075
ECJ 20 April 1999, Case 360/97, Nijhuis, [1999] *ECR* I-1919
ECJ 4 Mei 1999, Case 262/96, Sürül, [1999] *ECR* I-2685
ECJ 8 June 1999, Case 337/97, Meeusen, [1999] *ECR* I-3289
ECJ 10 February 2000, Case 202/97, Fitzwilliam, [2000] *ECR* I-883
ECJ 15 February 2000, Case 34/98, Commission *v.* France, [2000] *ECR* I-995
ECJ 15 February 2000, Case 169/98, Commission *v.* France, [2000] *ECR* I-1049
ECJ 30 March 2000, Case 178/97, Banks, [2000] *ECR* I-2005
ECJ 26 September 2000, Case 262/97, Engelbrecht, [2000] *ECR* I- I-7321
ECJ 9 November 2000, Case 75/99, Thelen, [2000] *ECR* I-19399
ECJ 9 November 2000, Case C-404/98, Plum, [2000] *ECR* I-9379
ECJ 23 November 2000, Case 135/99, Elsen, [2000] *ECR* I-10409
ECJ 8 MARCH 2001, Case 215/99, Jauch [2001] *ECR* I-1901
ECJ 15 March 2001, Case 444/98, De Laat, [2001] *ECR* I- 2229
ECJ 20 March 2001, Case 33/99, Fahmi and Esmoris Cerdeiro, [2001] *ECR* I-2452
ECJ 12 July 2001, Case 157/99, Peerbooms and Smits, [2001] *ECR* I- 5473
ECJ 12 July 2001, Case 368/98, Vanbraekel, [2001] *ECR* I-5363
ECJ 20 September 2001, case 184/99, Grzelczyk, [2001] *ECR* I- 6193
ECJ 11 October 2001, Case 95/99, Khalil, [2001] *ECR* I-7413
ECJ 16 October 2001, Case 212/00, Stallone, [2000] *ECR* I-7626
ECJ 25 October 2001, Case 189/00, Ruhr, [2000] *ECR* I-8225
ECJ 5 February 2002, Case 255/99, Humer, [2002] *ECR* I-1205
ECJ 5 February 2002, Case 277/99, Kaske, [2002] *ECR* I-1261
ECJ 7 February 2002 Case 28/00, Kauer [2002] *ECR* I-1343
ECJ 25 February 2003, Case 326/00, Ioannidis, [2003] ECR I-1703
ECJ 7 March 2002, Case 107/00, Insalaca, [2002] *ECR* I-2403
ECJ 19 March 2002, Cases C-393/99 and C-394/99, Hervein and Lorthiois [2002] ECR I-2829
ECJ 21 March 2002, Case 215/00, Rydergård, [2002] *ECR* I-1817
ECJ 25 February 2003, Case C-326/00, Ioannidis, [2003] ECR I-1703
ECJ 13 May 2003, Case 385/99, Müller-Fauré and Van Riet, [2003] *ECR* I-4509
ECJ 3 July 2003 Case 156/01, Van der Duin, [2003] *ECR* I-7045
ECJ 23 October 2003, Case C-56/01 Inizan [2003] *ECR* I-2403

ECJ 6 November 2003, Case 311/01, European Commission v. the Netherlands, [2003] ECR I-3103

ECJ 29 April 2004, Case C-160/02. Skalka, [2004] *ECR* I-5613

ECJ 7 September 2004, Case 456/02. Trojani, [2004] *ECR* I-7573

ECJ 11 November 2004, Case C-372/02, Adanez-Vega, [2004] *ECR* I-10761

ECJ 7 June 2005, Case C-543/03, Dodl-Oberhollenzer. [2005] *ECR* I-5049

ECJ 7 July 2005, Case 227/03, Van Pommeren-Bourgondien, [2005], *ECR* I-6101

ECJ 12 April 2005, Case C-145/03, Keller, [2005] ECR I-2529

ECJ 26 January 2006, Case C-2/05, Herbosch Kiere, [2006] *ECR* I-1081

ECJ 21 February 2006, Case C-286/03 Hosse [2006] *ECR* I-1771

ECJ 16 May 2006, Case C-372/04, Watts [2006] *ECR* I-4325

ECJ 6 July 2006, Case C-154/05, Kersbergen-Lap [2006] *ECR* I-6249

ECJ 18 July 2006, Case C-406/04, De Cuyper [2006] *ECR* I-6947

ECJ 26 October 2006 Case C-192/05, Tas Hagen, [2006] *ECR* I-10451

ECJ 9 November 2006, Case C-206/05, Nemec, [2006] *ECR* I-10745

ECJ 16 January 2007, Case C-265/05, Perez Naranjo [2007] *ECR* I-347

ECJ 18 July 2007, Case C-213/05, Geven, [2007] *ECR* I-6347

ECJ 18 January 2007, Case C-332/05 Celozzi,[2007] *ECR* I-563

ECJ 18 July 2007, Case C-212/05, Hartmann ,[2007] *ECR* I-6303

ECJ 11 September 2007, Case C-287/05, Hendrix, [2007] *ECR* I-6909

ECJ 18 October 2007, Case C-299/05, Commission v. European Parliament and Council, [2007] *ECR* I-8695

ECJ 1 April 2008, Case C-212/06, Walloon Government v. Flemish Government, [2008] *ECR* I-1683

ECJ 20 May 2008, Case C-352/06, Bosmann, [2008] *ECR* I-3827

ECJ 11 September 2008, Case C-228/07, Petersen, [2008] *ECR* I-6989

ECJ 18 November 2008, Case C-158/07, Jacqueline Föster, [2008] *ECR* I-8507

ECJ 1 October 2009, Case C-3/08, Leyman, not yet published

BIBLIOGRAPHY

Addison, en Siebert 1991

J. Addison en W. Siebert, 'The social charter of the European community: evolution and controversies', *ILRR* 1991, p. 597.

Amoroso 1990

B. Amoroso, 'A Danish perspective: the impact of the internal market on the labour unions and the welfare state', *Comparative labor law journal* 1990, p. 483 et seq.

Aposapori and Millar 2003

E. Aposapori and J. Millar, *The Dynamics of Social Exclusion in Europe*, Cheltenham and Northampton 2003

Arnull 1990

A. Arnull, *The General Principles of EEC Law and the Individual*, Leicester 1990.

Berghman and Okma 2002

J. Berghman and K. Okma, 'The Method of Open co-ordination: Open procedures or closed circuit? Social policy making between science and politics', *European Journal of Social Security* 2002, p. 331 ff.

Betten 1993

L. Betten, *International Labour Law,* Deventer 1993.

Betten 1998

L. Betten, 'The role of social partners in the Community's social policy law making: participatory democracy of furthering the interests of small elites', in: C. Engels and M. Weiss, *Labour Law and Industrial Relations at the Turn of the Century,* The Hague 1998, p. 239.

Betten and Mac Devitt 1996

L. Betten and D. Mac Devitt, *The Protection of Fundamental Social Rights in the European Union*, The Hague 1996.

Betten, Harris and Jaspers, 1989

L. Betten, D. Harris, and T. Jaspers, *The future of European Social Policy.* Deventer, 1989.

Blanpain 1998

R. Blanpain (ed.) et al, *Institutional Changes and European Social Policies after the Treaty of Amsterdam*, The Hague 1998.

Bogaerd, van den 1997

S. van den Bogaerd (ed.), *Social Security, Non-discrimination and Property*, Antwerpen 1997.

Bruce 1961

M. Bruce, *The Coming of the Welfare State*, London 1961.

Busquin 1990

Ph. Busquin, 'De sociale Slang en het Europees programma ter bestrijding van armoede', *BTSZ* 1990, p. 557.

Byre 1992

A. Byre, *EC Social policy and 1992*. Deventer 1992.

Carmichael 2001

L. Carmichael, 'The EU and the Fight against Exclusion: Maximising the Means to Match its Ambitions', in: D.G. Mayes, J. Berghman and R. Salais, *Social Exclusion and European Policy*, Cheltenham and Northampton, 2001, p. 233 ff.

Catala and Bonnet 1991

N. Catala and R. Bonnet, *Droit social européen*, Paris 1991.

Chassard 1991

Y. Chassard, 'Pour une convergence des politiques des Etats-Membres de la Communauté dans la domaine de la protection sociale', *Droit social* 1991, p. 157.

Christensen and Malmstedt 2000

Anna Christensen and Mattias Malmstedt, '*Lex Loci Laboris* versus *Lex Loci Domicilii* – an inquiry into the normative Foundations of European Social Security Law', *European Journal of Social Security* 2000, p. 69.

Clever 1989

P. Clever, 'Tendenzen zur Aufgabe des Territorialitätsprinzips', *Der Arbeitgeber* 1989, p. 988-990.

Cornelissen 1984

R.C. Cornelissen, *Europese coördinatie van invaliditeits- en weduwenverzekeringen*, Antwerpen 1984.

Cornelissen 1986

R.C. Cornelissen, 'Communautaire en Nederlandse jurisprudentie inzake conflictregels in het Europees sociaal zekerheidsrecht', *SEW* 1986, p. 799-823.

Cornelissen 1988

R. Cornelissen, 'Invaliditeit, Ouderdom en overlijden (pensioenen), Uitkeringen bij overlijden', in: Pieters 1988, p. 89-118.

Cornelissen 2007

R. Cornelissen, 'The New EU Coordination System for Workers who become Unemployed', *European Journal of Social Security*, 2007, p. 218.

Cornelissen 2008

R. Cornelissen, 'Third-Country Nationals and the European Coordination of Social Security', *European Journal of Social Security* 2008, p. 347.

Cornelissen 2009

R. Cornelissen, '50 Years of European Social Security Coordination', *European Journal of Social Security* 2009, p. 9 ff.

Cornelissen 2010

R. Cornelissen, 'Achievements of 50 years European social security coordination', in: Y. Jorens (ed), *50 years of Social Security Coordination. Past – Present – Future*, Euroepan Commission, Brussels, p. 55.

Cousins 1993

M. Cousins, 'The EC Recommendations on Social Protection: A Case Study in EC Social Policy', *Social Policy and Administration* 1993, p. 286.

Curtin 1987

D. Curtin, 'Occupational pension schemes and article 119: beyond the fringe?', *C.M.L.Rev.* 1987, p. 254.

Curtin 1990a

D. Curtin, 'Scalping the Community legislator: occupational pensions and 'Barber'', *C.M.L.Rev.* 1990, p. 475.

Curtin 1990b

D. Curtin, 'Directives: the effectiveness of judicial protection of individual rights.', *C.M.L.Rev.* 1990, p. 709.

Devetzi 2009

S. Devetzi, 'The Coordination of Family Benefits by Regulation 883/2004', *European Journal of Social Security* 2009, p. 205.

Donders 1995

P. Donders, Temporary employment across borders – posting in accordance with Regulation 1408/71 in practice, Utrecht 1995, mimeo.

Donders 2002

P. Donders, Current Practice in Posting According to Regulation 1408/71, Utrecht, 2002.

Eichenhofer 1993

E. Eichenhofer, 'Co-ordination of social security and equal treatment of men and women in employment: recent social security judgments of the Court of Justice', in: *C.M.L.Rev.* 1993, p. 1021.

Eichenhofer 1997

E. Eichenhofer (ed), *Social Security of Migrants in the European Union of Tomorrow*, Osnabrück, 1997.

Eichenhofer 2000

E. Eichenhofer, 'How to Simplify the Co-ordination of Social Security', *European Journal of Social Security* 2000, p. 229.

Eichenhofer 2010

E. Eichenhofer, *Sozialrecht derEuropaischen Union*, Berlin, 2010.

Eichenhofer and Zuleeg 1995

E. Eichenhofer and M. Zuleeg, *Die Rechtsprechung des Europäischen Gerichtshof zum Arbeits- und Sozialrecht im Streit*, Schriftenreihe der Europäischen Rechtsakademie Trier, Köln 1995.

European Commission 2002

European Commission, *Joint Report on Social Inclusion*, Luxemburg, 2002.

Fitzpatrick 1992

B. Fitzpatrick, 'Community social law after Maastricht', *ILJ* 1992, vol. 3, p. 199.

Forde 1980

M. Forde, 'The vertical conflict of social security law in the European Community', *LIEI* 1980, p. 21.

Fraser 1973

D. Fraser, *The Evolution of the British Welfare State*, London etc 1973.

Fuchs (ed) loosleaf

M. Fuchs (ed.), *Nomos Kommentar zum Europäischen Sozialrecht*, Baden-Baden, looseleaf.

Fuchs 2009

M. Fuchs, 'Accidents at Work and Occupational Diseases', *European Journal of Social Security* 2009, p. 163.

Fuchs 2010

M. Fuchs, 'The implementation of coordination regulations in active labour market policy provisions at national level', in: Y. Jorens (ed), *50 years of Social Security Coordination. Past – Present – Future*, Euroepan Commission, Brussels, p. 91.

Gauthier 1988

P. Gauthier, 'Les prestations familiales face au droit communautaire : suite du feuilleton « Pinna »', *Droit social* 1988, p. 288.

Gesellschaft für Versicherungswissenschaft und -gestaltung 2003

Gesellschaft für Versicherungswissenschaft und -gestaltung, *Social Security for Frontier Workers in Europe*. Conference 22-23 November 2001 in Aachen. Berlin, 2003.

Giesen 1999

R. Giesen, *Die Vorgaben des EG-Vertrages für das Internationale Sozialrecht*. Köln *et.al.*,1999.

Guild 2003

E. Guild, 'Economic and Social Challenges of Member and Accession States: Social Security in the Europe Agreements', *European Journal of Social Security* 2003, p. 55.

Heukels 1995

T. Heukels, 'Van Munster: een opmerkelijke uitspraak van het EG-Hof van Justitie inzake het vrij verkeer van werknemers met potentieel verstrekkende implicaties', *Ars Aequi* 1995, p. 296.

Houwerzijl and Pennings 1999

M. Houwerzijl and F. Pennings, 'Double Charges in case of Posting of Employees: the *Guiot* Judgment and its Effects on the Construction Sector', *European Journal of Social Security* 1999, p. 91.

Jaspers and Betten 1988

A. Jaspers and L. Betten (ed.), *25 Years European Social Charter*, Deventer 1988.

Jorens 1992

Y. Jorens, *Wegwijs in het Europees sociale zekerheidsrecht*, Brugge 1992.

Jorens 1997

Y. Jorens, *De rechtspositie van niet-EU-onderdanen in het Europese Socialezekerheidsrecht*, Brugge 1997.

Jorens 2003

Y. Jorens, 'Cross-Border Health Care in the European Union: Up to a Free Movement of Patients?', in: Gesellschaft für Versicherungswissenschaft und –gestaltung, *Social Security for Frontier Workers in Europe*. Berlin 2003, p. 90.

Jorens 2010

Y. Jorens, 'Towards new rules for the determination of the legislation applicable', in: Y. Jorens (ed), *50 years of Social Security Coordination. Past – Present – Future*, Euroepan Commission, Brussels, p. 168.

Jorens and Geenen 1999

Y. Jorens and S. Geenen, *De toepassing van de Verordening (EEG) nr. 1408/71 in België*, Brugge 1999.

Jorens and Schulte 1998

Y. Jorens and B. Schulte, *European Social Security Law and Third Country Nationals*, Brussel 1998.

Jorens and Schulte ed. 1999

Y. Jorens and B. Schulte (ed.), *Coordination of Social Security Schemes in connection with the accession of Central and Eastern European States – "The Riga Conference"*, Brussel 1999.

Jorens, Schulte and Schumacher 1999

Y. Jorens, B. Schulte and C. Schumacher, 'Co-ordination of the Social Security Systems and the Accession of Central and European Eastern European Countries to the European Union', *European Journal of Social Security* 1999, p. 269.

Jorens and Schulte 2001

Y. Jorens and B. Schulte, 'The Implementation of Regulation 1408/71 in the Member States of the European Union', *European Journal of Social Security* 2001, p. 237 e.v.

Jorens and Van Overmeiren 2009

Y Jorens and Van Overmeiren, 'General Principles of Coordination in Regulation 883/2004', *European Journal of Social Security* 2009, p. 47

Köbele and Leutschner 1995

Köbele, B. en G. Leutschner (ed.) (1995), *Dokumentation der Konferenz 'Europäischer Arbeitsmarkt Grenzenlos mobil?' 6 bis 8 März*, Bonn, 1995.

Köhler and Zacher 1983

P. Köhler and H. Zacher, *Beiträge zu Geschichte und aktueller Situation der Sozialversicherung*, Berlin 1983.

Langer and Sakslin 2000

R. Langer and M. Sakslin (ed), *Co-ordinating Work-Based and Residence-Based Social Security*, Helsinki, 2000.

Laske 1993

C. Laske, 'The impact of the Single European Market on Social protection for migrant workers', *C.M.L.Rev* 1993, 515.

Lyon-Caen 1993

G. and A. Lyon-Caen, *Droit social international et européen*, Paris 1993.

Marhold 2005

F. Marhold (ed), *Das neu Sozialrecht der EU*, Vienna 2005.

Marhold 2009

F. Marhold, 'Modernisation of European Coordination of Sickness Benefits', *European Journal of Social Security* 2009, 119.

Maydell, von, and Schulte 1995

B. von Maydell and B. Schulte, *Treatment of Third-Country Nationals in the EU and EEA Member States in Terms of Social Sercurity Law*, Leuven 1995.

Mayes, Berghman and Salais,

D.G. Mayes, J. Berghman and R. Salais, *Social Exclusion and European Policy*, Cheltenham and Northampton 2001.

Mei, van der 2001a

A.P. van der Mei, *Free Movement of Persons within the European Community. Cross-Border Access to Public Benefits*, Oxford, 2002.

Mei, van der 2001b

A.P. van der Mei, 'Free Movement and Financial Aid for Students: Some Reflections on *Grzelczyk* and *Fahmi and Esmoris-Cerdeiro Pinedo Amoris*', *European Journal of Social Security* 2001, p. 181.

Ministry of Labour and Social Security and European Commission 2001

Ministry of Labour and Social Security and European Commission, *The Free Movement of the Self-Employed within the European Union and the Co-ordination of National Social Security Systems*, Athens 2001.

Neal and Foyn 1995

A.C. Neal and S. Foyn, *Developing the Social Dimension in an Enlarged European Union*, Oslo 1995.

Nielsen and Szyszcak 1993

R. Nielsen and E. Szyszcak, *The social dimension of the European community*, Kopenhagen 1993.

Numhauser-Henning 2002

A. Numhauser-Henning, 'Freedom of Movement and Transfer of Social Security Rights', VII European Regional Congress, *Labour Law Congress 2002. Reports*, Stockholm 2002.

O'Keeffe 1981

D. O'Keeffe, 'The scope and content of social security regulation in European Community law', in: D. O'Keeffe en H. Schermers (red.), *Essays in European Law and Integration,* Leiden 1981, p. 105-122.

O'Keeffe 1985

D. O'Keeffe, 'Equal Rights for Migrants; the Concept of Social Advantages in Article 7(2), Regulation 1612/68', *YER* 1985, p. 93-123.

Pennings 1990

F. Pennings, *Benefits of Doubt. A Comparative Study of the Legal Aspects of Employment and Unemployment Schemes in Great Britain, Germany, France and the Netherlands,* Deventer 1990.

Pennings 1993

F. Pennings, 'Is the subsidiarity principle useful to guide the European integration process', *Tilburg Foreign law review* 1993, p. 153.

Pennings 1999

F. Pennings, 'The Potential Consequences of the *Gaygusuz* Judgment', *European Journal of Social Security* 1999, p. 181.

Pennings 2000

F. Pennings, 'Regulation 1408/71 and the Room for Manipulation of the Facts', in: A. Numhauser-Henning (ed), *Normativa Perspektiv,* Lund, 2000, p. 347.

Pennings 2001

F. Pennings, 'The European Commission Proposal to Simplify Regulation 1408/71', *European Journal of Social Security* 2001, p. 45.

Pennings 2005

F.Pennings,'Co-ordination of Social Security on the Basis of the State-of-employment Principle: Time for an Alternative?', *Common Market Law Review, 42*(1), 2005, p. 67-89

Pennings 2006

F. Pennings, 'Inclusion and Exclusion of Persons and Benefits in the New Co-ordination Regulation', in M. Dougan and E. Spaventa (eds.), *Social Welfare and EU Law,* Oxford 2006, p. 241-261.

Pennings 2009

F. Pennings, Introduction: Regulation 883/2004 – The Third Coordination Regulation in a Row', *European Journal of Social Security* 2009, p. 3.

Pennings 2009

F. Pennings, Coordination of Unemployment Benefits under Regulation 883/2004', *European Journal of Social Security* 2009, p. 177.

Pennings 2009

F. Pennings, 'Conclusion: Simplification, Modernisation and Regulation 883/2004', *European Journal of Social Security* 2009, p. 235 ff.

Perrin 1961

G. Perrin, 'Les prestations non contributives et la sécurité sociale', *Droit Social* 1961, p. 179-183.

Perrin 1969

G. Perrin, 'De aktie van de internationale arbeidsorganisatie ten gunste van de coördinering en van de harmonisering van de wetgevingen betreffende de sociale zekerheid', *BTSZ* 1969, p. 1165-1253.

Pfeil 1998

W. Pfeil (ed), *Soziale Sicherheit in Österreich und Europa. Durchführung der Verordnung (EWG) 1408/71 in Österreich*, Vienna, 1998

Pieters 1987

D. Pieters, *Europees en internationaal sociale zekerheidsrecht*, Antwerpen 1987.

Pieters 1988

D. Pieters (ed.), *Europees sociale zekerheidsrecht, commentaar*, Antwerpen 1988.

Pieters 1989a

D. Pieters, *Sociale Zekerheid na 1992: één over twaalf*, Tilburg, 1989.

Pieters 1989b

D. Pieters, 'Brengt '1992' coördinatie en harmonisatie van de sociale zekerheid?', *NJB* 1989, p. 831.

Pieters 1992

D. Pieters, *Sociale-zekerheidsrechtsvergelijking ten dienste van Europa*, Deventer 1992.

Pieters 1997

D. Pieters, 'Enquiry into the Legal Foundations of a Possible Extension of Community Provisions on Social Security to Third-Country Nationals Residing and/or Working in the European Union', in: P. Schoukens (ed)., *Prospects of Social Security Co-ordination*, Leuven, 1997, p. 15.

Pieters 1999

D. Pieters (ed.), *The Co-ordination of Social Security at Work*, Leuven, 1999.

Pieters 2000

D. Pieters, 'An overview of Alternative Solutions for Overcoming the Problematic Issues of Co-ordination', in: Ministry of Labour and Social Security and European Commission (ed), *The Free Movement of the Self-Employed within the European Union and the Co-ordination of National Social Security Systems*, Athens 2001, p. 127.

Pieters and Vansteenkiste 1993

D. Pieters and S. Vansteenkiste, *The Thirteenth State. Towards a European Community Social Insurance Scheme for Intra-Community Migrants*, s.l., 1993

Prechal 1995

S. Prechal, *Directives in European Community Law*, Oxford 1995.

Raepenbusch, van 1985

S. van Raepenbusch, 'La jurisprudence communautaire en matière de règles anticumul de sécurité sociale', *CDE* 1985, p. 251.

Rammeloo 1992

S.F. Rammeloo, *Das neue EG-Vertragskollisionsrecht*, Köln 1992.

Regenmortel van, and Jorens 1993

A. van Regenmortel and Y. Jorens (ed.), *Internationale Detachering*, Brugge 1993.

Regenmortel, Verschueren, Vervliet (ed) 2007

Regenmortel A. van, Verschueren, H., Vervliet, V. (eds.), *Sociale Zekerheid in het Europa van de markt en de burgers: enkele actuele thema's*, Brugge, die Keure, 2007.

Reimann 2009

A. Reimann, 'The Economic and Social Impact of Coordination', *European Journal of Social Security* 2009, p. 133.

Roberts 2000

S. Roberts, '"Our view has not changed": the UK's Response to the Proposal to Extend the Co-ordination of Social Security to Third Country Nationals', *European Journal of Social Security*, 2000, p. 189.

Roberts 2010

S. Roberts, 'A short history of social security coordination', in: Y. Jorens (ed), *50 years of Social Security Coordination. Past – Present – Future*, Euroepan Commission, Brussels, p. 8.

Sakslin 1997

M. Sakslin, 'Can the Principles of the Nordic Conventions on Social protection Contribute to the Modernisation and Simplification of Regulation (EEC) No. 1408/71', in: Swedish National Social Insurance Board and European Commission, *25 Years of Regulation (EEC) No. 1408/71 on Social Security for Migrant Workers-A Conference Report*, Stockholm 1997, p. 197.

Sakslin 2000

M. Sakslin, 'Social Security Co-ordination – Adapting to Change', *European Journal of Social Security* 2000, p. 169.

Sánchez-Rodas Navarro 1997

C. Sánchez-Rodas Navarro, *La aplicación del derecho comunitario a las prestaciones especiales no contributivas*, Granada, 1997.

Sánchez-Rodas Navarro 2010

C. Sánchez-Rodas Navarro (ed.), *Migrants and Social Security. The (EC) Regulations 883/2004 & 987/2009*, Madrid, 2010.

Schoukens 1997

P. Schoukens (ed), *Prospects of Social Security Co-ordination*, Leuven, Amersfoort 1997.

Schoukens 2000a

P. Schoukens, *De sociale zekerheid van de zelfstandige en het Europese Gemeenschapsrecht: de impact van het vrije verkeer van zelfstandigen*, Leuven, 2000.

Schoukens 2001

P. Schoukens, 'A Comparative Presentation of the National Social Security System for the Self-employed: Outstanding Issues of Co-ordination', in: Ministry of Labour and Social Security and European Commission, *The Free Movement of the Self-Employed within the European Union and the Co-ordination of National Social Security Systems*, Athens 2001, p. 195.

Schoukens 2002

P. Schoukens, 'How the European Union Keeps the Social Welfare Debate on Track: A Lawyer's View on the EU Instruments Aimed at Combating Social Exclusion', *European Journal of Social Security* 2002, 117.

Schoukens and Pieters 2009

P. Schoukens and D. Pieters, 'The Rules within Regulation 883/2004 for Determining the Applicable Member State Legislation', *European Journal of Social Security* 2009, p. 81.

Schuler 1985

R. Schuler, 'Zwischenstaatliche und gemeinschaftsrechtliche Sozialrechts-integration im Vergleich', *Europarecht* 1985, p. 113.

Schuler 1988

R. Schuler, *Das Internationale Sozialrecht der Bundesrepublik Deutschland*, Baden-Baden, 1988.

Schulte 1982

B. Schulte, 'Auf dem Weg zu einem europäischen Sozialrechts? – der Beitrag zur Entwicklung des Sozialrechts in der Gemeinschaft', *Europarecht* 1982, p. 357.

Schulte 1984

B. Schulte, 'Das Sozialrecht in der Rechtsprechung des Europäisches Gerichtshofs', in: G. Wannagat (ed.), *Jahrbuch des Sozialrechts der Gegenwart*, Band 6, Berlin 1984.

Schulte 1992

B. Schulte, 'Armut und Armutsbekämpfung in der Europäischen Gemeinschaft – Mindesteinkommenssicherung und Sozialhilfe in EG-Sozialrecht und EG-Sozialpolitik', *Zeitschrift für Sozialhilfe und Sozialgesetzbuch* 1992, p. 393.

Schulte 1992

B. Schulte, *Europäisches Sozialrecht*, Wiesbaden 1992.

Schulte 1995

B. Schulte, 'Konfliktfelder im Verhältnis zwischen mitgliedstaatlichem und europäischem Recht', in: Eichenhofer en Zuleeg 1995, p. 11.

Schulte 2002

B. Schulte, 'The new European 'Buzzword': Open Method of Co-ordination', *European Journal of Social Security* 2002, p. 343 ff.

Schulte and Zacher 1991

B. Schulte and H. Zacher, *Wechselwirkungen zwischen dem Europäischen Sozialrecht und dem Sozialrecht der Bundesrepublik Deutschland*, Berlin 1991.

Schultz 1991

Schultz, 'Grundsätze, Inhalte und institutionelle Verankerung im EWG-Vertrag', *Sozialer Fortschritt* 1991, p. 135.

Sieveking 2003

K. Sieveking, EU Agreements with the CEEC – Achievements and Problems with Special Reference to the Free Movement of Persons and Services and to Freedom of Establishment', *European Journal of Social Security* 2003, p. 38 ff.

Sociale Verzekeringsbank, Ministry of Social Affairs and Employment 1997

Sociale Verzekeringsbank, Ministry of Social Affairs and Employment, *Meeting the Challenge of Change*, Noordwijk 1997.

Spaventa 2010

E. Spaventa, 'The impact of Articles 12, 18, 39 and 43 of the EC Treaty on the coordination of social security systems', in: Y. Jorens (ed), *50 years of Social Security Coordination. Past – Present – Future*, Euroepan Commission, Brussels, p. 112.

Steen, van der, looseleaf

I. van der Steen, 'Thema Grensarbeid en sociale zekerheid', *Internationale Sociale Verzekering* (looseleaf), Deventer.

Steen, van der 2008

I.van der Steen, 'Zuivere interne situaties: geen omwenteling, wel inperking', *NTER*, nr. 11, 2008, p. 301 ff.

Stergiou

H.M. Stergiou, 'Op één been kan men niet lopen. Het arrest Watts een stap dichterbij de harmonisatie van patiëntenmobiliteit?', *NTER* 2006, p. 219.

Stiemer 1999

N. Stiemer, 'Sickness Insurance. Viewpoint of the EU-Member States', in: Y. Jorens and B. Schulte, *Co-ordination of Social Security Schemes in Connection with the Accession of Central and Eastern European States*, Brussels, 1999, p. 236.

Subsidiarity 1991

Subsidiarity: the Challenge of Change, Proceedings of the Jacques Delors Colloquium 1991, Maastricht 1991.

Swedish National Social Insurance Board and European Commission 1997

Swedish National Social Insurance Board and European Commission, *25 Years of Regulation (EEC) No. 1408/71 on Social Security for Migrant Workers – A Conference Report*, Stockholm 1997.

Tamburi 1983

G. Tamburi, "L'organisation intenationale du Travail et l'évolution des assurances sociales dans le monde', in: P. Köhler en H. Zacher, *Beiträge zu Geschichte und aktueller Situation der Sozialversicherung*, Berlin 1983, p. 647.

Tantaroudas 1976

C. Tantaroudas, *La protection jurdidque des travailleurs migrants*, Paris 1976.

Tantaroudas 1979

C. Tantaroudas, 'L'égalité de traitement en matière de sécurité sociale dans les règlements communautaires', *RTDE* 1979, p. 63.

Tegtmeier 1991

W. Tegtmeier, 'Wechselwirkungen zwischen dem Europäischen Sozialrecht und dem Sozialrecht der Bundesrepublik Deutschland – Erfahrungen und Vorstellungen aus deutscher Sicht', in: Schulte und Zacher 1991, p. 27.

Urbanetz 1991

H. Urbanetz, 'Modaliteiten voor het behoud van de rechten en de berekening van de prestaties in het Europees Verdrag inzake sociale zekerheid en andere samenordeningsinstrumenten', *BTSZ* 1991, p. 359.

Van Regenmortel, et al. Aeds.), *Sociale zekerheid in het Europa van de markt en de burgers: enkele actuele thema's*, Bruges, die Keure, 2007,.

Vansteenkiste 1991

S. Vansteenkiste, 'The idea of the thirteenth state system: towards a competition between a federal social insurance system and the national social security systems', in: Caixa Andorrana de seguretat social, *Colloqui international sobre seguretat social*, Andorra 1991.

Verschueren 1993,

H. Verschueren, 'Het arrest Taghavi en de tegemoetkoming van gehandicapten aan niet-EG-familileden van EG-werknemers', *MR* 1993/4, p. 75.

Verschueren 1997a

H. Verschueren, 'EC Social Security Coordination Excluding Third-Country Nationals: Still in Line with Fundamental Rights after the Gaygusuz Judgement?', *CMLRev* 1997, p. 991.

Verschueren 1997b

H. Verschueren, 'Na het arrest Taflan-Met: is er leven na de dood?', *Migrantenrecht* 1997, p. 29.

Verschueren 1999

H. Verschueren, 'The *Sürül* Judgment: Equal Treatment for Turkish Workers in Matters of Social Security', *European Journal of Migration and Law* 1999, p. 371.

Verschueren 2001

H. Verschueren, 'Financing Social Security and Regulation (EEC) 1408/71', *European Journal of Social Security* 2001, p. 7 ff.

Verschueren 2006

H. Verschueren, 'Sociale zekerheid en detachering binnen de Europese Unie. De zaak *Herbosch Kiere*: een gemiste kans in de strijd tegen grensoverschrijdende sociale dumpimg', *BTSZ* 2006, p. 403-449.

Verschueren 2007

H. Verschueren, 'De sociale bescherming van economisch niet (meer) actieve personen die zich binnen de Europese Unie verplaatsen', in: A Van Regenmortel et al (eds), *Sociale zekerheid in het Europa van de markt en de burgers: enkele actuele thema's*, Bruges, 2007, p. 213 ff.

Verschueren 2008

H. Verschueren, 'De regionalisering van de sociale zekerheid in België in het licht van het arrest van het Europese Hof van Justitie inzake de Vlaamse zorgverzekering', *Belgisch Tijdschrift Sociale Zekerheid*, 2008.

Verschueren 2009

Herwig Verschueren, 'Special Non-Contributory Benefits in Regulation 1408/71, Regulation 883/2004 and the Case Law of the ECJ', *European Journal of Social Security* 2009, p. 211 ff.

Villars 1979

B. Villars, *Le Code européen de sécurité sociale et le Protocole additionnel*, Genève 1979.

Vlemminckx and Berghman 2001

K. Vlemminckx and J. Berghman, 'Social Exclusion and the Welfare State', in: D.G. Mayes, J. Berghman and R. Salais, *Social Exclusion and European Policy*, Cheltenham-Northampton 2001, p. 34 ff

Watson 1980

Ph. Watson, *Social Security Law of the European Communities*, London 1980.

Watson 1991

Ph. Watson, 'The Community social charter', *CMLRev.* 1991, p. 37.

Watson 1993

Ph. Watson, 'Social policy after Maastricht,' *CMLRev.* 1993, p. 481.

Wiebringhaus 1983

H. Wiebringhaus, 'Die Sozialversicherung im Rahmen der Funktionen, der Möglichkeiten und der sozialpolitischen Vorhaben des Europarats', in: Köhler en Zacher 1983, p. 507.

Whiteford 1996

E.A. Whiteford, *Adapting to Change: Occupational Pension Schemes, Women and Migrant Workers*, The Hague, 1996.

Wienk 1999

M.A.B.L Wienk, *Europese coördinatie van aanvullende pensioenen*, Deventer 1999.

Zacher 1991

H. Zacher, 'Wechselwirkungen zwischen dem Europäischen Sozialrecht und dem Sozialrecht der Bundesrepublik Deutschland – Einführungsreferat aus sozialrechtlicher Sicht', in: Schulte and Zacher 1991, p. 11.

Zeben and Donders 2001

M. van Zeben and P. Donders, 'Co-ordination of Social Security – Developments in the Area of Posting', *European Journal of Social Security* 2001, p. 107.

INDEX ON CASES

SUBJECT INDEX

Intersentia